I M Coomber

Models covered

Skoda Estelle 105 S, L and Lux; 1046 cc
Skoda Estelle 120 L, LE, LS, GLS, LSE and Rapid; 1174 cc

Covers Estelle & Estelle 'Two' models and all Plus, Super & Cabriolet variants
Does not cover Estelle 130 range

ISBN 1 85010 196 5

Printed in England *(604 – 6L3)*

THE
BOOK

a30118 053044487b

ABCDE
FGHI

Haynes Publishing Group
Sparkford Nr Yeovil
Somerset BA22 7JJ England

Haynes Publications, Inc
861 Lawrence Drive
Newbury Park
California 91320 USA

British Library Cataloguing in Publication Data

Coomber, Ian
  Skoda Estelle owners workshop manual.–2nd ed–
  (Owners Workshop Manual/Haynes)
  1. Estelle automobile
  I. Title   II. Series
  629.28'722   TL215.E/
  ISBN 1-85010-196-5

Acknowledgements

Special thanks are due to Skoda (Great Britain) Limited for the supply of technical information and certain of the illustrations used in this manual. Castrol Limited supplied lubrication data and the Champion Sparking Plug Company supplied the illustrations showing the various spark plug conditions.

Our thanks are also due to Messrs Wareham and Sons Ltd of Gurney Slade Garage, Gurney Slade, Somerset, who very kindly supplied a vehicle for use when updating this manual. Finally, thank you to all the staff at Sparkford who assisted in the production of this manual.

About this manual

Its aim

The aim of this manual is to help you get the best value from your car. It can do so in several ways. It can help you decide what work must be done (even should you choose to get it done by a garage), provide information on routine maintenance and servicing, and give a logical course of action and diagnosis when random faults occur. However, it is hoped that you will use the manual by tackling the work yourself. On simpler jobs it may even be quicker than booking the car into a garage and going there twice to leave and collect it. Perhaps most important, a lot of money can be saved by avoiding the costs the garage must charge to cover its labour and overheads.

The manual has drawings and descriptions to show the function of the various components so that their layout can be understood. Then the tasks are described and photographed in a step-by-step sequence so that even a novice can do the work.

Its arrangement

The manual is divided into twelve Chapters, each covering a logical sub-division of the vehicle. The Chapters are each divided into Sections, numbered with single figures, eg 5; and the Sections into paragraphs (or sub-sections), with decimal numbers following on from the Section they are in, eg 5.1, 5.2, 5.3 etc.

It is freely illustrated, especially in those parts where there is a detailed sequence of operations to be carried out. There are two forms of illustration; figures and photographs. The figures are numbered in sequence with decimal numbers, according to their position in the Chapter – eg Fig. 6.4 is the fourth drawing/illustration in Chapter 6. Photographs carry the same number (either individually or in related groups) as the Section or sub-section to which they relate.

There is an alphabetical index at the back of the manual as well as a contents list at the front. Each Chapter is also preceded by its own individual contents list.

References to the 'left' or 'right' of the vehicle are in the sense of a person in the driver's seat facing forwards.

Unless otherwise stated, nuts and bolts are removed by turning anti-clockwise, and tightened by turning clockwise.

Vehicle manufacturers continually make changes to specifications and recommendations, and these when notified are incorporated into our manuals at the earliest opportunity.

Whilst every care is taken to ensure that the information in this manual is correct, no liability can be accepted by the authors or publishers for loss, damage or injury caused by any errors in, or omissions from, the information given.

Introduction to the Skoda Estelle

The Skoda Estelle was introduced in 1977 and was a replacement for the 'S' type models. Whilst the body style is definitely different from its predecessor, the mechanics are basically the same. The rear-mounted engine is of overhead valve design, with an aluminium cylinder block fitted with wet liners and a cast iron cylinder head. The engine is located at the rear of the car and is mounted in line with the gearbox and differential unit (which are integral). All models are fitted with a four-speed fully synchromesh gearbox. Drive is to the rear wheels by swinging half axles.

The front and rear suspensions are independent and the dual line

braking system employs disc front brakes and drum rear brakes.

A steel body is used and the front wing panels are bolted in position, enabling them to be removed if required for repair. The main luggage compartment is at the front.

Most jobs can be tackled with a basic tool kit but there are instances where special service tools are required and the owner mechanic should therefore study carefully any job to be undertaken prior to commencing work, in order to assess the prospects of completing the job at home satisfactorily.

Contents

Skoda 120 L. This is the project car which was dismantled in our workshop

Skoda 120 LSE. This is the top of the range model

General dimensions, weights and capacities

For modifications, and information applicable to later models, see Supplement at end of manual

Overall dimensions

Length	4.160 m (163.8 in)
Width	1.595 m (62.8 in)
Height (loaded)	1.4 m (55.2 in) approx
Ground clearance	170 mm (6.7 in)

Kerb weights (approximate)

105 S	855 kg (1885 lb)
105 L	875 kg (1929 lb)
120 L	875 kg (1929 lb)
120 LE, LS and LSE	885 kg (1951 lb)

Capacities

Engine oil:	
105 S and L, 120 L and LE	4 litres (7 pints)
120 GLS, LS and LSE	4.6 litres (8.1 pints)
Cooling system	12.5 litres (22 pints)
Gearbox and final drive:	
From dry	2.5 litres (4.4 pints)
Drain and refill	2.0 litres (3.5 pints)
Hydraulic system	0.5 litres (0.88 pints) approx
Steering box	0.16 litres (0.28 pints)
Fuel tank	38 litres (8.4 gal)

Buying spare parts
and vehicle identification numbers

Buying spare parts

Spare parts are available from many sources, for example, Skoda garages, other garages and accessory shops, and motor factors. Our advice regarding spare parts is as follows:

Officially appointed Skoda garages – this is the best source of parts which are peculiar to your car and otherwise not generally available (eg complete cylinder heads, internal gearbox components, badges, interior trim, etc). It is also the only place at which you should buy parts if your car is still under warranty; non-Skoda components may invalidate the warranty. To be sure of obtaining the correct parts it will always be necessary to give the storeman your car's engine and chassis number, and if possible, to take the old part along for positive identification. Remember that many parts are available on a factory exchange scheme – any parts returned should always be clean! It obviously makes good sense to go to the specialists on your car for this type of part for they are best equipped to supply you.

Other garages and accessory shops – these are often very good places to buy material and components needed for the maintenance of your car (eg, oil filters, spark plugs, bulbs, fan belts, oils and grease, touch-up paint, filler paste etc). They also sell general accessories, usually have convenient opening hours, often charge lower prices and can often be found not far from home.

Motor factors – good factors will stock all of the more important components which wear out relatively quickly (eg, clutch components, pistons, valves, exhaust systems, brake cylinders/pipes/hoses/seals/shoes and pads etc). Motor factors will often provide new or reconditioned components on a part exchange basis – this can save a considerable amount of money.

Vehicle identification numbers

The *engine number* is situated on the cylinder block adjacent to the water pump flange (photo).

The *chassis number* is stamped on a plate attached to the bulkhead panel inside the front luggage compartment (photo) on the rear bulkhead next to the engine compartment lid retainer and on the shroud above the radiator.

The engine number location

The chassis number plate location

Tools and working facilities

Introduction

A selection of good tools is a fundamental requirement for anyone contemplating the maintenance and repair of a motor vehicle. For the owner who does not possess any, their purchase will prove a considerable expense, offsetting some of the savings made by doing-it-yourself. However, provided that the tools purchased are of good quality, they will last for many years and prove an extremely worthwhile investment.

To help the average owner to decide which tools are needed to carry out the various tasks detailed in this manual, we have compiled three lists of tools under the following headings: *Maintenance and minor repair, Repair and overhaul,* and *Special.* The newcomer to practical mechanics should start off with the *Maintenance and minor repair* tool kit and confine himself to the simpler jobs around the vehicle. Then, as his confidence and experience grow, he can undertake more difficult tasks, buying extra tools as, and when, they are needed. In this way, a *Maintenance and minor repair* tool kit can be built-up into a *Repair and overhaul* tool kit over a considerable period of time without any major cash outlays. The experienced do-it-yourselfer will have a tool kit good enough for most repair and overhaul procedures and will add tools from the *Special* category when he feels the expense is justified by the amount of use to which these tools will be put.

It is obviously not possible to cover the subject of tools fully here. For those who wish to learn more about tools and their use there is a book entitled *How to Choose and Use Car Tools* available from the publishers of this manual.

Maintenance and minor repair tool kit

The tools given in this list should be considered as a minimum requirement if routine maintenance, servicing and minor repair operations are to be undertaken. We recommend the purchase of combination spanners (ring one end, open-ended the other); although more expensive than open-ended ones, they do give the advantages of both types of spanner.

Combination spanners - 8, 10, 11, 12, 13, 14 & 17 mm
Adjustable spanner - 9 inch
Spark plug spanner (with rubber insert)
Spark plug gap adjustment tool
Set of feeler gauges
Brake bleed nipple spanner
Screwdriver - 4 in long x $\frac{1}{4}$ in dia (flat blade)
Screwdriver - 4 in long x $\frac{1}{4}$ in dia (cross blade)
Combination pliers - 6 inch
Hacksaw (junior)
Tyre pump
Tyre pressure gauge
Grease gun
Oil can
Fine emery cloth (1 sheet)
Wire brush (small)
Funnel (medium size)

Repair and overhaul tool kit

These tools are virtually essential for anyone undertaking any major repairs to a motor vehicle, and are additional to those given in the *Maintenance and minor repair* list. Included in this list is a comprehensive set of sockets. Although these are expensive they will be found invaluable as they are so versatile - particularly if various drives are included in the set. We recommend the $\frac{1}{2}$ in square-drive type, as this can be used with most proprietary torque wrenches. If you cannot afford a socket set, even bought piecemeal, then inexpensive tubular box spanners are a useful alternative.

The tools in this list will occasionally need to be supplemented by tools from the *Special* list.

Sockets (or box spanners) to cover range in previous list
Reversible ratchet drive (for use with sockets)
Extension piece, 10 inch (for use with sockets)
Universal joint (for use with sockets)
Torque wrench (for use with sockets)
Mole wrench - 8 inch
Ball pein hammer
Soft-faced hammer, plastic or rubber
Screwdriver - 6 in long x $\frac{5}{16}$ in dia (flat blade)
Screwdriver - 2 in long x $\frac{5}{16}$ in square (flat blade)
Screwdriver - 1$\frac{1}{2}$ in long x $\frac{1}{4}$ in dia (cross blade)
Screwdriver - 3 in long x $\frac{1}{8}$ in dia (electricians)
Pliers - electricians side cutters
Pliers - needle nosed
Pliers - circlip (internal and external)
Cold chisel - $\frac{1}{2}$ inch
Scriber
Scraper
Centre punch
Pin punch
Hacksaw
Valve grinding tool
Steel rule/straight-edge
Allen keys
Selection of files
Wire brush (large)
Axle-stands
Jack (strong scissor or hydraulic type)

Special tools

The tools in this list are those which are not used regularly, are expensive to buy, or which need to be used in accordance with their manufacturers' instructions. Unless relatively difficult mechanical jobs are undertaken frequently, it will not be economic to buy many of these tools. Where this is the case, you could consider clubbing together with friends (or joining a motorists' club) to make a joint purchase, or borrowing the tools against a deposit from a local garage or tool hire specialist.

The following list contains only those tools and instruments freely available to the public, and not those special tools produced by the vehicle manufacturer specifically for its dealer network. You will find occasional references to these manufacturers' special tools in the text of this manual. Generally, an alternative method of doing the job without the vehicle manufacturers' special tool is given. However, sometimes, there is no alternative to using them. Where this is the case and the relevant tool cannot be bought or borrowed you will have to entrust the work to a franchised garage.

Valve spring compressor
Piston ring compressor
Balljoint separator
Universal hub/bearing puller
Impact screwdriver
Micrometer and/or vernier gauge
Dial gauge
Stroboscopic timing light
Dwell angle meter/tachometer
Universal electrical multi-meter
Cylinder compression gauge
Lifting tackle
Trolley jack
Light with extension lead

Buying tools

For practically all tools, a tool dealer is the best source since he will have a very comprehensive range compared with the average garage or accessory shop. Having said that, accessory shops often offer excellent quality tools at discount prices, so it pays to shop around.

Remember, you don't have to buy the most expensive items on the shelf, but it is always advisable to steer clear of the very cheap tools. There are plenty of good tools around at reasonable prices, so ask the proprietor or manager of the shop for advice before making a purchase.

Care and maintenance of tools

Having purchased a reasonable tool kit, it is necessary to keep the tools in a clean serviceable condition. After use, always wipe off any dirt, grease and metal particles using a clean, dry cloth, before putting the tools away. Never leave them lying around after they have been used. A simple tool rack on the garage or workshop wall, for items such as screwdrivers and pliers is a good idea. Store all normal spanners and sockets in a metal box. Any measuring instruments, gauges, meters, etc, must be carefully stored where they cannot be damaged or become rusty.

Take a little care when tools are used. Hammer heads inevitably become marked and screwdrivers lose the keen edge on their blades from time to time. A little timely attention with emery cloth or a file will soon restore items like this to a good serviceable finish.

Working facilities

Not to be forgotten when discussing tools, is the workshop itself. If anything more than routine maintenance is to be carried out, some form of suitable working area becomes essential.

It is appreciated that many an owner mechanic is forced by circumstances to remove an engine or similar item, without the benefit of a garage or workshop. Having done this, any repairs should always be done under the cover of a roof.

Wherever possible, any dismantling should be done on a clean flat workbench or table at a suitable working height.

Any workbench needs a vice: one with a jaw opening of 4 in (100 mm) is suitable for most jobs. As mentioned previously, some clean dry storage space is also required for tools, as well as the lubricants, cleaning fluids, touch-up paints and so on which become necessary.

Another item which may be required, and which has a much more general usage, is an electric drill with a chuck capacity of at least $\frac{5}{16}$ in (8 mm). This, together with a good range of twist drills, is virtually essential for fitting accessories such as wing mirrors and reversing lights.

Last, but not least, always keep a supply of old newspapers and clean, lint-free rags available, and try to keep any working area as clean as possible.

Spanner jaw gap comparison table

Jaw gap (in)	Spanner size
0.250	$\frac{1}{4}$ in AF
0.276	7 mm
0.313	$\frac{5}{16}$ in AF
0.315	8 mm
0.344	$\frac{11}{32}$ in AF; $\frac{1}{8}$ in Whitworth
0.354	9 mm
0.375	$\frac{3}{8}$ in AF
0.394	10 mm
0.433	11 mm
0.438	$\frac{7}{16}$ in AF
0.445	$\frac{3}{16}$ in Whitworth; $\frac{1}{4}$ in BSF
0.472	12 mm
0.500	$\frac{1}{2}$ in AF
0.512	13 mm
0.525	$\frac{1}{4}$ in Whitworth; $\frac{5}{16}$ in BSF
0.551	14 mm
0.563	$\frac{9}{16}$ in AF
0.591	15 mm
0.600	$\frac{5}{16}$ in Whitworth; $\frac{3}{8}$ in BSF
0.625	$\frac{5}{8}$ in AF
0.630	16 mm
0.669	17 mm
0.686	$\frac{11}{16}$ in AF
0.709	18 mm
0.710	$\frac{3}{8}$ in Whitworth; $\frac{7}{16}$ in BSF
0.748	19 mm
0.750	$\frac{3}{4}$ in AF
0.813	$\frac{13}{16}$ in AF
0.820	$\frac{7}{16}$ in Whitworth; $\frac{1}{2}$ in BSF
0.866	22 mm
0.875	$\frac{7}{8}$ in AF
0.920	$\frac{1}{2}$ in Whitworth; $\frac{9}{16}$ in BSF
0.938	$\frac{15}{16}$ in AF
0.945	24 mm
1.000	1 in AF
1.010	$\frac{9}{16}$ in Whitworth; $\frac{5}{8}$ in BSF
1.024	26 mm
1.063	$1\frac{1}{16}$ in AF; 27 mm
1.100	$\frac{5}{8}$ in Whitworth; $\frac{11}{16}$ in BSF
1.125	$1\frac{1}{8}$ in AF
1.181	30 mm
1.200	$\frac{11}{16}$ in Whitworth; $\frac{3}{4}$ in BSF
1.250	$1\frac{1}{4}$ in AF
1.260	32 mm
1.300	$\frac{3}{4}$ in Whitworth; $\frac{7}{8}$ in BSF
1.313	$1\frac{5}{16}$ in AF
1.390	$\frac{13}{16}$ in Whitworth; $\frac{15}{16}$ in BSF
1.417	36 mm
1.438	$1\frac{7}{16}$ in AF
1.480	$\frac{7}{8}$ in Whitworth; 1 in BSF
1.500	$1\frac{1}{2}$ in AF
1.575	40 mm; $\frac{15}{16}$ in Whitworth
1.614	41 mm
1.625	$1\frac{5}{8}$ in AF
1.670	1 in Whitworth; $1\frac{1}{8}$ in BSF
1.688	$1\frac{11}{16}$ in AF
1.811	46 mm
1.813	$1\frac{13}{16}$ in AF
1.860	$1\frac{1}{8}$ in Whitworth; $1\frac{1}{4}$ in BSF
1.875	$1\frac{7}{8}$ in AF
1.969	50 mm
2.000	2 in AF
2.050	$1\frac{1}{4}$ in Whitworth; $1\frac{3}{8}$ in BSF
2.165	55 mm
2.362	60 mm

Jacking and towing

Jacking

If the car is to be raised for service or repair operations it is essential that the correct jacking procedure be adhered to. It is most important that only the specified jack and support points are employed in order to prevent accidents and damage to the vehicle.

The jack supplied with the car is really only designed for the purpose of changing a wheel in the event of a puncture and should not be relied on for supporting the car during repair operations under the vehicle. Trolley or pillar jacks are more suitable for this purpose but even then they should be supplemented with axle stands or blocks to ensure complete working safety. Only jack up on firm level ground and chock the wheels to prevent the car rolling off the jack. Unless a wheel has to be removed most operations under the car are best carried out with the car on ramps if available.

If supporting the car on blocks or chassis stands position them at the points shown in the illustration.

Towing

In the event of the car breaking down or being in need of a tow, a front-mounted towing bracket is fitted and it must be used. Do not attach rope to suspension or steering components! The pin to which the tow rope is attached is located through the bracket and secured with a cotter pin. The tow pin and cotter pin were supplied with the car when new and should be used if available.

If a trailer is to be towed, only fit an approved towbar unit and ensure that the total weight towed is not in excess of 400 kg (881 lb) if the trailer itself is not fitted with brakes.

The Skoda sidewinder jack in position – ensure that it is fully engaged

Support the car at the points shown

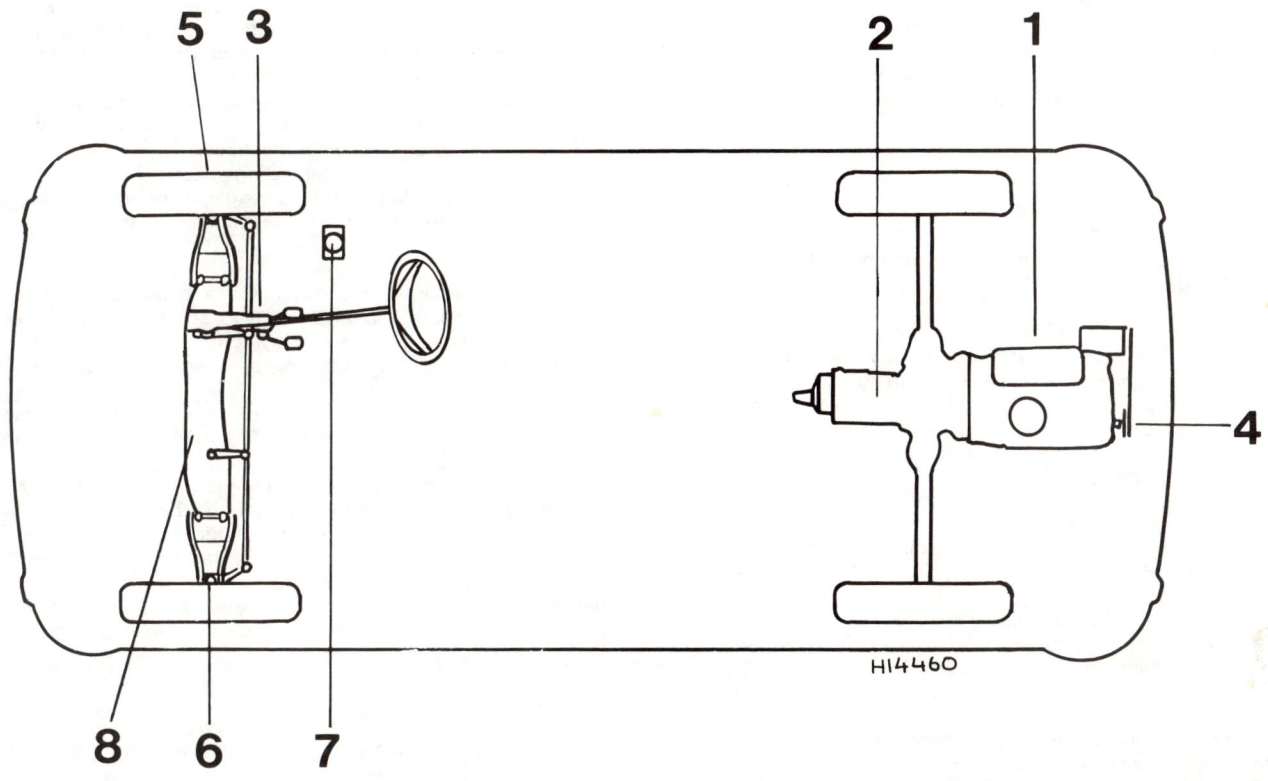

H14460

Recommended lubricants and fluids

Component or system	Lubricant type or specification
1 Engine	Multigrade engine oil
2 Transmission	Gear oil SAE 90EP
3 Steering box	Gear oil SAE 90EP or 140EP
4 Water pump	General-purpose grease
5 Front wheel bearings	General-purpose grease
6 Kingpins	General-purpose grease
7 Brake hydraulic system	Hydraulic fluid to SAE J1703
8 Steering rack	Gear oil SAE 90EP

Note: *The above are general recommendations only. Lubrication requirements vary from territory to territory and according to vehicle use. If in doubt consult the operator's handbook supplied with the vehicle.*

Safety first!

Professional motor mechanics are trained in safe working procedures. However enthusiastic you may be about getting on with the job in hand, do take the time to ensure that your safety is not put at risk. A moment's lack of attention can result in an accident, as can failure to observe certain elementary precautions.

There will always be new ways of having accidents, and the following points do not pretend to be a comprehensive list of all dangers; they are intended rather to make you aware of the risks and to encourage a safety-conscious approach to all work you carry out on your vehicle.

Essential DOs and DON'Ts

DON'T rely on a single jack when working underneath the vehicle. Always use reliable additional means of support, such as axle stands, securely placed under a part of the vehicle that you know will not give way.

DON'T attempt to loosen or tighten high-torque nuts (e.g. wheel hub nuts) while the vehicle is on a jack; it may be pulled off.

DON'T start the engine without first ascertaining that the transmission is in neutral (or 'Park' where applicable) and the parking brake applied.

DON'T suddenly remove the filler cap from a hot cooling system – cover it with a cloth and release the pressure gradually first, or you may get scalded by escaping coolant.

DON'T attempt to drain oil until you are sure it has cooled sufficiently to avoid scalding you.

DON'T grasp any part of the engine, exhaust or catalytic converter without first ascertaining that it is sufficiently cool to avoid burning you.

DON'T allow brake fluid or antifreeze to contact vehicle paintwork.

DON'T syphon toxic liquids such as fuel, brake fluid or antifreeze by mouth, or allow them to remain on your skin.

DON'T inhale dust – it may be injurious to health (see *Asbestos* below).

DON'T allow any spilt oil or grease to remain on the floor – wipe it up straight away, before someone slips on it.

DON'T use ill-fitting spanners or other tools which may slip and cause injury.

DON'T attempt to lift a heavy component which may be beyond your capability – get assistance.

DON'T rush to finish a job, or take unverified short cuts.

DON'T allow children or animals in or around an unattended vehicle.

DO wear eye protection when using power tools such as drill, sander, bench grinder etc, and when working under the vehicle.

DO use a barrier cream on your hands prior to undertaking dirty jobs – it will protect your skin from infection as well as making the dirt easier to remove afterwards; but make sure your hands aren't left slippery.

DO keep loose clothing (cuffs, tie etc) and long hair well out of the way of moving mechanical parts.

DO remove rings, wristwatch etc, before working on the vehicle – especially the electrical system.

DO ensure that any lifting tackle used has a safe working load rating adequate for the job.

DO keep your work area tidy – it is only too easy to fall over articles left lying around.

DO get someone to check periodically that all is well, when working alone on the vehicle.

DO carry out work in a logical sequence and check that everything is correctly assembled and tightened afterwards.

DO remember that your vehicle's safety affects that of yourself and others. If in doubt on any point, get specialist advice.

IF, in spite of following these precautions, you are unfortunate enough to injure yourself, seek medical attention as soon as possible.

Asbestos

Certain friction, insulating, sealing, and other products – such as brake linings, brake bands, clutch linings, torque converters, gaskets, etc – contain asbestos. *Extreme care must be taken to avoid inhalation of dust from such products since it is hazardous to health.* If in doubt, assume that they *do* contain asbestos.

Fire

Remember at all times that petrol (gasoline) is highly flammable. Never smoke, or have any kind of naked flame around, when working on the vehicle. But the risk does not end there – a spark caused by an electrical short-circuit, by two metal surfaces contacting each other, by careless use of tools, or even by static electricity built up in your body under certain conditions, can ignite petrol vapour, which in a confined space is highly explosive.

Always disconnect the battery earth (ground) terminal before working on any part of the fuel or electrical system, and never risk spilling fuel on to a hot engine or exhaust.

It is recommended that a fire extinguisher of a type suitable for fuel and electrical fires is kept handy in the garage or workplace at all times. Never try to extinguish a fuel or electrical fire with water.

Fumes

Certain fumes are highly toxic and can quickly cause unconsciousness and even death if inhaled to any extent. Petrol (gasoline) vapour comes into this category, as do the vapours from certain solvents such as trichloroethylene. Any draining or pouring of such volatile fluids should be done in a well ventilated area.

When using cleaning fluids and solvents, read the instructions carefully. Never use materials from unmarked containers – they may give off poisonous vapours.

Never run the engine of a motor vehicle in an enclosed space such as a garage. Exhaust fumes contain carbon monoxide which is extremely poisonous; if you need to run the engine, always do so in the open air or at least have the rear of the vehicle outside the workplace.

If you are fortunate enough to have the use of an inspection pit, never drain or pour petrol, and never run the engine, while the vehicle is standing over it; the fumes, being heavier than air, will concentrate in the pit with possibly lethal results.

The battery

Never cause a spark, or allow a naked light, near the vehicle's battery. It will normally be giving off a certain amount of hydrogen gas, which is highly explosive.

Always disconnect the battery earth (ground) terminal before working on the fuel or electrical systems.

If possible, loosen the filler plugs or cover when charging the battery from an external source. Do not charge at an excessive rate or the battery may burst.

Take care when topping up and when carrying the battery. The acid electrolyte, even when diluted, is very corrosive and should not be allowed to contact the eyes or skin.

If you ever need to prepare electrolyte yourself, always add the acid slowly to the water, and never the other way round. Protect against splashes by wearing rubber gloves and goggles.

When jump starting a car using a booster battery, for negative earth (ground) vehicles, connect the jump leads in the following sequence: First connect one jump lead between the positive (+) terminals of the two batteries. Then connect the other jump lead first to the negative (–) terminal of the booster battery, and then to a good earthing (ground) point on the vehicle to be started, at least 18 in (45 cm) from the battery if possible. Ensure that hands and jump leads are clear of any moving parts, and that the two vehicles do not touch. Disconnect the leads in the reverse order.

Mains electricity

When using an electric power tool, inspection light etc, which works from the mains, always ensure that the appliance is correctly connected to its plug and that, where necessary, it is properly earthed (grounded). Do not use such appliances in damp conditions and, again, beware of creating a spark or applying excessive heat in the vicinity of fuel or fuel vapour.

Ignition HT voltage

A severe electric shock can result from touching certain parts of the ignition system, such as the HT leads, when the engine is running or being cranked, particularly if components are damp or the insulation is defective. Where an electronic ignition system is fitted, the HT voltage is much higher and could prove fatal.

Routine maintenance

For modifications, and information applicable to later models, see Supplement at end of manual

The maintenance instructions listed below are basically those recommended by the vehicle manufacturer. They are supplemented by additional maintenance tasks which, through practical experience, the author recommends should be carried out at the intervals suggested.

The additional tasks are primarily of a preventive nature in that they will assist in eliminating the unexpected failure of a component due to fair wear and tear.

The levels of the engine oil, cooling water, windscreen washer water and battery electrolyte, also the tyre pressures, should be checked weekly or more frequently if experience dictates this to be ncessary. Similarly it is wise to check the level of the fluids in the clutch and brake master cylinder reservoir at monthly intervals. If not checked at home, it is advantageous to use regularly the same garage for this work as they will get to know your preferences for particular

oils and the pressures at which you like to run your tyres.

Every 250 miles (400 km) travelled or weekly

Engine

Check the engine oil level with the car parked on level ground. Withdraw the dipstick, wipe it clean, reinsert it and double check the reading. Top up the level if necessary to the full mark (photo). Check the radiator coolant level and top up the reservoir if required (photo).

Check the battery electrolyte level and top up if necessary as described in Chapter 10.

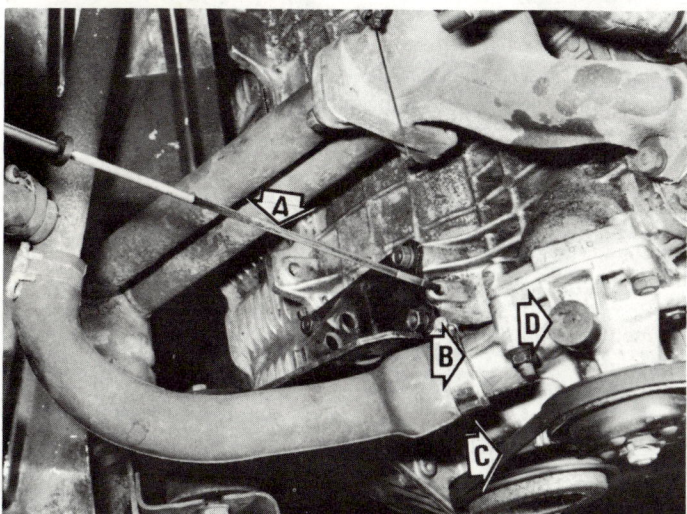

Remove dipstick (A) to check engine oil level
Other maintenance check points shown are:

B   *Coolant hoses and connections for leaks and security*
C   *Drivebelt for tension and condition*
D   *Water pump bearing lubricator*

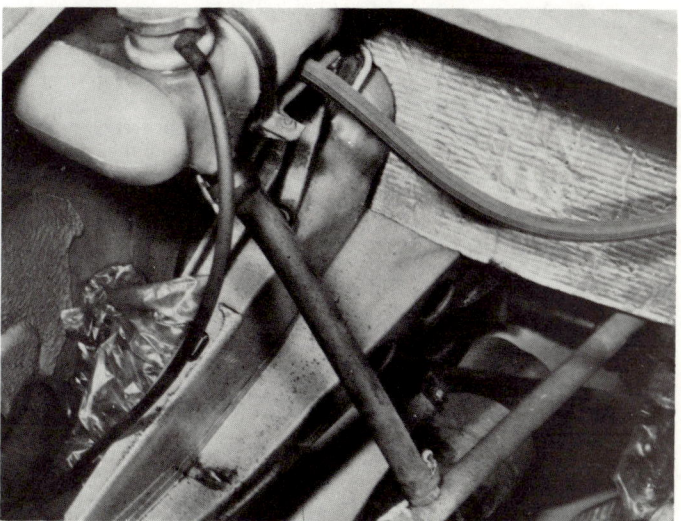

Check coolant level in header tank in engine compartment

Brakes and clutch

Check the hydraulic fluid level in the brake and clutch reservoir (photo). Top up the prescribed level if necessary with the specified fluid type. A sudden drop in fluid level indicates a leakage in one of the systems which must be repaired without delay. Refer to Chapter 5 or 9 for further details.

Tyres

Check the tyre pressures (using a gauge known to be accurate) and adjust the pressures if necessary (see Chapter 7). Check the pressure in the spare tyre monthly.

Examine tyres for wear and damage. If uneven wear has taken place, check the steering and suspension alignments.

Lights, wipers and horn

Switch on the lights and check that they all operate. The indicators must function at the correct speed.

Check the operation of the windscreen wipers and washer. Top up the washer reservoir if level is low. Check that the horn works.

Every 3000 miles (5000 km) or three months

(In addition to the work specified in the weekly schedule)

Engine

Change the engine oil and filter – pre 1984 models only. Drain the engine oil when hot and refill with the specified grade and quantity of fresh oil. Remove the oil filter casing, clean it out and refit with a new element and sealing washers. Recheck the oil level after running the engine. The oil should be changed more frequently if the car is used under adverse conditions (extremes of heat or cold, or mainly short journeys).

Check the water pump housing bolts for tightness and the drivebelt for tension and condition. Retension or renew if necessary as described in Chapter 10.

Lubricate the water pump bearings by unscrewing the lubricator cap, filling with grease and screwing it back into position.

Inspect the radiator core and coolant hose joints for leakage.

Inspect the engine and transmission for oil leaks and, if found, determine and rectify the cause.

Fuel system

Remove the fuel pump cover and clean the filter. Renew the cover gasket if necessary.

Inspect and clean the air filter element as described in Chapter 3.

Remove the carburettor fuel inlet pipe and clean the strainer – pre 1984 models only.

Check and adjust the slow running adjustment as described in Chapter 3.

Ignition system

Remove, clean and regap the spark plugs as described in Chapter 4. Check the condition of the HT leads.

Clean and regap the contact breaker points if necessary, refer to Chapter 4. Clean the inside of the distributor cap and the rotor arm. Lubricate the distributor sparingly: two drops of oil to the centre of the cam spindle and through the baseplate, one drop of oil to the contact breaker pivot, and a smear of grease on the cam. Wipe off any excess lubricant.

Clutch

Lubricate the clutch release bearing. Remove the central floor cover behind the rear seats, detach the slave cylinder cover and pour 10 to 12 drops of oil into the central recess of the release lever. The oil will run down and lubricate the bearing. Do not overlubricate!

Adjust the clutch if necessary as described in Chapter 5.

Steering and suspension

Check the steering joints for excessive play and the column mountings for security.

Check the front hub endfloat and adjust if necessary as described in Chapter 8. Apply clean grease to the cap.

Grease the kingpins – one nipple on each side (photo). Check the kingpin play and if necessary adjust as described in Chapter 8.

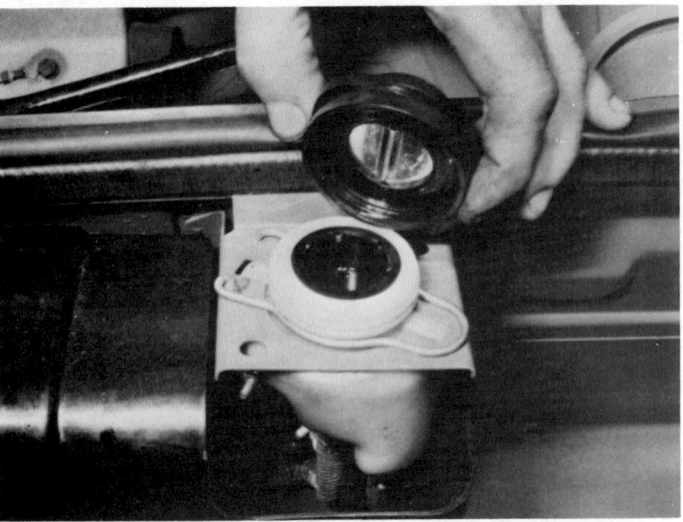

Hydraulic fluid reservoir – level must be maintained

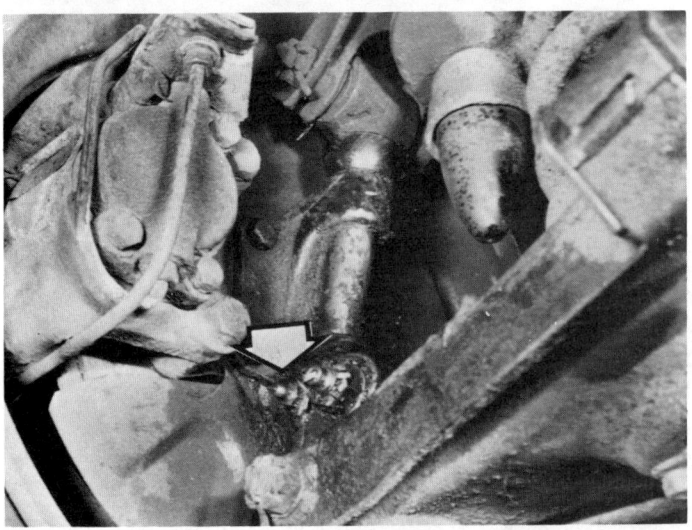

Kingpin grease nipple location (arrowed)

Braking system

Inspect all hydraulic pipes, hoses and unions for damage or leakage and renew if necessary. Check the operation of the brakes.

Every 6000 miles (10 000 km) or six months

(In addition to the work specified in the previous schedules)

Engine

Check the valve clearances and adjust if necessary as described in Chapter 1.

Change the engine oil and filter – models 1984 on.

Fuel system

Remove the carburettor fuel inlet pipe and clean the strainer – models 1984 on.

Steering

Have the front wheel alignment checked if steering is heavy or uneven tyre wear is noted.

Check the steering rack for damage or leaks. Top up the oil, if necessary.

Braking system

Inspect the front disc pads and renew if necessary – refer to Chapter 9.

Lights and wipers

Check headlamp alignment.

Renew windscreen wiper blades if necessary.

Transmission drain plugs – gearbox (1) and differential housing (2). Also shown are the level plug (3) and reversing light switch (4)

Renew the transmission oil, filling through tube to correct level

General
Lubricate locks, hinges, catches, seat runners etc.
Clean the interior of the car and wash and polish the exterior.

Every 12 000 miles (20 000 km) or twelve months

(In addition to the work specified in the previous schedules)
Engine
Check starter motor mounting bolts for tightness.

Fuel system
Renew the air cleaner element.
Check carburettor, manifold and exhaust fittings for tightness.
Examine exhaust system for leaks.

Ignition system
Renew the spark plugs.
Renew the contact breaker points.

Transmission
Drain and renew the transmission oil – pre 1984 models only (photo). The correct oil level is 8 mm (0.3 in) above the dipstick upper index line.

Steering
Check and if necessary top up the steering box oil via the filler/level plug.

Every 24 000 miles (40 000 km) or two years

(In addition to the work specified in the previous schedules)
Transmission
Drain and renew the transmission oil – models 1984 on.

Every 36 000 miles (60 000 km) or three years

(In addition to the work specified in the previous schedules)
Engine
Check engine mountings for damage or deterioration and renew if necessary.

Driveshafts
Inspect rubber boots for damage or deterioration and renew if necessary.

Suspension and steering
Check rubber bushes for damage or deterioration and renew if necessary.
Repack the front hub bearings with grease – see Chapter 8.

Braking system
Inspect rear brake linings and renew if necessary.
Renew all rubber seals and flexible hydraulic hoses and refill system with fresh hydraulic fluid – see Chapter 9.

General
Have the engine compartment and the underside of the car body steam cleaned. Inspect for rust damage, frayed wiring etc and make good as necessary.

Fault diagnosis

Introduction

The car owner who does his or her maintenance according to the recommended schedules should not have to use this section of the manual very often. Modern component reliability is such that, provided those items subject to wear or deterioration are inspected or renewed at the specified intervals, sudden failure is comparatively rare. Faults do not usually just happen as a result of sudden failure, but develop over a period of time. Major mechanical failures in particular are usually preceded by characteristic symptoms over hundreds or even thousands of miles. Those components which do occasionally fail without warning are often small and easily carried in the car.

With any fault finding, the first step is to decide where to begin investigations. Sometimes this is obvious, but on other occasions a little detective work will be necessary. The owner who makes half a dozen haphazard adjustments or replacements may be successful in curing a fault (or its symptoms), but he will be none the wiser if the fault recurs and he may well have spent more time and money than was necessary. A calm and logical approach will be found to be more satisfactory in the long run. Always take into account any warning signs or abnormalities that may have been noticed in the period preceding the fault – power loss, high or low gauge readings, unusual noises or smells, etc – and remember that failure of components such as fuses or spark plugs may only be pointers to some underlying fault.

The pages which follow here are intended to help in cases of failure to start or breakdown on the road. There is also a Fault Diagnosis Section at the end of each Chapter which should be consulted if the preliminary checks prove unfruitful. Whatever the fault, certain principles apply. These are as follows:

Verify the fault. This is simply a matter of being sure that you know what the symptoms are before starting work. This is particularly important if you are investigating a fault for someone else who may not have described it very accurately.

Don't overlook the obvious. For example, if the car won't start, is there petrol in the tank? (Don't take anyone else's word on this particular point, and don't trust the fuel gauge either!) If an electrical fault is indicated, look for loose or broken wires before digging out the test gear.

Cure the disease, not the symptom. Substituting a flat battery with a fully charged one will get you off the hard shoulder, but if the underlying cause is not attended to, the new battery will go the same way. Similarly, changing oil-fouled spark plugs for a new set will get you moving again, but remember that the reason for the fouling (if it wasn't simple an incorrect grade of plug) will have to be established and corrected.

Don't take anything for granted. Particularly, don't forget that a 'new' component may itself be defective (especially if it's been rattling round in the boot for months), and don't leave components out of a fault diagnosis sequence just because they are new or recently fitted. When you do finally diagnose a difficult fault, you'll probably realise that all the evidence was there from the start.

Electrical faults

Electrical faults can be more puzzling than straightforward mechanical failures, but they are no less susceptible to logical analysis if the basic principles of operation are understood. Car electrical wiring exists in extremely unfavourable conditions – heat, vibration and chemical attack – and the first things to look for are loose or corroded connections, and broken or chafed wires, especially where the wires pass through holes in the bodywork or are subject to vibration.

Carrying a few spares may save you a long walk

All metal-bodies cars in current production have one pole of the battery 'earthed', ie connected to the car bodywork, and in nearly all modern cases it is the negative (–) terminal. The various electrical components – motors, bulb holders etc – are also connected to earth, either by means of a lead or directly by their mountings. Electric current flows through the component and then back to the battery via the car bodywork. If the component mounting is loose or corroded, or if a good path back to the battery is not available, the circuit will be incomplete and malfunction will result. The engine and/or gearbox are also earthed by means of flexible metal straps to the body or subframe; if these straps are loose or missing, starter motor, generator and ignition trouble may result.

Assuming the earth return to be necessary, electrical faults will be due either to component malfunction or to defects in the current supply. Individual components are dealt with in Chapter 10. If supply wires are broken or cracked internally this results in an open-circuit, and the easiest way to check for this is to bypass the suspect wire temporarily with a length of wire having a crocodile clip or suitable connector at each end. Alternatively, a 12V test lamp can be used to verify the presence of supply voltage at various points along the wire and the break can be thus isolated.

If a bare portion of a live wire touches the car bodywork or other earthed metal part, the electricity will take the low-resistance path thus formed back to the battery: this is known as a short-circuit. Hopefully a short-circuit will blow a fuse, but otherwise it may cause burning of the insulation (and possible further short-circuits) or even a fire. This is why it is inadvisable to bypass persistently blowing fuses with silver foil or wire.

Spares and tool kit

Most cars are only supplied with sufficient tools for wheel changing; the *Maintenance and minor repair* tool kit detailed in *Tools and working facilities*, with the addition of a hammer, is probably sufficient for those repairs that most motorists would consider attempting at the roadside. In addition a few items which can be fitted without too much trouble in the event of breakdown should be carried. Experience and available space will modify the list below, but the following may save having to call on professional assistance:

Spark plugs, clean and correctly gapped
HT lead and plug cap – long enough to reach the plug furthest from the distributor
Distributor rotor, condenser and contact breaker points
Drivebelt – emergency type may suffice
Spare fuses
Set of principal light bulbs
Tin of radiator sealer and hose bandage
Exhaust bandage
Roll of insulating tape
Length of soft iron wire
Length of electrical flex
Torch or inspection lamp (can double as test lamp)
Battery jump leads
Tow-rope
Ignition waterproofing aerosol
Litre of engine oil
Sealed can of hydraulic fluid
Emergency windscreen
Tyre valve core

If spare fuel is carried, a can designed for the purpose should be used to minimise risks of leakage and collision damage. A first aid kit and a warning triangle, whilst not at present compulsory in the UK, are obviously sensible items to carry in addition to the above.

When touring abroad it may be advisable to carry additional spares which, even if you cannot fit them yourself, could save having to wait while parts are obtained. The items below may be worth considering:

Throttle cable
Cylinder head gasket
Alternator brushes
Fuel pump repair kit

One of the motoring organisations will be able to advise on availability of fuel etc in foreign countries.

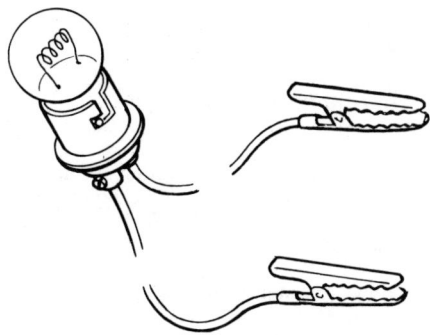

A simple test lamp is useful for investigating electrical faults

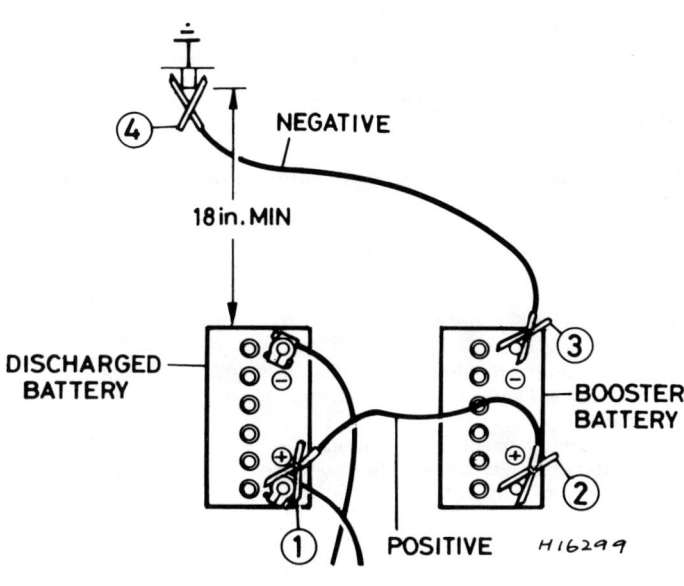

Jump start lead connections for negative earth – connect leads in order shown

Engine will not start

Engine fails to turn when starter operated
Flat battery (recharge, use jump leads, or push start)
Battery terminals loose or corroded
Battery earth to body defective
Engine earth strap loose or broken
Starter motor (or solenoid) wiring loose or broken
Automatic transmission selector in wrong position, or inhibitor switch faulty
Ignition/starter switch faults
Major mechanical failure (seizure) or long dususe (piston rings rusted to bores)
Starter or solenoid internal fault (see Chapter 10).

Starter motor turns engine slowly
Partially discharged battery (recharge, use jump leads, or push start)
Battery terminals loose or corroded
Battery earth to body defective
Engine earth strap loose
Starter motor (or solenoid) wiring loose
Starter motor internal fault (see Chapter 10)

Starter motor spins without turning engine
    Flat battery
    Starter motor pinion sticking on sleeve
    Flywheel gear teeth damaged or worn
    Starter motor mounting bolts loose

Engine turns normally but fails to start
    Damp or dirty HT leads and distributor cap (crank engine and
    check for spark)
    Dirty or incorrectly gapped contact breaker points
    No fuel in tank (check for delivery at carburettor)
    Excessive choke (hot engine) or insufficient choke (cold engine)
    Fouled or incorrectly gapped spark plugs (remove, clean and
    regap)
    Other ignition system fault (See Chapter 4)
    Other fuel system fault (see Chapter 3)
    Poor compression (See Chapter 1)
    Major mechanical failure (eg camshaft drive)

Engine fires but will not run
    Insufficient choke (cold engine)
    Air leaks at carburettor or inlet manifold
    Fuel starvation (see Chapter 3)
    Other ignition fault (see Chapter 4)

Engine cuts out and will not restart

Engine cuts out suddenly – ignition fault
    Loose or disconnected LT wires
    Wet HT leads or distributor cap (after traversing water splash)
    Coil or condenser failure (check for spark)
    Other ignition fault (see Chapter 4)

Engine misfires before cutting out – fuel fault
    Fuel tank empty
    Fuel pump defective or filter blocked (check for delivery)
    Fuel tank filler vent blocked (suction will be evident on releasing
    cap)
    Carburettor needle valve sticking
    Carburettor jets blocked (fuel contaminated)
    Other fuel system fault (See Chapter 3)

Engine cuts out – other causes
    Serious overheating
    Major mechanical failure (eg camshaft drive)

Engine overheats

Ignition (no-charge) warning light illuminated
    Slack or broken drivebelt – retension or renew (Chapter 10)

Ignition warning light not illuminated
    Coolant loss due to internal or external leakage (see Chapter 2)
    Thermostat defective
    Low oil level
    Brakes binding
    Radiator clogged externally or internally
    Electric cooling fan not operating correctly
    Engine waterways clogged
    Ignition timing incorrect or automatic advance malfunctioning
    Mixture too weak

Note: *Do not add cold water to an overheated engine or damage may
result.*

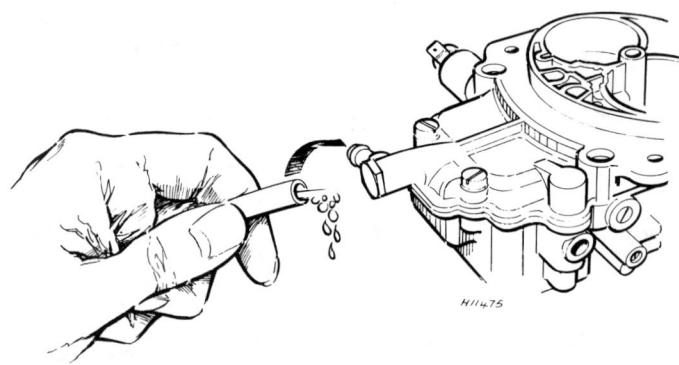

**Remove fuel pipe from carburettor and check that fuel is being
delivered**

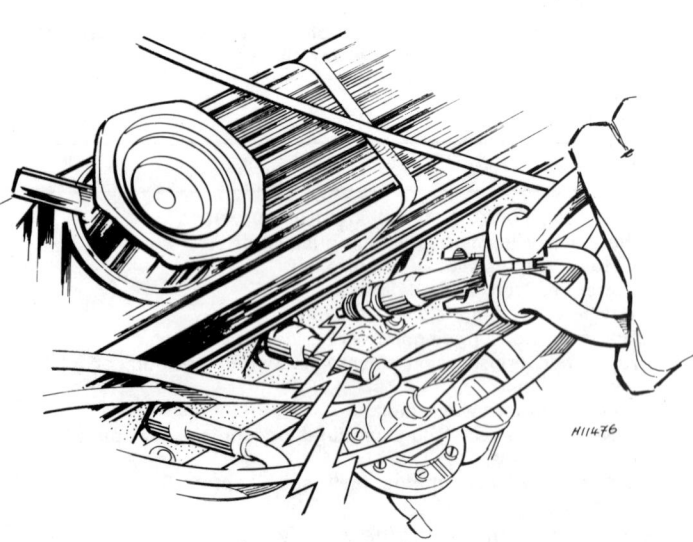

**Crank engine and check for a spark. Note use of insulated pliers –
dry cloth or a rubber glove will suffice**

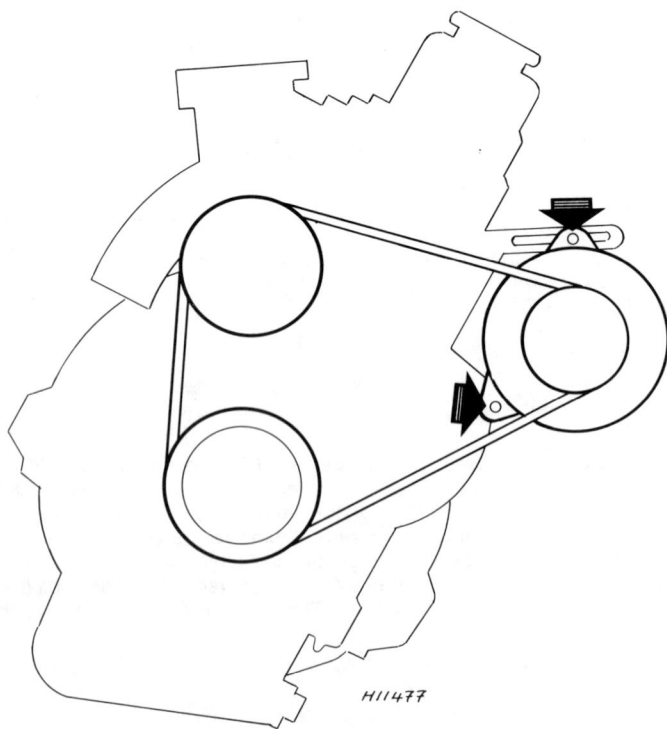

**A slack drivebelt may cause overheating and battery charging
problems**

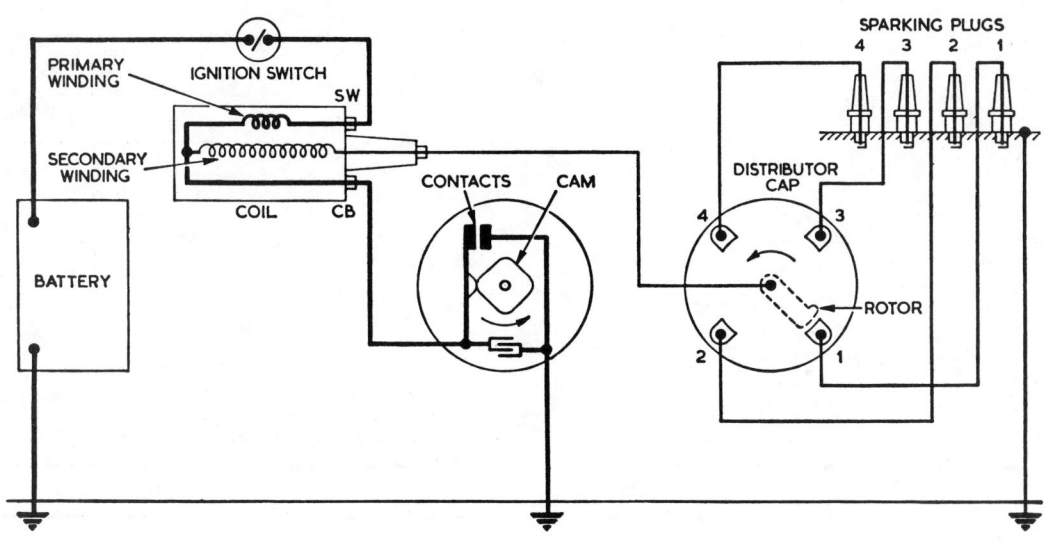

Schematic ignition circuit diagram

Low engine oil pressure

Gauge reads low or warning light illuminated with engine running
   Oil level low or incorrect grade
   Defective gauge or sender unit
   Wire to sender unit earthed
   Engine overheating
   Oil filter clogged or bypass valve defective
   Oil pressure relief valve defective
   Oil pick-up strainer clogged
   Oil pump worn or mountings loose
   Worn main or big-end bearings

Note: *Low oil pressure in a high-mileage engine at tickover is not necessarily a cause for concern. Sudden pressure loss at speed is far more significant. In any event, check the gauge or warning light sender before condemning the engine.*

Engine noises

Pre-ignition (pinking) or acceleration
   Incorrect grade of fuel

   Ignition timing incorrect
   Distributor faulty or worn
   Worn or maladjusted carburettor
   Excessive carbon build-up in engine

Whistling or wheezing noises
   Leaking vacuum hose
   Leaking carburettor or manifold gasket
   Blowing head gasket

Tapping or rattling
   Incorrect valve clearances
   Worn valve gear
   Worn timing chain
   Broken piston ring (ticking noise)

Knocking or thumping
   Unintentional mechanical contact (eg fan blades)
   Worn fanbelt
   Peripheral component fault (generator, water pump etc)
   Worn big-end bearings (regular heavy knocking, perhaps less under load)
   Worn main bearings (rumbling and knocking, perhaps worsening under load)
   Piston slap (most noticeable when cold)

Chapter 1 Engine

For modifications, and information applicable to later models, see Supplement at end of manual

Contents

Specifications

General

Engine type	4-cylinder, 4-stroke, water-cooled, ohv
Engine type number:	
Models 105S and 105L	742.10
Models 120L and LE	742.12
Models 120LS, GLS and LSE	742.12X
Bore x stroke (mm):	
742.10	68 x 72
742.12 and 742.12X	72 x 72
Cubic capacity (cc):	
742.10	1046
742.12 and 742.12X	1174
Compression ratio:	
742.10 and 742.12	8.5 : 1
742.12X	9.5 : 1
Firing order	1 – 3 – 4 – 2 (No 1 cylinder at crankshaft pulley end)
Engine oil capacity:	
742.10 and 742.12	7 pints (4 litres)
742.12X	8 pints (4.6 litres)

Cylinder liners

Maximum permissible bore wear	0.1 mm (0.004 in)

Internal diameter (mm):	Class mark	742.10	742.12 and 12X
Standard	A	68.00	72.00
	B	68.01	72.01
	C	68.02	72.02
First rebore	1A	68.25	—
	1B	68.26	—
	1C	68.27	—
Second rebore	2A	68.50	—
	2B	68.51	—
	2C	68.52	—
Internal diameter tolerance	+0.009 mm (0.00035 in)		
Protrusion above block	0.125 to 0.155 mm (0.005 to 0.006 in)		
Shim sizes available	0.10 to 0.14 mm (0.004 to 0.0055 in)		

Pistons

Type	Light alloy, flat crown (except 742.12X which has convex crown)		
Diameter (mm):	Class mark	742.10	742.12 and 12X
Standard	A	67.95	71.95
	B	67.96	71.96
	C	67.97	71.97
First oversize	1A	68.20	—
	1B	68.21	—
	1C	68.22	—
Second oversize	2A	68.45	—
	2B	68.46	—
	2C	68.47	—
Diameter tolerance	-0.009 mm (0.00035 in)		

Gudgeon pins

	Nominal	Tolerance
Diameter	20 or 20.05 mm	-0.003 mm
Small-end bush diameter	20 or 20.05 mm	+0.005 to -0.001 mm
Pin bore in piston	20 or 20.05 mm	-0.004 to -0.010 mm

Crankshaft

Journal diameters (mm):	Main bearing	Big-end bearing
Standard	55.00	45.00
First regrind	54.75	44.75
Fourth regrind	54.00	44.00
Journal diameter tolerance	-0.010 to -0.029 mm	-0.009 to -0.025 mm
Bearing shell thickness (mm):		
Standard	1.497	1.490
First regrind	1.622	1.615
Second regrind	1.747	1.740
Third regrind	1.872	1.865
Fourth regrind	1.997	1.990
Shell bearing tolerance	-0.007 mm	-0.007 mm
Main bearing journal width and guide ring thickness (mm):	Main bearing	Guide ring
Standard	31.5	1.490
First regrind	31.625	1.615
Second regrind	31.75	1.740
Third regrind	31.875	1.865
Fourth regrind	32.00	1.990
Journal width and guide ring tolerance	+0.025 mm	-0.01 mm
Thrust ring minimum thickness	3.75 mm (0.148 in)	
Crankshaft endfloat	0.04 to 0.10 mm (0.0016 to 0.0039 in)	

Oil pump

Type	Gear driven, force feed	
Clearances:	Standard	Wear limit
Driveshaft-to-bearing	0.02 to 0.06 mm (0.0008 to 0.002 in)	0.15 mm (0.006 in)
Pin-to-driven gear	0.014 to 0.050 mm (0.0006 to 0.0019 in)	0.10 mm (0.004 in)
Gears-to-cap	0.045 to 0.158 mm (0.0018 to 0.006 in)	0.20 mm (0.008 in)

Camshaft

	Standard	Oversize
Camshaft bearing diameter in block (mm):		
No 1	39.0 +0.025	39.2 +0.025
No 2	38.5 +0.025	38.7 +0.025
No 3	30.0 +0.021	30.2 +0.025
Crankshaft journal diameter (mm):		
No 1	39.0 -0.050	39.2 -0.050 to -0.025
No 2	38.5 -0.025	38.7 -0.050 to -0.025
No 3	30.0 -0.041 to -0.020	30.2 -0.050 to -0.025

Valves and valvegear

Valve stem diameter:		
Inlet	7.5 mm -0.013 to -0.028 mm (0.295 in -0.0005 to -0.001 in)	
Exhaust	7.5 mm -0.025 to -0.040 mm (0.295 in -0.001 to -0.0016 in)	
Valve guide internal diameter (inlet and exhaust)	7.5 mm +0.022 mm (0.295 in +0.0009 in)	
Tappet diameter:		
Standard	21 mm -0.020 mm (0.826 in -0.0007 in)	
Oversize	21.1 mm -0.007 in (0.835 in -0.0003 in)	
Tappet bore diameter	As tappet diameter but +0.021 mm (+0.0008 in)	
Valve spring free length:		
Inner	43.6 mm (1.717 in)	
Outer	45.85 mm (1.805 in)	
Valve timing:	Opens	Closes
Inlet (all models)	14° 30' BTDC	45° 30' ABDC
Exhaust (742.10 and 742.12)	40° 10' BBDC	13° 30' ATDC
Exhaust (742.12X)	46° 30' BBDC	7° 30' ATDC
Valve clearances (cold):		
Inlet (742.10 and 742.12)	0.15 mm (0.006 in)	
Inlet (742.12X)	0.20 mm (0.008 in)	
Exhaust (all models)	0.20 mm (0.008 in)	

Torque wrench settings

	Nm	lbf ft
Main bearing nuts	40 to 45	29.5 to 33.1
Connecting rod nuts	25 to 28	18.4 to 20.6
Rocker cover nut	4 to 6	3 to 4
Rocker pedestal bolts	30 to 35	22.1 to 25.8
Cylinder head nuts	25 to 28	18.4 to 20.6
Cylinder head bolts	50 to 55	36.8 to 40.5
Camshaft gear bolt	30 to 35	22.1 to 25.8
Flywheel bolt	55 to 65	40.5 to 48
Crankshaft pulley bolt	100 to 120	73.7 to 88.5
Sump bolts	7 to 9	5 to 6.6
Drain plug	30 to 35	22.1 to 25.8
Oil pressure relief valve bolt	22 to 25	16.2 to 18.4
Oil pressure switch socket	50 to 55	36.8 to 40.5
Oil pressure switch	20 to 25	14.7 to 18.4
Spark plugs	20 to 30	14.7 to 22.1

1 General description and maintenance

The engine fitted to all models covered is of similar design, being a four-stroke, 4-cylinder in-line unit with an overhead valve layout. The crankcase is cast in aluminium whilst the cylinder head is iron. The engine is water-cooled.

The crankshaft has three main bearings. The clutch and flywheel assembly are located onto its rear flange whilst a double sprocket fitted onto its front end serves to drive the camshaft via the double row timing chain. The main bearings and the big-end bearings are of the shell type whilst the connecting rod small-end bearings are of the bronze bush type, being pressed into the connecting rod and reamed to suit.

The camshaft has a helical gear on its front end which drives the distributor. The camshaft also drives the oil pump.

The force feed lubrication system consists of a gear-driven pump unit which draws oil from the sump through a strainer, and circulates the lubricant to the various engine components via a filter mounted externally on the crankcase. On some models an oil cooler is fitted and some 120 models are fitted with a ribbed sump to aid oil cooling. The oil pressure is controlled by an automatic pressure relief valve.

Engine – maintenance

The engine is the heart of the car and, as such, should be treated with respect. Weekly checks should be made on the oil and coolant levels, and they should be topped up if required. As detailed in the Maintenance Section at the front of this book, engine oil should, periodically, be drained and replenished.

Look for coolant and oil leaks around the engine and, if found, repair as required.

All the electrical connections should be clean and secure, and cables and pipes should be kept clear of 'hot spots' and not allowed to chafe.

Careful and regular maintenance will ensure a long and reliable life for your engine.

2 Major operations possible – engine in car

The following operations are possible with the engine in the vehicle:

Cylinder head – removal and refitting
Timing cover and timing sprockets and chain assemblies – removal and refitting
Camshaft – removal and refitting
Pistons and connecting rods and cylinder liners – removal and refitting

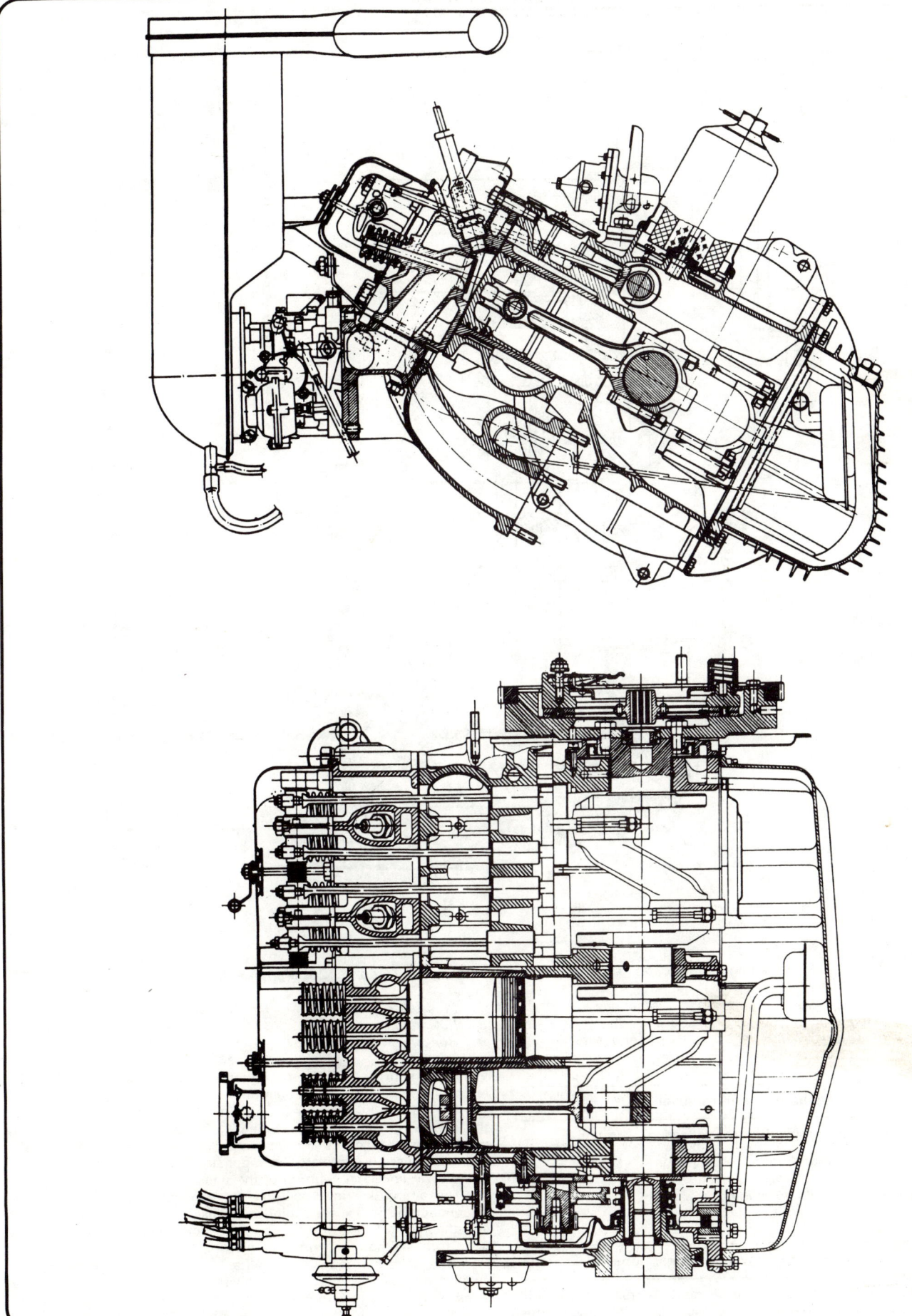

Fig. 1.1 Sectional views of 120LS engine (Sec 1)

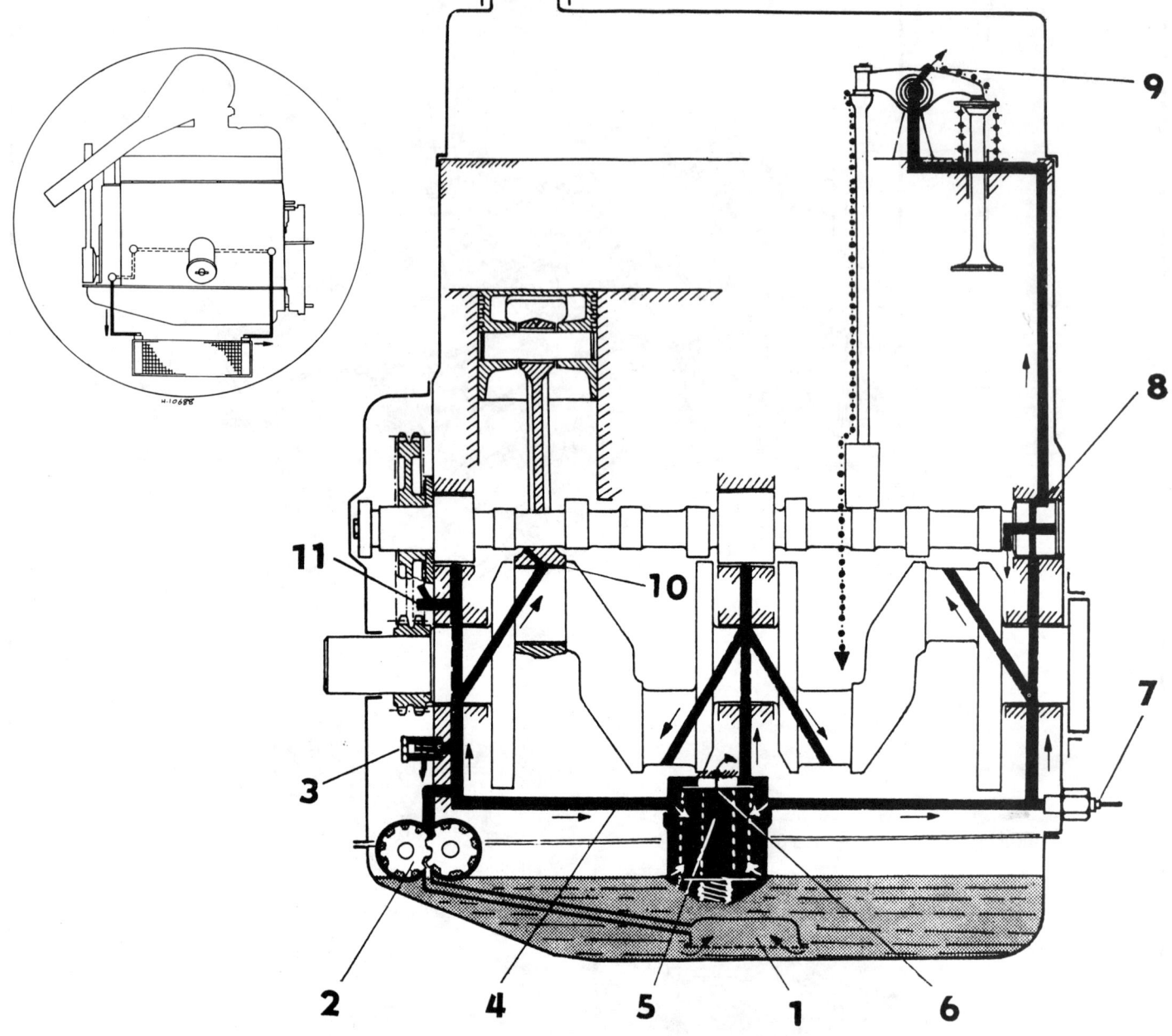

Fig. 1.2 Engine lubrication system. Inset shows oil cooler fitted to 120LS engine (Sec 1)

1	Pick-up strainer	4	Main oilway	7	Pressure switch
2	Oil pump	5	Filter	8	Pulsating chamber
3	Pressure relief valve	6	Filter bypass	9	Rockers

10	Connecting rod splash hole
11	Timing chain splash screw

3 Major operations requiring engine removal

The engine must be removed for the following operations:

Crankshaft – removal and refitting
Clutch – removal and refitting
Transmission – removal and refitting

4 Engine and transmission removal – general notes

The engine may be removed with or without the transmission unit as required. There are two methods of actually withdrawing the engine/transmission, the method employed depending on facilities for removal and on personal preference.

The easiest method for the DIY mechanic is probably to remove the rear body panel (as described in Chapter 11), which not only provides better access for disconnecting and reattaching the engine/transmission-associated components, but also allows for easy withdrawal and later refitting of the units.

The alternative method (and the one that we employed) is to disconnect the respective engine/transmission-associated components and then to raise the rear of the body sufficiently high to allow the units to be withdrawn from underneath.

Whichever method is used, suitable axle stands will be needed to support the rear of the body. If available, a trolley jack will be a great asset and a pillar jack, preferably hydraulic, should also be at hand.

When the engine/transmission is ready for removal the trolley jack will be needed to support the unit. The driveshafts can be left connected to the transmission but must be disconnected together with the suspension radius arm and shock absorber coil spring. Do not detach the radius arm from the driveshaft housing or the rear suspension alignment will be disturbed.

5 Engine and transmission – removal

1   Raise and support the car at the rear. Make secure by placing an axle stand each side just forward of the radius arm pivot point.
2   Disconnect the battery terminals. The battery is situated behind the rear seats and access to it is gained by removing the seat backs and lifting the rear storage compartment floor covering. Remove the battery cover and disconnect the terminals.
3   Drain the engine oil into a container having at least 1 gallon (4.6 litres) capacity. Refit the drain plug afterwards to ensure it does not get mislaid.
4   If the transaxle assembly is also being removed this should also be drained. The gearbox and axle housing capacity on all models is 4.5 pints (2.5 litres).
5   Drain the cooling system (see Chapter 2) and remove the central undertray.
6   Disconnect the carburettor air cleaner and remove it (refer to Chapter 3 if necessary). Also disconnect the throttle linkage, the choke cable, the lead to the carburettor solenoid (if fitted) and the petrol pump feed pipe (photo). Plug the fuel pipe to prevent leakage or dirt ingress.
7   Remove the engine dirt protector plate from its position on the inside of the right-hand rear wing. There are two nuts on top and five bolts underneath.
8   Disconnect the starter motor leads.
9   Remove the oil pressure switch cable from its terminal (located in front of the oil filter).
10   On 120LS models detach the oil cooler outlet and inlet pipes from the engine and drain the oil into a container. The ends of the oil pipes are best wrapped in a polythene bag or piece of rag to prevent further spillage. If in good condition the pipe junction sealant washers may be used again but it is generally recommended that they be renewed.
11   Remove the distributor cap, rotor arm and HT leads from the spark plugs and coil. Place a piece of rag over the distributor to protect it.
12   Disconnect the two alternator leads – yellow from top, blue from engine side – and tuck the cables out of the way behind the coil.
13   Detach the water temperature wire from its location near the thermostat housing.
14   Disconnect the hoses from the thermostat housing and water pump. The original Skoda hose clips are somewhat awkward to undo and can get distorted. It is therefore suggested that these be changed for worm drive clips during reassembly.
15   Detach the heater hose from the interconnecting pipe to the thermostat (on the right-hand side).
16   Although not essential, it is advisable to remove the thermostat and housing complete at this stage to protect it from damage during engine removal. Therefore either remove the thermostat complete as given in Chapter 2, or disconnect it from the engine but leave the hoses attached.
17   Undo the bolts securing the nearside dirt shield to the underbody

above the exhaust silencer, and remove it.
18   Remove the central inspection cover in the rear storage compartment to gain access to the clutch slave cylinder. This in turn is protected by a cover retained by a spring: cover and spring must be removed, together with the slave cylinder retaining bolts. Unhook the two clutch release fork springs. The slave cylinder can now be disconnected and tucked out of the way, being still connected to the hydraulic hose.
19   Disconnect the handbrake by removing the two cable adjusting nuts on the handbrake link. Access to this assembly is gained by removing the inspection cover at the rear end of the central drive tunnel, in front of the rear seats. The cables should then be pulled through the guide holes in the body and left to hang free under the car.
20   Disconnect the telescopic shock absorbers. Fold back the carpet from the wheel arch at the rear on each side and prise free the plastic cover for access to the upper shock absorber mounting. Hold the top of each shock absorber with a pair of grips to prevent the shaft from turning and then unscrew the retaining nut. Remove the nut, washer and bushed washer. If the wheels have been removed a jack should be positioned under each brake drum to support the suspension arm at the correct height.
21   Unscrew and remove the shock absorber lower retaining plate bolts. Lower and remove the shock absorbers. **Do not** detach or disturb the half axle-to-suspension arm retaining bolts.
22   From underneath remove the two cables from the reversing light switch, located on the forward end of the gearbox on the right-hand side (photo).
23   Disconnect the rear brake hydraulic pipes. To prevent spillage through the breather hole of the brake fluid reservoir, remove the filler cap, place a piece of polythene over the filler neck and refit the cap. Disconnect each of the two rear brake hydraulic connections from the respective backplates. These are 'banjo' type connectors, and the copper sealing washers should always be renewed on refitting.
24   Select 1st or 3rd gear, then release the gear selector rod from underneath by undoing the locknut and loosening off the selector rod locking bolt (photo). Push the selector shaft forward to disconnect. Should the shaft fail to move, check that the locking bolt is slackened off sufficiently and move the gear selector lever to the rear to obtain more leverage.
25   Next remove the bolt through the speedo cable clamp. Withdraw it from its driveshaft and pull the cable clear.
26   Disconnect the suspension arm (each side) at its forward pivot point. Unscrew the retaining nut from the pivot bolt and then withdraw the pivot bolt with its special spacer/bush washer. Prise the arm free from its location.
27   Disconnect the yoke limiting strap on each side.
28   Position a trolley jack under the engine/transmission and raise to support (not lift) the unit.
29   If the driveshafts are to be removed prior to engine/transmission withdrawal, disconnect them at the transmission flange by removing the nuts, then refer to Chapter 8 and disconnect the shock absorbers at the top and bottom.
30   Lower the jacks supporting the suspension arms and driveshaft assemblies and remove them, the coil springs and shock absorbers.
31   Check that the trolley jack is securely located under the engine/transmission assemblies and just supporting their weight. Now disconnect the engine/transmission crossmember support bars from

5.6 Disconnect the choke cable and carburettor solenoid (arrowed)

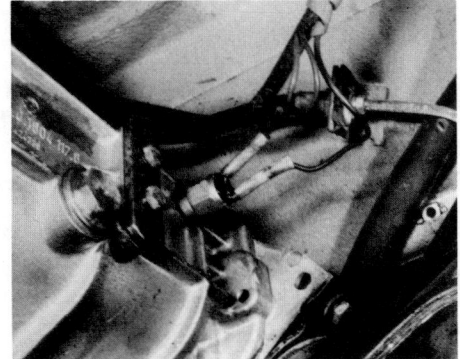
5.22 Disconnect the reversing light switch leads

5.24 Disconnect the selector shaft (arrowed)

5.31a Engine support bar and ...

5.31b ... gearbox support bar location

their locations to the body on each side (photos).

32 Check that all wiring, hoses and fittings are detached and folded back out of the way of the engine and transmission and then carefully withdraw the power pack from the rear of the car.

33 If the driveshafts are still attached, the body will have to be raised sufficiently to allow the coil springs to be removed prior to withdrawing the power pack. Alternatively, remove the wheels temporarily and fully lower the suspension arms to withdraw the springs.

34 Having removed the power pack it can be wheeled to a suitable spot for further dismantling, cleaning and inspection.

6 Engine only – removal

1 If only the engine is to be removed it can either be detached from the transmission unit, supported and the body raised sufficiently to allow the engine to be withdrawn from underneath, or the rear body panel can easily be removed (see Chapter 11) and the engine withdrawn rearwards without having to lift the body. To disengage the engine from the transmission it is necessary to withdraw it rearwards by 70 mm (2.75 in).

2 The latter of the above two engine removal methods is recommended if no trolley jack is available on which to support the engine and wheel it rearwards.

3 Proceed as detached in the previous Section, paragraphs 1 to 15, then as follows.

4 Position a jack in under the engine to support (not raise) it. If removing the engine with rear panel removed, locate the lifting sling securely in place round the engine so that it will lift the engine squarely without tilting it. Ensure that the sling will not interfere with any protruding engine attachments liable to be damaged when the full weight is taken up. Jack or block up the gearbox to support it.

5 Working through the central access aperture behind the rear seats, unscrew and remove the engine-to-transmission retaining nuts.

6 Disconnect the gearchange linkage from the gearbox as detailed in the previous Section, paragraph 24. **Note:** *This is not necessary if removing the engine with the rear panel removed.*

7 Remove the flywheel guard from the transmission case flange and remove the two nuts securing the engine to the transmission on each side.

8 Unscrew and remove the engine mounting bolts.

9 If removing the engine under the rear body panel, lower the engine and transmission jacks sufficiently to allow the engine to clear the rear body panel when being withdrawn. If necessary increase the raised height of the body at the rear.

10 Before withdrawing the engine from the transmission ensure that all engine fittings and attachments are detached and clear of the engine. It is important during removal that the engine and transmission are kept parallel (although the engine will be tilted downwards to the rear) so that no undue strain will be placed on the gearbox input shaft.

11 Support the engine and carefully withdraw it from the transmission and clear of the car.

7 Engine dismantling (general)

Owners who have dismantled engines will know the need for a strong workbench and the many tools and pieces of equipment, which make their life much easier when going through the process of dismantling an engine. For those who are doing a dismantling job for the first time, there are a few 'musts' in the way of preparation which, if not done, will only cause frustration and long delays in the job.

It is essential to have sufficient space in which to work. Dismantling and reassembly are not going to be completed all in one go and it is therefore absolutely essential that you have sufficient area to leave things as they are, when necessary. A strong workbench is also necessary together with a good engineer's vice, and lastly but by no means least, your work area, bench and tools must be clean; if any dirt is conveyed into the engine during dismantling or reassembly, your work will be wasted completely.

The necessity for cleanliness also applies to the engine and transmission assembly; therefore once the assembly is clear of the car thoroughly clean the outside of the units. Remove all traces of oil and congealed dirt. A good grease solvent will make the job easier, as, after the solvent has been applied and allowed to stand for a time, the grease and dirt may be washed off with a jet of water. Finally the unit may be wiped dry and clean in preparation for dismantling.

Once the ancillary components together with the transmission unit have been removed from the engine, it may be lifted onto a clean bench for the main dismantling task.

During dismantling, clean the components in a solvent such as paraffin and carefully store them in clean containers – in readiness for assembly.

Never clean components with oilways (eg crankshaft) in petrol or paraffin, but wipe down carefully with a petrol-dampened rag. Nylon pipe cleaners or compressed air may be used to clear and clean the oilways.

It is false economy to re-use old gaskets. New gasket kits are available and with correct assembly, ensure first rate joints. The old gaskets may be useful as templates for new gaskets, if a replacement is not immediately available from a Skoda dealer.

8 Engine – ancillary components removal

1 Having cleaned off the external surfaces of the engine, the ancillary components and fittings can then be removed as required.

2 If the engine and transmission were removed together and are to be separated, first unbolt and remove the starter motor (photo). Unscrew and remove the engine-to-transmission retaining nuts and

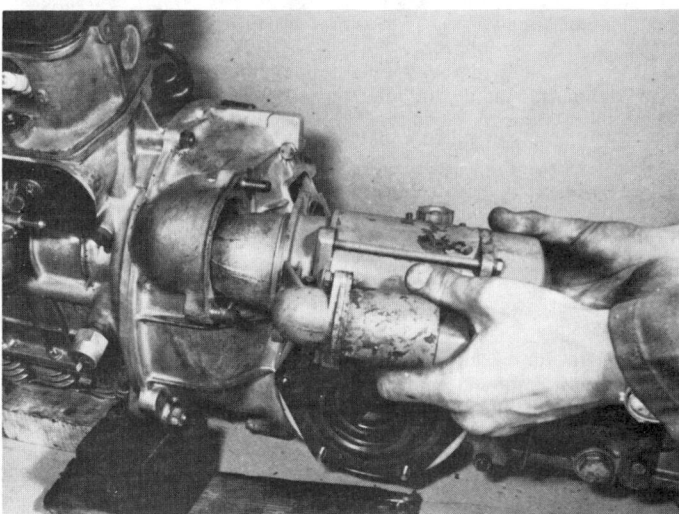

8.2 Remove the starter motor

8.3 Remove the inlet manifold and ...

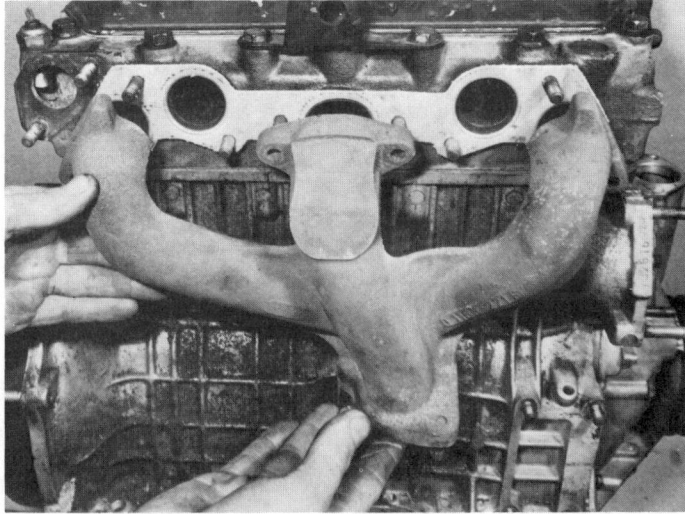

8.4 ... the exhaust manifold

the clutch belly guard plate. Pull the engine from the gearbox, being careful not to allow the weight of the engine to rest on the transmission input shaft.

3   Remove the carburettor and inlet manifold. Disconnect the fuel line from the pump and the vacuum tube from the carburettor, then unscrew the four carburettor-to-manifold nuts and unclip the throttle connecting rod linkage to release. Remove the inlet manifold by unscrewing the four retaining nuts (photo).

4   Remove the exhaust manifold (photo). The exhaust manifold can be removed complete with the downpipe(s) and silencer by undoing the manifold nuts and silencer support bracket bolts. Alternatively, if the head only is being removed, or a new manifold gasket being fitted, it can be parted at the manifold and downpipe flange by undoing the clamp nuts.

5   Remove the alternator. To disconnect the alternator, remove the adjustment strap bolt at the top and the hinge bolt from the mounting bracket. If the engine is being stripped, the adjustment strap and mounting bracket should also be removed.

6   Remove the distributor. Scratch mark the relative position of the distributor with the crankshaft on TDC – see Chapter 4. Remove the two distributor extension tube flange bolts to the timing chest and withdraw the distributor. Avoid moving the preset clamp plate if possible.

7   Remove the water pump. Undo the retaining nuts and remove the water pump complete with pulley and gasket from its position on the front of the block.

8   Remove the fuel pump. Undo the fixing nuts and remove the fuel pump/insulating washer and gaskets.

9   Remove the clutch unit. Prior to clutch removal, mark the adjacent positions of the flywheel and clutch cover, assuming they are to be refitted. This is because the clutch, flywheel and crankshaft were fully balanced as a unit, and should therefore be kept in unison on reassembly. Undo the six clutch retaining bolts half a turn at a time, in diagonal fashion. This method will relieve the spring pressure without distorting the cover or putting excessive strain on individual bolts. Remove the clutch complete.

10   Remove the flywheel. Mark the flywheel-to-crankshaft relative position, bend flat the four locktabs of the washer and undo the four bolts to remove.

11   Remove the pilot bearing from its recess in the crankshaft and flange.

12   The engine is now stripped of all ancillary equipment and is ready for the final dismantling.

9   Cylinder head – removal

1   If the cylinder head is to be removed with the engine in the car, drain the coolant (Chapter 2), remove the air cleaner unit (Chapter 3) and disconnect the choke and throttle cables, the fuel lines and the vacuum hose to the carburettor. Then continue as follows.

2   Remove the rocker cover complete with gasket and washers. Disconnect the rocker shaft pedestals, there are four bolts for the pedestals. Note that on some models the pedestals are retained by two long Allen screws at each end which also double as cylinder head bolts.

3   Carefully lift clear the rocker assembly, and dismantle for inspection. Note the oil feed hole in one of the pedestals, and keep all parts in the order of original assembly. To dismantle the rockers, remove the circlip from the end of the shaft and slide off the rockers, pedestals, etc.

4   Remove the pushrods, keeping them in the relative order in which they were removed. The easiest way to do this is to push them through a sheet of thick paper or thin card in the correct sequence.

5   Undo the four head nuts in front of the spark plug holes and the nine head bolts. These should be undone in the reverse order to the tightening sequence as shown in Fig. 1.12.

6   Remove the water temperature gauge sender.

7   If the engine is in the car, disconnect the exhaust manifold-to-downpipe connection.

8   The cylinder head may now be removed. If it is reluctant to come off, use the exhaust manifold as a handle and try to rock the head to break the seal. If this fails to work, strike the head sharply with a plastic or wooden-headed hammer, at the same time pulling upwards. **Do not** try to lever the head away from the block with a screwdriver or chisel as damage to the mating surfaces may result.

9   If the engine is to be dismantled completely, it may be possible to free the head by turning the engine, when the compression in the cylinders will lift the head. This is not advised if it is only wished to work on the head, since the cylinder liners may be disturbed in their seats which would entail additional unwanted work.

10 Cylinder block – dismantling

1   Remove the tappet side cover by removing the four nuts and flat washers. Withdraw complete with gasket. It may help to prise it off with a screwdriver but be careful not to damage the cover, as oil leakage will occur on reassembly if distorted.
2   Lift and remove to the bench the cam followers, keeping in order of removal (photo).
3   Remove the oil filter. Place a container under the oil filter and remove the complete filter with element and sealing ring by undoing the centre stud bolt.
4   Remove the right-hand engine mounting bracket, complete with earth strap and rubber shock absorbers.
5   Remove the clutch belly plate cover, two bolts with flat and shakeproof washers (which should be replaced if worn flat).
6   Undo the sump bolts and remove the sump. If stuck, lightly tap the protruding tabs on the sump with a soft-headed mallet.
7   Remove the oil suction tube and filter, by undoing the four bolts to the base of the timing case, and the support stay bolt located on the middle main bearing cap.
8   Now remove the timing chest by undoing the seven screws. If tight, place a screwdriver in the screw slot and lightly tap a hammer, directly in line with the screw, then try unscrewing. Remove the alternator mounting bracket to allow the cover to be removed.
9   Bend the lockwasher tab flat and undo the camshaft gear retaining nut. To stop the crankshaft and camshaft revolving, place a block of wood between the cylinder wall and the crankshaft.
10 Withdraw the distributor driving gear from the camshaft, followed by the crankshaft and camshaft sprockets, complete with timing chain. The sprockets are a sliding fit on their respective shafts, being located by Woodruff keys and thrust washers, which are also removed at this stage.
11 Undo the three setscrews and remove the camshaft thrust plate, and withdraw the camshaft.
12 Remove the rear oil seal and housing complete, by undoing the five screws.
13 Unscrew the retaining nuts and remove the connecting rod bearing caps. Note that the connecting rods and caps are marked on the right-hand side, and the locknuts are fitted with the flat flange face to the cap.
14 Prior to removing the respective piston and rod assemblies, consider whether or not the cylinder liners are to be withdrawn. If they are then the piston/rod assemblies can be withdrawn complete with

each liner in turn. If the liners are to stay in position in the crankcase they should be clamped in position by fitting suitable bolts and washers as shown (photo).
15 With the shells removed, push a hammer handle against the rod and withdraw the piston and rod through the top of the cylinder bores. Lay out the connecting rod assemblies and shells on a worktop, in sequence, ready for cleaning and careful inspection.
16 Now remove the three main bearing caps and note their markings. If unmarked, mark them yourself to ensure correct refitment. Care should be taken to keep the shells with their respective caps if it is intended to re-use them. Note, as with the big-end shells, it is probably false economy to re-use old main bearing shells unless they are virtually as new.
17 Lift the crankshaft clear of the crankcase. Clean ready for inspection.
18 Remove the oil pressure relief valve assembly by unscrewing the retaining nut directly beneath the alternator bracket.
19 The cylinder block should now be fully cleaned inside, and out, prior to inspection.

11 Engine – component examination and renovation (general)

With the engine stripped down and the various components cleaned, they can be thoroughly examined for wear or other damage.
At this stage it can be decided whether only a partial engine overhaul is required, or a complete reconditioning. If the latter is the case, an exchange reconditioned unit is often the best solution. If an exchange 'short engine' is to be purchased, the main components in the existing short block (ie pistons, connecting-rods, crankshaft) should be loosely reassembled prior to exchanging the unit.
The items covered in the following Sections must be checked, and where necessary, renewed or renovated before the engine can be rebuilt.

12 Crankshaft – examination and renovation

1   Examine the crankpin and main journal surfaces for signs of scoring or scratches, check the ovality of the crankpins at different positions with a micrometer. If more than 0.001 inch (0.025 mm) out of round, the crankpins will have to be reground. They will also have to be reground if there are any scores or scratches. Check the big-end journals in the same fashion.
2   If it is necessary to regrind the crankshaft and fit new bearings, your local Skoda garage or engine reconditioning specialist will be able to decide on how much metal needs to be ground off and also the size of replacement bearing shells.
3   If it is decided to fit new bearing shells without regrinding, *note that oversize shells are not necessarily marked* – have the crankshaft

10.2 Withdraw the cam followers

10.14 Cylinder retainers in position

measured if you suspect that it may have been reground by a previous owner.

13 Big-end and main bearings – examination and renovation

1 Big-end bearing failure is recognised by a noisy knocking from the crankcase and a slight drop in oil pressure. Main bearing failure is accompanied by vibration, which can be quite severe as the engine speed rises and falls, and a drop in oil pressure.

2 Bearings which have not broken up, but are badly worn, will give rise to low oil pressure and some vibration. Inspect the big-ends and main bearing shells and the crankshaft thrust washers for signs of general wear, scoring, pitting and scratches. The bearings should be matt grey in colour. With lead bronze bearings, should a trace of copper colour be noticed the bearings are badly worn as the lead bearing material has worn away to expose the indium underlay. Renew the bearings if they are in this condition or if there is any sign of scoring or pitting. We recommend that bearing shells and thrust washers are renewed as a matter of course – regardless of their condition.

3 The undersizes available are designed to correspond with the regrind sizes. The bearings are in fact slightly more than the stated undersize as running clearances have been allowed for during their manufacture.

4 Very long engine life can be achieved by changing big-end bearings at intervals of 30 000 miles and main bearings at intervals of 50 000 miles, irrespective of bearing wear. Crankshafts normally have to be reground because of scoring due to bearing failure.

14 Cylinder bores – examination and renovation

1 Cylinder bores must be examined for taper, ovality, scoring and scratches. Start by carefully examining the top of the cylinder bores; if they are at all worn, a very slight ridge will be found on the thrust side. This marks the top of the piston travel. The owner will have a good indication of the bore wear prior to dismantling the engine or removing the cylinder head. Excessive oil consumption accompanied by blue smoke from the exhaust, is a sure sign of worn cylinder bores and piston rings.

2 Measure the bore diameter just under the ridge with a micrometer and compare it with the diameter at the bottom of the bore which is not subject to wear. If the difference between the two measurements is more than 0.004 in (0.1 mm), then it will be necessary to fit special piston rings or to have the cylinders rebored and fit oversize piston and rings. If no micrometer is available, remove the rings from the pistons and place the piston in each bore in turn about $\frac{3}{4}$ in (19 mm) below the top of the bore. If an 0.010 in (0.25 mm) feeler gauge can be slid between the piston and the cylinder wall on the thrust side of the bore, then remedial action must be taken.

3 Liners for the 742.10 (1046 cc) engine can be rebored to the limits given in the Specifications, and oversize pistons obtained to suit. Liners for the 742.12 and 12X (1174 cc) engines cannot be rebored, neither are oversize pistons available, so renewal is the only course possible if the bores are excessively worn.

4 If the bores are slightly worn, but not so badly worn as to justify

reboring or renewing them, special oil control rings can be fitted to the existing pistons, which will restore the compression and stop the engine burning excessive quantities of oil. Several different types are available and the manufacturer's instructions concerning their fitting must be followed closely.

5 To ensure that new rings fitted to a worn bore bed in correctly the bores must be deglazed, and if possible, the top ridge in the bore removed. If a de-ridging tool or deglazing hone are not available, suitable results can be obtained by rubbing the interior of the bore with a fine grade emery paper in a criss-cross fashion on the horizontal. Never deglaze in a vertical line down the bore! If deglazing with a hone powered by a drill, with the liners clamped in position in the block, take care not to foul the cylinder block casing which protrudes just below the base of the bores.

6 Each cylinder liner is marked, on its top face (Fig. 1.3) with an A, B or C – this denotes the cylinder tolerance class (these are given in the Specifications Section). Check each cylinder prior to ordering any pistons and/or rings to ensure the correct replacements as specified.

15 Pistons and rings – examination and renovation

1 If the existing pistons are to be refitted, carefully remove the piston rings and then thoroughly clean them. Take care not to cut your fingers – piston rings are sharp! Use a piece of old piston ring or similar to clean out the piston ring grooves, taking care not to scratch the aluminium.

2 If new rings are to be fitted to the old pistons, then the top ring should be stepped so as to clear the ridge left above the previous top ring. If an unstepped new ring is to be fitted it will hit this ridge in the cylinder bore and break, this is because the new ring will not have worn in the same way as the old – which will have worn in unison with the ridge.

3 Before fitting the rings on the pistons each should be inserted part way down the cylinder bore and the gap in the ring measured with a feeler gauge. This should be between 0.009 in and 0.015 in (0.22 mm and 0.38 mm) (photo). It is essential that the gap is measured at the bottom of the ring travel. If it is measured at the top of the worn bore only and gives a perfect fit, it could easily seize at the bottom. If the ring gap is too small rub down the ends of the ring with a very fine file until the gap when fitted, is correct. To keep the rings square in the bore for measurement, line each up in turn with an old piston. Use the piston, upside-down, to push the ring down. Remove the piston and measure the piston ring gap.

4 When fitting new pistons and rings to rebored or new liners, the ring gap can be measured at the top of the bore, as the bore will not taper. When fitting new oil control piston rings it may be necessary to have the grooves widened, by machining, to accept new wider rings. In this instance the manufacturer's representative will make this quite clear and will supply the address to which the pistons must be sent for machining.

5 When new pistons are fitted take great care to fit the exact size best suited to the particular bore of your engine. Skoda go one stage further than merely specifying one size of piston for all standard bores. Because of very slight differences in cylinder machining during production, it is necessary to select just the right piston for the bore.

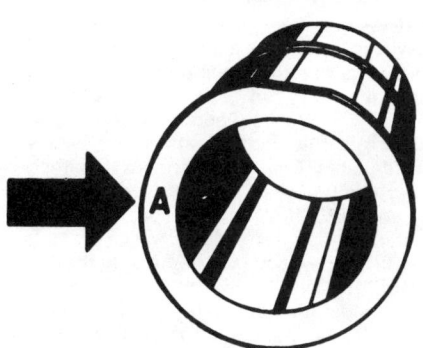

Fig. 1.3 Cylinder liner tolerance class mark (arrowed) (Sec 14)

15.3 Checking the ring gaps in the respective cylinder bores

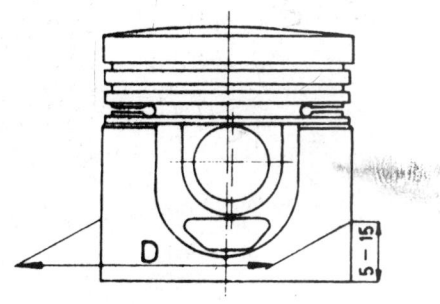

Fig. 1.4 Piston diameter measuring point (Sec 15)

A range of different sizes is available either from the piston manufacturers or the Skoda dealer.
6   The tolerance class, for standard sized pistons, is stamped on top
of the piston. The relevant tolerance classes are given in the
Specifications.

16 Gudgeon pin and small-end – examination and renovation

1   If the existing pistons are to be used again it is advisable to check
the gudgeon pin and small-end bush. The gudgeon pin is removed by
removing the circlips from the grooves in the pistons and pressing or
drifting the gudgeon pins out. They should be an interference fit in the
piston and a sliding fit in the small-end bush.
2   Providing the gudgeon pin is not badly worn, it is re-usable but it
is well worthwhile fitting new small-end bushes to the connecting
rods, considering the relatively small cost involved. The bush size
required is obtained by measuring the gudgeon pin with a micrometer,
and then referring to Specifications.
3   Fit the bush with the oil hole in line with the corresponding oil hole
in the small-end boss in the connecting rod. Ream the bush to suit.
This task is best undertaken by your Skoda agent, or an engine
rebuilding specialist, as they are not only better equipped, but can also
check the piston and rod alignment at the same time.

17 Camshaft and camshaft bearings – examination and reno- vation

1   Carefully examine the camshaft for wear. Slight scoring of the
cams may be removed by gently rubbing down with a fine emery cloth
or oilstone. The greatest care should be taken to keep the cam profiles
smooth.
2   Carefully examine the camshaft bearings in the cylinder block. If
they are badly worn, an oversize camshaft will have to be fitted and the
existing bearing apertures in the block reamed out. This is a job for
your Skoda agent as a line reamer is required.

18 Oil pressure relief valve – removal, inspection and reassembly

1   To prevent excessive oil pressure, for example when the engine is
cold, an oil pressure relief valve is built into the oilway system and
consists of a spring and ball valve which opens according to pressure.
2   Very little wear takes place in this assembly but in order to clean
the oilway out or to check for a suspected faulty oil pressure reading,
remove, as follows, from its location beneath the alternator bracket.
3   Undo the retaining bolt and remove complete with spring ball and
sealing washer. Should the ball not come out, insert a small magnet or
a rod with a smear of grease on the end to extract it.
4   Clean and inspect the parts for signs of deterioration and renew as
necessary.
5   Reassemble in the reverse sequence and be sure to fit a new
sealing washer under the bolt head.

19 Oil pump – removal, inspection and assembly

1   The oil pump is located in the case of the timing case and is driven
by a shaft from one of the gears which is located in the driving
mechanism of the distributor, see Fig. 1.6.
2   To examine the gears of the pump with the engine assembled, it
is necessary to remove the sump (see Section 10) and the oil suction
strainer assembly.
3   Inspect the gears and pump body for signs of wear and ensure
clearances are as given in the Specifications (photos). Renew the
pump assembly if in any doubt.
4   Prior to assembly, the gears of the pump and the driving shaft
must be lubricated with engine oil.
5   Reassembly is the reverse sequence of removal but always be sure
to fit a new suction strainer gasket. If a manufacturer's replacement is
not available, it can be made from a suitable gasket paper of 0.003 in
(0.1 mm) thickness. **This thickness is critical** since it provides the
necessary axial clearance for the gears, when assembled.

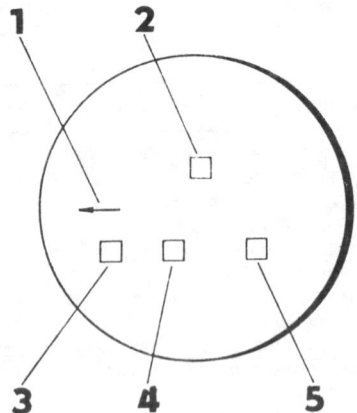

Fig. 1.5 Piston crown markings (Sec 15)

1   Arrow shows direction of   3   Dimension class
     crankshaft rotation   4   Tolerance class
2   Manufacturer's mark   5   Weight

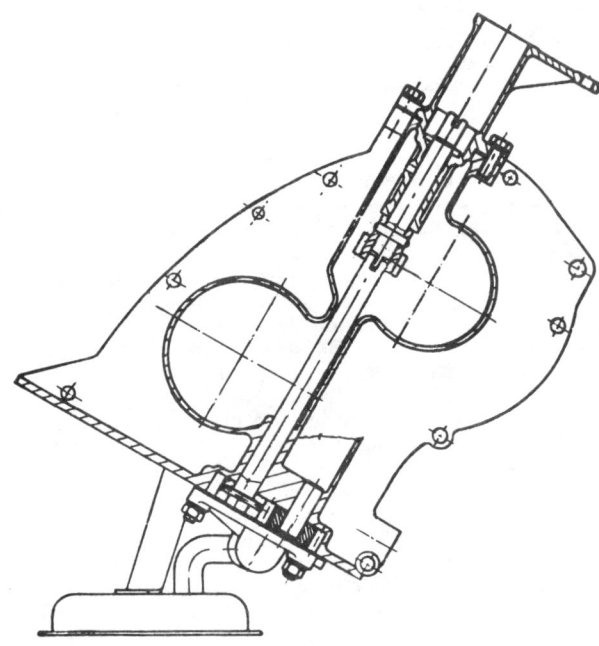

Fig. 1.6 Sectional view of timing case showing oil pump drive
(Sec 19)

20 Flywheel and starter ring – removal and refitting

1   If the teeth on the flywheel starter ring are badly worn or some are
missing, then it will be necessary to remove the ring and fit a new one.
2   To remove, either split the ring with a cold chisel after initially
making a cut with a hacksaw blade between two teeth, or use a
copper headed mallet to knock the ring off, striking it evenly and
alternately at equally spaced points. Take great care not to damage the
flywheel in any way during this process.
3   Clean and polish with emery cloth four evenly spaced areas on the
outside face of the new starter ring.
4   Heat the ring evenly with an oxy-acetylene flame until the polished
portions turn dark blue (356° to 392°F/180° to 200°C).
5   Keep the ring at this temperature for a few minutes and then
quickly but carefully fit it to the flywheel. **Do not overheat the ring.**
6   The ring should be tapped evenly onto its location and left to cool
naturally. The contraction of the metal during cooling, ensures a tight
and permanent fit.

19.3a Checking the oil pump gear-to-body clearance

19.3b Checking the gear endplay

22.4 Renew the oil filter element

21 Timing sprockets and chain – examination and renovation

1   Examine the teeth on both the crankshaft sprocket and the camshaft sprocket for wear. Each tooth forms an inverted 'V' with the gearwheel periphery and if worn the side of each tooth under tension will be slightly concave in shape when compared with the other side of the tooth. If any sign of wear is present the gearwheels must be renewed.
2   Examine the links of the chain for side slackness by bending the chain sideways. If excessive slackness is noticeable the chain should be renewed. It is a sensible precaution to renew the chain at about 30 000 miles and at lesser mileage if the engine is stripped down for a major overhaul. The actual rollers on a very badly worn chain may be slightly grooved.
3   Examine the distributor driving gear and the locating Woodruff keys. Any sign of excessive wear necessitates renewal.

22 Oil filter – removal and renewal

1   The oil filter is of the cylinder type and is located on the right-hand side of the engine. To remove, place a receptacle underneath (to catch any oil left inside), unscrew the centre bolt, and withdraw the filter body from the block.
2   Withdraw the element and discard.
3   Wash the filter bowl out with petrol.
4   Install the new element over the centre bolt and against the retaining spring, and smear some oil around the sealing washer under the bolt head – this will ensure ease of removal at a later date. Always fit a new sealing washer and sealing ring for the filter bowl as a matter of course (photo).
5   Never overtighten the centre bolt.
6   Having refitted the filter, a check should be made for leaks around the sealing ring and washer areas as soon as the engine is restarted. If leakage does occur it is probably due to distortion of the seals and the bowl will have to be reseated.

23 Sump – renovation

1   It is essential that the oil sump should be thoroughly cleaned inside with petrol, ensuring that all signs of old oil and any metal particles are removed.
2   Scrape all traces of the old sump gasket from the mating flange and clean out the external cooling fins (where applicable).
3   Remove the sump internal baffle (if fitted) so that thorough cleaning may be carried out.

24 Oil cooler – removal and refitting

1   The oil cooler (when fitted) is located in the engine compartment on the right-hand side.
2   To remove the cooler unit, disconnect the inlet and outlet hoses from the cooler connections and drain any oil spillage into a suitable container or soak up with a cloth.
3   Unbolt the cooler retaining bolts and withdraw the unit.
4   Flush the cooler with petrol or cellulose thinners and dry with compressed air.
5   Refit in reverse and check on completion that there are no leaks from the pipes when the engine is running.
6   Run the engine for an initial period to allow the oil to circulate and then recheck and top up the oil level as required.

25 Cylinder head, pistons and bores – decarbonisation

This can be carried out with the engine in or out of the car. With the cylinder head off (see Section 9), carefully remove with a wire brush and blunt scraper all traces of carbon deposits from the combustion spaces and ports. The valve head stems and valve guides should also be freed of any carbon deposits. Wash the combustion spaces and ports down with petrol and scrape the cylinder head surface free of any foreign matter with a brass scraper, or one made of a similar soft metal.

Clean the pistons and top of the cylinder bores. If the pistons are still in the block then it is essential that great care is taken to ensure that no carbon falls down the side of the pistons as this could scratch the cylinder walls or cause damage to the piston and rings. To ensure this does not happen, first fit liner retaining bolts and turn the crankshaft so that two of the pistons are at the top of their bores. Stuff rag into the other two bores or seal them off with paper and masking tape. The waterways should also be covered with small pieces of masking tape to prevent particles of carbon entering the cooling system and damaging the water pump.

There are two schools of thought as to how much carbon should be removed from the piston crown. One school recommends that a ring of carbon should be left round the edge of the piston and on the cylinder bore wall as an aid to low oil consumption. Although this is probably true for early engines with worn bores, on modern type engines the thought of the second school can be applied, which is that for effective decarbonisation all traces of carbon should be removed.

If all traces of carbon are to be removed, press a little grease into the gap between the cylinder walls and the two pistons which are to be worked on. With a blunt scraper carefully scrape away the carbon from the piston crown, taking great care not to scratch the aluminium. Also scrape away the carbon from the surrounding lip of the cylinder wall. When all carbon has been removed, scrape away the grease which will now be contaminated with carbon particles, taking care not to press any into the bores. To assist prevention of carbon build-up the piston crown can be polished with a metal polish. Remove the rags or masking tape from the other two cylinders and turn the crankshaft so that the two pistons which were at the bottom are now at the top. Place rag or masking tape in the cylinders which have been de-carbonised and proceed as just described.

26 Valves – removal

1   The valves can be removed from the cylinder head by compressing each spring in turn with a valve spring compressor, until the two halves of the collets can be removed (photo). Then slowly release the compressor and remove the spring retainer and springs (photo).
2   If, when the valve spring compressor is screwed down, the valve spring retaining cap refuses to free to expose the split collet, do not continue to screw down on the compressor as there is a likelihood of damaging it.
3   Gently tap the top of the tool directly over the cap with a light hammer. This will free the cap. To avoid the compressor jumping off the valve spring retaining cap when it is tapped, hold the compressor firmly in position with one hand.
4   It is essential that the valves are kept in their correct sequence unless they are so badly worn that they are to be renewed. If they are going to be kept and used again, place them in a sheet of card having eight holes numbered 1 to 8 corresponding with the relative positions the valves were in when originally installed. Also keep the valve springs, washers and collets in their original sequence.

27 Valves and valve seats – examination and renovation

1   Examine the heads of the valves for pitting and burning, especially the exhaust valves. The valve seats should also be examined at the same time. If pitting is only slight on valves and seats they may be renovated by grinding.
2   Valve grinding is carried out as follows: Smear a trace of coarse carborundum paste on the seat face and apply a suction grinder tool to the valve head. With a semi-rotary motion, grind the valve head to its seat, lifting the valve occasionally to redistribute the grinding paste. When a dull matt even surface is produced on both the valve seat and the valve, then wipe off the paste and repeat the process with fine carborundum paste, lifting and turning the valve to redistribute the paste as before. A light spring placed under the valve head will greatly ease this operation. When a smooth, unbroken ring of light grey matt finish is produced, on both valve and valve seat faces, the grinding operation is complete. This can be further checked with the use of 'Engineer's Blue', if available.
3   Scrape away all carbon from the valve head and the valve stem. Carefully clean away every trace of grinding compound, taking great care to leave none in the ports or in the valve guides. Clean the valves and valve seats with a paraffin soaked rag then with a clean rag, and finally, if an airline is available, blow the valves, valve guides and valve ports clean.
4   Where bad pitting has occurred to the valve seats, it will be necessary to recut them and fit new valves. If the valve seats are so worn that they cannot be recut, then it will be necessary to fit new valve seat inserts. These latter two jobs should be entrusted to the local Skoda agent or engineering works. In practice it is very seldom that the seats are so badly worn that they require renewal. Normally, it is the valve that is too badly worn for re-use, and the owner can easily purchase a new set of valves and match them to the seats by valve grinding.

28 Valve guides – examination

The valve guides are formed within the cylinder head casing itself – there are no separate guide sleeves. It therefore follows that if a guide bore is badly worn and the valves are a loose fit, the bores will have to be reamed and bushes fitted. This is a job for your Skoda dealer as he is equipped for this operation. Oversize valves are not supplied by Skoda.

29 Rockers and rocker shaft – dismantling and inspection

With the rocker shaft assembly removed from the cylinder head, dismantle as follows:
1   Release the circlip from the end of the shaft (photo) and remove the rockers, pedestals, springs and washers, keeping in order of removal.
2   Clean the individual components for inspection.
3   Check the rocker shaft for straightness by rolling it on a perfectly flat surface; a sheet of plate glass is ideal. A slightly bent shaft should be straightened if possible; if not, a replacement shaft is required. This is also the case if the shaft has signs of excessive wear, such as ridges worn by the rocker arms.
4   Slide the rocker arms onto their respective locations on the shaft and inspect for excess wear. No sloppiness should be apparent.

26.1a Compress valve spring to extract collets

26.1b Remove the springs

29.1 Remove circlip to dismantle rockers

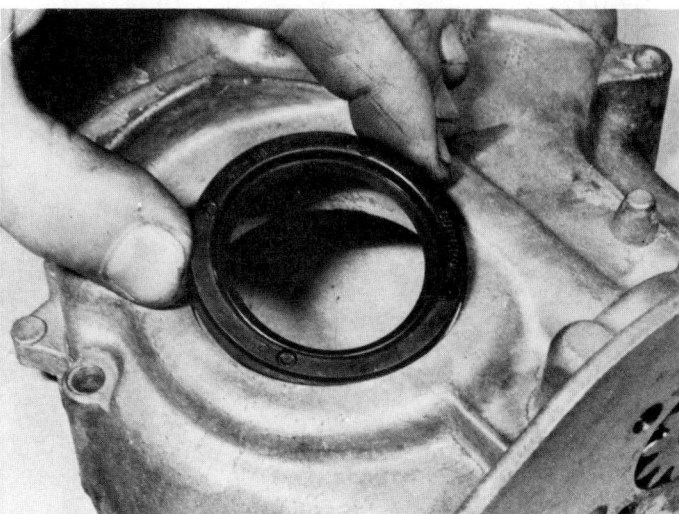

31.4a Renew front cover seal and ...

31.4b ... crankshaft rear seal with ...

31.4c ... arrow marking on seal to outer face of housing

5   Inspect the wear face of the rocker arms, and the ball-ends of the adjusting screws, which locate in the pushrods. If there are any signs of cracking or wear through the case-hardening of these components, they must be renewed.
6   Check the pushrods correspondingly, and also roll them on a flat surface to check for straightness. Any defective ones should be renewed.

30 Tappets (cam followers) – examination and renovation

1   Clean and inspect the tappet wear faces, which bear on the camshaft lobes. Any indentations or cracks in the surface indicate serious wear, and therefore, the need for renewal.
2   Check each tappet in its respective bore; if any are loose and can readily be rocked, they should be renewed. It is most unusual to have badly worn tappet side faces.
3   Oversize tappets are available as listed in the Specifications, but it will be necessary to have your Skoda dealer ream the tappet bores in the block to suit.

31 Engine – reassembly (general)

1   To ensure maximum life with minimum trouble from a rebuilt engine, not only must everything be correctly assembled, but all the parts must be spotlessly clean. All the oilways must be clear, locking washers and spring washers must always be fitted where indicated. Before assembly begins renew any bolts or studs, the threads of which are in any way damaged, and whenever possible use new spring washers.
2   Apart from your normal tools, a supply of clean rag, an oil can filled with engine oil (an empty plastic detergent bottle, thoroughly cleaned and washed out, will do just as well), a new supply of assorted spring washers and a set of new gaskets should be gathered together. A torque wrench is essential as the engine is largely made from aluminium. If a torque wrench cannot be bought then one must be borrowed as if one is not used, then it is almost a certainty that trouble will be experienced after a few thousand miles through aluminium components distorting.
3   Lubricate all bearings and friction surfaces with clean engine oil prior to assembly.
4   All oil seals must be renewed during reassembly (photos).

32 Crankshaft – refitting

1   Ensure that the crankcase is thoroughly clean and that all oilways are clear. A thin drill or a pipe cleaner is useful for cleaning them out. If possible, blow them out with compressed air. Treat the crankshaft in the same fashion and then inject engine oil into the crankshaft oilways.
2   Note that at the back of each bearing is a tab which engages in locating grooves in either the crankcase or the main bearing cap housings (photo).
3   If new bearings are being fitted, carefully clean away all traces of the protective grease with which they are coated.
4   If the old main bearing shells are to be re-used (a false economy unless they are virtually new), fit the three upper halves (ie those in the actual cylinder block casting) of the main bearing shells to their location in the crankcase (photo), after wiping the locations clean.
5   With the three upper bearing shells securely in place, wipe the lower bearing cap housings and fit the three lower shell bearings to their caps, ensuring that the right shell goes into the right cap, if the old bearings are being refitted.
6   Fit the thrust washer onto the front main bearing journal of the crankshaft (photo), and lubricate. The lubrication grooves on the washer must face the crankshaft web.
7   Generously lubricate the crankshaft journals and the upper and lower main bearing shells and carefully lower the crankshaft into place (photos).
8   The next task is to fit the rear main bearing cap. The seal strips in the side joints of the rear main bearing cap must be fitted with jointing compound sparingly applied to the joint faces and also to the block location recess. Thin shims (old feeler gauges are ideal) will assist when fitting the strips (photo). Tap the main bearing cap home with a wooden or plastic hammer. Fit the retaining nuts and lockwashers,

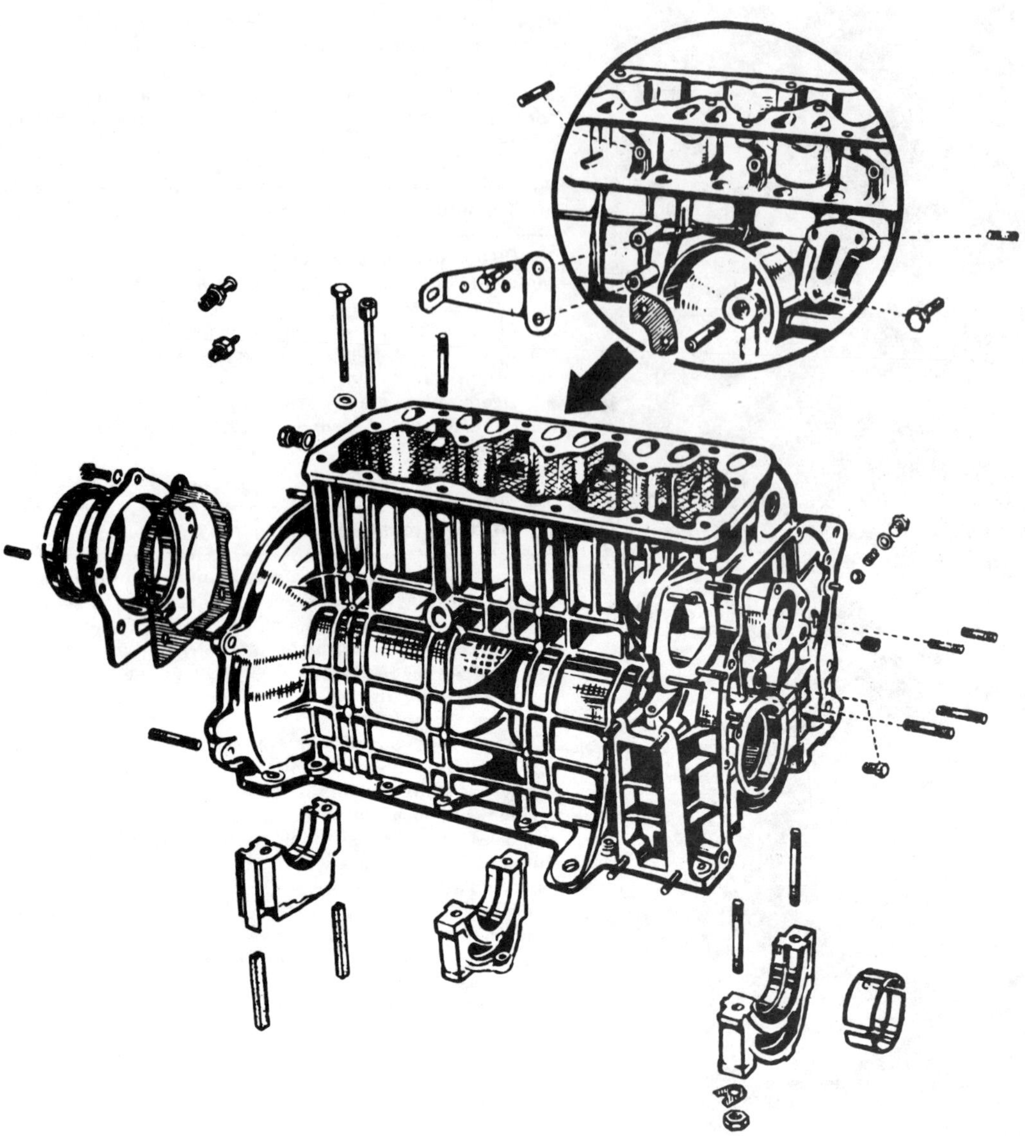

Fig. 1.7 Crankcase and fixed components (Sec 32)

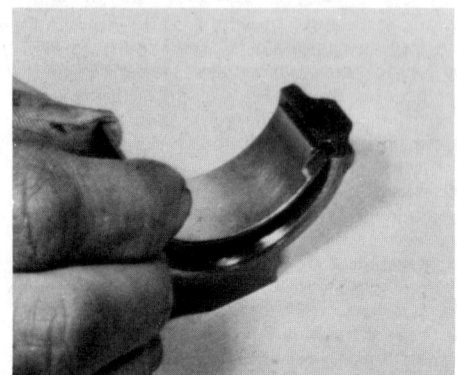

32.2 Locate bearing tongue into groove

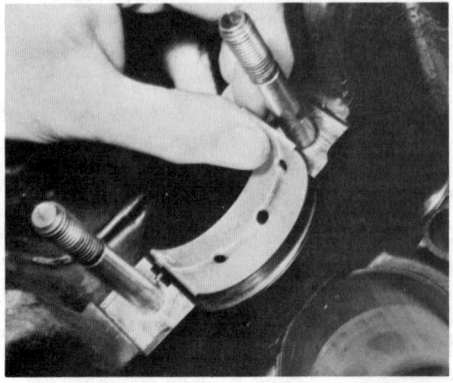

32.4 Insert the upper bearing half shells — note tab location

32.6 Fit front thrust washer with lubrication grooves towards crankshaft web

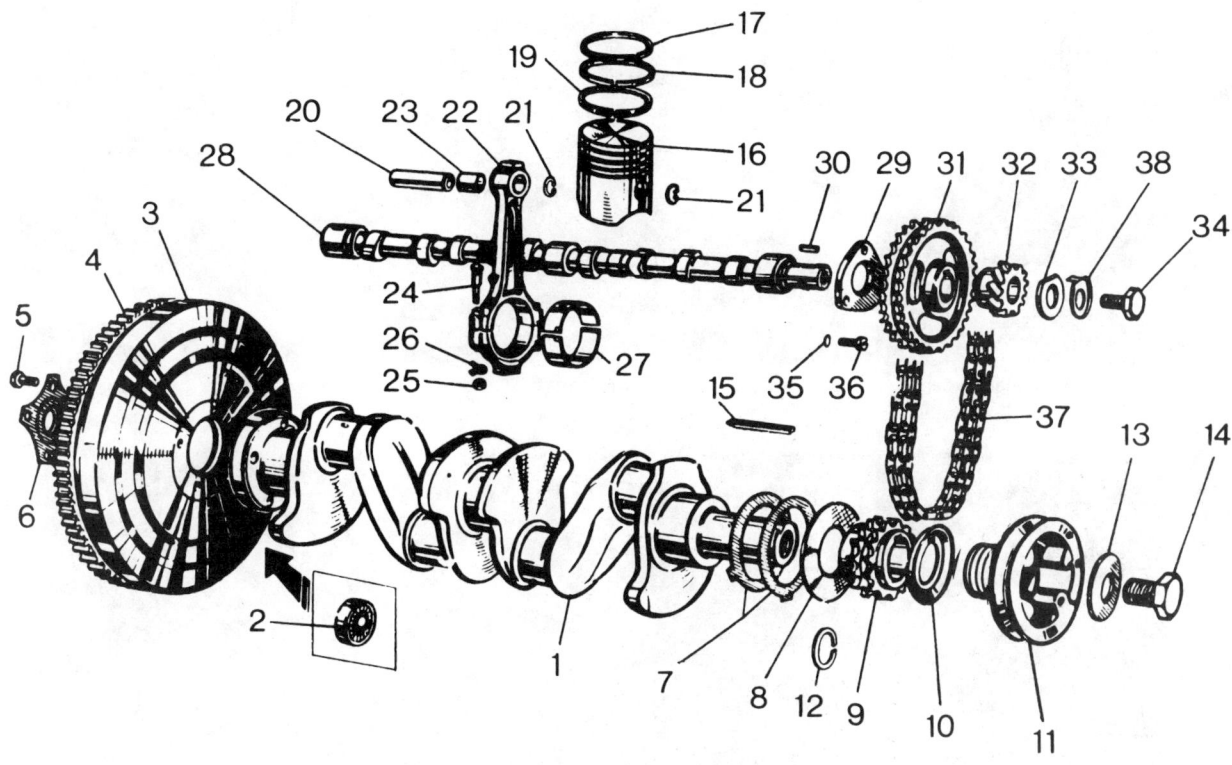

Fig. 1.8 Crankshaft and camshaft assemblies (Sec 32)

1 Crankshaft	11 Crankshaft pulley	21 Circlip	30 Woodruff key
2 Bearing	12 Compensating washer	22 Connecting rod assembly	31 Sprocket
3 Flywheel	13 Washer	23 Bush	32 Worm wheel
4 Ring gear	14 Fixing screw	24 Connecting rod bolt	33 Washer
5 Flywheel screw	15 Woodruff key	25 Connecting rod nut	34 Bolt
6 Bearing cover	16 Piston	26 Tab washer	35 Spring washer
7 Thrust ring	17 Top piston ring (chromium)	27 Big-end bearing shell	36 Screw cheesehead
8 Support ring	18 Stepped piston ring	28 Camshaft	37 Timing chain (Duplex)
9 Sprocket	19 Oil control piston ring	29 Thrust plate	38 Lockwasher
10 Oil thrower	20 Gudgeon pin		

32.7a Lubricate the journals, bearings and ...

32.7b ... then lower the crankshaft into position

32.8a Fitting the rear main bearing oil seal strips and cap. Note use of shims between crankcase and seals to assist fitting

tightening just enough to retain the cap. Fit the centre (photo) and front main bearing caps in a similar fashion. The location tag of the thrust washer must face upwards and fit in the slot of the front main bearing cap.

9   To check the crankshaft endfloat, temporarily fit the following onto the crankshaft: The thrust ring with oil grooves facing away from the block (photo), the support ring (photo), the compensating washer (photo), the Woodruff key, the timing chain sprocket (photo), the dished washer, the fan pulley (photo) and its washer and bolt. Tighten

the bolt to the specified torque.

10   Lever the crankshaft back and forth with a screwdriver against the centre bearing and measure the endfloat with a feeler gauge as shown (photo). The endfloat must be within the limits given in the Specifications; if not, dismantle the assembly and substitute a thrust washer of suitable thickness. When the correct endfloat is achieved, remove the pulley and sprocket components except for the support ring.

11   Tighten the main bearing cap nuts to the specified torque (photo) and bend up the lockwasher tabs.

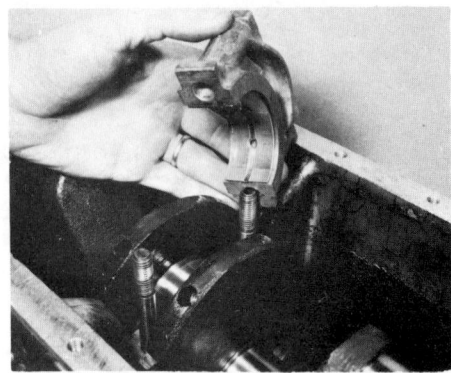

32.8b Fitting the centre main bearing cap

32.9a Temporarily fit the front thrust ring washer, ...

32.9b ... the support ring, ...

32.9c ... the compensating washer, ...

32.9d ... the sprocket ...

32.9e ... and the pulley

32.10 Check the endfloat of the crankshaft

32.11 Tighten the main bearing cap bolts to the specified torque

33.4 Arrow on piston crown on opposite side to oil splash hole in connecting rod

12 Check the crankshaft for freedom of rotation. If new bearing shells have been fitted it may be fairly stiff, but so long as the stiffness is uniform there should be no cause for alarm. In the unlikely event of the crankshaft being impossible to turn, or showing high spots of resistance, a careful inspection of the shaft and bearings must be made, preferably by a qualified mechanic equipped with a micrometer.

33 Pistons and connecting rods – assembly

1 If the existing pistons are being re-used, then they must be mated to the same connecting rod with the same gudgeon pin. If new pistons are being fitted it does not matter with which connecting rod or gudgeon pin they are used.
2 Place the correct piston adjacent to each connecting rod and remember that the same rod and piston must go back into the same bore. If new pistons are being used it is only necessary to ensure that the right connecting rod is placed in each bore.

3 Fit a new circlip in position at one end of the gudgeon pin hole in the piston.
4 Place one piston in boiling water for a few minutes. Remove it from the water and quickly wipe away any excess water with a non-fluffy rag. Take care not to burn yourself during this process. **Note:** *It is essential that the piston is assembled to the connecting rod with the arrow mark on the piston crown on the opposite side to the oil splash hole in the connecting rod big-end (photo).*
5 Hold the connecting rod in position inside the piston. Push the gudgeon pin through the piston and connecting rod small-end until it contacts the fitted circlip. Fit the remaining circlip in its groove. Repeat this process with the other three pistons and connecting rods.
6 When all four pistons are assembled to their connecting rods, the following items should be checked:

(a) *When the piston and connecting rod assembly is held horizontal, the connecting rod should be free to fall by its own weight*
(b) *Gripping the piston firmly with one hand and the connecting*

rod with the other, ensure that the connecting rod cannot be rocked from side to side on the gudgeon pin. It is normal for there to be sliding movement from one side to the other

(c) *Check that all the gudgeon pin retaining circlips are firmly seated in their grooves. It is essential that new circlips are used*

34 Piston rings – refitting

1 Check that the piston ring grooves and oilways are thoroughly clean and unblocked. Piston rings must always be fitted over the head off the piston and never from the bottom.
2 The easiest method to use when fitting rings is to wrap a 0.020 in (0.50 mm) feeler gauge, round the top of the piston and place the rings one at a time, starting with the bottom oil control ring, over the feeler gauge.
3 The feeler gauge, complete with ring, can then be slid down the piston over the other piston ring grooves until the correct groove is reached. The piston ring is then slid gently off the feeler gauge into the groove.
4 An alternative method is to fit the rings by holding them slightly open with the thumbs and both of your index fingers. This method requires a steady hand and great care as it is easy to open the ring too much and break it. When fitting the top ring ensure the chamfered

35.4 Refitting the pistons to the cylinders with the aid of a piston ring compressor

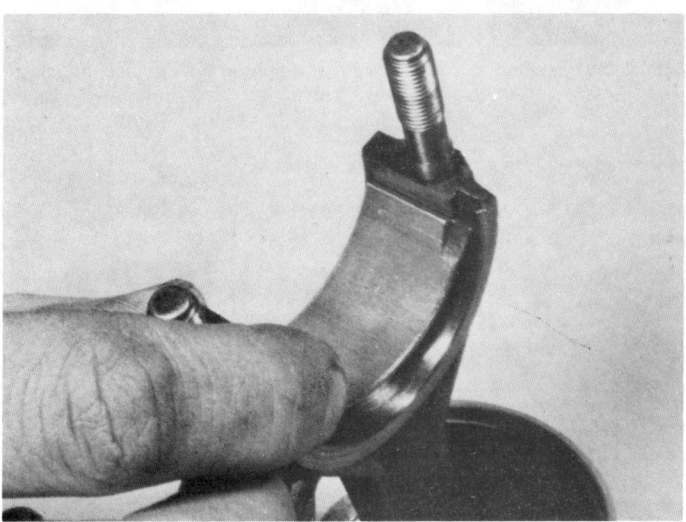

37.1 Locate the tongue of the bearing into the rod groove

edge faces up or if fitting a set of replacement rings into a worn bore, the top ring may be stepped and this step should face upwards. This acts as a safeguard to avoid the ring fouling the wear ridge at the top of the cylinder bore. Always gap check the new rings in their respective bores (see Section 15). Always follow the manufacturer's instructions most carefully when fitting a replacement ring set to used pistons.

35 Pistons and connecting rods – refitting

1 Clean and lubricate each cylinder bore with engine oil.
2 It is essential that each piston and connecting rod assembly is fitted into the bore from which it was originally removed.
3 Locate the piston rings on each piston so that the ring gaps are staggered in relation to each other by 120°.
4 Lubricate the pistons and rings and install them into their respective cylinders. The piston rings should be compressed with a ring compressor. Ensure when clamped round the piston that it is squarely located and is compressing all of the rings (photo).
5 The pistons must be inserted down the bores with the marking arrow to the camshaft. Where the liners are removed, the arrow mark on the piston must face the liner tolerance mark on its top face.

36 Cylinder liners – fitting to crankcase

1 The cylinder liners can be fitted into position in the crankcase with their respective pistons and connecting rods as an assembly. Each piston connecting rod and cylinder liner must be refitted to its original location. Where new pistons and/or liners are to be fitted then their position doesn't matter, but once fitted they should be marked accordingly.
2 Prior to fitting the liners, check that their mating surfaces are perfectly clean.
3 As each liner is pressed into position (thumb pressure is all that should be required), use a straight-edge and feeler gauges to check the amount of liner protrusion above the cylinder block. Tap the liner down to ensure that it is seated properly, then place the straight-edge across the liner top face and measure the clearance between the underside of

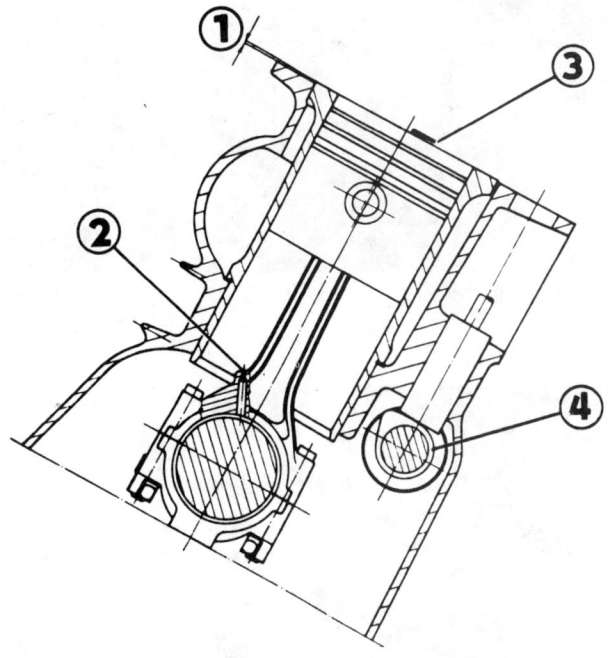

Fig. 1.9 End sectional view of crankcase (Sec 36)

1 *Liner projection above top face*   3 *Arrow on piston crown*
2 *Splash hole in connecting rod*   4 *Camshaft*

the straight-edge and the top face of the crankcase.

4   Each liner should protrude by the amount given in the Specifications. If necessary adjustment can be made by altering the shim thickness under the liner mating flange. Shims are available in thicknesses as listed in the Specifications.

5   To assist final location of the cylinder liner assembly (having selected the correct shim requirement), grease the cylinder flange and shims to retain them in position when finally fitting the liner. Ensure that it seats correctly.

6   To retain the liners in position in the crankcase during subsequent operations (assuming the engine has been completely dismantled), insert two short bolts down into the cylinder head bolt holes on one side between number 1 and 2 cylinders and also number 3 and 4 cylinders and lightly tighten with a suitable flat washer under the bolt heads to secure the liners until the cylinder head is ready for fitting.

37 Connecting rods to crankshaft – reassembly

During the following procedures it is essential that the utmost cleanliness is observed as any dirt caught between the crankpins and bearings will score the crankshaft journals and will thus lead to early bearing failure.

1   Wipe the connecting rod half of the big-end bearing cap and the underside of the shell bearing clean, and fit the shell bearing in position with its locating tongue groove engaged with the corresponding rod (photo).

2   If the old bearings are nearly new and are being refitted, then ensure they are replaced in their correct locations on the corect rods.

3   Generously lubricate the crankpin journals with engine oil and turn the crankshaft so that the crankpin is in the most advantageous position for the connecting rod to be drawn onto it.

4   Wipe the connecting rod bearing cap and back of the shell bearing clean and fit the shell bearing in position ensuring that the locating tongue at the back of the bearing engages with the locating groove in the connecting rod cap.

5   Generously lubricate the shell bearing and offer up the connecting

rod bearing cap to the connecting rod (photo). Note that each rod and cap are numbered as a pair according to their respective bores. Therefore always fit the cap and rod numbers opposite each other.

6   Fit the connecting rod bolt self-locking nuts and tighten to the specified torque (photo).

7   When all the connecting rods have been fitted, rotate the crankshaft to check that everything is free, and that there are no high spots causing binding.

38 Crankshaft oil seal (rear) – refitting

1   To fit the new oil seal into its housing, place the housing onto a flat surface on the workbench.

2   Insert the seal into its housing recess so that the coil spring side faces inwards (the serrated lip and direction arrow facing out).

3   Before fitting to the engine, smear some sealing compound lightly over the inner face of the housing and fit the gasket over the two location pegs, then lightly smear the gasket with some sealant.

4   Fit the seal carefully over the crankshaft rear flange and insert and tighten the five retaining screws and spring washers (photo).

5   Trim off any protruding seal strip flush with the crankcase mating face (photo).

6   If the crankshaft pilot bearing is to be renewed now is the time to fit it (photo).

39 Camshaft – refitting

1   Insert the camshaft into position in the block, having first lubricated the location apertures (photo).

2   Oil and refit the camshaft thrust plate, and retain with the three bolts and spring washers (photo).

3   Rotate the camshaft to ensure it turns freely.

37.5 Refit the bearing end cap

37.6 Tighten the big-end nuts to the specified torque

38.4 Locate and tighten the rear seal housing retaining screws

38.5 Trim off the excess seal strip

38.6 Rear seal assembly and crankshaft pilot bearing fitted

39.1 Insert the camshaft and ...

39.2 ... fit the thrust plate

40.4 Locate the timing chain and sprockets – note position of keyways and dot markings on sprockets

40.5 Locate the distributor drive pinion

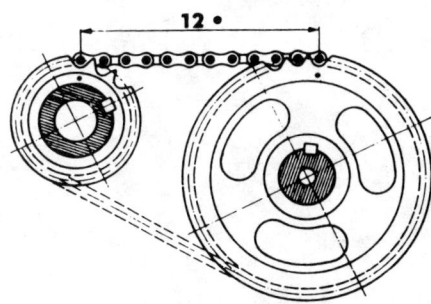

Fig. 1.10 Crankshaft and camshaft timing marks are separated by twelve links (Sec 40)

40 Timing sprockets, chain and cover – refitting

1   Locate the selected crankshaft thrust washer and shims onto the shaft.
2   Fit the crankshaft and camshaft keys to their respective shafts.
3   Locate the camshaft and crankshaft chain sprockets into the chain so that there are twelve link hinge pins between the respective marking dots on the sprocket outer faces (see Fig. 1.10).
4   Turn the two shafts so that the keys line up with the sprocket keyway, and fit the chain and sprockets as a single assembly, to the shafts (photo).
5   Now fit the distributor driving pinion with the boss facing towards the camshaft sprocket. Fit the retaining washers and bolt (photo). Tighten to the specified torque but before bending over the tab washer to secure the bolt, check that the crankshaft and camshaft sprockets are in alignment by placing a straight-edge across their front faces. Any measurable difference (check with a feeler gauge) should not exceed 0.004 in (0.1 mm). Adjustment washers 0.006 in (0.16 mm) thick are available to overcome any misalignment between the sprockets. When alignment is correct, bend over the lockwasher of the camshaft bolt.
6   It will be observed that there is no timing chain tensioner fitted, and therefore if the chain appears to be too slack or possibly tight then an alternative chain and/or camshaft sprocket should be fitted. The grade size of the camshaft sprocket is stamped next to the punch mark, except for grade A. Three sprocket sizes are available being A, B and C.
7   The chain assembly has a split link to facilitate chain removal and fitting without removing the gears if necessary. The chain coupling link must be fitted with the front face and the clip to the rear (pointing in the opposite direction to chain travel). When the chain is being reconnected ensure that the camshaft and crankshaft timing positiions are correct as in paragraph 3.
8   Fit the dished oil thrower washer to the crankshaft and locate over the Woodruff key, so that the concave side faces away from the crankshaft sprocket (photo).
9   Apply some jointing compound to the timing chest and block flanges and locate the gasket in position on the block. Lubricate the chain and sprockets, then carefully fit the timing cover into position, complete with the oil pump gears (photo). Secure the timing chest with the setscrews, but do not over-tighten.

41 Oil pump suction unit and sump – assembly

1   Lubricate the gears and then smear the location flanges of the pump suction tube and timing chest with sealing compound and place the gasket in position. Note that it is essential that the gasket be 0.0039 in (0.1 mm) thick to provide the correct pump gear clearance.
2   Carefully fit the suction tube unit and retain with the bolts and spring washers, over the pump, and the tube filter to the middle main bearing cap (photo).
3   Ensure that the sump and block facing flanges are clean, smear them with jointing compound and fit together complete with the gasket (photo). Insert the retaining bolts and washers and tighten to the specified torque.

40.8 Fit the dished washer onto the crankshaft

40.9 Refit the timing cover

41.2 Locate the suction tube unit

41.3 Refit the sump

42.1 Fit the crankshaft pulley and ...

42.2 ... tighten the retaining bolt to the specified torque

42.4a Locate the flywheel ...

42.4b ... and tighten the retaining bolts

42.4c Method of jamming flywheel to tighten flywheel and crankshaft pulley retaining bolts

42 Crankshaft pulley and flywheel – assembly

1   Slide the pulley over the crankshaft, locating the keyway over the Woodruff key (photo).
2   Fit the flat washer over the bolt and screw into the crankshaft. Tighten to the specified torque (photo).
3   Fit to the clutch housing the belly plate cover.
4   Now fit the flywheel so that the crankshaft and flywheel markings are in line and retain with the locking washer plate and bolts. Tighten the bolts to the specified torque and bend over the ears of the locking tabs to retain in position (photos).
5   With the flywheel fully bolted in position the clutch unit may now be fitted. The assembly procedure is fully described in Chapter 5.

43 Valves and valve springs – refitting

1   Fit each valve in turn, wiping down and lubricating each valve stem as it is inserted into the same valve guide from which it was removed.
2   Build up each valve assembly by first fitting the valve springs and then the valve spring shroud.
3   With the base of the valve compressor on the valve head, compress the valve spring until the cotters can be slipped into place in the cotter grooves. Gently release the compressor.
4   Repeat this procedure until all eight valves and valve springs are fitted.
5   Tap the end of each valve stem in turn on completion to open the

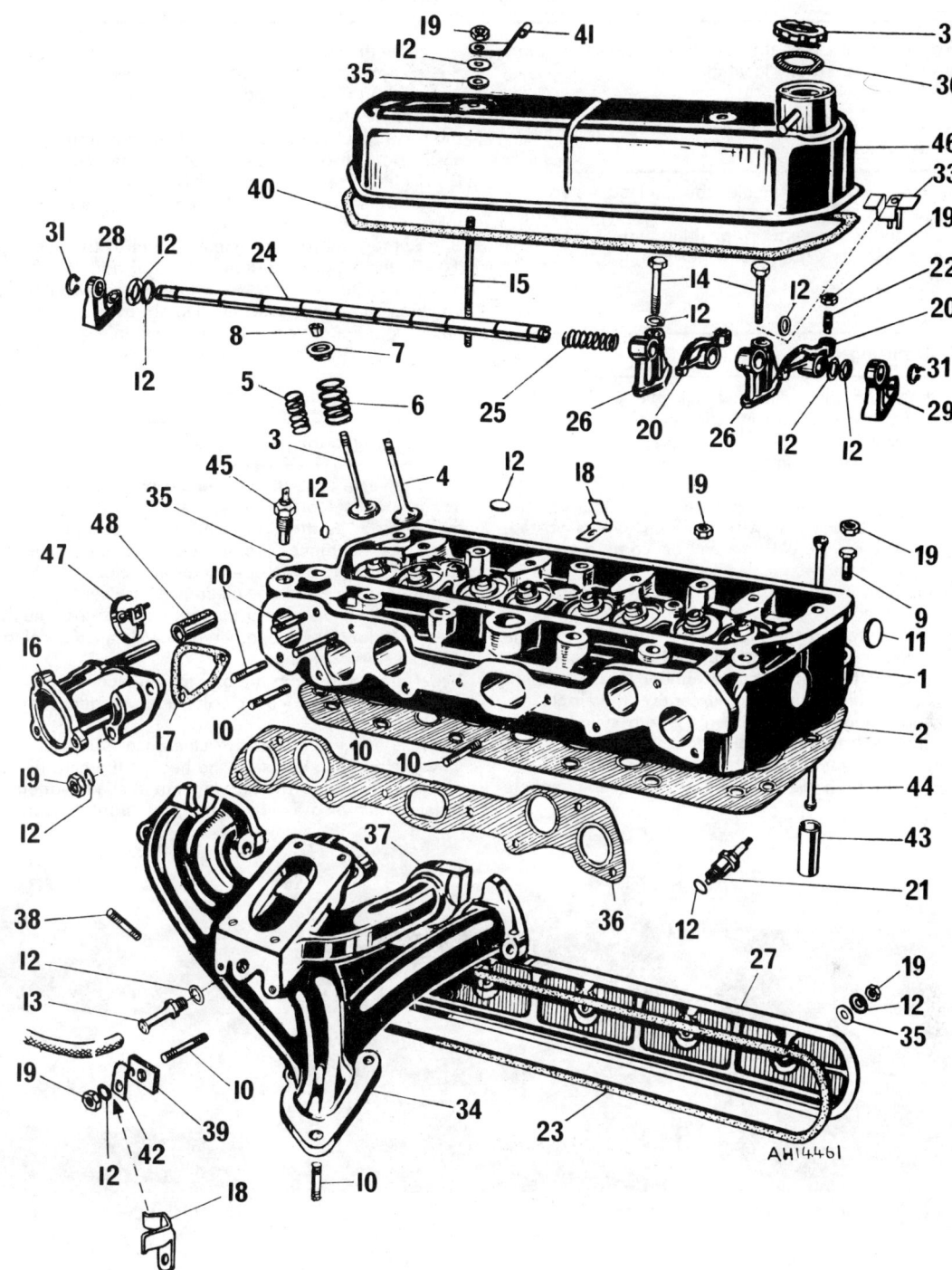

Fig. 1.11 Cylinder head and associated components (Sec 45)

1	Cylinder head	14	Rocker pedestal bolt
2	Cylinder head gasket	15	Rocker cover stud
3	Inlet valve	16	Thermostat housing
4	Exhaust valve	17	Gasket
5	Valve spring (inner)	18	Bracket
6	Valve spring (outer)	19	Nut
7	Valve spring shroud	20	Rocker arm
8	Cotters	21	Spark plug
9	Bolt for generator strut	22	Rocker arm adjuster
10	Manifold stud	23	Gasket
11	Core plug	24	Rocker shaft
12	Washer	25	Rocker shaft spring
13	Hose adaptor		

26	Rocker pedestal
27	Tappet side cover
28	Rocker pedestal (rear)
29	Rocker pedestal (front)
30	Gasket
31	Circlip
32	Oil filler cap
33	Channelled plate washer
34	Exhaust manifold
35	Sealing washer
36	Manifold gasket
37	Inlet manifold

38	Carburettor stud
39	Adaptor
40	Gasket
41	Fuel feed pipe support bracket
42	Pipe clip
43	Tappet
44	Pushrod
45	Coolant temperature transmitter
46	Rocker cover
47	Clip
48	Hose

respective valves and to ensure that the valves are seated correctly and also that the cotters are correctly located.

44 Rocker shaft – assembly

1   Oil the rocker shaft and reassemble the pedestals, springs, washers, etc, in the reverse sequence to that used for dismantling.
2   When the retaining circlips are in position, check that the individual rockers and pedestals turn freely (except for the spring tension) on the shaft.

45 Cylinder head – refitting

1   After checking that both the cylinders/block and cylinder head mating surfaces are perfectly clean, lubricate each cylinder with engine oil.
2   Remove the cylinder liner retaining bolts and washers where fitted.
3   Locate the new cylinder head gasket into position on the crankcase (photo). It only fits one way with the word OBEN on top. Always use a new gasket as the old one will be compressed and incapable of giving a good seal.
4   Place the cylinder head in position over the gasket (photo) and insert the respective retaining bolts, screwing them down finger-tight. The alternator bracket is fitted to the first bolt on the lower flange whilst the water pipe holder is secured by the third bolt on the lower flange row. The air cleaner bracket is located under the two upper bolts. Bolt washers are fitted in all instances except on the air cleaner bracket bolts, the lower flange bolts and (on 72 mm cylinder bore engines) the rocker arm shaft outer support bolts.
5   Lubricate and insert the tappets into their respective apertures.
6   Insert the pushrods through the head and locate in the tappets (photo).

7   Refit the rocker assembly to the cylinder head, carefully locating the rocker arms to pushrods and insert the location bolts and flat washers and at the ends, the two Allen screws. Note that the 4th rocker pedestal has a gasket 0.1 mm thick (maximum) fitted between the head and base to prevent oil leakage from the oilway to the rocker shaft. Note also the position of the channelled washer (photos).
8   Tighten the bolts, nuts and Allen screws gradually in the tightening sequence shown in Fig. 1.1 and finally tighten in sequence to the torque quoted in the Specifications.
9   Tighten the rocker pedestal bolts to the specified torque (photo).
10 Fit the tappet side cover (photo) and gasket – which should be smeared with a sealing solution. Retain with the four nuts, rubber washers and dished washers. Do not overtighten. Note that the tappet cover only fits correctly in one position.

46 Valve clearances – adjustment

1   The valve adjustments should be made with the engine cold. The importance of correct rocker arm/valve stem clearances cannot be overstressed as they vitally affect the performance of the engine.
2   If the clearances are set too open, the efficiency of the engine is reduced as the valves open later and close earlier than was intended. If, on the other hand, the clearances are set too close there is a danger that the stem and pushrods will expand upon heating and not allow the valves to close properly which will cause burning of the valve head and possible warping.
3   If the engine is in the car, to gain access to the rockers, undo and remove the rocker cover bolts and washers. Carefully lift away the rocker cover.
4   It is important that the clearance is set when the tappet of the valve being adjusted is on the heel of the cam (ie opposite the peak). This can be done by carrying out the adjustments in the following order, which also avoids turning the crankshaft more than necessary:

45.3 Locate the new cylinder head gasket

45.4 Refit the cylinder head

45.6 Insert the pushrods

45.7a Fit the gasket to the 4th rocker pedestal location ...

45.7b ... and refit the rocker shaft assembly

45.7c Channelled plate washer is fitted to the 2nd pedestal bracket from the front

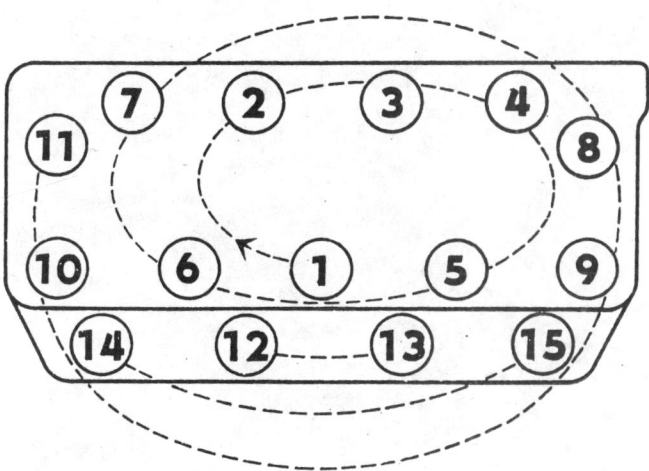

Fig. 1.12 Cylinder head bolt tightening/slackening sequence
(Sec 45)

Valves fully open	Check and adjust
Valve No 8	*Valve No 1 (Ex)*
Valve No 6	*Valve No 3 (In)*
Valve No 4	*Valve No 5 (Ex)*
Valve No 7	*Valve No 2 (In)*
Valve No 1	*Valve No 8 (Ex)*
Valve No 3	*Valve No 6 (In)*
Valve No 5	*Valve No 4 (Ex)*
Valve No 2	*Valve No 7 (In)*

5   The correct valve clearance is given in the Specifications at the beginning of this Chapter. It is obtained by slackening the hexagonal locknut with a spanner while holding the ball-pin against rotation with a screwdriver as shown (photo). Then still pressing down with the screwdriver, insert a feeler gauge of the required thickness between the valve stem head and the rocker arm and adjust the ball-pin until the feeler gauge will just move in and out without nipping. Then, still holding the ball-pin in the correct position, tighten the locknut and recheck.

6   Smear the rocker cover gasket with sealant and refit complete with cover over the rockers, securing with bolts and washers (photo).

45.9 Tighten the rocker pedestal retaining bolts

45.10 Fit the tappet side cover

46.5 Method of adjusting the valve clearances

46.6 Refit the rocker cover

47 Engine – final assembly

1 The engine ancillary items can now be refitted. If the rear body panel was removed to withdraw the engine, then all components can be fitted. If not, it is advisable to leave the refitting of the distributor, carburettor and thermostat until after the engine is refitted.

2 Refit the fuel pump complete with new gasket and the insulating washer.

3 Insert the new oil filter into its bowl. Don't forget the spring and thrust plate which must face outwards. Lubricate the seal ring and locate it into the groove in the housing, then refit the filter unit and tighten the central retaining bolt. Note that some filter elements are fitted with a bottom seal in the plate, in which case invert the element so that the seal faces the thrust plate and spring.

4 Refit the water pump with new gasket. Smear the gasket faces with sealant before fitting.

5 Place the manifold gasket over the studs and refit the exhaust manifold and inlet manifold. It is vitally important that the manifold mating faces are cleaned of any previous gasket pieces that may have stuck in position, if the manifolds are to seal correctly. The manifolds fit over the studs and are retained by nuts and washers. Note the special square section washers that are bridged over the studs between the inlet and exhaust manifolds. Also fit the vacuum tube retaining clip between the nut and square washer of the inlet/exhaust retaining stud. If they are not already fitted, the downpipe(s) and silencer assembly can be fitted to the exhaust manifold pipe flange, complete with gasket. Again, check that the flange faces are clean. Refit the clutch housing belly plate when fitting the exhaust location bracket.

6 Attach the right-hand rear engine mounting bracket in correct relative position to the protruding flange face with the two bolts. The upper bolt also retains the alternator which can also be fitted at this stage together with the drivebelt (photo).

7 Refit the engine mounting bars to their brackets, slotting into position with rubbers and tightening the nuts to secure.

8 If the transmission has been removed and separated from the engine it can now be refitted. Proceed carefully when inserting the gearbox input shaft into the clutch disc and crankshaft bearing. Do not force the gearbox and ensure that it is supported during assembly to avoid putting unnecessary strain on the input shaft. If difficulty in fully engaging the two is experienced, check that the clutch disc is centralised. When in position refit the nuts and bolts to secure.

9 Refit the starter motor.

48 Half axles – refitting

1 Refit the half axle assemblies complete with wheel hubs and struts. This procedure is the reverse of the dismantling sequence, but be sure to refit the exact number and thickness of bearing preload shims (photo) to each side as were originally extracted. Always fit a new gasket with the bearing cover and ensure that the breather hole is at the top, as in the axle flange on the gearbox. If on assembly the half axle radial movement is stiff, fit another or thicker gasket as required. If a new crownwheel and pinion assembly has been fitted, the correct number and thickness of preload shims must be fitted to ensure the correct meshing of the crownwheel and pinion (see Chapter 6).

2 An assistant will be required to support the brake drum end of the half axle assembly when fitting to the transaxle.

3 Smear some sealant solution over the respective flange faces and fit the gasket over the studs.

4 Offer the half axle to the transaxle. Rotate the brake drum to align the knuckle with the slot in the differential. When in place, slide home the outer cover and fit the six nuts and spring washers (photo). Check when in place that the half axles swivel freely.

49 Engine and transmission – refitting

Refitting is basically a direct reversal of the removal procedure, depending on the method employed. Reposition the engine and transaxle assembly under the car and then proceed as follows

1 Attach the hoist around the engine securely, to give a centrally balanced lift; then raise the assembly slightly.

47.6 Right-hand engine mounting bracket and earth strap

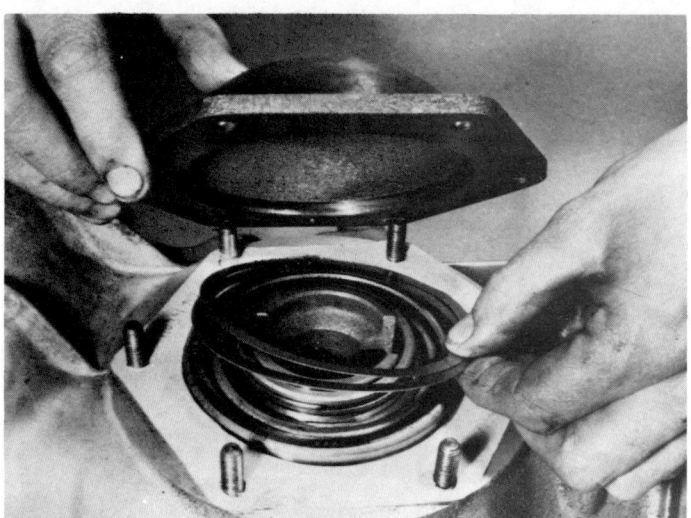

48.1 Fit gasket with breather hole at top and exact number of shims

48.4 Refitting half axle assembly to the transaxle unit

2 Place a jack under the gearbox.

3 Raise slightly the engine/transaxle assembly. If the distributor is in position on the engine, ensure when lifting that the diaphragm does not foul the rear panel, if this is also in position. At the forward end, the thermostat housing, if fitted, should clear the rear body bulkhead panel.

4 Insert the rear suspension coil springs into their location channels.

5 Now continue raising the engine and transaxle in unison and locate the coil springs into their recess channels in the body at the top. The shock absorber studs at the bottom are located through their respective holes in the radius struts. This can be made easier if a further jack is available to raise the brake drum and outer axle, so that the nut, spring washers and rubber bushes can be fitted to retain the shock absorber, and spring in position.

6 Align the gearbox mountings and fit the retaining bolts, flat and spring washers (photo).

7 Align the engine bearer bar each side under the body and retain with the bolts, springs and flat washers. Fit the earth strap to the right-hand mounting bolt (photo).

8 Locate the thrust arms over their location studs and retain with nuts and spring washers.

9 Now tighten the engine, gearbox mounting, shock absorber, strut arm retaining nuts and bolts, to the respective torques as given in the Specifications.

10 Remove the hoist and jack and refit the half axle limiting strap each side.

11 Refit the brake pipes and cables. The system will have to be bled and the brakes checked for adjustment (see Chapter 9).

12 Reconnect the speedometer cable.

13 Reconnect the gear selector rod. An assistant is useful to operate the gear lever in the car: select 1st or 3rd gear and then locate the locking bolt into the recess in the rod and retain in position by tightening the nut.

14 Refit the coolant pipe/fuel tank guard plate, the right-hand engine splash plate and left-hand splash plate.

15 If still to be attached, refit the carburettor, the thermostat and distributor units referring to Chapters 3, 2 and 4 respectively for full details on settings and adjustments.

16 Connect the radiator bottom hose to the water pump.

17 Where fitted, reconnect the oil cooler pipes, ensuring that the pipes are in good condition and securely connected.

18 Refit the spark plugs, after checking that their gaps are correctly set. Then refit the plug leads, distributor cap and the vacuum tube from the carburettor.

19 Refill the engine (photo) and gearbox with the recommended lubricants (ensure the drain plugs and level plug in the gearbox are in place and tightened to the correct torque).

20 Refit the clutch slave cylinder to the top of the gearbox and reconnect the hydraulic pipe. Adjust the clearance of the operating rod, as described in Chapter 5, and refit the protection cover and spring clamp.

21 Refill the cooling system and check for leaks.

22 Remake all electrical connections (except the battery). Check that all the fittings and attachments are securely in position and then reconnect the battery (negative terminal last).

23 Refit the air filter unit.

24 The car is now ready for starting (see following Section).

50 Engine – initial start-up after overhaul

1 Make sure that the battery is fully charged and that all lubricants, coolant and fuel are replenished.

2 If the fuel system has been dismantled it will require several revolutions of the engine on the starter motor to pump the petrol up the carburettor.

3 As soon as the engine fires and runs, keep it going at a fast tickover only (no faster) and bring it up to normal working temperature.

4 As the engine warms up there will be odd smells and some smoke from parts getting hot and burning off oil deposits. The signs to look for are leaks of water or oil which will be obvious, if serious. Check also the exhaust pipe and manifold connections as these do not always find their exact gastight position until the warmth and vibration have acted on them and it is almost certain that they will need tightening further. This should be done, of course, with the engine stopped.

5 When normal running temperature has been reached, adjust the

49.6 Gearbox mounting – right-hand side

49.7 Earth strap location on right-hand engine mounting

49.19 Refill the engine with oil

engine idle speed as described in Chapter 3.

6   Stop the engine and wait a few minutes to see if any lubricant or coolant is dripping out when the engine is stationary.

7   Recheck the fan and alternator belt tensions and adjust if necessary.

8   Road test the car to check that the timing is correct and that the engine is giving the necessary smoothness and power. Do not race the engine – if new bearings and/or pistons have been fitted it should be treated as a new engine and run in at a reduced speed for, at least, the first 300 miles (500 km).

51 Fault diagnosis – engine

When investigating engine faults, do not be tempted into snap diagnosis. Adopt a logical checking procedure and follow it through – it will take less time in the long run. Poor engine performance in terms of power or fuel economy is not always easy to diagnose.

Symptom	Reason(s)
Engine fails to turn when starter operated	Battery flat, or connections loose or corroded Gear engaged Earth strap(s) broken or loose Starter (or solenoid) wiring loose or broken Starter or solenoid internal fault (see Chapter 10) Major mechanical failure (seizure)
Engine cranks but will not start	Battery partly discharged, or connections loose or corroded (engine cranks slowly) Fuel tank empty Insufficient or excessive choke Ignition system fault (Chapter 4) Fuel system fault (Chapter 3) Incorrect valve timing (after rebuild) Major mechanical failure
Engine misfires or idles unevenly	Valve clearances incorrect Valve(s) burnt or badly seated Valve spring(s) broken Ignition system fault (Chapter 4) Fuel system fault (Chapter 3) Severe overheating (Chapter 2) Incorrect valve timing (after rebuild) Poor compression on one or more cylinders
Lack of power and poor compression	Incorrect valve clearances Valve(s) burnt or badly seated Valve spring(s) broken Blowing head gasket Worn pistons, rings and/or bores Ignition system fault (Chapter 4) Fuel system fault (Chapter 3) Overheating (Chapter 2) Incorrect valve timing (after rebuild)
Engine pinks under load	Ignition over-advanced (Chapter 4) Excessive carbon build-up in engine Wrong grade of fuel in use Incorrect valve timing (after rebuild)
Excessive oil consumption	Leakage (clean engine and inspect) Overfilling Worn valve stems and/or guides Worn pistons, rings and/or bores Piston oil return holes choked
Unusual mechanical noises	Valve clearances too wide (tapping noise from top of engine) Blowing head gasket (whistling or wheezing noises) Broken piston ring(s) (ticking noise) Piston slap (worst when cold) Worn small-end(s) (light tapping noise) Worn big-end bearing(s) (heavy knocking, perhaps decreasing under load) Worn main bearing(s) (rumbling and vibration, perhaps worsening under load) Worn timing chain and/or gears (thrashing noise from front of engine) Peripheral component fault (eg water pump) Unintentional mechanical contact (eg fan blades)

Chapter 2 Cooling system

For modifications, and information applicable to later models, see Supplement at end of manual

Contents

Specifications

General

System type .... Pressurised, pump-assisted, thermostatically controlled. Electrically – operated cooling fan

System capacity .... 12.5 litres (22 pints)

Test pressure .... 1.2 kgf/cm² (17 lbf/in²)

Thermostat

Starts to open .... 80° ± 2° C (176° ± 4° F)

Fully open .... 90° ± 4° C (194° ± 7° F)

Fully open lift .... 11 mm (0.43 in)

Fan thermoswitch

Cut-in temperature .... 92° ± 3° C (198° ± 5° F)

Cut-out temperature .... 85° ± 3° C (185° ± 5° F)

Pressure cap

Blow-off pressure .... 0.4 kgf/cm² (5.6 lbf/in²)

Vacuum relief pressure .... 0.1 kgf/cm² (1.4 lbf/in²)

Torque wrench setting

	Nm	lbf ft
Water pump pulley nut	12 to 16	9 to 12

---

1 General description and maintenance

The cooling system is of thermo-syphon, pump assisted type. The radiator is mounted at the front of the car, where it benefits most from the inrush of cold air created by the car's motion. When airflow provides insufficient cooling – eg idling in heavy traffic – an electric fan is actuated by means of a thermoswitch.

The system is of the sealed type, ie it incorporates a storage tank into which coolant is displaced when the volume of the circulating coolant increases due to expansion, and from which coolant is sucked back on subsequent contraction. The need for topping up is therefore minimal compared with the older, 'open' type systems. Topping up and level checking is carried out via the storage tank and not the radiator.

The filler cap incorporates a pressure release valve to vent steam to the atmosphere should the coolant boil, and a vacuum relief valve to admit air as the system cools down. Since the system is pressurised, the boiling point of the coolant is increased above that obtaining at atmospheric pressure. If the cap is removed when the system is hot, sudden boiling may occur, with risk of scalding. Take care, therefore if removing the cap when the system is hot. It is also important to make sure that the filler cap is in good condition and that the spring behind the sealing washer has not weakened.

The system functions in the following fashion. Cold water in the bottom of the radiator circulates up the lower radiator hose to the water pump, where it is pushed round the water passages in the cylinder block, helping to keep the cylinder bore and pistons cool.

The water then travels up into the cylinder head and circulates round the combustion spaces and valve seats absorbing more heat, and then, when the engine is at its optimum operating temperature, travels out of the cylinder head, past the open thermostat into the upper radiator hose and so into the radiator tank.

The water travels down the radiator where it is rapidly cooled by the in-rush of cold air through the radiator core, which is created by the motion of the car. Above certain coolant temperatures the electric fan comes into operation to assist in cooling. The fan is attached to a housing connected to the rear of the radiator and is switched on or off as required by the thermo switch which is screwed into the radiator and thereby senses the coolant temperature.

When the engine is cold, the thermostat (a valve which opens and closes according to the temperature of the water), maintains the circulation of the same water in the engine. Only when the correct minimum operating temperature has been reached (see Specifications), does the thermostat begin to open, allowing water to return to the radiator.

Maintenance

1 Normal maintenance of the cooling system is minimal. A weekly check should be made on the coolant level in the storage tank. If necessary, top it up using a coolant solution with the correct amount of antifreeze (so that its effectiveness is retained).

2 Periodically, check the exterior of the radiator core and remove any

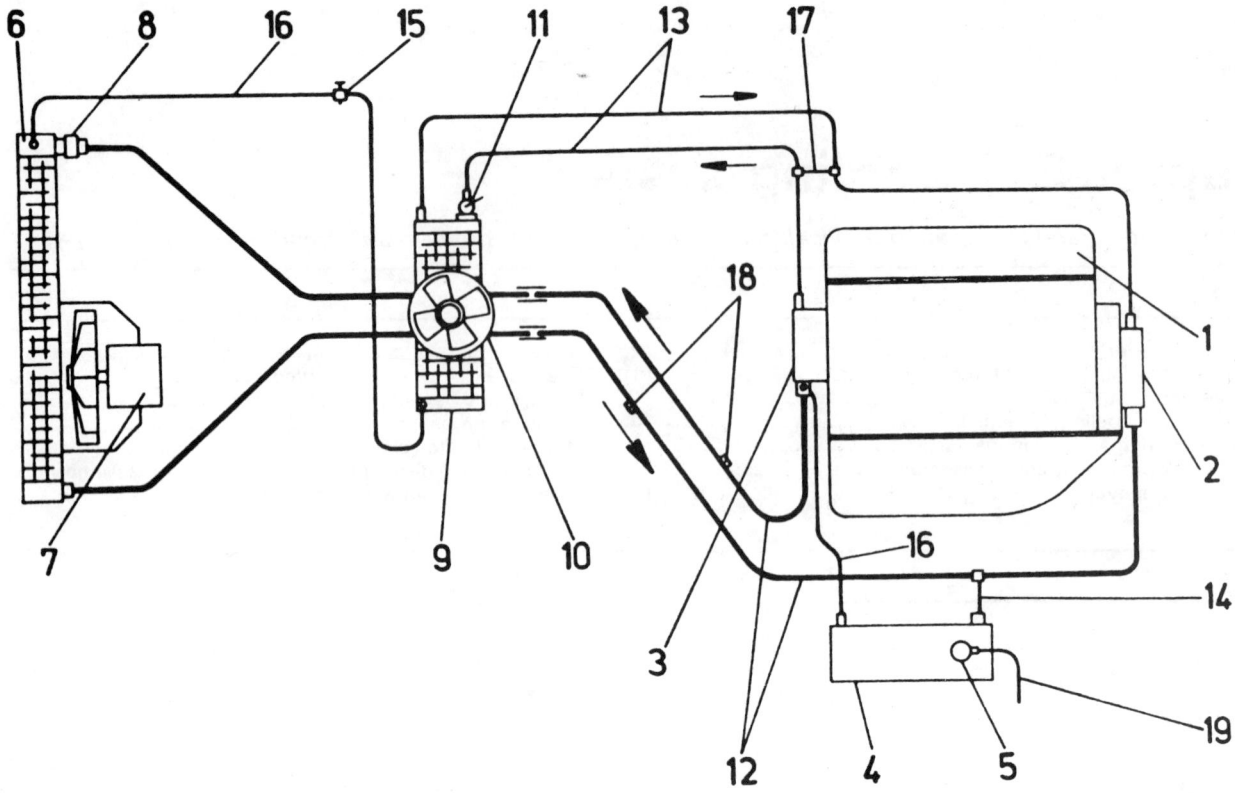

Fig. 2.1 Cooling system layout (Sec 1)

1	Engine	7	Radiator fan
2	Water pump	8	Fan thermoswitch
3	Thermostat	9	Heater
4	Storage tank	10	Heater fan
5	Filler cap	11	Heater valve
6	Radiator		

12	Radiator supply and return pipes
13	Heater supply and return pipes
14	Storage tank filler pipe

15	Bleed valve
16	Bleed pipes
17	Bypass pipe
18	Drain screws
19	Overflow pipe

debris that may have gathered by hosing or blowing through with an air line.

3 Check the hose connections for chafing, cracking and leakage. Renew as required.

4 At the specified intervals, lubricate the water pump bearings via the lubricator provided (photo). Unscrew the cap, fill with grease, then screw fully into position.

2 Cooling system – draining

1 When draining the cooling system, the car should be parked as level as possible, but bear in mind that you will have to raise the car and suitably support it for access to the drain plugs of the main pipes. If a pit or ramps are available these should be used.

2 If the engine is hot having just been run, allow it to cool prior to draining to avoid the possibility of scalding.

3 Where the coolant contains antifreeze, this can be saved for re-use, so drain it into a clean container of suitable capacity. Under normal circumstances, the actual amount of coolant drained will be about 85% of the total capacity (see Specifications) and therefore you must have a container with a minimum capacity of 10.5 litres (18.5 pints).

4 Release and remove the coolant storage (expansion) tank filler cap (photo).

5 Open the bleed cock under the boot lid (photo) and open the heater control valve by moving the heater lever on the facia panel to the ON position.

6 Raise and support the vehicle so that you can work underneath.

7 With the car raised, unscrew and release the respective pipe drainplugs (photo) and drain the coolant into the container. You may

need to probe the drain holes with a piece of wire to clear any minor blockage preventing the coolant from emerging.

8 When the coolant ceases to flow from the pipes the drain plugs can be retightened and any work necessitating engine dismantling can be commenced. However, if the coolant pipes between the pump and

1.4 Water pump bearing lubricator

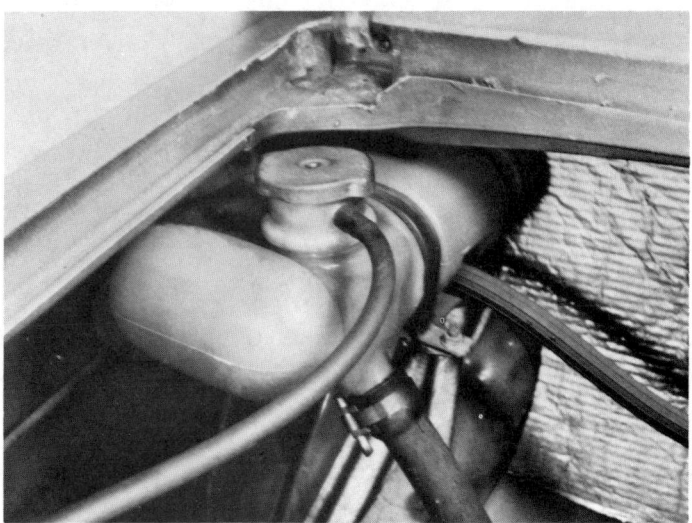
2.4 Remove expansion tank cap

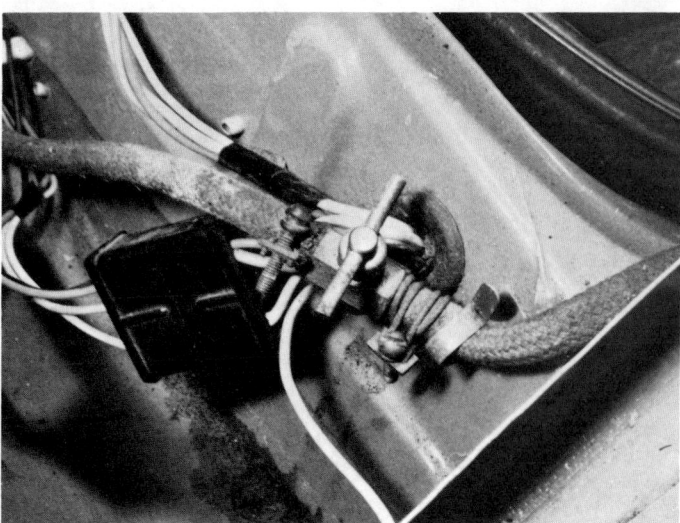
2.5 Bleed cock tap

2.7 The drain plugs (arrowed) in the supply and return coolant pipes

4.7 Radiator cooling fan (viewed from underneath)

heater and thermostat housing and heater are disconnected, also if the crankcase drain plug is removed, allow for a further small amount of coolant drainage. Again blockages may have occured in the system at these points in which case they can be cleared by probing with a suitable piece of wire.

3 Cooling system – flushing

1 Over a period of time the cooling system will lose its efficiency as the waterways and radiator tubes become clogged with rust scales, lime deposits and other sediment. Use of hard water when topping up (rainwater is to be preferred) and failure to use antifreeze or some corrosion inhibitor in summer may accelerate the clogging process.
2 To flush the cooling system, first drain it as described in Section 2.
3 Working underneath the car, disconnect the radiator inlet hose. Insert a garden hose into the radiator hose connection – it will be necessary to fabricate some kind of adaptor to get a reasonable seal – and run water through the system until it is coming out of the inlet hose fairly clean.
4 If it is wished to reverse flush the system, insert the hose into the radiator inlet hose and allow the water to flow out of the radiator hose connection.

5 In severe cases, a proprietary de-scaling compound may be used in accordance with the maker's instructions. Make sure that such compounds are suitable for use in aluminium engines.
6 Refill the system on completion as described in Section 11. Use new hose clips if necessary – the originals may not retighten satisfactorily.

4 Radiator – removal and refitting

1 Drain the coolant as described in Section 2.
2 Disconnect the coolant inlet and outlet hoses from the radiator (working underneath the car).
3 Detach the bleed hose from its location clips on the outer edge of the luggage boot.
4 Disconnect the thermoswitch leads from the switch on the radiator rear side.
5 Disconnect and remove the radiator grille and lower front body panel as described in Chapter 11.
6 Unscrew and remove the radiator retaining bolts from each headlight spacer and then carefully lift the radiator clear. Loosen the retaining clip and disconnect the bleed hose.
7 The cooling fan asssembly (photo) can be removed from the radiator on removal as can the thermoswitch.

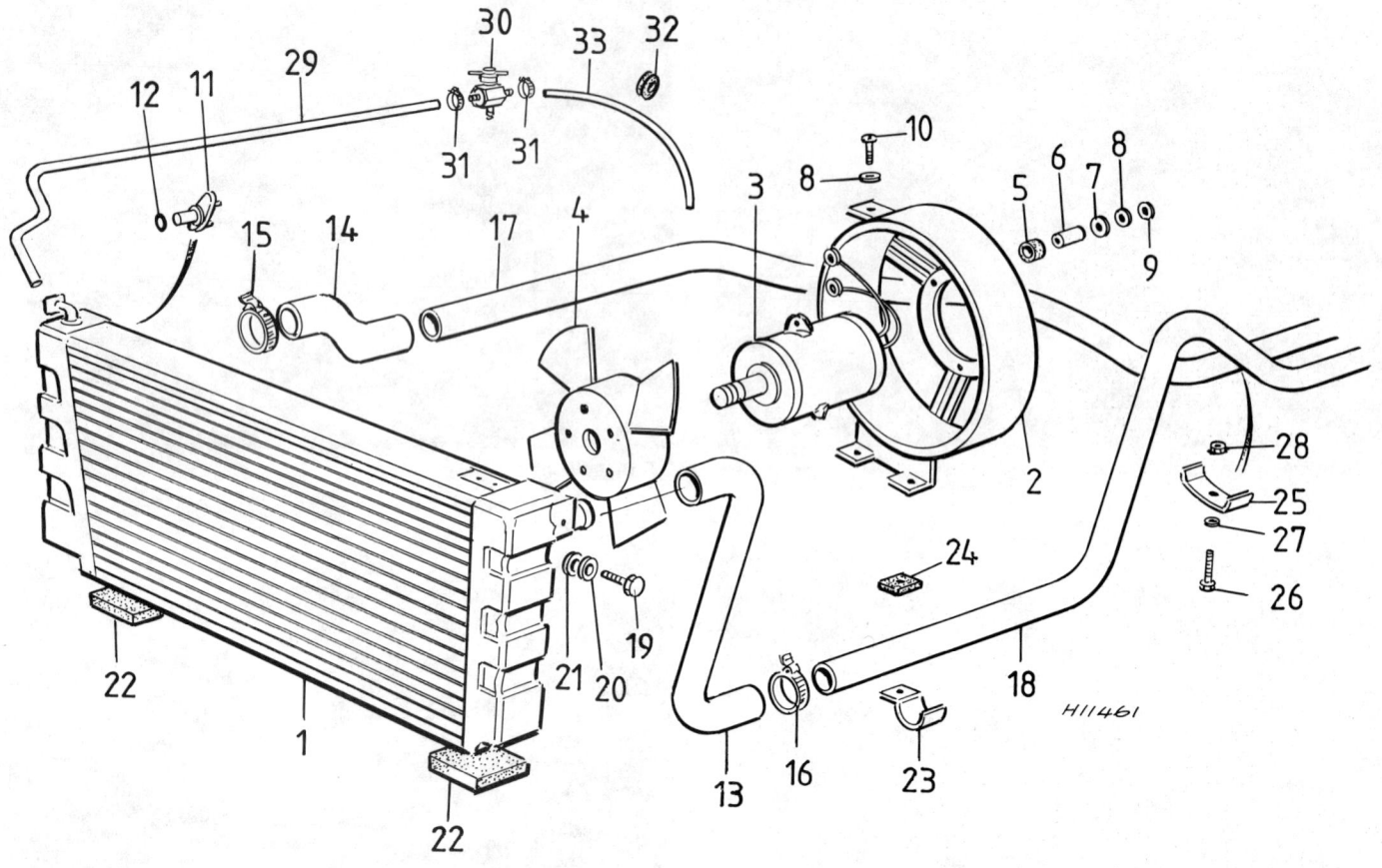

Fig. 2.2 Radiator, cooling fan and associated components (Sec 4)

1	Radiator	10	Cap screw
2	Fan cowling	11	Thermoswitch
3	Fan motor	12	Sealing ring
4	Fan	13	Outlet hose
5	Rubber bush	14	Inlet hose
6	Spacer	15	Hose clip
7	Washer	16	Hose clip
8	Washers	17	Feed pipe
9	Washer		

18	Return pipe	26	Bolt
19	Retaining bolt	27	Washer
20	Washer	28	Nut
21	Washer	29	Bleed hose
22	Rubber mountings	30	Bleed cock
23	Pipe clip	31	Clips
24	Rubber mounting	32	Grommet
25	Pipe clip	33	Bleed hose

8   Refitting the radiator is a reversal of the removal procedure. Take care not to damage the radiator when lifting it into position and locate it on the rubber pads. If the thermoswitch has been removed ensure that it is refitted with a new sealing ring.

9   Refill the system on completion as described in Section 11. Use new hose clips if necessary.

5 Radiator – inspection

1   With the radiator out of the car any leaks can be soldered or repaired with a proprietory compound. Clean out the radiator by flushing, as described in Section 3. It should be mentioned that solder repairs are best completed professionally. It is too easy to damage other parts of the radiator by excessive heating.

2   Clean the exterior of the radiator by hosing down the radiator matrix with a strong jet of water to clean away road dirt, dead flies etc.

3   Inspect the radiator hoses for cracks, internal and external, perishing and damage caused by over-tightening of the hose clips. Renew the hoses as necessary.

4   Examine the hose clips and renew them if they are rusted or distorted.

6 Storage tank – removal and refitting

1   Detach the three hoses and drain the tank contents.

2   Unscrew the tank retaining strap nuts, release the strap and remove the tank.

3   Refitting is the reverse of the removal procedure.

7 Thermostat – removal, testing and refitting

1   To remove the thermostat, first drain the cooling system as described in Section 2.

2   The thermostat is located at the rear (bulkhead end) of the cylinder head, attached to a flange on the left-hand side (photo). Disconnect the hoses and undo the housing flange nuts. Remove the housing. If it sticks in position, soak the studs and joint area with penetrating oil. The main body can be left in position on the cylinder head.

3   Extract the thermostat from its housing and inspect it to make sure that no riveted or soldered joints are broken or loose. Check that the jiggle pin is in position and moves freely.

4   To test for correct opening, hang the thermostat by a string in a

7.2 Thermostat unit

8.4 Removing the water pump

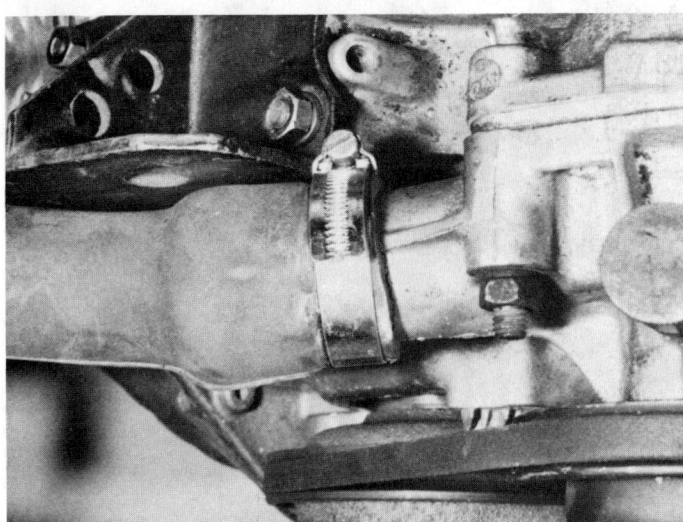

8.5 Renew hose clips where necessary

saucepan of cold water. Heat the water, stirring occasionally and monitoring the water temperature with a thermometer.

5   The thermostat should start to open at the temperature given in the Specifications. Continue to heat the water and check that fully opening is also achieved at the specified temperature. Check whilst the thermostat is open that there is no dirt or scale around the valve seat.

6   Remove the thermostat from the hot water and immerse it in cold water. It should close completely in 15 to 20 seconds.

7   If the thermostat fails any of the above tests it should be discarded and a new unit obtained. In an emergency it is possible to run the engine without a thermostat in the housing, but warm-up will be prolonged (perhaps indefinitely) and fuel consumption will suffer.

8   Refitting is the reverse of the removal procedure. Use a new gasket lightly smeared with jointing compound. Renew hose clips where necessary.

9   Refill the cooling system as described in Section 11. Check the thermostat housing for leakage on completion.

8   Water pump – removal and refitting

1   To remove the pump, first drain the cooling system as described in Section 2.

2   Loosen the alternator clamping bolts and remove the drivebelt.

3   Disconnect the hoses from the pump body.

4   Undo the flange fixing nuts and remove the pump (photo). If the pump is stuck, apply penetrating oil to the studs and the flange. **Do not** strike the pump with a metal hammer or lever against the flange.

5   Refitting is the reverse of the removal procedure. Ensure that the mating faces are free of old gasket and jointing compound. Always use a new gasket, and if necessary renew the hose clips (photo).

6   Refill the cooling system on completion as described in Section 11. Check for signs of joint leakage when the engine is run.

9   Water pump – dismantling, inspection and reassembly

1   If the water pump bearings or seals are defective, they can be renewed but it should be borne in mind, prior to dismantling, that considering the time and cost involved, it will probably be more practical to obtain a new or exchange pump unit complete. It is also unlikely that the pump spares will be readily available. However, if the pump is to be dismantled proceed as follows (refer to Fig. 2.3).

2   Undo and remove the pulley nut and washer.

3   Withdraw the pulley from the shaft. A puller may be required, and care should be taken not to distort the pulley.

4   Remove the Woodruff key from the shaft keyway and press, or drive out, the pump shaft. Remove the housing plate.

5   Remove the bearing retaining ring and drive out the bearings and

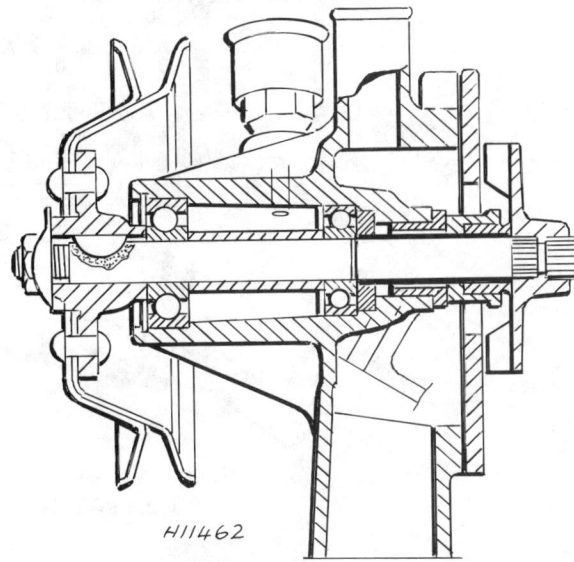

H11462

Fig. 2.3 Sectional view of water pump (Sec 9)

spacer tube from opposing ends with a suitable drift.
6   Remove the rubber sealing ring from the pump body.
7   Clean and inspect all the parts, in particular the bearings and
rubber seal. Renew as required if showing signs of wear.
8   Reassembly is the reverse sequence of dismantling, but be sure to
grease the bearings and ensure the rubber seal is located correctly.
Tighten the pulley nut to the specified torque.
9   Fill the greaser with bearing grease and screw it into position to
lubricate the bearings. Leave the grease cap in the tightened position
to prevent it from coming loose.
10 The water pump bearings must be lubricated at the intervals given
in the Routine Maintenance Section at the front of this book.

10 Temperature gauge sensor unit

1   A water temperature warning sensor unit is fitted, and is located
at the top of the cylinder head. Removal of this unit is only required if
the temperature gauge fails to work, and the gauge and wiring are
known to be in good order. It is not possible to repair either the gauge
or sensor unit and they must therefore be renewed if at fault. Prior to
removal of the gauge or sensor unit, check the wiring for breaks using
an ohmmeter or continuity tester. The sensor and gauge can be tested
by substitution.
2   The sensor unit is removed from the head after draining half of the
coolant from the system, and disconnecting the electrical terminal.
Unscrew the unit with a spanner of the correct size.
3   Replacement is a reversal of the above procedure.
4   For details of removing the temperature gauge, see Chapter 10.

11 Cooling system – refilling and antifreeze

1   Reconnect any hoses that were detached and tighten the drain
taps.
2   If the heater system has been drained, open the heater inlet valve.
3   Refill the cooling system through the storage tank, ensuring that
the heater control valve is open and also the bleed valve.
4   Top up slowly and watch for leaks in the system. Close the bleed
valve and refit the pressure cap. Run the engine for a few minutes
when the correct level is reached, then recheck the level and top up
further if required.

5   The storage tank is marked MAX and MIN on some models and
the coolant level must be between these marks when refilled. If these
marks are not shown on the tank, refill to the half-full mark which is
indicated by the dividing seam.

6   If the engine has overheated due to lack of water, **do not top-up
immediately with cold water!** Wait for the engine to cool naturally.
Alternatively, refill with hot water with the engine ticking over.

7   If an antifreeze solution is to be used, and this is obviously
essential during the winter months, be sure to use a good quality type,
having a mixture that is non-corrosive to aluminium. It should have a
glycol or ethylene base. The amount of dilution with water varies, but
strictly follow the antifreeze manufacturer's instructions, bearing in
mind the temperature variations which may be encountered.

8   If antifreeze is not used, a corrosion inhibitor should be used in the
cooling system.

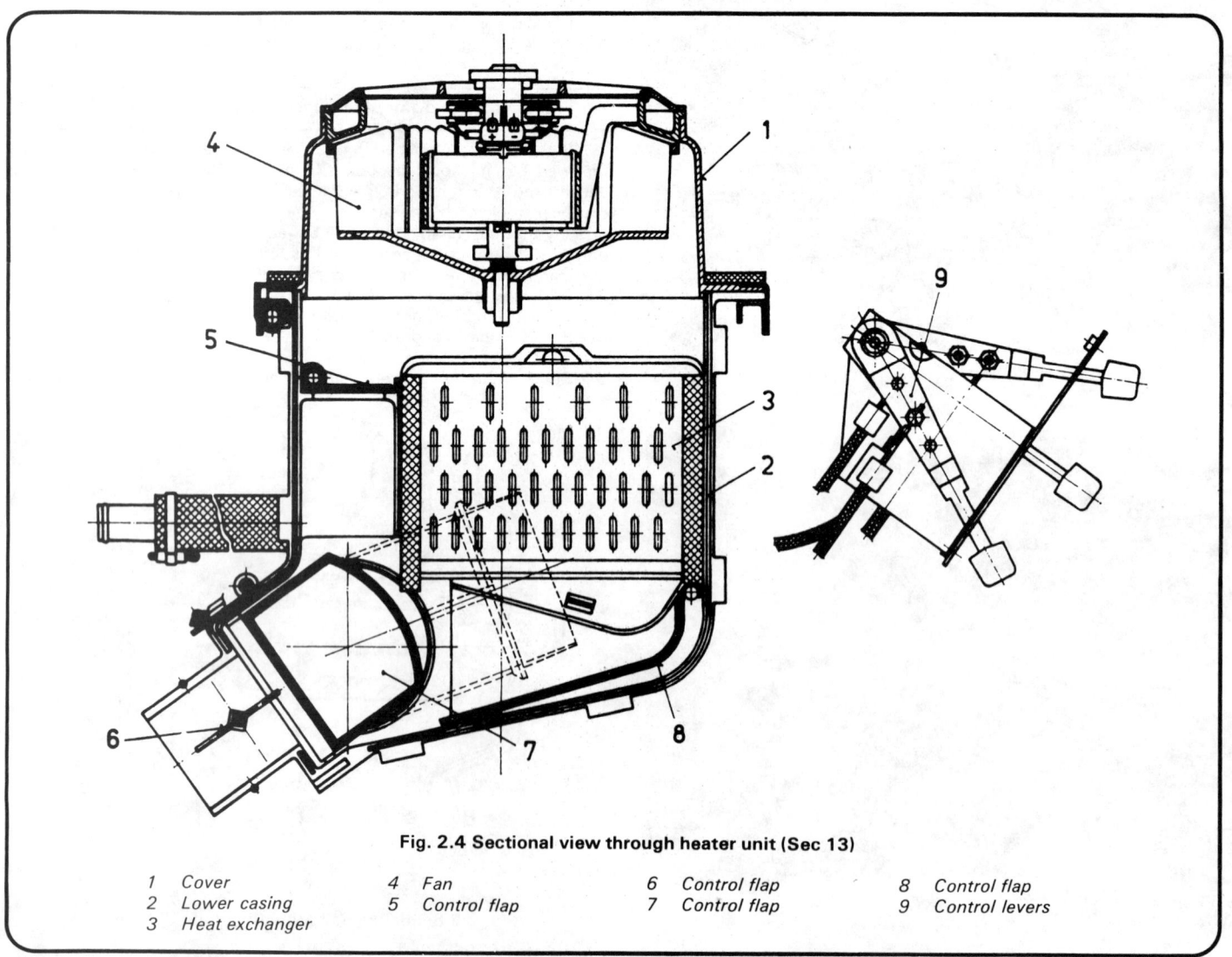

Fig. 2.4 Sectional view through heater unit (Sec 13)

1 Cover	4 Fan	6 Control flap	8 Control flap
2 Lower casing	5 Control flap	7 Control flap	9 Control levers
3 Heat exchanger			

12 Heater unit – removal and refitting

1 Refer to Section 2 and drain the cooling system.
2 Disconnect the battery earth lead.
3 Prise free the hose guard-to-floor tunnel pin, loosen the screw on top of the guard and sliding it down the cutaway, remove the guard.
4 Pull the air hose from the heater.
5 Detach the terminal board connectors, but not the motor cable (in the luggage compartment). Detach the earth cable and lug from the windscreen wiper bracket.
6 Disconnect the bleed hose from the bleed cock.
7 Pull and remove the heater control grip buttons from their levers on the facia. Detach the panel.
8 Disconnect the hazard warning terminal (where fitted).
9 Compress and detach the heater air ducts from the heater sides.
10 Detach the heater hoses from the unit.
11 Unscrew the four unit-to-body retaining nuts and remove the heater.
12 Refit in the reverse sequence. Ensure that the heater hoses are securely located. Lubricate the heater control cables with a few drops of oil before reconnecting.
13 On completion check the operation of the heater unit and also the hazard warning lights (if fitted).

13 Heater unit – dismantling and reassembly

1 Detach the heater control cables from the levers.

2 Remove the heater gasket from the flange face, loosen the brace locks and disconnect the braces, cover and fan.
3 Remove the heater control valve.
4 Detach the hose clips and remove the second inlet hose and bleed hose from the exchanger. Do not disconnect the valve lever link.
5 Disconnect the rear face flap links and the case flap links (retained by lock rings, washers and levers).
6 Remove the bottom socket flap lockring with washer and spring.
7 Prise the case flange clips free and separate the casing halves. The side elbows can be removed by simply pulling them free.
8 To remove the fan unit, unscrew the three cap screws and washers, detach the grille and remove the fan and bracket. If necessary unscrew and remove the resistor from the case cover. To dismantle the fan motor refer to Chapter 10.
9 Reassemble in the reverse order, employing a sealing ring when fitting the valve. The bowden cables must be correctly connected as follows:

  a) Connect the left-hand lever to the link on the heater rear side
  b) Connect the central lever to the lever on the heater right side
  c) Connect the right-hand lever to the first bowden cable from the lever pivot on the left-hand side of the heater. The second cable is attached to the control valve

10 To adjust the bowden cables and links (not normally necessary unless link screws have been loosened), locate the bracket and levers with the surface face at the grips at an angle of 35° with the centre-line of the heater. The top corner is about 40 mm (1.57 in) from the flange. Set the levers on the brackets and heater to extreme positions and then lock the cable link screws.

14 Fault diagnosis – cooling system

Symptom	Reason(s)
Overheating	Low coolant level
	Low oil level
	Water pump drivebelt slack or broken
	Radiator fan, wiring or thermoswitch defective
	Thermostat faulty (jammed shut)
	Radiator internal blockage or external obstruction
	Engine waterways blocked or hoses collapsed
	Water pump defective
	Ignition timing incorrect
	Mixture too weak
	Exhaust system blockage
	Blown cylinder head gasket
	New engine not yet run-in
	Brakes binding
	Gauge reading incorrect
Overcooling	Thermostat defective (jammed open), missing, or incorrect type
	Radiator fan thermostat defective (fan running continuously)
	Mixture too rich
	Gauge reading incorrect
Coolant loss (external)	Hoses perished or clips loose
	Radiator core leaking
	Pressure cap defective
	Thermostat or water pump leaking
	Heater core leaking
	Blown head gasket (combustion gases forcing coolant down overflow pipe)
Coolant loss (internal)	Blown head gasket (steam in exhaust and/or water in oil)
	Cracked, distorted or badly seated cylinder liner
	Cracked head or block
Poor heater output	Overcooling (see above)
	Air-lock in heater line (bleed system)
	Internal blockage (flush, de-scale or renew)

Chapter 3 Fuel and exhaust systems

For modifications, and information applicable to later models, see Supplement at end of manual

Contents

Specifications

Carburettor

Make and type .... Jikov 32 EDSR twin choke downdraught

Specification number:
- 105 S and 105 L 443 751 290 100
- 120 L and LE 443 751 319 800
- 120 LS, GLS and LSE 443 751 290 000

Carburettor specifications:

	105S, 105L		120L and LE		120 LS, GLS and LSE	
Choke no	*1*	*2*	*1*	*2*	*1*	*2*
Atomizer cone diameter	21 mm	22 mm	22 mm	23 mm	22 mm	23 mm
Main petrol jet	105	120	112	125	112	130
Main air jet	170	160	170	160	170	160
Pilot jet	50	45	50	45	50	45
Pilot air jet	140	–	140	–	140	–
Auxiliary pilot jet	–	60	–	60	–	60
Econostat petrol jet	60	–	60	–	70	–
Econostat mixture jet	95	–	110	–	110	–
Econostat air jet	70	–	70	–	70	–
Choke petrol jet	90		100		100	
Choke air jet diameter	4.5 mm		4.5 mm		4.5 mm	
Diaphragm control air valve	130	80	160	80	160	80
Pump bypass orifice	40		40		40	
Injector	50	–	50	–	50	–
Needle valve diameter	1.5 mm		1.5 mm		1.5 mm	
Suction connection diameter	1.2 mm		1.2 mm		1.2 mm	
Accelerator pump discharge	7 to 9 cc per 10 strokes					

Fuel pump

Make and type	Jikov MF 3407 diaphragm
Actuation	Mechanical from camshaft
Stroke	4 mm
Suction head	1.5 m
Delivery head	2 m
Discharge rate at 2000 strokes per minute	30 litres (6.6 gal) per hour

Fuel octane requirement

120 LS, GLS and LSE	95 minimum (UK 3-star)
All other models	90 minimum (UK 2-star)

Engine idle speed .... 780 to 830 rpm

1 General description

Fuel from the tank is delivered to the carburettor by a fuel pump, which is mechanically operated, and located on the cylinder block in line with the camshaft. A lever from the pump is actuated by the camshaft.

The carburettor and fuel pump on all models are of Jikov manufacture. The carburettor is a downdraught twin choke type.

Maintenance of the system consists of the following, which should be checked at the intervals given in the Routine Maintenance Section at the front of the book:

(a) Check the idle speed setting (Section 4)
(b) Clean the fuel pump filter (Section 8)
(c) Clean/renew the air filter element (Section 2)
(d) Lubricate the throttle and choke cables and check settings
(e) Check the system for any signs of fuel leakage

2   Air filter – servicing, removal and refitting

1   The carburettor air cleaner must be serviced regularly at the specified maintenance intervals. Servicing consists of removing and cleaning the filter element and casing, and when necessary renewing the element.
2   To remove the element, unclip and remove the filter cover lid, then depressing the cross brace retaining the element, twist it to disengage it and extract the element (photos).
3   Lightly tap and shake the element to remove most of the dirt from it. Wipe clean the inside of the element housing, then refit the element and re-engage the cross brace to secure.
4   At the specified intervals the element must be discarded and a new one fitted. The time intervals should be reduced when the vehicle is operating in hot, dusty or particularly adverse conditions whereby the element will clog up quicker.
5   In the winter months the air cleaner should be fitted with the hot air hose duct to assist in rapid warm-up. The hose (which is supplied

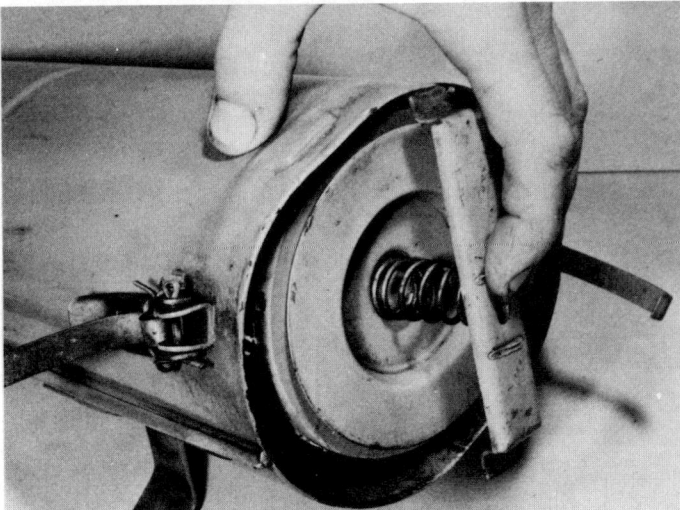

2.2a Depress cross brace and twist it to release ...

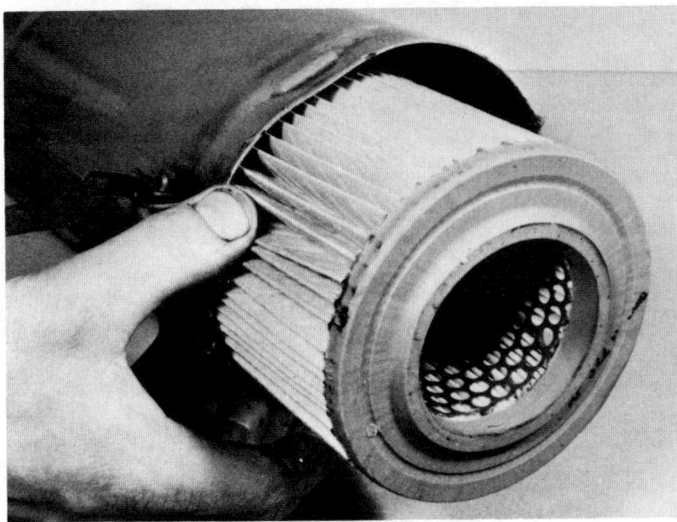

2.2b ... then withdraw the air filter element

with the car) is located between the air cleaner unit and the exhaust manifold.
6   To fit the hose, remove the rubber cap from the extension arm of the cover and use it to plug the arm mouth. Now locate the guide extension into the clear aperture of the arm and fit the corrugated paper hose into the extension and the holder of the inlet and exhaust manifold. Bend the hose to shape, allowing a finger width clearance between it and the exhaust manifold.
7   In moderate to warm temperatures, remove the hose and refit the rubber cap into its original position in the extension arm.
8   To remove the element case complete, disconnect its attachment to the carburettor and support brackets on the cylinder head (photo).
9   Refit in the reverse order and set the seasonal adjustment accordingly as given above. Take care that the casing does not foul the carburettor solenoid valve connection.

3   Carburettor – description

All models are fitted with a Jikov twin choke downdraught carburettor (photo). The various systems are as follows.
Both choke chambers have their own individual system, the initial air and fuel mixture being regulated by the emulsion tube, and final mixture adjustment being in accordance with the airflow when the throttle valve is opened the required amount.
The idle system of stage I (primary choke) and the bypass system of stage II (secondary choke) are interconnected to the emulsion orifice. The idle adjuster screw and fast idle screw are incorporated into these circuits. A solenoid valve is used in the stage I operation to prevent running on (dieseling) when the ignition is switched off. The idle orifice and mixture chamber are interconnected to provide a smooth transfer to the main system.
The bypass hole in stage II ensures satisfactory connections between stages I and II.
The econostat (rich mixture system) operates in stage I when the engine is operating under higher work loading and it functions according to the atomizer pressure and airflow into the engine.
The accelerator pump is a mechanical diaphragm type. It sucks fuel from the float chamber and directs it through a non-return valve either to the injector, or via a bypass orifice back to the float chamber. Under sudden acceleration, the required amount of fuel travels through the injector and into the choke tube.
The choke unit for cold starting consists of a fuel reservoir, petrol jet, vacuum control and throttle. The choked fuel mixture enters the venturi underneath the throttle valve, the choke control being manually

2.8 Air filter case showing main attachments and fittings

A   Retaining bolt to carburettor
B   Release clip to extension arm
C   Rubber plug for seasonal hot air hose
D   Unit bracket mounting on rocker cover
E   Engine breather tubes junction

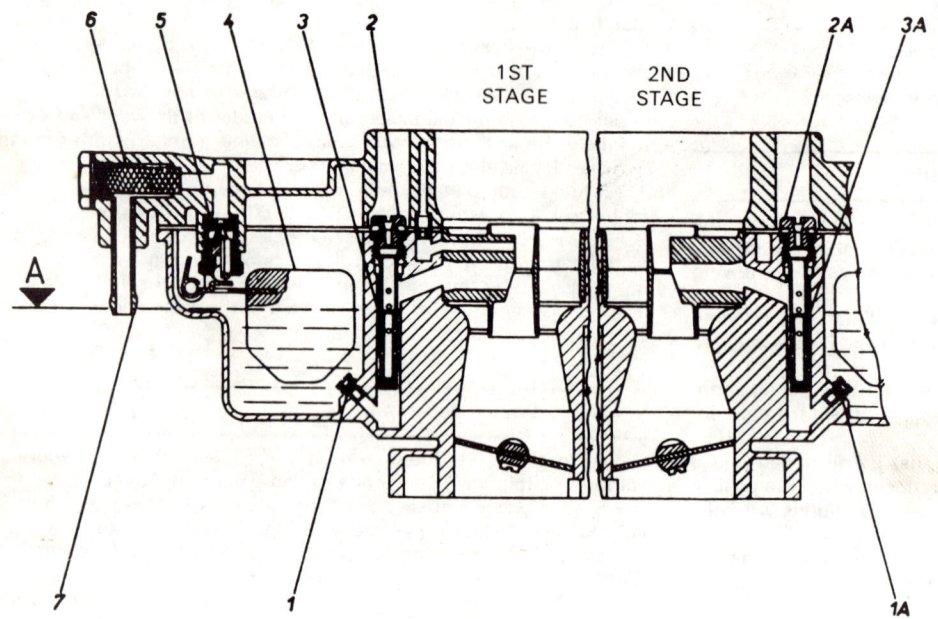

Fig. 3.1 Sectional view of Jikov
carburettor (Sec 3)

1   Primary main jet
1A Secondary main jet
2   Primary main air jet
2A Secondary main air jet
3   Primary emulsion tube
3A Secondary emulsion tube
4   Float
5   Needle valve
6   Fuel strainer
7   Fuel intake
A   Fuel level (20 ± 1 mm)

3.0 The Jikov carburettor

A   Solenoid valve   D   Throttle balljoint
B   Choke lever   E   Idle mixture screw location
C   Diaphragm pump

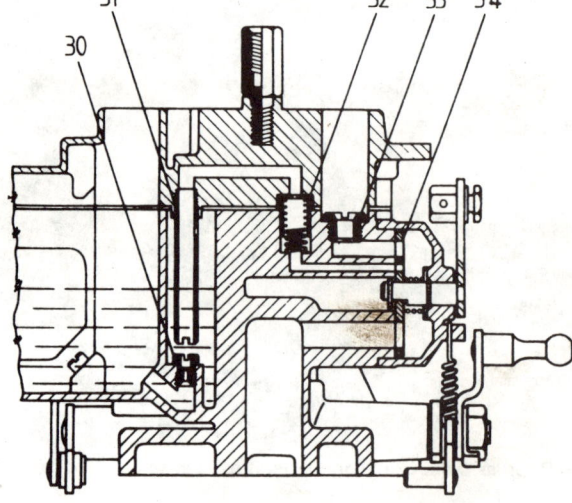

Fig. 3.2 Details of choke system (Sec 3)

30 Choke jet   33 Choke air jet
31 Choke pipe   34 Throttle valve
32 Choke valve

operated from the dashboard.

A vacuum connection from the crankcase to below the second stage throttle valve allows crankcase fumes to be drawn into the combustion chamber and burnt when the engine is running above idling speed.

4   Carburettor – adjustment

1   To adjust the carburettor it is essential that the engine be at its normal operating temperature, and the air cleaner in position. The idle mixture screw is normally covered by a 'tamperproof' plug which can be prised free using a needle. Its location can be determined by referring to photo 3.0.

2   Before making any adjustments ensure that the ignition timing is correct, the valve adjustments are correct and that the air filter is in position and in serviceable condition.

3   For accurate adjustment a tachometer should be used to give the correct engine speed readings. Connect the tachometer in accordance with its manufacturer's instructions.

4   Check that the throttle pedal has the correct free play, as described in Section 13.

5   Run the engine at a fast tickover for a few minutes so that it reaches normal operating temperature, then adjust as follows:

(a)   Adjust the air correction screw (photo) to set the engine speed at the specified level

(b)   The idling mixture screw should now be screwed out until the engine shows signs of stalling, then gradually screwed back in until the engine just runs smoothly (photo)

(c)   Now turn the air correction screw to regain the specified idle speed

6   To further check for correct adjustment and operation, the throttle should be opened quickly and the increase in engine speed should be accomplished smoothly. Turn the engine off and restart. This should be achieved without using the throttle and must be immediate.

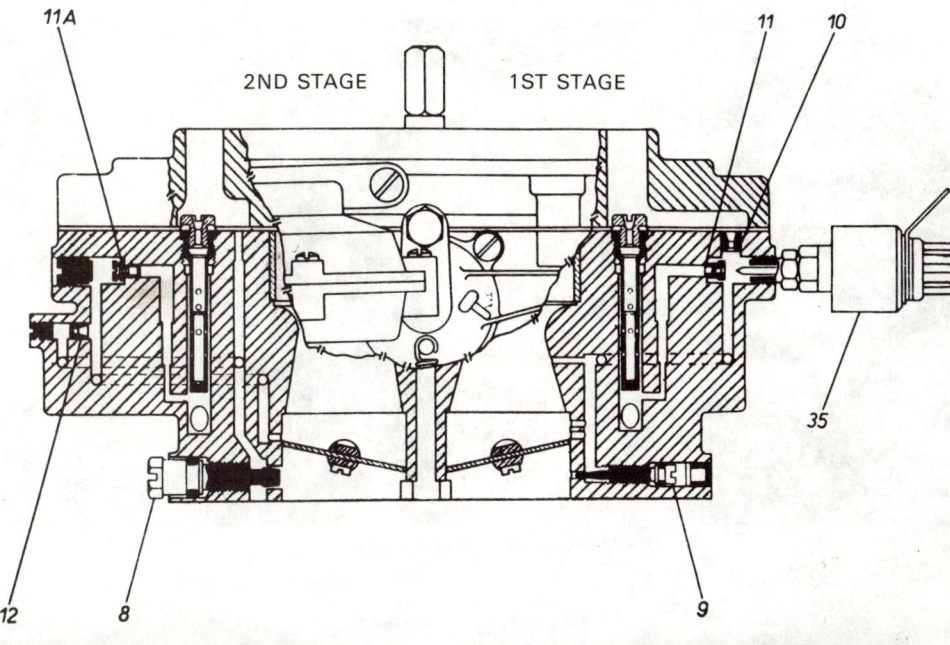

2ND STAGE   1ST STAGE

Fig. 3.3 Details of idling system (Sec 3)

8   Air screw
9   Mixture screw
10 Primary pilot air jet
11 Primary pilot jet
11A Secondary pilot jet
12 Secondary pilot air jet
35 Solenoid valve

4.5 Adjusting the air correction screw

5.8 Disconnect the balljoint retaining clip

5.9 Removing the carburettor from the manifold

7   If backfiring occurs then the idling mixture screw should be turned in slightly and the air correction screw adjusted to compensate if necessary.
8   Refit the plug over the idle mixture screw on completion.

5 Carburettor – removal and refitting

1   The carburettor can be easily removed from the engine but prior to doing so a new carburettor-to-manifold flange gasket should be obtained. If the carburettor is to be dismantled get a complete gasket kit.
2   Referring to Section 2, remove the air cleaner unit.
3   Disconnect the choke cable and tuck it out of the way. Likewise disconnect the throttle cable.
4   Disconnect the lead from the solenoid valve.
5   Disconnect the fuel supply pipe to the carburettor.
6   Unscrew the distributor vacuum tube retaining bolt from its position adjacent to the air cleaner bracket, and slide the pipe clear of the carburettor along its guide.
7   Remove the four carburettor-to-manifold nuts.
8   Disconnect the throttle control rod balljoint connection by prising free its retaining clip (photo).
9   Now lift the carburettor clear of the manifold (photo).
10 Refit in the reverse order, taking care not to overtighten fastenings, and if available use a new carburettor-to-manifold gasket. Adjust the choke and throttle cables as described in Sections 14 and 13 respectively.

6 Carburettor – dismantling, inspection and reassembly

1   Remove the carburettor to the workbench and clean off the exterior, prior to dismantling. Dismantle on a sheet of clean newspaper and lay the individual parts out, taking note of the removal sequence. **Do not clean the jets out with wire** – wash in petrol and blow through with compressed air.
2   To remove the top section, unscrew and remove the six retaining screws and the diaphragm retaining rod from the lower operating shaft by unclipping the C-clip (photo).
3   Lift the upper section clear, taking care not to damage the gasket – it may need to be used as a template if a replacement is not available.
4   Drain any remaning fuel from the carburettor and remove the float by withdrawing the spindle (photo).
5   Pull out of its location the accelerator injector jet (photo).
6   Unscrew the 1st and 2nd emulsion tubes and remove (photo).
7   Remove the idling air bleed supply jet and the cold start mechanism, which is retained by four screws, and the cold start air supply jet.
8   Remove the remaining jets and wash the various components thoroughly in petrol, and blow dry with an airline.
9   Inspect the various components for signs of wear, or damage. Shake the float to ensure that petrol has not leaked into it. Check the accelerator pump jet O-ring for distortion or signs of cracking. Renew if necessary. Check the choke unit (photo). The seal valve should move smoothly and the spring should have adequate tension. Although it rarely needs attention, the vacuum timing control for the second stage can be unscrewed from its flange on the upper section. Its upper and

6.2 Remove the upper section retaining screws

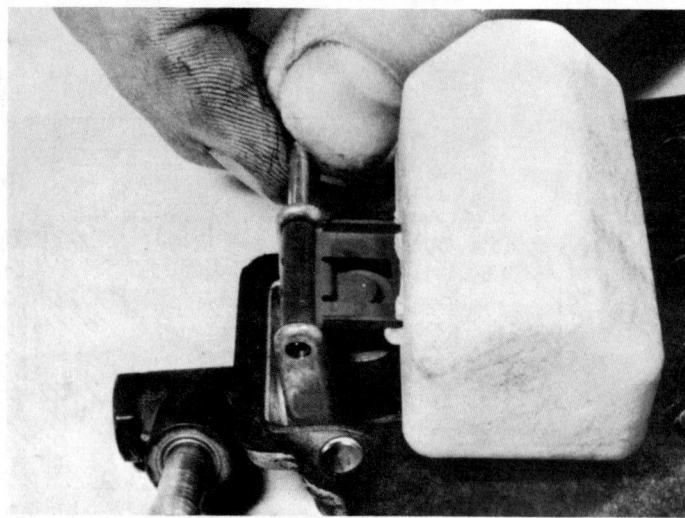

6.4 Withdraw the float spindle

6.5 Top view of carburettor

A   Accelerator injector   D   Choke jet
B   Emulsion tubes   E   Choke air jet
C   Stage 1 main jet

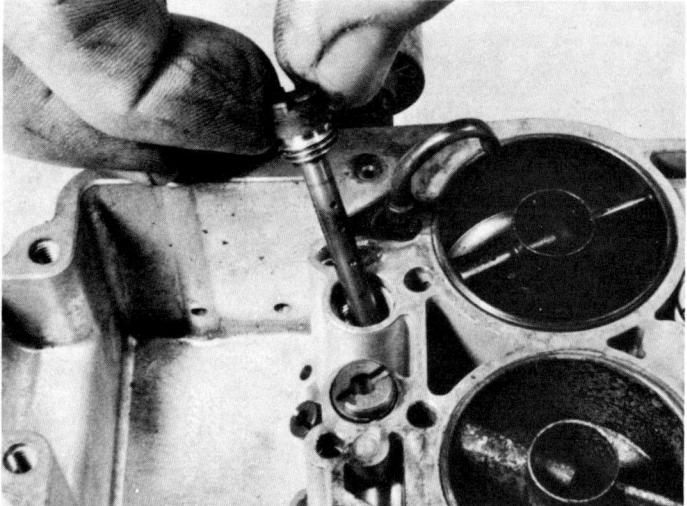

6.6 Removing an emulsion tube

lower body retaining screws are then removed and the unit split for inspection. Remove any traces of dirt and check the spring tension and diaphragm.

10 Reassembly and refitting are a reversal of dismantling and removal. Before refitting the upper body check and if necessary adjust the float level setting as follows. This is essential if the needle valve has been renewed (photo).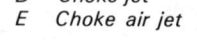

11 Hold the top cover section in the vertical position and then carefully check the float lip to gasket face clearance (with gasket in position). The correct clearance is 10 mm (0.39 in) and this can be achieved by bending the float pivot lip accordingly should it be necessary (Fig. 3.4). The shank of a suitable drill will suffice for a gauge rod.

12 When assembling the carburettor, be sure to fit the new gasket the correct way. Do not over-tighten the retaining screws or nuts and ensure all sealing faces are perfectly clean.

7   Fuel pump – removal and refitting

1   Disconnect the fuel inlet and outlet pipes from the pump body. Plug the feed pipe from the tank.

6.9 The choke valve and spring

6.10 The float needle valve (shown with float removed)

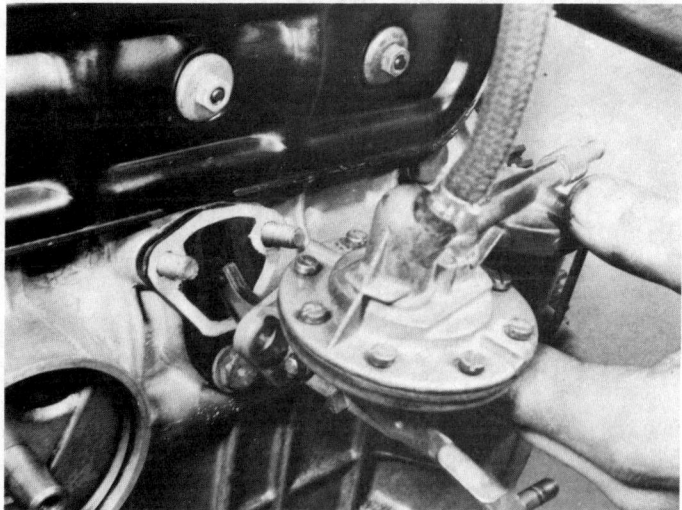

7.4 Refitting the fuel pump – note new gasket in position on flange

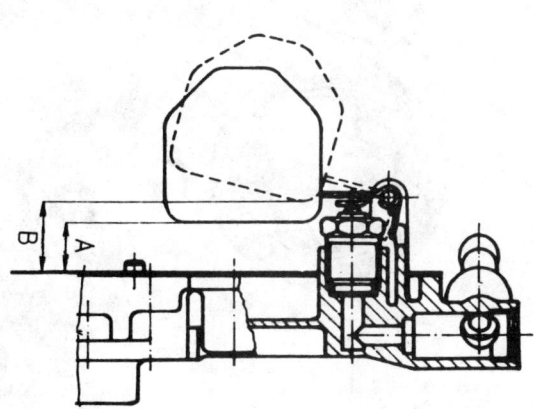

Fig. 3.4 Checking float level position (Sec 6)

A = 10 mm   B = 13.5 ± 1 mm

2   Undo the two pump flange retaining nuts and remove the pump complete with gasket.

3   Refitting is a reversal of the above procedure. However, ensure that the pipe connections are secure (but not over-tightened – worm drive clips are suggested as replacements for the original Skoda split pin type clips).

4   Always refit the pump with a new gasket of the same thickness as the one originally fitted (photo).

5   It should be noted that the filter in the pump can be removed and cleaned without removing the pump from the car.

8   Fuel pump – dismantling, inspection and reassembly

1   Unscrew and remove the eight upper pump body retaining screws and carefully lift it clear, noting the relative positions of the upper and lower body sections. Care must be taken not to split or damage the diaphragm (photo).

2   To remove the inlet and outlet valves from the roof of the upper section, unscrew the bridge plate screws and prise each valve from its recess, noting the location of each (photo).

3   To remove the filter, unscrew the retaining clamp screw and withdraw the bowl (photo). Wash the bowl and filter in clean petrol.

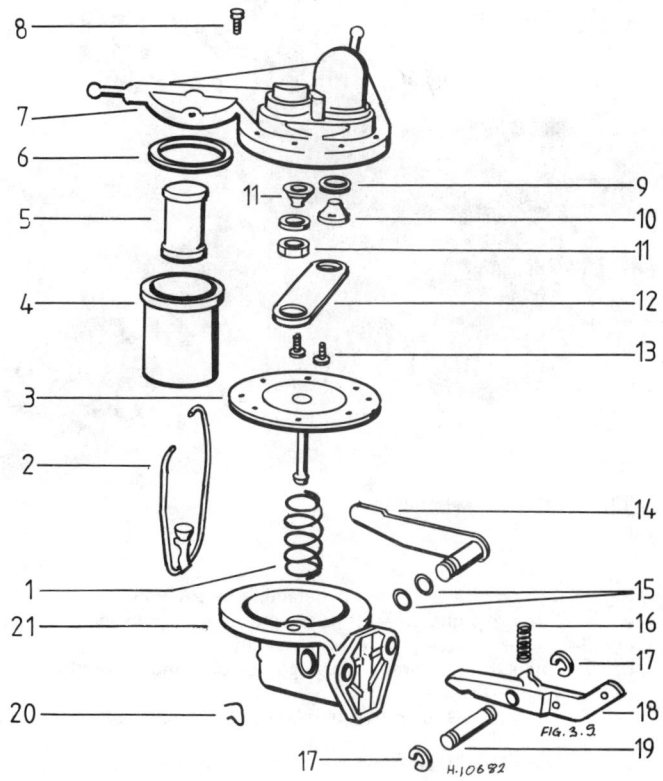

Fig. 3.5 Exploded view of fuel pump (Sec 8)

1 Spring	12 Bridge plate
2 Yoke	13 Screw
3 Diaphragm	14 Priming lever
4 Filter	15 Rings
5 Strainer	16 Spring
6 Seal	17 C-clips
7 Top section	18 Operating lever
8 Screw	19 Lever pivot
9 Seal	20 C-clip
10 Valve	21 Lower section
11 Spacer	

8.1 Remove the upper body section

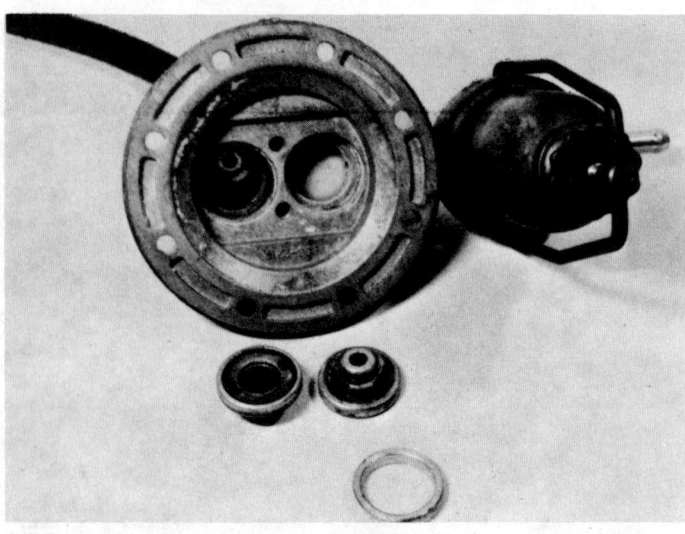

8.2 The inlet and outlet valves removed for cleaning and inspection

8.3 The filter, bowl and seal

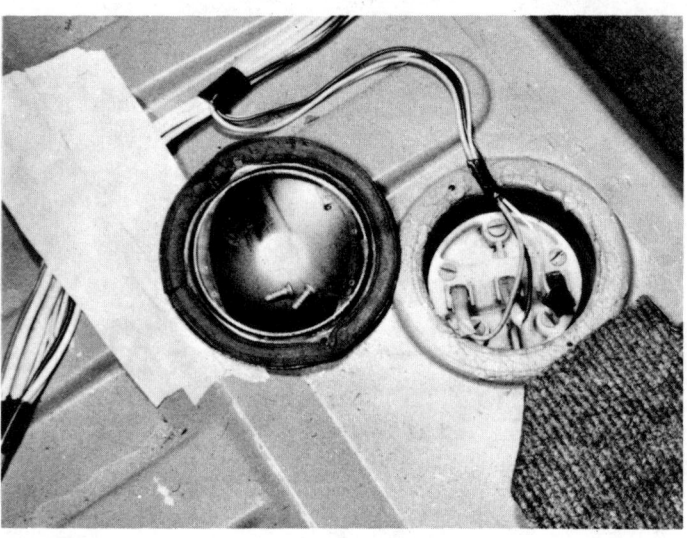

9.5 The fuel tank sender unit with cover removed

Renew the bowl seal rubber if defective in any way.

4   If there are signs of wear in the pump lever pivot pin, pump lever and link bushes, they should be renewed.

5   Examine the diaphragm for signs of cracking or perforation and renew if necessary.

6   To remove the diaphragm release the C-clips of the actuation lever.

7   Reassemble in reverse sequence, ensuring that all parts are perfectly clean.

8   When the pump is reassembled the suction and delivery pressure can be felt at the inlet and outlet ports when the lever arm is operated. Be careful not to block the inlet port completely when testing suction. If the rocker arm were to be operated strongly and the inlet side was blocked the diaphragm could be damaged.

9   Fuel tank – removal and refitting

1   Raise the rear of the vehicle and support it. Chock each side of the front wheels for security.

2   Drain the cooling system as described in Chapter 2.

3   Disconnect the battery earth cable from its terminal.

4   Drain any remaining fuel in the tank by removing the drain plugs on the underside of the tank. The tank is situated under the rear

passenger seats.

5   Remove the rear passenger seat on the right-hand side and remove the cover from the floor panel to expose the fuel gauge sender unit in the top of the tank (photo). Disconnect the sender unit wires from their connectors.

6   Working underneath the vehicle, unbolt and remove the central undertray.

7   Disconnect and detach the lower coolant and heater hose connections at the rear. Remove the rear sections of the coolant pipes.

8   Disconnect the fuel filler tube underneath on the right-hand side.

9   Select 1st or 3rd gear and then disconnect and remove the gear selector rod between the gearlever and gearbox.

10 Disconnect the speedometer drive cable from the gearbox.

11 Refer to Chapter 9 and disconnect the handbrake cables, then pull them through underneath.

12 Disconnect the choke and throttle cables at the carburettor end. On models so equipped, disconnect the servo vacuum hose at the inlet manifold.

13 Disconnect and plug the main fuel supply line at the pump end or fuel tank inlet as preferred.

14 Disconnect and plug the clutch hydraulic line at the bracket on the vertical floor panel to the rear of the tank.

15 Pull all lines and cables out of the way. Place a jack under the gearbox to support it, then loosen off the transmission cross bearer at

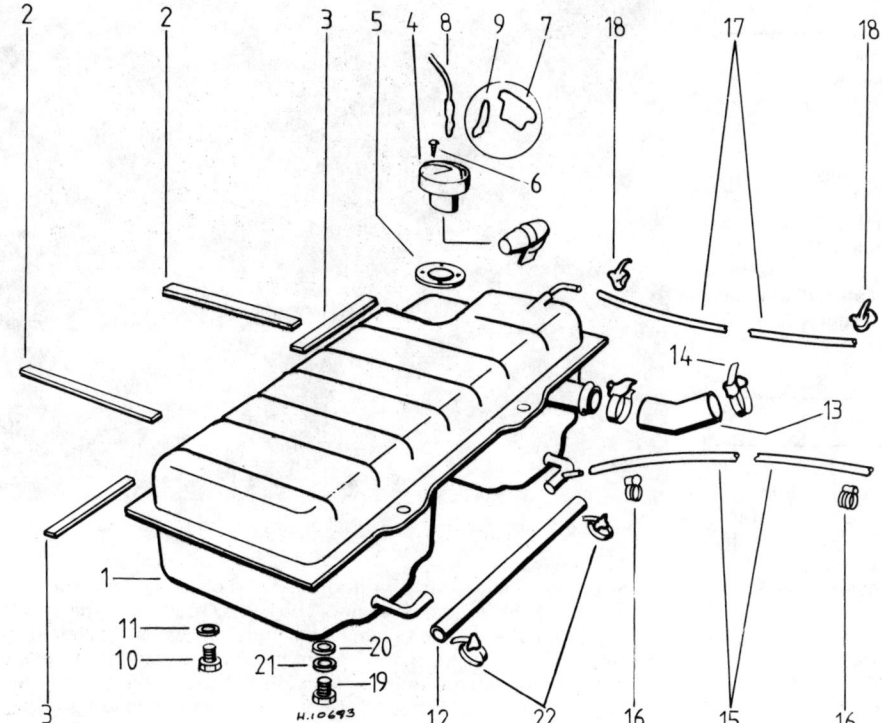

Fig. 3.6 Fuel tank and fittings (Sec 9)

1   Tank
2   Upper cover bands
3   Sealing strips
4   Fuel gauge float unit
5   Gasket
6   Screw
7   Float resistance strip
8   Connector
9   Float sliding wire
10 Drain plug
11 Sealing ring
12 Hose (balance)
13 Filler hose
14 Hose clip
15 Supply hose
16 Clips
17 Vent hose
18 Clips
19 Screw
20 Washer
21 Washer
22 Clips

the body mountings.

16 Support the fuel tank and remove its fastenings to the floor. Lower the jack under the transmission and simultaneously move the tank backwards and downwards, then tilting downwards and forwards to remove it. If it is found that the brake pipes interfere with removal of the tank they will have to be disconnected accordingly.

17 The tank is refitted in the reverse sequence but note the following:

(a) Renew any defective hoses and/or retaining clips
(b) Check that all connections are secure
(c) Refill the cooling system as given in Chapter 2
(d) Top up the clutch hydraulic fluid (and brake system if disturbed) and bleed as described in Chapters 5 and 9 respectively
(e) Reconnect and check the adjustment and correct operation of the choke and throttle cables
(f) On completion check for signs of fuel and/or coolant leakages from the disturbed connections

10 Fuel tank – cleaning and repair

1   With time, it is likely that sediment will collect in the bottom of the fuel tank. Condensation, resulting in rust and other impurities, will usually be found in the fuel tank of any vehicle more than three years old.

2   When the tank is removed it should be swilled out using several changes of clean paraffin and finally rinsed out with clean petrol. Remember that the float mechanism is delicate and the tank should not be shaken violently, or turned upside-down quickly, in case damage to the sender unit is incurred.

3   If the tank is leaking, it should be taken to a specialist firm for repair. **Do not attempt to solder, braze or weld the tank yourself; it is most dangerous.** A temporary repair may be made with fibreglass or similar material, but a new tank should be fitted or a permanent repair made as soon as possible.

11 Fuel gauge sender unit – removal and refitting

1   Before removing the sender unit, disconnect the battery earth terminal cable.

2   The sender unit is located in the top of the tank on the right-hand

side. Access to it is gained by tilting forward the right-hand rear passenger seat, unscrewing the cover screws and prising the cover free.

3   Disconnect the sender unit wires from their terminals.

4   Unscrew the five screws retaining the sender unit to the tank and then withdraw the unit, taking care not to damage the gasket and/or the float mechanism.

5   Cover the sender unit hole with a piece of polythene or similar and temporarily refit the cover to avoid petrol fumes building up inside the car.

6   Refitting is the reverse of the removal procedure.

12 Fuel tank filler pipe – removal and refitting

1   Disconnect the battery earth cable from its terminal.

2   Drain the fuel from the tank into a suitable sealed container.

3   Detach the filler pipe attachment bolt on the inside of the wing panel at the top.

4   Disconnect the pipe attachment bracket bolt to the chassis member where it curves forwards.

5   Disconnect the filler pipe to the tank and remove the pipe.

6   Refit in the reverse sequence, ensuring that all connections are secure. When the tank has been refilled with petrol check for any signs of leakage from the filler hose and connections.

13 Throttle pedal and cable – removing and refitting

1   Disconnect the throttle cable at the carburettor end and the engine-mounted relay lever.

2   Remove the pedal bearing retaining cap screws, then press the pedal lightly and withdraw it from the floor together with the bearing and cable.

3   The cable can be removed from the pedal after loosening off the retaining clamp.

4   Refit in the reverse sequence, but ensure that the cable is well lubricated with engine oil.

5   When adjusting the cable at the carburettor end it must be tightened in such a position that it is neither too tight nor too slack when the throttle pedal is in the fully retracted position.

14 Choke cable – removal and refitting

1   Disconnect the choke cable at the carburettor end.
2   Fold back the central floor tunnel mat. If a single piece mat is used you will have to remove a door sill strip on one side to fold the carpet over.
3   Disconnect the choke lever retaining bracket from the tunnel.
4   Working underneath the car, remove the fuel tank guard and the air duct cover.
5   Remove the choke control and guide the cable through to remove.
6   Refit in the reverse order and adjust the choke cable. Tip the cable lever towards the tunnel when attaching the cable to the carburettor.
7   Adjust the cable so that when fully released it has a small amount of slack at the choke lever connection. This ensures that when the cable is released, the choke is fully off.

15 Exhaust system

1   The exhaust system on the Skoda is simple and compact. It comprises a cast iron manifold and one or two pipes running from the manifold to the silencer which is mounted on the left-hand side of the engine (photo). When repairing the system, it is wise only to use the original type of exhaust clamps and proprietary made systems.
2   When any one section of the exhaust system needs renewal it often follows that the whole lot is best renewed.
3   It is most important when fitting exhausts that the twists and contours are carefully followed and that each connecting joint overlaps the correct distance. Any stress or strain imparted, in order to force the system to fit, will result in early fractures and failures.
4   When fitting a new part or a complete system, it is well worth

15.1 The exhaust silencer and bracket viewed from underneath

removing the whole system from the car and cleaning up all the joints so that they fit together easily. The time spent struggling with obstinate joints whilst flat on your back under the car is eliminated and the likelihood of distorting or even breaking a section is greatly reduced. Do not waste a lot of time trying to undo rusted and corroded clamps and bolts. Cut them off. New ones will be required anyway if they are that bad.

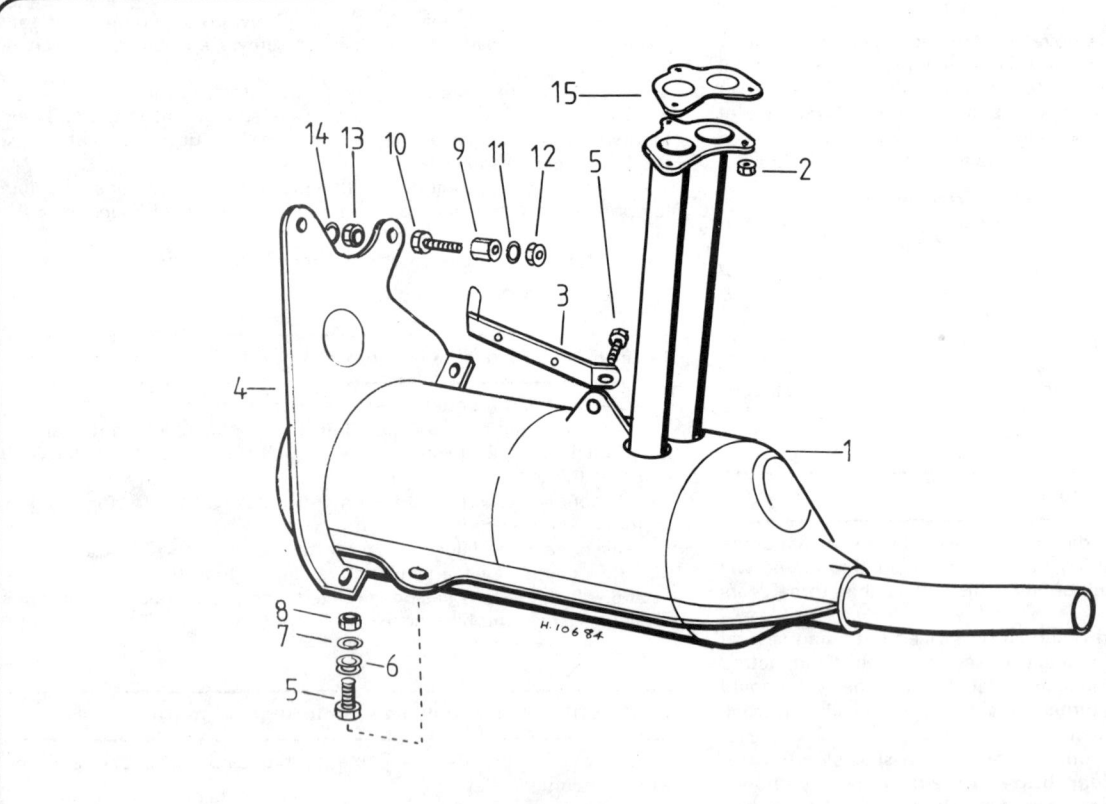

Fig. 3.7 Exhaust system components (Sec 15)

1 Silencer	5 Bolt	9 Spacer	13 Nut
2 Self-locking nut	6 Washer	10 Bolt	14 Washer
3 Front bracket	7 Washer	11 Washer	15 Gasket
4 Rear bracket	8 Nut	12 Nut	

16 Fault diagnosis – fuel and exhaust systems

Unsatisfactory engine performance and excessive fuel consumption are not necessarily the fault of the fuel system or carburettor. In fact they more commonly occur as a result of ignition and timing faults. Before acting on the following it is necessary to check the ignition system first. Even though a fault may lie in the fuel system it will be difficult to trace unless the ignition is correct. The faults below, therefore, assume that this has been attended to first (where appropriate).

Symptom	Reason(s)
Smell of petrol when engine is stopped	Leaking fuel lines or unions Leaking fuel tank
Smell of petrol when engine is idling	Leaking fuel line unions between pump and carburettor Overflow of fuel from float chamber due to wrong level setting, ineffective needle valve or punctured float
Excessive fuel consumption for reasons not covered by leaks or float chamber faults	Worn jets Over-rich setting (inspect spark plugs for evidence) Sticking mechanism Air filter blocked Choke cable maladjusted Binding brakes Overcooling (see Chapter 2)
Engine will not idle	Defective or disconnected carburettor solenoid valve Carburettor adjustment incorrect Idle jet(s) blocked Carburettor and/or manifold gasket(s) leaking (listen for hissing noise) Air filter blocked Float level incorrect
Difficult starting, uneven running, lack of power, cutting out	One or more jets blocked or restricted Float chamber fuel level too low or needle valve sticking Fuel pump not delivering sufficient fuel Faulty or disconnected carburettor solenoid valve Air filter blocked Secondary choke not opening correctly
Hesitation on acceleration	Mixture too weak Accelerator pump defective or jet blocked

Chapter 4 Ignition system

Contents

Specifications

General
System type .... Contact breaker and coil
Firing order .... 1-3-4-2 (No 1 cylinder at water pump end)

Spark plugs
Type:
    105, 120 L and 120 LE models .... PAL N7Y, Bosch W200T35, Champion L87Y, or equivalent
    120 LS, 120 GLS and 120 LSE models .... PAL N8Y, Bosch W5BC, Champion L87Y, or equivalent
Electrode gap (all models) .... 0.7 mm (0.028 in)

Distributor
Make and type:
    105 models .... PAL Magneton 443.213-204.480
    120 models .... PAL Magneton 443.213-204.460
Direction of rotation .... Clockwise
Contact breaker points gap .... 0.4 mm (0.016 in)
Dwell angle .... 49.5° ± 4.5° (55% ± 5%)

Ignition timing
Static timing:
    105 models .... 3° BTDC ± 2°
    120 models .... 5° BTDC ± 2°
Dynamic timing (vacuum hose disconnected):
    105 models .... 8° BTDC approx @ 800 rpm
    120 models .... 10° BTDC @ 800 rpm

Torque wrench setting

	Nm	lbf ft
Spark plugs	20 to 30	15 to 22

1 General description and maintenance

In order that the engine can run correctly it is necessary for an electrical spark to ignite the fuel/air mixture in the combustion chamber at exactly the right moment in relation to engine speed and load. The ignition system is based on feeding low tension voltage from the battery to the coil where it is converted to high tension voltage. The high tension voltage is powerful enough to jump the spark plug gap in the cylinders many times a second under high compression pressures, providing that the system is in good condition and that all adjustments are correct.

The ignition system is divided into two circuits: the low tension circuit and the high tension circuit.

The low tension (sometimes known as the primary) circuit consists of the battery, lead to the control box, lead to the ignition switch, lead from the ignition switch to the low tension or primary coil windings, and the lead from the low tension coil windings to the contact breaker points and condenser in the distributor.

The high tension circuit consists of the high tension or secondary coil windings, the heavy ignition lead from the centre of the coil to the centre of the distributor cap, the rotor arm, and the spark plug leads and spark plugs.

The system functions in the following manner. Low tension voltage is changed in the coil into high tension voltage by the opening and closing of the contact breaker points in the low tension circuit. High tension voltage is then fed via the carbon brush in the centre of the distributor cap to the rotor arm of the distributor. The rotor arm revolves inside the distributor cap, and each time it comes in line with one of the four metal segments in the cap, which are connected to the spark plug leads, the opening and closing of the contact breaker points causes the high tension voltage to build up, jump the gap from the rotor arm to the appropriate metal segment and so via the spark plug lead to the spark plug, where it finally jumps the spark plug gap before going to earth.

The ignition is advanced and retarded auotmatically, to ensure the spark occurs at just the right instant for the particular load at the prevailing engine speed.

The ignition advance is controlled both mechanically and by a vacuum operated system. The mechanical governor mechanism comprises two lead weights, which move out from the distributor shaft as the engine speed rises due to centrifugal force. As they move outwards they rotate the cam relative to the distributor shaft, and so advance the spark. The weights are held in position by two light springs and it is the tension of the springs which is largely responsible for correct spark advancement.

The vacuum control consists of a diaphragm, one side of which is connected via a small bore tube to the carburettor, and the other side to the contact breaker plate. Vacuum in the inlet manifold and carburettor, which varies with engine speed and throttle opening, causes the diaphragm to move, so moving the contact breaker plate, and advancing or retarding the spark. A fine degree of control is achieved by a spring in the vacuum assembly.

Maintenance

Correct and regular maintenance of the ignition system is essential if you are to have a reliable and efficient engine. The servicing procedures for the ignition system are easy and do not require a great deal of time, energy or special tools to keep in order. Refer to the respective Sections for full details and to the Routine Maintenance Section at the front of the book for the necessary time or mileage intervals between services.

2 Contact breaker points – adjustment

1   To adjust the contact breaker points to the correct gap, first release the two distributor cap retaining clips and lift the cap out of the way.
2   With a dry cloth, clean the cap inside and out and examine the four segments (photo). If these are badly burned or scored the cap should be renewed, but a temporary improvement may be made by scraping the segments clean with a small penknife.
3   Check that the carbon brush is located correctly on its spring and that it has a free movement within the cap.
4   Carefully prise the contact breaker points apart for inspection. If they are pitted or dirty, they will have to be removed for cleaning or replacement (see Section 3).
5   Assuming the points to be in satisfactory condition, adjust them as follows:

   (a) *Remove the rotor arm, then turn the engine until the contact breaker heel is on the very peak of one of the four cam lobes*
   (b) *With a feeler gauge, measure the gap between the contact points, which will now be fully open (photo). The correct gap is given in the Specifications*
   (c) *If the gap is incorrect it can be adjusted by loosening the contact plate screw slightly, inserting a screwdriver into the notched recess in the end of the plate (photo), and then moving the plate in the relevant direction to open or close the contact gap as required. The gap is correct when a feeler gauge of the correct size may be moved between the points without binding or slackness*
   (d) *Tighten the contact plate screw, and recheck the gap*

6   Refit the rotor arm and distributor cap.
7   If a dwell meter is available, the dwell angle may be measured instead of physically measuring the points gap. (Dwell angle is the number of degrees of distributor cam rotation during which the points remain closed during the ignition cycle of one cylinder.)
8   Connect up the dwell meter in accordance with its maker's instructions and measure the dwell angle. The correct dwell angle is given in the Specifications. If the indicated dwell angle is too large, increase the points gap as described above. If it is too small, reduce the gap. Recheck the dwell angle after each adjustment.
9   Whenever the contact breaker gap is altered, the ignition timing must be checked and if necessary reset as described in Section 7 or 8.

3 Contact breaker points – removal and refitting

1   Unclip the retaining springs and remove the distributor cap complete with leads, then remove the rotor arm.
2   Loosen the LT lead terminal screw and detach the lead from the moving contact spring.
3   Remove the points retaining screw and lift the points clear. Unclip the low tension lead from behind the points spring. Be careful not to drop the small pivot plate screws down through the baseplate holes.
4   Inspect the faces of the contact points (photo). If they are only lightly burned or pitted then they may be ground square on an oilstone or by rubbing carborundum strip between them. Where the points are found to be severely burned or pitted, then they must be renewed and at the same time the cause of the erosion of the points established. This is most likely to be due to poor earth connections from the battery negative lead to body earth or the engine to earth strap. Remove the connecting bolts at these points, scrape the surfaces free from rust and corrosion and tighten the bolts using a star type lockwasher. Other screws to check for security are: the baseplate-to-distributor body securing screws, the condenser securing screw and the distributor body-to-lockplate bolt. Looseness in any of these could contribute to a poor earth connection. Check the condenser (Section 4).
5   Refitting the contact breaker assembly is a reversal of removal. When fitted, adjust the points gap as described in the preceding Section, apply a smear of grease to the high points of the cam.

4 Condenser (capacitor) – removal and refitting

1   The condenser, or capacitor as it is sometimes known, is fitted to ensure that when the contact breaker points are open, there is no excessive sparking across them to cause waste voltage and additional contact face wear. A faulty condenser will cause misfiring or complete failure. Although it is possible to test a condenser, special equipment is required. It is therefore advisable to replace a suspected faulty unit with a new one as they are relatively inexpensive.
2   If the contact points become pitted after a low mileage and if starting is difficult, then it is a good idea to replace the condenser when replacing the points. Another way to check is to remove the distributor cap and rotor arm and turn the engine so that the points are closed. Then switch on the ignition and open the points, using an

2.2 Check inside the distributor cap for cracks and dampness and clean the segments (A). The carbon brush (B) must also be checked

2.5a Measure the contact gap with a feeler gauge

2.5b Adjusting the contact breaker gap

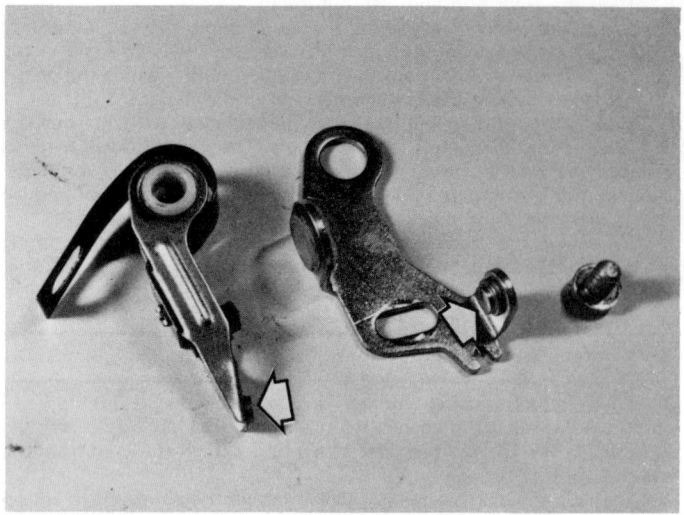

3.4 Check the contact faces (arrowed) for wear or damage

4.3 The condenser unit location

5.1 Set the crankshaft pulley notch opposite the O (TDC) position as shown

5.3 Remove the vacuum tube (A) and distributor cap (B). Do not loosen clamp plate screw (C) unless absolutely necessary

insulated screwdriver. There should be a small blue spark visible but if the condenser is faulty there will be a fat blue spark, or none at all.

3   The condenser is external to the workings of the distributor, and can be removed by undoing the lead from the condenser to the fixing point on the side of the distributor, and the retaining screws on the distributor body (photo).

4   Fit a new replacement in the reverse order to removal.

5   Distributor – removal and refitting

1   To assist during reassembly, the timing of the distributor can be marked before it is removed. This is achieved by turning the crankshaft to TDC which can be seen by aligning the V nick in the crankshaft pulley with the O marked on the timing chest (photo). With a fine-toothed hacksaw blade or small file, mark the position of the two flanges and, on top of the distributor body, mark the point to which the rotor arm is facing.

2   The distributor is best removed by undoing the two retaining bolts on the extension tube flange to timing chest. If disconnected at the top of the extension tube, the preset timing will be disturbed: this should be avoided if possible.

3   Remove the vacuum tube (photo).

4   Disconnect the low tension lead.

5   The distributor may now be withdrawn.

6   Refitting is a reversal of the above procedure, but if the engine has been turned at all since distributor removal, the ignition should be retimed. This is also necessary if the clamp plate at the top of the extension tube has been disturbed. See Section 7 to check and adjust ignition timing.

7   When inserting the distributor ensure that the oil pump drive is correctly aligned for engagement with the distributor shaft.

6   Distributor – dismantling, inspection and reassembly

1   If the distributor is causing trouble, it is often a good idea to fit a completely new unit. Without the proper test equipment it is difficult to diagnose whether or not the centrifugal advance mechanism is performing as it should. However, play in the shaft bushes can be detected by removing the rotor arm and gripping the end of the distributor shaft and trying to move it sideways. If there is any movement then it means that the cam cannot accurately control the contact points gap. This must receive attention.

2   With the distributor removed, take off the rotor, condenser and contact points.

3   Remove the vacuum unit complete, by undoing the two screws (one retains the condenser connector), and lifting the control rod from

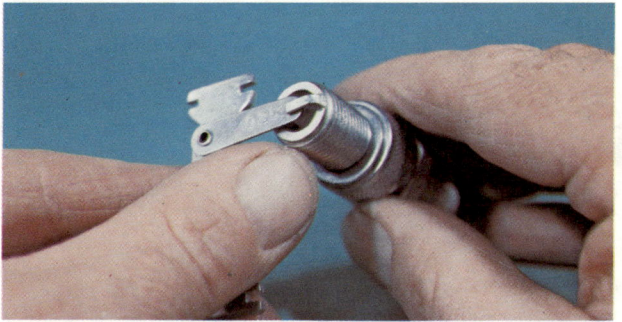

Measuring plug gap. A feeler gauge of the correct size (see ignition system specifications) should have a slight 'drag' when slid between the electrodes. Adjust gap if necessary

Adjusting plug gap. The plug gap is adjusted by bending the earth electrode inwards, or outwards, as necessary until the correct clearance is obtained. Note the use of the correct tool

Normal. Grey-brown deposits, lightly coated core nose. Gap increasing by around 0.001 in (0.025 mm) per 1000 miles (1600 km). Plugs ideally suited to engine, and engine in good condition

Carbon fouling. Dry, black, sooty deposits. Will cause weak spark and eventually misfire. Fault: over-rich fuel mixture. Check: carburettor mixture settings, float level and jet sizes; choke operation and cleanliness of air filter. Plugs can be re-used after cleaning

Oil fouling. Wet, oily deposits. Will cause weak spark and eventually misfire. Fault: worn bores/piston rings or valve guides; sometimes occurs (temporarily) during running-in period. Plugs can be re-used after thorough cleaning

Overheating. Electrodes have glazed appearance, core nose very white – few deposits. Fault: plug overheating. Check: plug value, ignition timing, fuel octane rating (too low) and fuel mixture (too weak). Discard plugs and cure fault immediately

Electrode damage. Electrodes burned away; core nose has burned, glazed appearance. Fault: pre-ignition. Check: as for 'Overheating' but may be more severe. Discard plugs and remedy fault before piston or valve damage occurs

Split core nose (may appear initially as a crack). Damage is self-evident, but cracks will only show after cleaning. Fault: pre-ignition or wrong gap-setting technique. Check: ignition timing, cooling system, fuel octane rating (too low) and fuel mixture (too weak). Discard plugs, rectify fault immediately

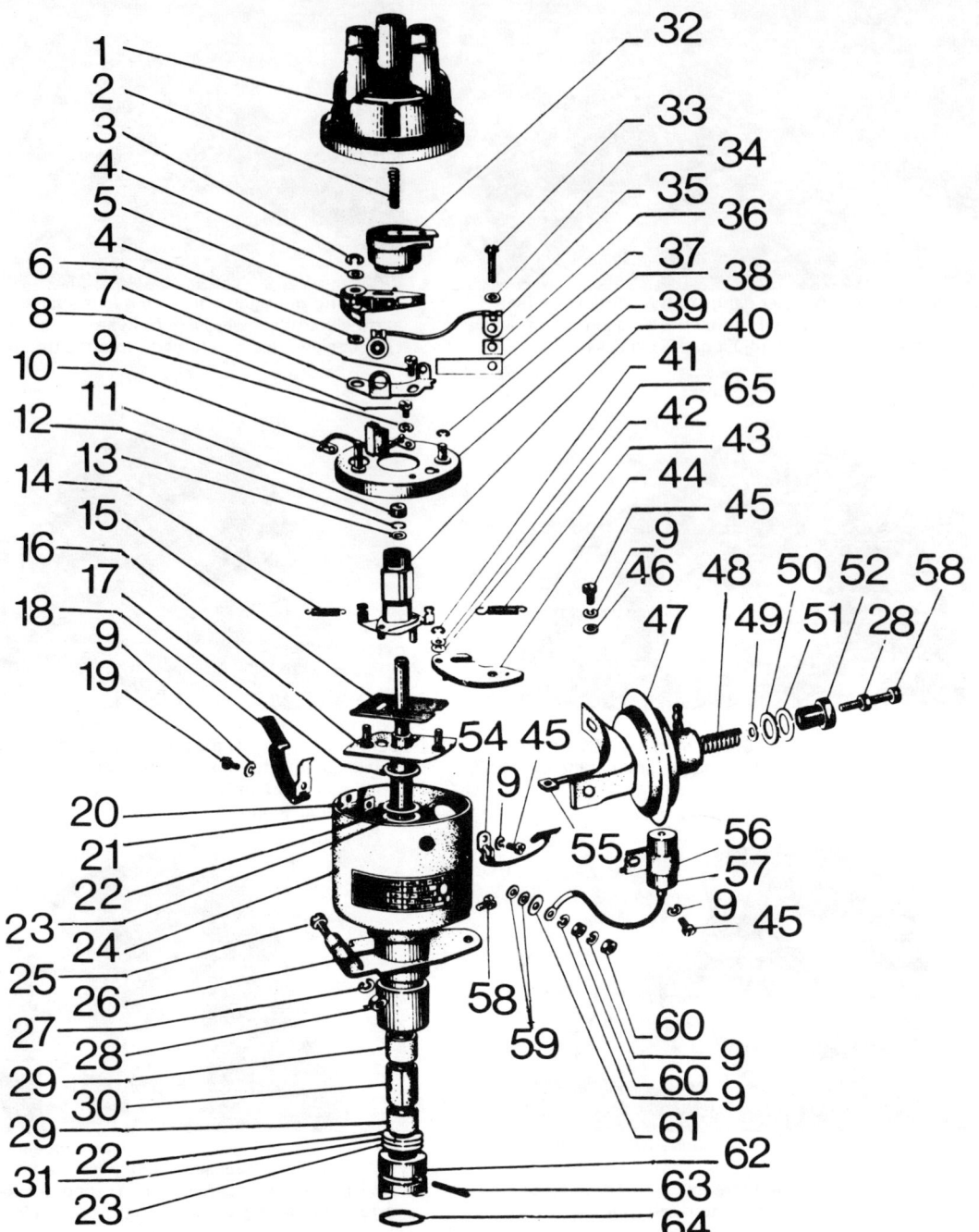

Fig. 4.1 Exploded view of the distributor (Sec 6)

1 Distributor cap assembly	17 Washer	33 Screw	49 Distance washer
2 Carbon brush	18 Cap securing clip	34 Washer	50 Seal
3 Safety washer	19 Screw	35 Arm connection	51 Distance washer
4 Distance washers	20 Packing piece	36 Insulating washer	52 Reduction screw
5 Contact breaker arm	21 Nuts	37 Insulating band	54 Cap securing clip
6 Screw	22 Washers	38 Safety ring	55 Pull rod
7 Fixed contact	23 Washers	39 Baseplate	56 Retainer
8 Screw	24 Casing of distributor	40 Cam complete	57 Capacitor
9 Spring washers	25 Screw	41 Safety ring	58 Screw
10 Earthing connection	26 Clamp plate	42 Washer	59 Insulating washers
11 Lubricating packing	27 Spring washer	43 Governor spring	60 Nuts
12 Securing spring	28 Nut	44 Governor weight	61 Insulating washer
13 Washer	29 Self-lubricating bearings	45 Screws	62 Driving coupling
14 Governor spring	30 Lubricating felt	46 Washer	63 Coupling pin
15 Washer	31 Washer	47 Vacuum chamber	64 Securing ring
16 Shaft complete	32 Distributor rotor arm	48 Spring	65 Distance washer

its location pin having detached the C-clip (photo).

4   Undo the distributor cap retaining clip screws and remove the clips, then lift out the baseplate.

5   By now you should not have taken too much time dismantling the distributor, and after cleaning the components in petrol or carbon tetrachloride they may be examined for wear. It should be noted that individual components are not particularly easy to obtain. Serious consideration should be given to a new or exchange assembly. If, however, you feel you must proceed to dismantle and renovate your distributor further, continue as follows.

6   Remove the felt pad from its recess in the cam head and then the C-clip and washer.

7   From the bottom of the shaft, remove the serrated location pin from the drive coupling by drifting it out.

8   Remove the coupling from the shaft and withdraw the camshaft, complete with the governor springs and weight assembly.

9   The bushes and felt lubricator can now be removed from the distributor body.

10 Check the condition of the contact breaker points. Check the distributor cap for signs of tracking, indicated by a thin black line between the segments. Renew the cap if any signs of tracking are found.

11 If the metal portion of the rotor arm is badly burned or loose, renew the arm. If slightly burnt clean the arm with a fine file.

12 Check that the carbon brush moves freely in the centre of the distributor cover.

13 Examine the fit of the breaker plate on the bearing plate and also check the breaker arm pivot for looseness or wear and renew as necessary.

14 Examine the balance weights and pivot pins for wear, and renew the weights or cam assembly if a degree of wear is found.

15 Examine the shaft and fit of the cam assembly on the shaft. If the clearance is excessive compare the items with new units, and renew either, or both, if they show excessive wear.

16 If the shaft is loose in the distributor bushes, it will be necessary to fit a new shaft, and bushes and felt bush (located between the bushes). The old bushes are simply pressed out and the new bushes pressed in. The felt bush should be thoroughly soaked in oil (Shell Clavus or equivalent) prior to assembly. It will be noted that there is a grub screw located at an angle in the exterior of the distributor body approximately in line with the bushes. This grub screw should be periodically removed and oil squirted through the aperture to re-lubricate the felt bush. This will prolong both the shaft and bush life.

17 Examine the length of the balance weight springs and compare them with new springs. If they have stretched they must be renewed.

18 Reassembly is a straight reversal of the dismantling process, but there are several points which should be noted in addition to those already given in the section on dismantling.

19 Lubricate with engine oil, the balance weights and other parts of the mechanical advance mechanism; the distributor shaft; and the portion of the shaft on which the cam bears, during assembly. Do not oil excessively but ensure these parts are adequately lubricated.

20 Check the action of the weights in the fully advanced and fully retarded positions and ensure they are not binding.

21 Tighten the micrometer adjusting nut to the middle position on the timing scale.

22 Finally, set the contact breaker gap to the correct clearance.

7 Ignition timing (static) – checking and adjustment

1   Whenever the contact breaker gap has been altered, or the position of the distributor disturbed, the ignition timing must be checked and if necessary adjusted. For checking the static ignition timing as described here, a 12V test lamp with leads and crocodile clips will be required.

2   The correct static timing for the various Estelle models is given in the Specifications in degrees BTDC (before top dead centre). There is a plate on the timing chest, just above the crankshaft pulley, with marks every 5° from 40° BTDC to TDC. Identify the mark on the plate which corresponds with the correct static timing for your model. When the notch in the crankshaft pulley coincides with this mark, the points should just be separating.

3   Remove the distributor cap so that the engine cannot fire. Connect the test lamp between the distributor LT terminal (to which the coil LT lead is connected) and earth. Switch on the ignition. When the points

6.3 Release the vacuum control rod C-clip (A), the cap clip bolt (B) and LT wiring (C)

are open, the lamp will light.

4   The crankshaft must now be turned in the normal direction of rotation to bring the timing marks into alignment. This may be achieved in several ways:

(a) With a spanner on the crankshaft pulley nut
(b) By engaging top gear and pushing the car forwards
(c) By engaging top gear, jacking up the car so that one rear wheel is clear of the ground and rotating the wheel

Whichever method is adopted, it will be easier to turn the crankshaft if the spark plugs are removed first.

5   As the timing marks come into alignment, the test lamp should just light, indicating that the points have just separated. If the lamp lights too early (ignition advanced) or too late (ignition retarded), slacken the distributor clamp bolt and rotate the distributor body as necessary (clockwise to retard the ignition, anti-clockwise to advance it). Tighten the clamp bolt and recheck.

6   It will be appreciated that either No 1 or No 4 cylinder may be on the firing stroke when the timing marks are aligned. For checking the timing when the distributor has not been disturbed this is of no practical consequence, but if the timing has been lost completely, or when rebuilding the engine, it will be necessary to determine when No 1 cylinder is on the firing stroke. This is when there is free play on both rocker arms for that cylinder, ie both valves closed. There is a line scribed on the distributor cap adjacent to No 1 plug lead: when No 1 cylinder is firing, the rotor arm should be pointing to this line.

7   The amount of wear in the engine, grade of petrol used, and amount of carbon in the combustion chambers, all contribute to make the recommended ignition timing setting no more than nominal ones. To obtain the best setting under running conditions, first start the engine and allow it to warm up to normal temperature and then accelerate in top gear from 30 to 50 mph, listening for heavy pinking. If this occurs, the ignition needs to be retarded slightly until just the faintest trace of pinking can be heard under these operating conditions.

8   Since the ignition timing adjustment enables the firing point to be related correctly in relation to the grade of fuel used, the fullest advantage of any change of fuel will only be attained by readjustment of the ignition settings.

8 Ignition timing using a stroboscopic light

1   This is becoming an increasingly popular method of checking the ignition timing and is generally the more accurate method, although

the static check previously described is quite satisfactory in most instances. The advantage of the strobe light is that it enables the timing to be checked at engine idle speed and also at higher speeds so that the advance/retard mechanism can be checked for correct operation.

2 Initially check the contact breaker points gap or dwell angle as given in Section 2.
3 Mark the notch on the crankshaft pulley with chalk or white paint.
4 Mark in a similar manner, the appropriate line on the timing cover scale (see Specifications for timing figure according to engine and vehicle type).
5 Disconnect the vacuum pipe which runs from the vacuum capsule on the distributor to the carburettor. Disconnect the pipe from the distributor end and plug the pipe.
6 Connect a stroboscope in accordance with the maker's instructions (usually interposed between No 1 spark plug and HT lead).
7 Start the engine (which should previously have been run to normal operating temperature) and let it idle (see recommended speeds in Specifications), otherwise the mechanical advance will operate and give a false ignition timing.
8 Point the stroboscope at the ignition timing marks when they will appear stationary and if the ignition timing is correct, in alignment. If the marks are not in alignment, loosen the distributor clamp plate screw and turn the distributor accordingly so that they do, then retighten the clamp.
9 If the engine speed is now increased, the pulley mark should appear to drift anticlockwise away from the timing chest mark as the distributor automatic advance comes into operation. An additional advance of 14° to 18° can be expected at the engine speeds of 3600 rpm and above; if this is not the case, or if the advance seems jerky or erratic, the distributor automatic advance mechanism should be examined.
10 If the distributor vacuum capsule is now reconnected, a further advance of approximately 5° should be seen at light throttle openings. If this is not the case, the vacuum capsule may be defective.

9 Spark plugs and HT leads – general

1 The correct functioning of the spark plugs is vital for the correct running and efficiency of the engine.
2 At intervals of 3000 miles (5000 km), the plugs should be removed, examined, cleaned, and if worn excessively, renewed. The condition of the spark plug will also tell much about the overall condition of the engine.
3 If the insulator nose of the spark plug is clean and white, with no deposits, this is indicative of a weak mixture, or too hot a plug. (A hot plug transfers heat away from the electrode slowly – a cold plug transfers it away quickly).
4 If the top and insulator nose are covered with hard black looking deposits, then this is indicative that the mixture is too rich. Should the plug be black and oily, then it is likely that the engine is fairly worn, as well as the mixture being too rich. A hotter plug may relieve this condition temporarily.
5 If the insulator nose is covered with light tan to greyish brown deposits, then the mixture is correct and it is likely that the engine is in good condition.
6 If there are any traces of long brown tapering stains on the outside of the white portion of the plug, then the plug will have to be renewed, as this shows that there is a faulty joint between the plug body and the insulator, and compression is being allowed to leak away.
7 Plugs should be cleaned by a sand blasting machine, which will free them from carbon more thoroughly than cleaning by hand. The machine will also test the condition of the plugs under compression. Any plug that fails to spark at the recommended pressure should be renewed.
8 The spark plug gap is of considerable importance, as, if it is too large or too small, the size of the spark and its efficiency will be seriously impaired.
9 To set it, measure the gap with a feeler gauge, and then bend open, or close, the outer plug electrode until the correct gap is achieved. The centre electrode should never be bent as this may crack the insulation and cause plug failure, if nothing worse.
10 When refitting the plugs, remember to use new plug washers, and refit the leads from the distributor in the correct firing order, which is 1,3,4,2, number 1 cylinder being the one nearest the crankshaft pulley.

11 The only routine attention required by the HT leads is to be kept clean and dry. At 3000 mile (5000 km) intervals, remove the leads, one at a time, wipe them clean and remove any dirt, damp or corrosion from the brass and clips. Clean out the distributor cap collars and refit the leads.
12 Renew the spark plugs regularly at 12 000 miles (20 000 km) intervals.

10 Coil – general

1 The coil, mounted on the inside panel of the right-hand rear wing normally requires very little attention, apart from checking that the HT and low tension lead connections are clean and secure (photo).
2 The coil should always be tested at its working temperature: so, if possible, allow the engine to warm up first. The basic coil testing procedures are given in the following Section. For a more detailed check remove the coil and take it to your Skoda dealer or automotive electrician who has the specialised equipment necessary.
3 If required, the coil can easily be removed by disconnecting the leads and undoing the clamp location stud nuts. Reassembly is the reverse procedure.

11 Fault diagnosis – ignition system

1 By far the majority of breakdown and running troubles are caused by faults in the ignition system, either in the low tension or high tension circuit. There are two main symptoms indicating ignition faults. Either the engine will not start or fire, or the engine is difficult to start and misfires. If it is a regular misfire, ie the engine is only running on two or three cylinders, the fault is almost sure to be in the secondary, or high tension, circuit. If the misfiring is intermittent, the fault could be in either the high or low tension circuits. If the car stops suddenly, ot will not start at all, it is likely that the fault is in the low tension circuit. Loss of power and overheating, apart from faulty carburation settings, are normally due to faults in the distributor or incorrect ignition timing.

Engine fails to start
2 If the engine fails to start and the car was running normally when it was last used, first check there is fuel in the petrol tank. If the engine turns over normally on the starter motor and the battery is evidently well charged, then the fault may be in either the high or low tension circuits. First check the HT circuit.
3 One of the commonest reasons for bad starting is wet or damp spark plug leads and distributor. Remove the distributor cap. If condensation is visible internally, dry the cap with a rag and wipe over the leads. Refit the cap.

10.1 The coil and voltage regulator location

4   If the engine still fails to start, check that current is reaching the plugs, by disconnecting each plug lead in turn at the spark plug end, and holding the end of the cable with a pair of pliers with insulated handles about $\frac{3}{16}$ in (5 mm) away from the cylinder block. Spin the engine on the starter motor.

5   Sparking between the end of the cable and the block should be fairly strong with a regular blue spark. If current is reaching the plugs, then remove them and clean and regap them. The engine should now start.

6   If there is no spark at the plug leads, take off the HT lead from the centre of the distributor cap and hold it to the block as before. Spin the engine on the starter once more. A rapid succession of blue sparks between the end of the lead and the block indicates that the coil is in order and that the distributor cap is cracked, the rotor arm faulty or the carbon brush in the top of the distributor cap is not making good contact with the spring on the rotor arm. Possibly the points are in bad condition. Clean and reset them.

7   If there are no sparks from the end of the lead from the coil, check the connections at the coil end of the lead. If it is in order start checking the low tension circuit.

8   Use a 12 voltmeter or a 12 volt bulb and two lengths of wire. With the ignition switch on and the points open, test between the low tension wire to the coil (SW or +) and earth. No reading indicates a break in the supply from the ignition switch. Check the connections at the switch to see if any are loose. Refit them and the engine should run. A reading shows a faulty coil or condenser or broken lead between the coil and the distributor.

9   Take the condenser wire off the points assembly and with the points open, test between the moving point and earth. If there now is a reading, then the fault is in the condenser. Fit a new one and the fault is cleared.

10 With no reading from the moving point to earth, take a reading between earth and the CB or (–) terminal of the coil A reading here indicates a broken wire which must be renewed between the coil and distributor. No reading confirms that the coil has failed and must be renewed. Remember to connect the condenser lead to the points assembly. For these tests it is sufficient to separate the contact breaker points with a piece of paper.

Engine misfires

11 If the engine misfires regularly, run it at a fast idling speed. Pull off each of the plug caps in turn and listen to the note of the engine. Hold the plug cap in a dry cloth or with a rubber glove as additional protection against a shock from the HT supply.

12 No difference in engine running will be noticed when the lead from the defective circuit is removed. Removing the lead from one of the good cylinders will accentuate the misfire.

13 Remove the plug lead from the end of the defective plug and hold it about $\frac{3}{16}$ in (5 mm) away from the block. Restart the engine. If the sparking is fairly strong and regular, the fault must lie in the spark plug.

14 The plug may be loose, the insulation may be cracked, or the points may have burnt away, giving too wide a gap for the spark to jump. Worse still, one of the points may have broken off. Either renew the plug, or clean it, reset the gap, and then test it.

15 If there is no spark at the end of the plug lead, or if it is weak and intermittent, check the ignition lead from the distributor to the plug. If the insulation is cracked or perished, renew the lead. Check connections at the distributor cap.

16 If there is still no spark, examine the distributor cap carefully for tracking. This can be recognised by a very thin black line running between two or more electrodes, or between an electrode and some other part of the distributor. These lines are paths which now conduct electricity across the cap, thus letting it run to earth. The only answer is a new distributor cap. Temporary relief may be obtained by filing or drilling at each end of the tracking path to interrupt the current flow.

17 Apart from the ignition timing being incorrect, other causes of misfiring have already been dealt with under the section dealing with the failure of the engine to start. To recap, these are that:

(a) *The coil may be faulty giving an intermittent misfire*
(b) *There may be a damaged wire or loose connection in the low tension circuit*
(c) *The condenser may be short-circuiting*
(d) *There may be a mechanical fault in the distributor (broken driving spindle or contact breaker spring)*

18 If the ignition timing is too far retarded, it should be noted that the engine will tend to overheat, and there will be quite a noticeable drop in power. If the engine is overheating and the power is down, and the ignition timing is correct, then the carburettor should be checked, as it is likely that this is where the fault lies.

Chapter 5 Clutch

For modifications, and information applicable to later models, see Supplement at end of manual

Contents

Specifications

General
Clutch type .... Dry, single plate, coil springs
Actuation .... Hydraulic

Friction disc
Thickness:
   New .... 8.5 mm (0.335 in)
   Minimum allowable after wear .... 7.0 mm (0.276 in)
Diameter .... 170 mm (6.7 in)
Maximum ovality .... 0.5 mm (0.02 in)

Clutch pedal free play
After correct adjustment .... 40 to 50 mm (1.6 to 2.0 in)
Minimum allowable .... 10 to 15 mm (0.4 to 0.6 in)

Torque wrench setting

	Nm	lbf ft
Clutch housing-to-flywheel bolts	23 to 28	17 to 21

1 General description

The dry, single plate type clutch has been used on all models since the introduction of the Estelle in 1977.

Basically, it comprises a cover plate, incorporating the coil springs and a pressure plate, which bolts onto the flywheel. The friction disc is positioned between the pressure plate and the flywheel and is free-floating on the gearbox input shaft splines.

The mode of operation is that when the clutch pedal is depressed, the thrust bearing moves towards the clutch. The thrust bearing acts on three levers thereby lifting the pressure plate away from the friction disc.

The friction disc is now free and the gearshift can be used. When the clutch pedal is released the thrust bearing withdraws from the clutch and the pressure plate is allowed to bear on the friction disc and flywheel. With the disc firmly retained against the flywheel by the force in the coil springs, the clutch will transmit the driving torque from the engine to the gearbox.

The actuating system is hydraulic, drawing on fluid from the same reservoir as the brake system.

The master cylinder is located in the front boot, mounted on the bulkhead panel.

Hydraulic lines connect the master cylinder to the slave cylinder and this is mounted on top of the gearbox. It is accessible from within the car via an inspection panel in the floor of the rear luggage compartment. A plastic cover is located in position over the slave cylinder by a spring retainer. This cover prevents the ingress of dirt into the bellhousing aperture. To remove this cover simply prise the spring back.

2 Clutch – adjustment and bearing lubrication

Adjustment

1   To check the clutch operating rod and release lever adjustment (essential after a replacement clutch unit has been fitted or the hydraulic actuating system has been overhauled), is a relatively easy task. Proceed as follows.

2   Remove the central cover of the floor in the luggage area behind the rear seats. Disconnect the spring and lift clear the release cylinder cover (photo).

3   Prise the release lever from the protruding rod (having disconnected the tension springs). The clearance between the two should be at least 2 mm (0.078 in). Loosen the rod locknut and turn the release finger accordingly to obtain the correct clearance of 4 to 5 mm (0.16 to 0.20 in). Retighten the locknut to secure the release finger in position on the rod.

4   Check that the adjustment is correct by measuring the clutch pedal free play which should be as specified.

5   Should the procedure given fail to provide the specified adjustment, then the disc linings are probably worn down considerably. In this instance the clutch will have to be removed for inspection as described in Sections 3 and 4.

6   It may be found that although worn, the lining thickness is still within the specified amount and it may therefore be possible to adjust the clutch unit itself to counteract this wear. Such adjustment however necessitates the use of a special tool and this task is therefore best entrusted to your Skoda dealer who will be able to advise you accordingly on the best course of action.

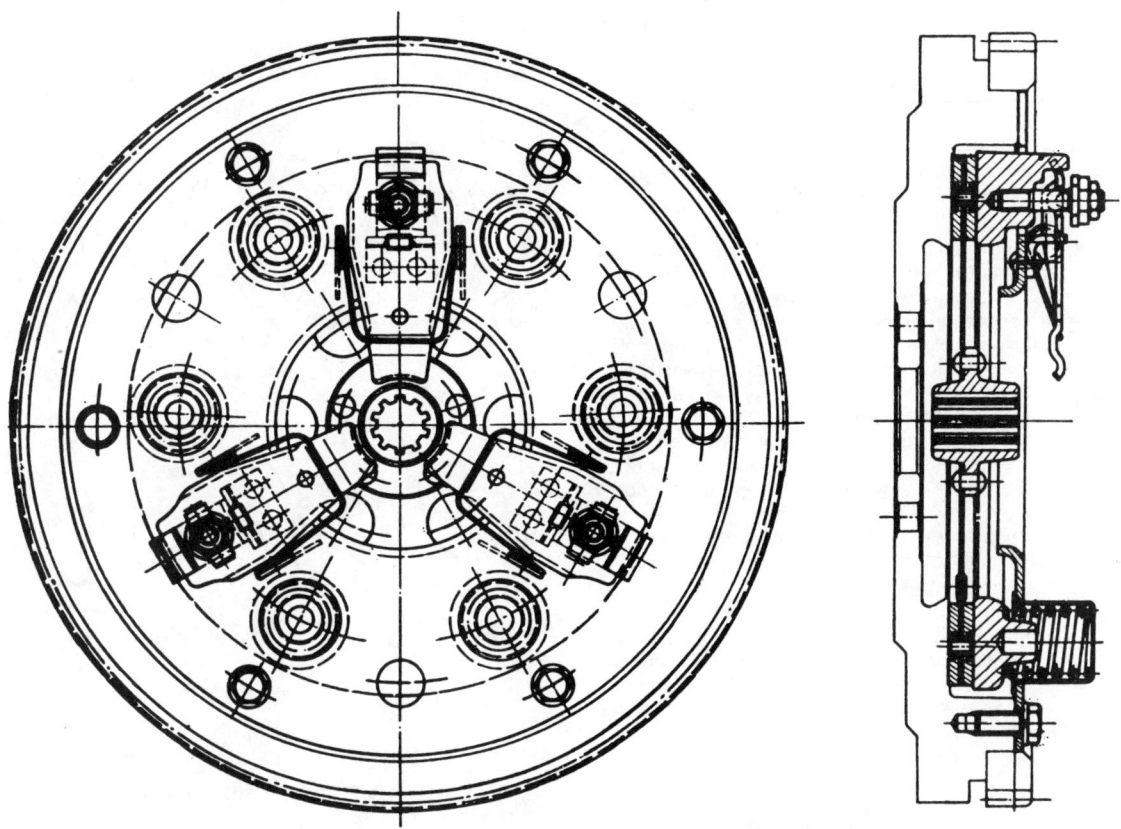

Fig. 5.1 Sectional views of clutch unit (Sec 1)

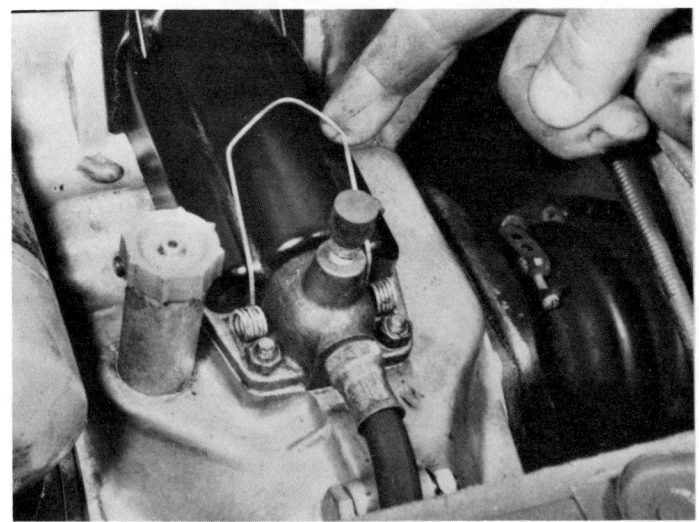

2.2 Pull spring back to release cover

2.8 Lubricating the release bearing

Clutch release bearing – lubrication

7   To lubricate the clutch release bearing it is necessary to remove the central floor cover under the floor covering in the compartment behind the rear seats. This done, release the spring and remove the plastic cover over the slave cylinder.

8   With a suitable oil can, preferably having an adjustable nozzle, apply 10 to 12 drops of oil to the central slot of the clutch release lever (photo).

9   Also lubricate the clutch release bearing sleeve recess with the pad in it. **Note**: *Be careful not to squirt any oil in the direction of the clutch plate assembly!*

3   Clutch – removal and dismantling

To renew the friction disc or examine the clutch assembly, it is necessary to remove the engine from the gearbox. To remove the engine only, follow the instructions given in Chapter 1. With the engine removed from the car proceed as follows.

1   Mark the pressure (cover) plate in relation to the flywheel so that it can be refitted in the same relative position.

2   Slacken off the cover plate retaining bolts half a turn at a time in a diagonal sequence, to relieve the tension of the coil springs evenly

thus preventing distortion.

3   On removing the bolts, the friction disc will be released, together with the cover plate.

4 Clutch – inspection

To check the condition of the clutch assembly proceed as follows.

Friction disc

1   Visually inspect the facing material. There should be no evidence of oil contamination, deep scoring, pitting or signs of uneven wear. Also ensure that the friction disc thickness is not worn beyond the minimum allowed. Glazing of the lining material is acceptable as long as the lining material pattern can clearly be seen through the glaze.

2   Next check the friction disc for distortion. Note that it can easily be damaged by the transaxle input shaft when the engine and transaxle are mated. To test the disc for distortion, slide it onto the input shaft splines. Rotate the disc against a fixed object. Any distortion will become immediately apparent. Whilst the disc is on the input shaft, ensure that it runs up and down the splines freely. Renew the friction disc if the splines are worn or if any of the previously described faults are in evidence. **Note:** *If fitting a new friction disc, ensure that it is a good sliding fit on the input shaft splines with no tight spots.*

Pressure plate assembly

3   Clean this assembly before inspection. Do not dismantle as the adjustment on the clutch fingers is preset and should not be disturbed.

4   Inspect the pressure plate friction face for any signs of scoring or pitting – if present, renew the assembly as a unit. Look for broken springs through the retaining cups, and also the finger return springs.

5   Inspect the clutch release sleeve assembly, checking for wear on the front face and the bearing.

6   Ensure that the release fork and the return and retaining springs are in good condition – any distortion, or signs of wear, will necessitate renewal (see Section 6). Any sign of oil on the clutch assembly when dismantling indicates that the gearbox input shaft and/or crankshaft oil seals are faulty and should therefore be renewed at this time. Also examine the camshaft core plug and oilway plug for signs of leakage (see Chapter 1).

5 Clutch – refitting

1   It is important that no oil or grease gets on the clutch disc friction linings or the pressure plate and flywheel faces. It is advisable to refit the clutch with clean hands and to wipe down the pressure plate and flywheel faces with a clean dry rag before assembly begins.

2   Place the clutch disc against the flywheel with the longer end of the hub facing outwards, away from the flywheel (photo). On no account should the clutch disc be refitted with the longer end of the centre hub facing in to the flywheel as on reassembly it will be found quite impossible to operate the clutch with the friction disc in this position. Often the friction disc will be marked 'Flywheel Side' to aid refitting.

3   Refit the clutch cover assembly, with markings in line with those made on the flywheel. Replace the six retaining bolts and spring washers. Tighten them finger tight so that the clutch disc is gripped, but can still be moved.

4   The clutch disc must now be centralised so that when the engine and gearbox are mated, the gearbox input shaft splines will pass through the splines in the centre of the friction plate hub.

5   Centralise the clutch disc by inserting a round bar or long screwdriver into the hole in the centre of the clutch, so that the end of the bar rests in the crankshaft bearing for the input shaft. Ideally an old input shaft should be used for this purpose.

6   Using the input shaft bearing in the crankshaft as a fulcrum point, move the bar sideways, or up and down, as required, to centralise the clutch disc.

7   Centralisation can be judged by removing the bar and viewing the clutch disc splined hub in relation to the input shaft bearing in the crankshaft. When the two appear in line, the clutch bolts may be tightened to the correct torque in a diagonal sequence to ensure that the pressure (cover) plate is pulled down evenly and without distortion.

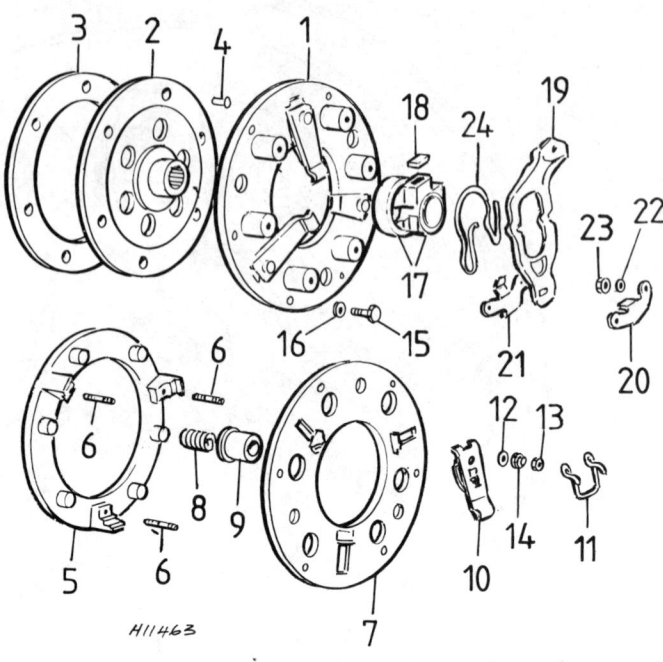

H11463

Fig. 5.2 Clutch components (Sec 4)

1 Cover plate	13 Locknut
2 Clutch plate (friction disc)	14 Adjuster nut
3 Friction lining	15 Cap screw
4 Rivet	16 Washer
5 Pressure plate	17 Release bearing
6 Screw	18 Felt insert
7 Housing	19 Release arm
8 Spring	20 Support
9 Spring cap	21 Spring-loaded holder
10 Release lever	22 Washer
11 Return spring	23 Nut
12 Shim	24 Retaining spring

5.2 Locate the disc

5.8a Method of checking that the release finger clearances are equal, using a feeler gauge and a piece of wire fixed to the housing

5.8b Adjusting a finger clearance

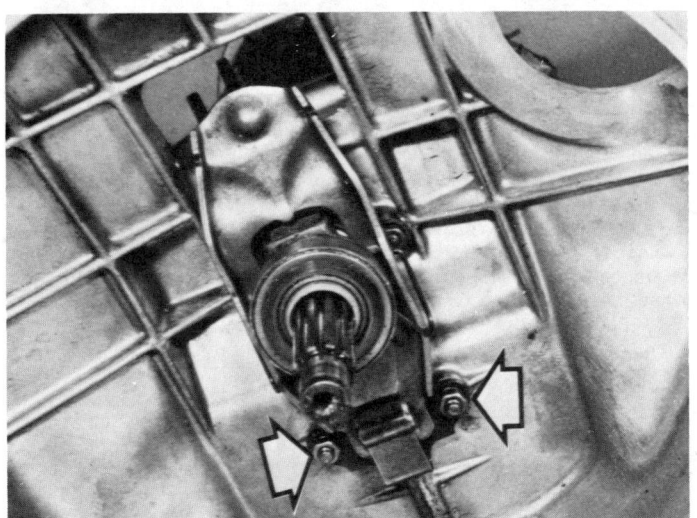

6.3 The clutch release bearing unit showing the retaining clip nuts (arrowed)

6.4 The release bearing and retaining clip

To prevent the flywheel turning when tightening the cover plate bolts, a screwdriver may be placed to locate between the teeth at the flywheel and a bellhousing stud.

8   If a new pressure plate has been fitted, a check should be made to ensure that the three release fingers are equally adjusted. Although Skoda dealers use a special tool for this purpose (MP 2-109), we found that a length of welding rod attached to the crankcase at the rear and bent round the clutch to just make contact with the fingers will suffice (photo). Adjust the end of the rod so that it is just in contact with one of the release fingers, then rotate the flywheel so that as the other fingers come round to align with the rod, their clearances can be compared. If necessary adjust the finger(s) by loosening the locknut and turning the adjuster as required (photo). A maximum deviation of 1 mm (0.039 in) is available. Retighten the locknut on completion. Do not allow the locknut to protrude over the end of the thread.

9   When the engine is refitted into the car, the clutch adjustment must be checked as described in Section 2.

6   Clutch release bearing and gearbox oil seal – removal and refitting

1   To inspect the clutch release bearing it is necessary to remove the engine from the gearbox as described in Chapter 1.

2   The release bearing and fork form an integral unit, which is retained in position by the release fork holder at the bottom, whilst the bearing which locates over the protruding oil seal sleeve from the gearbox, is fixed with the release fork by means of a special spring.

3   To remove the release bearing and fork, simply undo and remove the two fork retaining clip nuts and remove complete (photo).

4   To disconnect the release fork and bearing, unclip the spring from the rear face (photo).

5   If oil is leaking from the gearbox, the sleeve and seal should also be removed and the seal renewed at this stage. This can be achieved by first partly draining the gearbox, undoing the two sleeve plate retaining nuts and then removing the sleeve complete with seal from its aperture.

6   After renewing the seal the sleeve can be reassembled over the spigot shaft and with a small amount of sealing solution smeared around its location housing in the gearbox, pressed into position.

7   Smear some grease over the sleeve prior to fitting the release bearing assembly into position.

7   Master cylinder – removal and dismantling

1   To remove the master cylinder, it is first necessary to disconnect

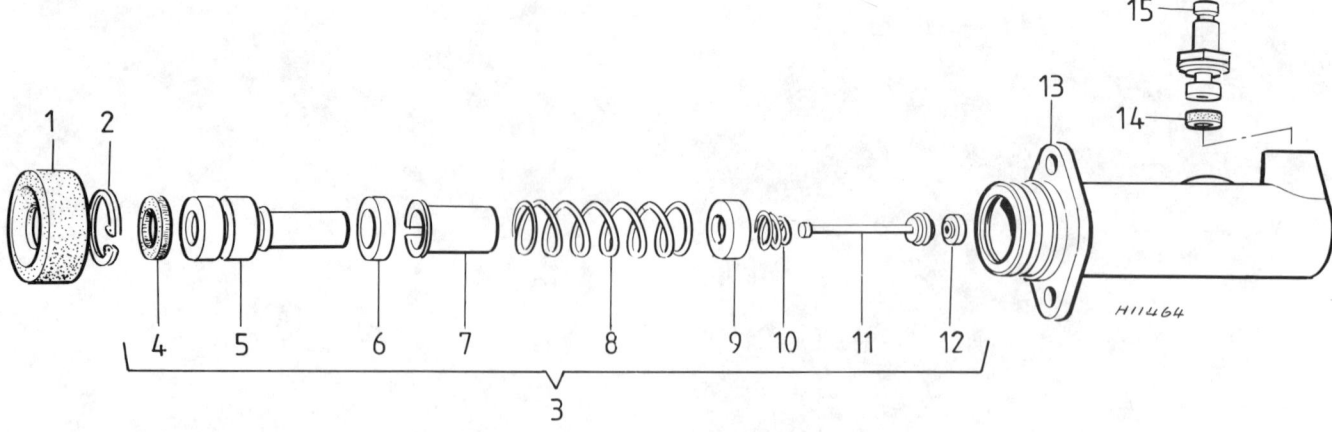

Fig. 5.3 Clutch master cylinder components (Sec 7)

1	Boot	4	Seal	8	Spring	12	Valve
2	Circlip	5	Piston	9	Bush	13	Cylinder body
3	Piston, seal and valve	6	Cup	10	Spring	14	Seal
	assembly	7	Spring seat	11	Shank	15	Union

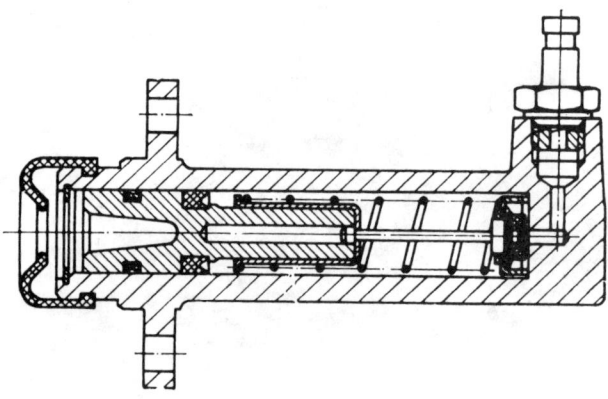

Fig. 5.4 Sectional view of clutch master cylinder (Sec 7)

the hydraulic fluid feed pipe from the reservoir. Place a piece of newspaper around the base of the cylinder to prevent any spillage which might damage the paintwork. Undo the union bolt and double the hose back on itself, with a piece of rag over the end, to prevent spillage. Tie the hose back out of the way.

2   Undo the two flange retaining nuts, and remove together with the spring washers.

3   Disconnect the feed pipe from the side of the cylinder whch goes to the slave cylinder.

4   Now withdraw the master cylinder from the bulkhead, leaving the piston operating rod attached to the pedal linkage.

5   The master cylinder assembly can now be removed to the workbench where the various components can be dismantled, cleaned and laid out in sequence on a sheet of clean newspaper.

6   Dismantle as follows, referring to Fig. 5.3.

7   Remove the rubber boot from the cylinder.

8   Remove the circlip, cover, piston assembly, and valve assembly.

9   If required, the valve assembly in the outlet pipe to the slave cylinder can be removed by unscrewing the end plug.

8   Master cylinder – renovation

1   Once the unit has been dismantled, thoroughly clean all parts in hydraulic fluid – never contaminate any part associated with clutch or brake hydraulic systems with any other solvent.

2   Wipe the components dry with a non-fluffy rag and carefully

examine the cylinder bore for wear, scratches or score marks. Renew the cylinder if necessary.

3   Always use a complete set of new rubbers and, prior to assembly on the piston, thoroughly wet the primary and secondary cups in **clean** hydraulic fluid.

4   With all components laid out on a spotlessly clean surface, make sure your hands are free from grease and foreign matter and that your tools are spotlessly clean.

5   Assembly of the master cylinder is the reverse of the dismantling sequence – be careful not to damage the fine lips on the piston cups when introducing the piston assembly back into the cylinder.

6   Refitting is the reverse sequence to removal, except that the hydraulic system must be bled – see Section 11.

9   Clutch slave cylinder – removal and dismantling

1   It is possible to remove the slave cylinder without lowering the engine or transaxle assemblies. The first step is to disconnect the inlet pipe (plug it to prevent leakage) and then remove the cylinder cover.

2   Unscrew the nuts which retain the cylinder to the gearbox and remove the release fork springs. With the nuts removed the cylinder and pushrod may be lifted clear (photo).

3   Dismantling of the cylinder assembly should be done on a clean bench, and begins with the withdrawal of the operating rod, followed by the removal of the rubber boot over the end of the cylinder and then removal of the circlip.

4   The piston may now be extracted and the bleed screw removed (also the seal and spring on some early models).

5   Thoroughly clean all parts in clean brake fluid or methylated spirit, ready for inspection.

6   Temporarily cover the aperture in the bellhousing with a piece of rag, or similar, to prevent the entry of bolts, washers or dirt into the housing.

10   Clutch slave cylinder – renovation, assembly and refitting

1   Having thoroughly cleaned all parts of the cylinder assembly, examine as follows.

2   Inspect the piston and cylinder for scratching and the rubber seal and boot for wear or perishing.

3   If the cylinder bore or periphery of the piston are badly scratched, it is advisable to renew the whole unit, as it is not practical to repair these items.

4   Should the rubbers only be at fault, then these can be renewed from a seal kit.

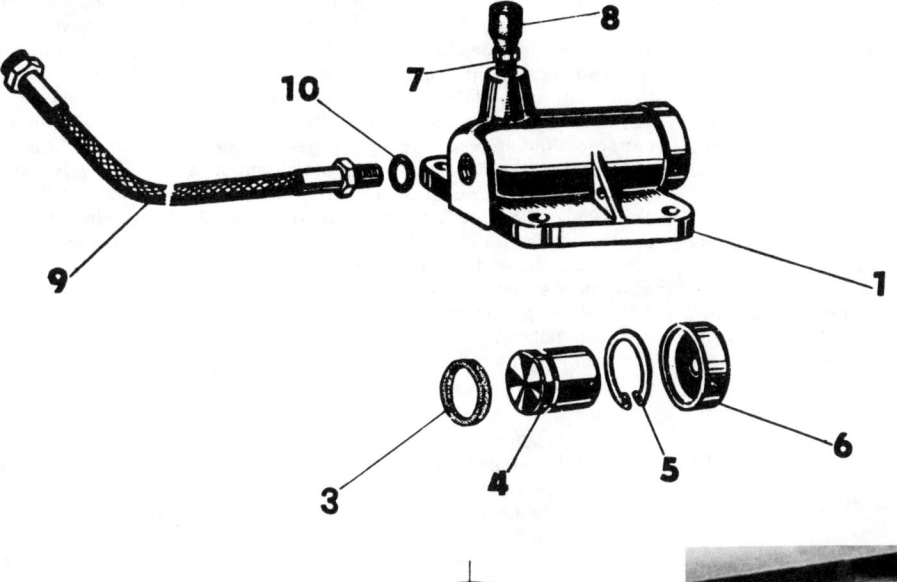

Fig. 5.5 The component parts of the clutch slave cylinder (Sec 9)

1 Slave cylinder
3 Seal
4 Piston
5 Circlip
6 Dust cover
7 Bleed screw
8 Rubber cap
9 Clutch hose
10 Seal

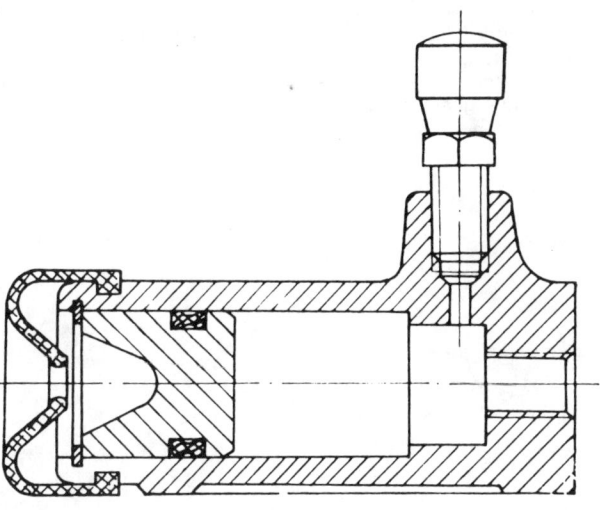

Fig. 5.6 Sectional view of clutch slave cylinder (Sec 9)

9.2 Removing the slave cylinder and pushrod

5 Smear all parts of the piston assembly with hydraulic fluid and carefully reassemble and refit the slave cylinder in the reverse order of removal and dismantling.
6 After refitting the slave cylinder, bleed the system, as described in Section 11, and adjust, as described in Section 2.

11 Clutch hydraulic system – bleeding

1 Gather together a clean glass jar, length of rubber tubing which fits tightly over the bleed nipple in the slave cylinder and a tin of hydraulic brake fluid. The services of an assistant will also be required.
2 Check that the master cylinder is full and if not, fill it, and cover the bottom two inches of the jar with hydraulic fluid.
3 Remove the rubber dust cap from the bleed nipple on the slave cylinder and with a suitable spanner open the bleed nipple $\frac{1}{2}$ to $\frac{3}{4}$ of a turn.
4 Place one end of the tube securely over the nipple and insert the other end in the jar so that the tube orifice is below the level of the fluid.
5 The assistant should now pump the clutch pedal until air bubbles cease to emerge from the end of the tubing. It is essential that the end of this tube should stay immersed at all times. Your assistant should also ensure that the fluid reservoir is kept topped up, as if this empties, air will enter the system and it will be necessary to start again.
6 When no more air bubbles appear, tighten the bleed nipple during a slow downstroke. This done, remove the bleed tube from the nipple

and refit the rubber dust cap. Top up the fluid reservoir.
7 Do not re-use hydraulic fluid bled from the system.

12 Fault diagnosis – clutch

There are four main faults to which the clutch and release mechanism are prone. They may occur by themselves or in conjunction with any of the other faults. They are clutch squeal, slip, spin, and judder.

Clutch squeal
1 If on taking up the drive or when changing gear, the clutch squeals, this is a sure indication of a badly worn clutch release bearing.
2 As well as regular wear due to normal use, wear of the clutch release bearing is much accentuated if the clutch is ridden, or held down for long periods in gear, with the engine running. To minimise wear of this component the car should always be taken out of gear at traffic lights and for similar hold-ups.
3 The clutch release bearing is not an expensive item, but difficult to get at. **Note** *Ensure engine squeal does not originate from the alternator drivebelt or water pump.*

Clutch slip
4 Clutch slip is a self-evident condition which occurs when the clutch friction plate is badly worn, the release arm free travel is

insufficient, oil or grease have got onto the flywheel or pressure plate faces, or the pressure plate itself is faulty.

5   The reason for clutch slip is that, due to one of the faults listed above, there is either insufficient pressure from the pressure plate, or insufficient friction from the friction plate to ensure solid drive.

6   If small amounts of oil get onto the clutch, they will be burnt off under the heat of clutch engagement, and in the process, gradually darken the linings. Excessive oil on the clutch will burn off leaving a carbon deposit which can cause quite bad slip, or fierceness, spin and judder.

7   If clutch slip is suspected, and confirmation of this condition is required, there are several tests which can be made.

8   With the engine in second or third gear and pulling lightly up a moderate incline, sudden depression of the accelerator pedal may cause the engine to increase its speed without any increase in road speed. Easing off on the accelerator will then give a definite drop in engine speed without the car slowing.

9   In extreme cases of clutch slip the engine will race under normal acceleration conditions.

10   If slip is due to oil or grease on the linings a temporary cure can sometimes be effected by squirting carbon tetrachloride into the clutch. The permanent cure is, of course, to renew the clutch driven plate and trace and rectify the oil leak.

Clutch spin

11   Clutch spin is a condition which occurs when there is a leak in the clutch hydraulic actuating mechanism, the release arm free travel is excessive, there is an obstruction in the clutch either on the primary gear splines, or in the operation lever itself, or oil may have partially burnt off the clutch linings and have left a resinous deposit which is causing the clutch disc to stick to the pressure plate or flywheel.

12   The reason for clutch spin is that due to any, or a combination of, the faults just listed, the clutch pressure plate is not completely freeing from the centre plate even with the clutch pedal fully depressed.

13   If clutch spin is suspected, the condition can be confirmed by extreme difficulty in engaging first gear from rest, difficulty in changing gear, and very sudden take-up of the clutch drive at the fully depressed end of the clutch pedal travel as the clutch is released.

14   Check the clutch master cylinder and slave cylinders and the connecting hydraulic pipe for leaks. Fluid on one of the rubber boots fitted over the end of either the master or slave cylinders is a sure sign of a leaking piston seal.

15   If these points are checked and found to be in order then the fault lies internally in the clutch, and it will be necessary to remove the clutch for examination.

Clutch judder

16   Clutch judder is a self-evident condition which occurs when the gearbox or engine mountings are loose or too flexible, when there is oil on the faces of the clutch friction plate, or when the clutch pressure plate has been incorrectly adjusted.

17   The reason for clutch judder is that due to one of the faults just listed, the clutch pressure plate is not freeing smoothly from the friction disc, and is snatching.

18   Clutch judder normally occurs when the clutch pedal is released in first or reverse gears, and the whole car shudders as it moves backwards or forwards.

Chapter 6 Transmission

For modifications, and information applicable to later models, see Supplement at end of manual

Contents

Specifications

Gearbox

Number of gears	4 forward, 1 reverse
Synchromesh	On all forward gears
Gear ratios:	
1st	3.8 : 1
2nd	2.12 : 1
3rd	1.41 : 1
4th	0.96 : 1
Reverse	3.27 : 1

Final drive

Type	Swinging half axles with independent suspension
Differential	Spiral bevel gears
Final drive ratio:	
Standard	4.22 : 1
Optional	4.44 : 1
Crownwheel/pinion backlash	0.13 to 0.18 mm (0.005 to 0.007 in)

Torque wrench settings

	Nm	lbf ft
Gearcase clamp bolt/nuts	22 to 25	16 to 18
Primary shaft nut	35 to 45	26 to 33
Pinion nut	40 to 50	30 to 37
Pinion bearing cap nut	14 to 17	10 to 12.5
Release sleeve nut	6 to 8	4 to 6
Front cover nuts	19 to 25	14 to 18
Speedometer shaft clip bolt/nut	7 to 9	5 to 7
Speedometer drive bearing bolt/nut	7 to 9	5 to 7
Reverse gear pin bolt/nut	17 to 20	12.5 to 15
Reverse gear pin bolt	7 to 9	5 to 7
Shift fork bolts	14 to 17	10 to 12.5
Detent cover bolts	7 to 9	5 to 7
Silentblock bolt	30 to 40	22 to 30
Axle housing bolt	20 to 30	14 to 22
Crownwheel gear bolts	70 to 80	52 to 59
Drain plug and level plug	30 to 35	22 to 26
Reversing light switch	7 to 9	5 to 7

1 General description and maintenance

General description

The transmission unit fitted to all models contains four forward speeds and one reverse. The gearchange lever is of floor-mounted, remote control type.

The gearbox and final drive unit form an integral assembly within a single aluminium casing. For inspection or repairs, this has to be removed from the car, the two halves of the casing separated, and the front cover removed. It is not possible to remove the differential or gearbox separately from the car.

For maintenance there is a drain plug, level plug and a special filler tube projects from the top of the gearbox casing between the starter

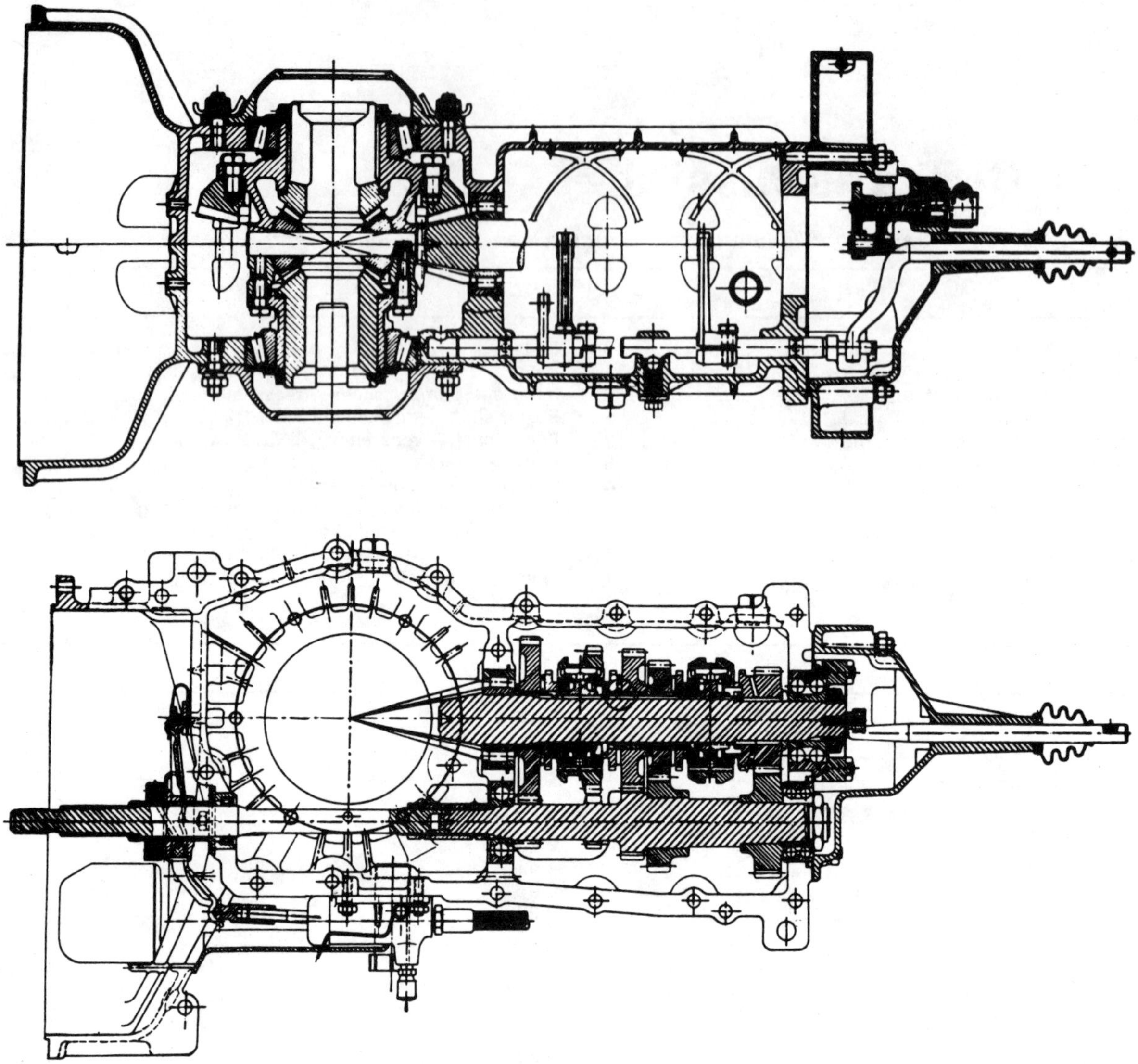

Fig. 6.1 Sectional views of gearbox and final drive assembly (Sec 1)

motor and clutch slave cylinder.

Crownwheel and pinion – special note

If on stripping the gearbox and differential units, the pinion or crownwheel unit are found to be damaged, they will have to be renewed as a pair. Each crownwheel and pinion are run in together at the Skoda factory and are marked as such (see Fig. 6.2). The crownwheel is located in the differential housing between the tapered roller bearings, which are preloaded by the shims fitted between the half-axle flanges and the bearing cups.

The pinion adjustment is by half-shims fitted between the front pinion shaft bearing flange and bearing cover.

To predetermine the thickness of the shims required for accurate meshing of the two gears, special tools are required. It is not possible to accurately check the mesh of the two gears when the gearbox/differential units are fully assembled.

In view of these problems, if you have to renew the pinion unit it is best left to your local Skoda agent, unless he is prepared to pre-check the gearbox/differential tolerances to determine the respective shim requirements.

Similarly, if the crownwheel unit is damaged or suspect, do not strip it down but take it to your Skoda dealer for checking. The crownwheel and sunwheels have preset adjustments and require specialised tools for resetting.

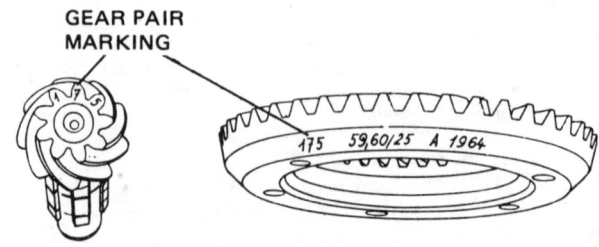

Fig. 6.2 Crownwheel and pinion showing pair marking (Sec 1)

Maintenance

The transmission maintenance details are given in the Routine Maintenance Section at the front of the book. Apart from the lubrication details given, an occasional visual check should be made to ensure that no excessive leaks are visible from the gearbox/differential housing joints. Also check the transmission rubber mountings for signs of deterioration or damage.

2 Transmission unit – removal and refitting

1 To remove the transmission it is necessary to withdraw it from the car together with the engine and half axle units, as described in Chapter 1. Also read Section 4 of Chapter 1, before proceeding.

2 When the transmission/engine unit has been removed the two units can be separated by undoing the nuts and bolts around the periphery of the bellhousing, and the starter motor removed.

3 This done the units can be gently pulled apart and the transmission unit is ready for dismantling to begin. It is a good idea to thoroughly wash the exterior of the transmission unit with paraffin or a water-soluble grease solvent. This will simplify dismantling considerably and also help to prevent the ingress of dirt into the internal working parts.

4 Refitting of the transmission assembly is accomplished in the reverse sequence. Refer to Chapter 1, Section 49 for full details.

3 Transmission – removal of half axle assemblies

With the transmission removed from the car and disconnected from the engine unit, proceed as follows.

1 Place a drip tray under the axle housing to catch any oil which may remain. Now remove one of the half axle assemblies by undoing the six nuts retaining the universal coupling cover and withdraw complete with shims, knuckle and guide blocks. The guide blocks should be kept in their respective positions; this is best achieved by retaining them on their pegs with a rubber band around them. Retain the correct number of shims on each side.

2 Repeat for the second half axle assembly.

4 Gearbox front cover – removal

Unscrew the cover retaining nuts and remove with washers. Detach the cover from the transmission housing complete with gasket.

5 Gearbox bellhousing – dismantling

1 Dismantle the clutch release unit from the gearbox by undoing the two nuts from the studs, on which the release lever retaining plate is located. Then withdraw the release bearing and lever unit, complete from the input shaft.

2 Unscrew and remove the input shaft plate nuts and withdraw the plate.

6 Gearbox and differential – dismantling

1 Remove the reversing light switch (photo).

2 Remove the front cover and gasket, complete with the gear selection control rod, by undoing the six retaining nuts.

3 Remove the pinion shaft bearing cover by undoing the four nuts.

4 Carefully remove from the pinion shaft the half shims (photo), keeping in order, and tie together through the holes with a piece of wire, or place in a safe spot keeping in respective positions.

5 Remove the C-clip and slide off the speedometer drivegear from its splined shaft (photo).

6 Undo the retaining nut and remove.

7 Drain any remaining oil in the gearbox by tilting over a drip tray. The gearbox is now ready to be separated by undoing the six upper and eight lower housing flange nuts, the clamp nut inside the bellhousing (photo) and the nut to the right of the clutch slave cylinder. The gearbox can now be laid on its side (either), and separated by levering with a screwdriver in the opposing recess in the flange bosses, wriggling the two halves free over the studs.

8 Lift out the differential unit complete.

9 Lift out the primary shaft assembly complete.

10 Lift out the pinion shaft assembly complete.

11 From the right-hand gearbox housing, remove the detent plate and the three springs and balls.

12 Slacken the selector clamp bolts and remove the 1st and 2nd, 3rd and 4th and the reverse selector fork rods (photo).

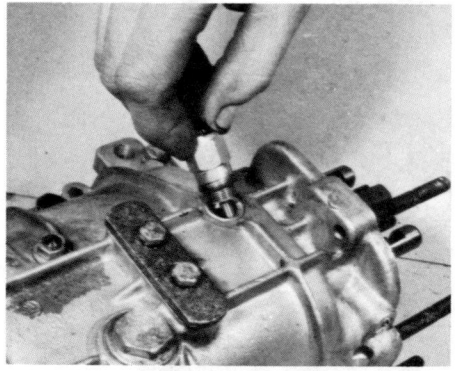

6.1 Remove the reversing light switch. Note detent retaining plate and plug in foreground

6.4 Remove the pinion shaft location half shims

6.5 Remove C-clip and speedometer drivegear

6.7 The half casing flange nut (arrowed) in the bellhousing

6.12 General view of selectors showing respective clamp bolts (arrowed)

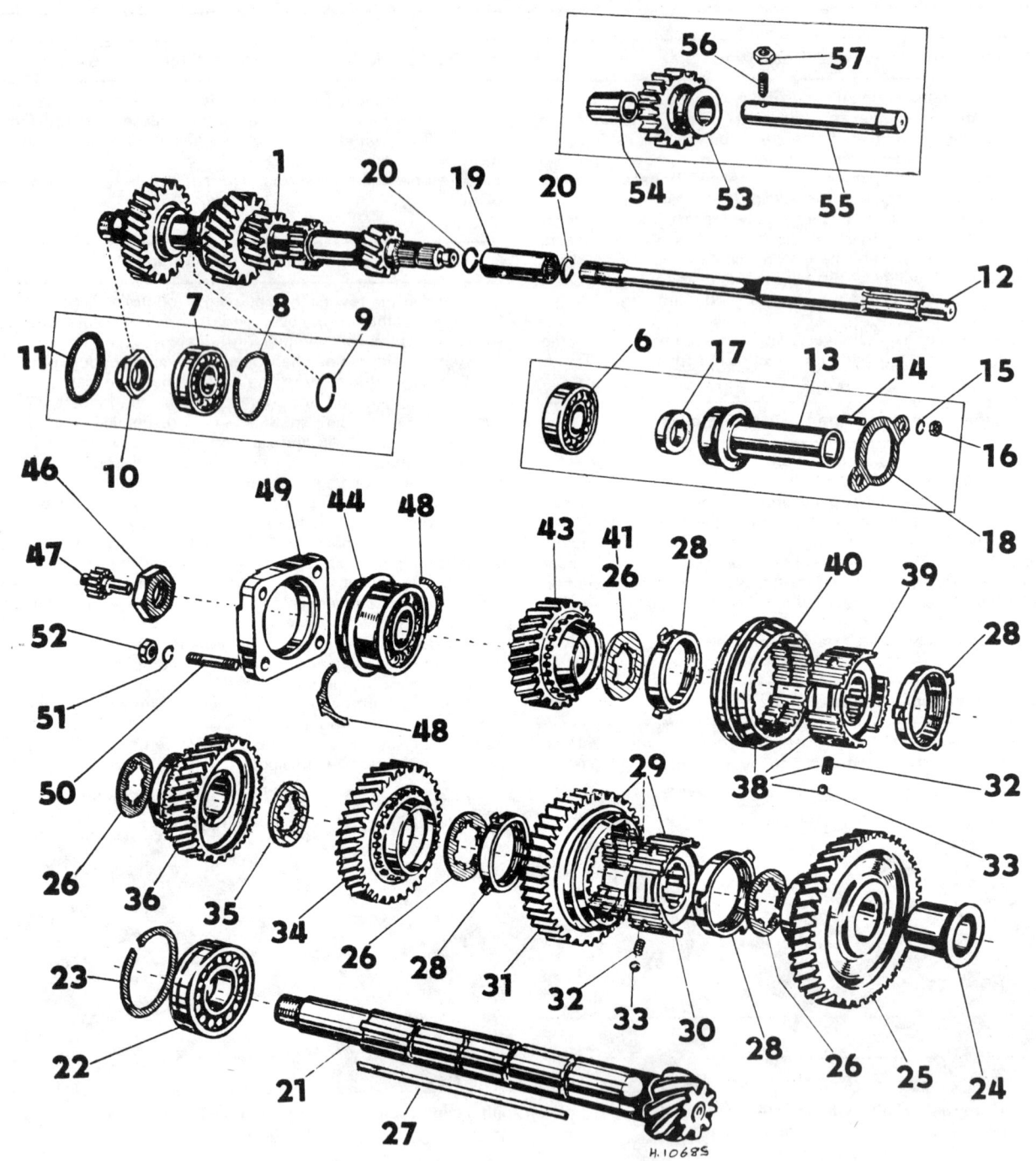

Fig. 6.3 Main gearbox components (Sec 7)

1	Primary shaft	19	Muff coupling
6	Ball bearing	20	Securing clip
7	Ball bearing	21	Pinion shaft with pinion
8	Bearing distance ring	22	Roller bearing
9	Ring	23	Bearing distance ring
10	Nut	24	Bush – 1st gear
11	Compensating washer	25	1st speed gear
12	Input shaft	26	Friction rings
13	Sleeve clutch release	27	Locking slide bar
	bearing	28	Synchromesh rings
14	Stud	29	1st and 2nd selector hub
15	Spring washer		assembly
16	Nut	30	1st and 2nd selector hub
17	Oil seal		centre
18	Sleeve retaining ring		

31	1st and 2nd selector hub	43	4th speed gear
	sleeve	44	2-row ball bearing
32	Spring	46	Nut
33	Ball bearing	47	Speedometer drivegear
34	2nd speed gear	48	Compensating washer
35	Friction ring (2nd/3rd)	50	Stud
36	3rd speed gear	51	Spring washer
38	3rd and 4th selector hub	52	Nut
	assembly	53	Reverse gear with bush
39	3rd and 4th selector hub	54	Bush
	centre	55	Reverse gear shaft
40	3rd and 4th selector hub	56	Setscrew
	sleeve	57	Nut
41	Friction ring		

13 The interlock pins can now be extracted from their position in the end of the casing, via the selector rod holes.
14 To remove the reverse gear, undo the locknut and unscrew the locating stud from the casing on the outside, then punch out the carrier shaft towards the front of the casing away from the differential housing.

7 Pinion shaft – dismantling

1 If prior to dismantling, the gears show signs of excessive wear and/or damage, serious consideration must be given to obtaining a new gearbox and this is due to the following factors:

(a) *If the bevel pinion and/or crownwheel are worn or damaged then they must be renewed as a matching pair (see Section 1)*

(b) *If the transmission gears on the pinion shaft are defective then it is probable that their mating primary shaft gears are also in need of replacement. It is not generally recommended to renew a single gear since when meshed with a worn one, its operation will almost certainly be noisy.*

Therefore in view of the above, a generally worn gearbox and/or differential assembly are better exchanged for a new or rebuilt unit as the cost difference will probably be marginal and you should also get a guarantee with a replacement unit. Should you decide to dismantle the gear assemblies continue as follows.
2 Refer to Fig. 6.3. Remove the bearing, a two-row special type with a protruding flange around the outside periphery, by supporting the main assembly and applying a puller over the bearing. In order not to damage the speedometer gear shaft, place a suitable tube or socket and T-bar head over the shaft and locate the puller screw on it.
3 Remove fourth gear.
4 Withdraw the locking slide bar (photo).
5 After noting which way round it is fitted, remove the 3rd/4th gear synchro-hub assembly, and the 3rd gear synchro-hub centre, which can be refitted in the hub.
6 Remove 3rd gear and friction ring.
7 Remove the friction ring and 2nd gear.
8 Remove the synchro-ring and the 1st and 2nd synchro-hub assembly.
9 Remove the friction ring and 1st gear complete with synchro-ring and bush.
10 Slide off the roller bearing outer case and, if necessary, the inner roller bearing race, taking great care not to damage the pinion teeth. It is suggested that your Skoda dealer remove this bearing race, as he is equipped with a special removal tool.

8 Synchro-hub – dismantling

Carefully press the synchro-hub centre through the synchro sleeve, and collect and retain the springs and balls, as they are ejected. Keep in order of dismantling.

9 Input and primary shafts – dismantling

1 The primary and input shafts can be split by removing the spring clips from the splined connector sleeve and parting the two shafts.
2 Remove the ball bearing, if required, with a puller. At the opposing end of the shaft, undo the nut and locating ring from the outer bearing cage and then remove the bearing.

10 Speedometer drivegear cluster – removal

This assembly is located in the front cover and is removed by undoing the cotter pin nut and driving out the pin.

11 Gearbox mountings – general

1 The gearbox mounting rubbers should be removed and cleaned at

7.4 Remove the locking slide bar

this stage, and if showing signs of wear, renewed.
2 They are bonded to small flat plates, which are bolted to the underside of the front cover casing. When in position the mountings are sandwiched between the casing and the mounting bracket which support the gearbox.

12 Gearbox components – examination and renovation

1 All parts should be thoroughly washed in paraffin or petrol and then laid out on a sheet of clean newspaper.
2 Generally examine the gearwheels and bearings for excessive wear, distortion, slackness of fit and damage to machined faces and threads.
3 The most likely components to be worn are the selector forks. Wear will be immediately apparent as the ends of each fork will be badly grooved. If the selector forks are badly worn, the selector should be renewed. A badly worn selector will eventually lead to jumping out of gear and difficult engagement.
4 The synchro-rings are bound to be worn and it is false economy not to renew them. New rings will improve the smoothness and speed of the gearchange considerably.
5 The reverse pinion gearwheel will possibly be badly worn and is the main cause of buzz and vibration during reversing. If your vehicle is suffering from this malady the gearwheel should be renewed.
6 If the input shaft bearings are worn they will cause the gearbox to be very noisy and to suffer from vibration. Bearings can be checked by feeling for slackness of the bearings in races and also by listening for excessive noise when the bearings are spun.
7 Always fit a new front cover gasket and input shaft seal. Also, if renewing pinion gears, renew the corresponding gear on the input shaft and vice versa.
8 Lastly check the condition of the transmission casing joint faces.
9 A generally worn gearbox is best exchanged for a new or rebuilt unit, see Section 7.

13 Gearbox – reassembly (general)

Before proceeding with reassembly all parts should be laid out on a sheet of clean newspaper. Absolute cleanliness is extremely important. If any traces of old jointing compound are still present they should be removed with methylated spirit and **not** scraped under any circumstances. Each component should be lightly lubricated as it is assembled.

Before commencing assembly of the pinion shaft you will require a good selection of friction washers of varying thicknesses for tolerance selection.

14 Pinion shaft – reassembly

1   Press the needle roller bearing into position against the back of the pinion gear with the flange ring groove offset, away from the pinion gear.

2   Fit the bearing distance ring to its groove on the bearing outer race.

3   Next slide the 1st gear coupling bush down the shaft so that the flanged end butts against the bearing.

4   With the coupling bush pressed against the bearing, slide the friction ring down the shaft with the oil groove face towards the pinion, and locate in the groove in the shaft. Rotate the ring to determine its suitability. Different thicknesses of friction ring are available and a fairly tight fit in the groove, against the bush, is required (see Fig. 6.4). The friction ring thicknesses available range from 3.5 mm (0.138 in) to 3.8 mm (0.150 in).

5   When a ring of the correct thickness has been selected, remove it from the shaft, lubricate the bush and fit the 1st gear over it (photo), followed by the friction ring (oilways to pinion) (photo), and turn the ring, using a drift, to align with the grooves on the shaft (photo). Now check that the gear is free to rotate.

6   Do not fit the locking slide bar at this stage, but try it in the groove to ensure the friction ring is correctly located. **Note:** *Each time a friction ring is fitted, slide the bar down its groove to check location.*

7   Now select a suitable friction ring for the third groove from the pinion end (omitting the 2nd). This ring has oil grooves on both faces. Again select a ring giving the tightest fit, giving a clearance of 0 + 0.02 mm (0 + 0.0008 in). Having selected a suitable ring for this groove, remove it until ready for fitting.

8   Now select a ring for the omitted (2nd) groove in a similar manner to that described for the third groove, fit 2nd gear and lock it in position with the selected ring. Check the axial clearance of the gear (photo) which should be 0.1 + 0.07 mm (0.004 + 0.003 in). Remove the 2nd gear and selected ring from the shaft.

9   Place the 1st and 2nd hub centre on the workbench so that the teeth face downwards (photo). Insert the springs into their location

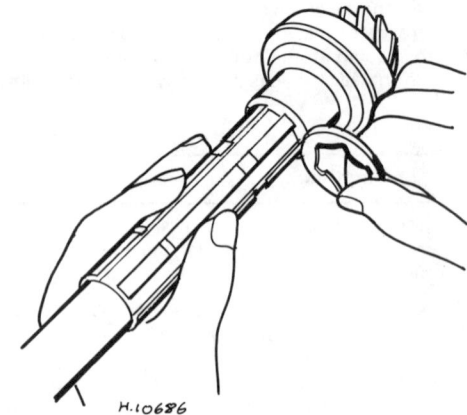

Fig. 6.4 Checking the thickness requirement of the friction ring in the location groove on the pinion shaft (Sec 14)

holes. Smear some grease round them to locate them in position, and place the balls on the springs (photo).

10   With the short end of the hub facing upwards (away from the gearteeth), depress the balls and springs and slide the hub centre into the 1st/2nd selector hub (photo).

11   Now insert the synchro-ring into the hub centre from the reverse side of the gear, and slide the completed assembly onto the pinion shaft, with the gear facing away from the pinion (photo).

12   Fit the synchro-ring to the other side of the hub unit, followed by the previously selected friction ring, which can be located in its shaft groove (photo). Ensure that the ring is located with its oil grooves towards the gear.

13   Fit 2nd speed gear, with teeth offset away from the pinion end, and lock in position with the friction ring previously selected.

14.5a Fit 1st gear over the bush

14.5b Fit the selected friction ring

14.5c Align the friction ring with the shaft grooves

14.8 Check the axial clearance between friction ring and gear

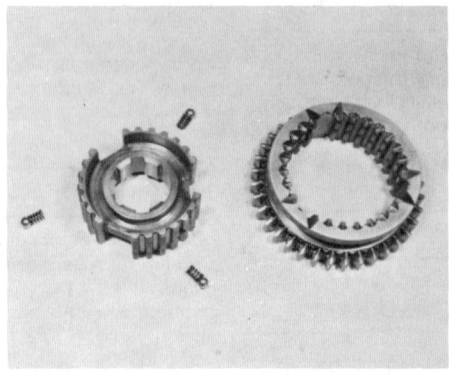

14.9a 1st and 2nd synchro-hub unit ready for assembly

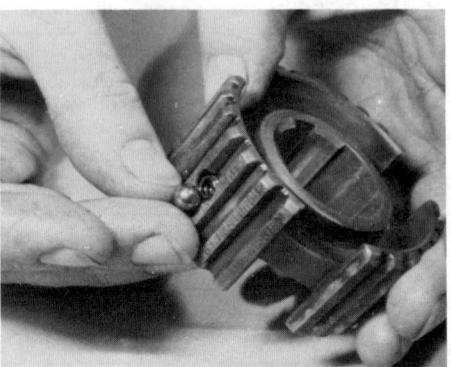

14.9b Insert the springs and balls into the hub centre

14.10 The assembled synchro-hub

14.11 Slide 1st/2nd selector hub into position

14.12 Friction ring in position in shaft groove

14.16 Fit the 3rd/4th synchro-hub unit

14.17 Friction ring in position together with locking slide bar

14.19 Locknut, bearing and 4th gear in position

14 Now locate 3rd gear with teeth offset towards the pinion and then select a suitable friction ring to provide an axial clearance of 0.1 + 0.07 mm. (0.004 + 0.003 in). When fitted the friction ring oil groove faces towards the gear.

15 Select a friction ring for the end groove of the shaft in a similar manner to that given in paragraph 4. Locate 4th gear and fit the pinion nut, using a suitably thick collar in place of the bearing temporarily. The collar must be dimensionally the same as the bearing and its inner bore edge chamfered at 45°. Mark the nut side of the collar to avoid damage to the gear face of the collar. When the collar is fitted and the nut tightened to the correct torque the gear clearance must be 0.1 + 0.07 mm (0.004 + 0.003 in). Select a ring accordingly then remove the nut, collar, gear and ring.

16 Assemble the 3rd/4th selector hub unit in a similar fashion to the 1st and 2nd, and insert the synchro-ring with its locktabs offset to the pinion. Slide the unit onto the shaft with the larger flange on the inner hub facing away from the pinion (photo). Then insert the other synchro-ring into the opposite side of the hub with its locktabs facing away from the pinion.

17 Fit the selected friction ring with its oil groove away from the shaft. When in position, push (or lightly tap) the locking slide bar down the shaft groove, passing through all of the friction rings, until when fully home its tail end is level with the end of the shaft splines (photo).

18 Fit the 4th gear onto the shaft with the teeth offset away from the pinion. Now press the double row ball bearing onto the pinion shaft.

19 Fit the locking nut (photo) and tighten to the specified torque wrench setting. Bend over the locking tab in the nut with a punch to lock in position in the wedged slot in the shaft.

20 If the speedometer drivegear has been removed, this can now be relocated with its splined shaft in the end of the pinion shaft, and locked in position with the C-clip. There should be a clearance of 0 to 0.5 mm (0.019 in) between the gear front face and the rear face of the pinion nut when fitted.

15 Input and primary shafts – reassembly

1 Assuming the 3rd and 4th gears are in place on the shaft and the

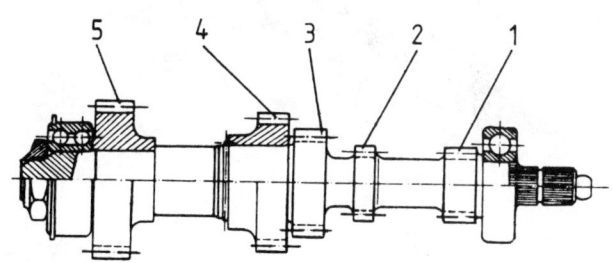

Fig. 6.5 Primary shaft gears (Sec 15)

1	1st gear	4	3rd gear
2	Reverse gear	5	4th gear
3	2nd gear		

bearings in position, proceed as follows.

2 Fit the location ring to its bearing location groove.

3 Fit the retaining nut and tighten to the specified torque; lock by bending the locking tab in the nut boss into the wedged slot in the shaft.

4 Join the primary and input shafts by fitting the intermediate collar, and retain with the spring clips (photos).

16 Reverse gears – refitting

1 The reassembly sequence of the reverse gear and shaft is a reversal of the dismantling procedure, but ensure that all parts are thoroughly cleaned and well lubricated.

2 Check that the gear runs freely on completing the assembly (photo).

15 4a Primary shaft gears and bearings shown together with the input shaft and interconnecting collar and lock spring

15.4b Input and primary shafts assembled and retained by spring clips

16.2 Reverse gear in position

17.2 Reverse gear selector and shaft in position

17 Gear selector shafts – reassembly

1   Stand the right-hand half of the gearbox casing on the clutch housing.
2   Insert the circlip into its groove on the reverse selector shaft, and pass the shaft through the aperture, in the forward end of the gearbox. As it passes through, place the reverse selector onto the shaft (photo). The shaft continues through the gearbox and locates in the gearbox-to-differential wall. Locate the selector clamp locking bolt in position – there is a slight recess in the shaft to locate it.
3   Insert the interlock pins into the aperture within the selector rod location holes (Fig. 6.6).
4   Insert the 1st/2nd selector rod circlip to its groove, pass the rod through the box and fit the selector and then fit with the 3rd/4th selector rod (photo).

18 Gearbox – final assembly

1   Place the pinion shaft assembly carefully into position in the gearcase as shown (photo), locating in the selector and bearings. Rotate the assembly to ensure it spins freely.
2   Slide the input shaft seal into position on the shaft to locate in the

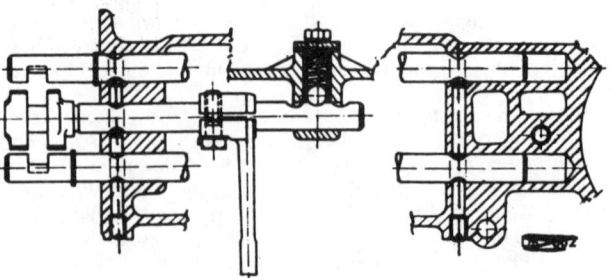

Fig. 6.6 Selector shafts showing interlock assembly (Sec 17)

half-aperture in the differential housing wall. To protect the seal, wrap tape over the shaft splines and remove when seal and housing are fitted (photos).
3   Insert the input shaft assembly, checking that the selectors engage correctly and that the gears do not bind. Note the position of the oil hole (photo).
4   The crownwheel unit is now fitted into position (crownwheel teeth facing down to mesh with pinion) (photo).
5   Ensure that the gearbox mating flanges are perfectly clean and

17.4 Selector rods and C-clips in position

18.1 Install the pinion shaft

18.2a Fit a new input shaft seal into its housing

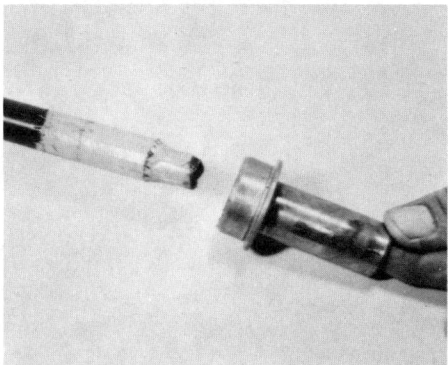
18.2b Bind shaft with tape to protect when fitting seal into position

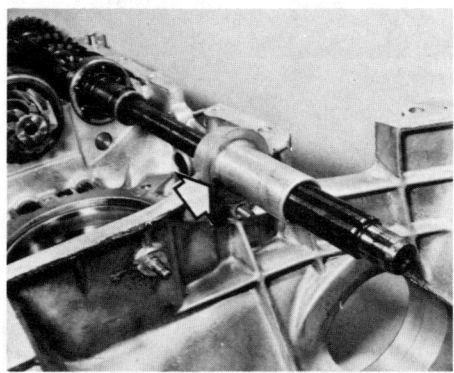
18.3 Install the primary/input shaft unit with oil hole (arrowed) as shown

18.4 Fit the crownwheel unit into position

18.7 Reassembling the gearbox half casings

18.10 Locate bearing cover over studs

19.1 Fit shim(s) to the primary shaft bearing

smear with jointing compound.

6   Ensure that all the gears are well lubricated.

7   Refit the left-hand gearbox half casing into position over the studs, and use a soft-headed hammer or block of wood to tap lightly home. Ensure flanges are a neat fit all round (photo).

8   Refit the flange nuts and bolts, do not tighten at this stage (do not forget the clamp bolt in the bellhousing).

9   Reinsert the pinion half shims, exactly as they were removed, or as has been specified by your Skoda specialist (see special note regarding crownwheel and pinion).

10   Refit the end housing bearing cover over the four location studs and retain with nuts and spring washers (photo). Tighten the nuts to the specified torque. Note that the housing does not fit flush to the gearbox endhousing, but against the bearing. Do not overtighten.

11   Ensure the crownwheel and pinion movement is free by rotating the halfshaft location housings.

12   Now tighten the gearbox casing nuts to the specified torque.

19 End cover – reassembly

1   Fit shim(s) to the primary shaft bearing (photo) such that the top shim protrudes above the housing surface by 0.1 ± 0.05 mm (0.004 ± 0.002 in).

2   If removed, oil and refit the selector rod into the end cover housing so that it protrudes through the guide tab (photo). Refit the rubber boot and retain with a length of wire twisted to grip the rubber over the cover tube (photo). Do not overtighten the wire, it will distort and possibly cut the rubber.

3   Smear some sealing compound over the end cover and gearbox mating faces and fit the gasket over the studs.

4   Initially hold the selector rod back, and place the end cover over the location studs, then as the cover closes onto the end face of the gearbox, guide the selector rod into the selector channels (photo). Secure the end cover with the nuts and washers. Check that the

19.2a Selector cover showing selector rod and speedometer drivegears

19.2b Refit the protective rubber boat

19.4 Fitting the end cover – note gasket in position and selector engaging with shafts

19.5 Locate the detent springs and balls

selector mechanism is working correctly by gripping the end of the protruding selector rod and push, pull and turn it to ensure correct engagement. Due to the lack of leverage the movement will be stiff, but if it fails to engage as required, do not force or hit with a hammer. Undo and remove the end cover to check that the selector rod is correctly engaged.

5   Fit the three detent balls and springs into their respective apertures in the gearbox outer casing next to the level plug (photo). Retain with plate, gasket and two bolts, which should be tightened to the specified torque.

6   Refit the reversing light switch.

20 Bellhousing – refitting

1   Check that the half-casings clamp bolt is in position on the gearbox front face and tightened to the correct torque.

2   Reassemble the clutch release fork assembly by fitting the spring round the groove in the clutch release sleeve, and locate the sleeve and spring into the fork.

3   Clip on the release fork holder to the fork.

4   Refit the release sleeve guide retaining plate over the two studs and tighten the two nuts and spring washers.

5   Refit the clutch release fork and retain the support over the two

lower studs with nuts and spring washers.

6   Assuming the end cover mounting suspension rubbers are bolted in position, the transmission is now ready for reassembly to the engine. To prevent the ingress of foreign matter into the aperture in which the clutch slave cylinder is located, place a piece of cardboard over the studs.

21 Gearshift linkage and lever – removal and refitting

1   The gearshift layout is divided into two main units, the gearlever and housing assembly, and the shifter rod and link with the gearbox.

2   To remove the lever housing and link, fold back the mat(s) from the front and rear floor compartment. Where a single mat is fitted, partially remove the door sill strips on one side to release the covering.

3   Unscrew and remove the lever housing screws, prise the cover plate free between the seats, and working through the floor aperture, detach the link from the shift rod by removing the bolt.

4   Lift the housing and lever up through the aperture. Twist the lever to prevent the shift rod fouling the housing bearing.

5   If the link is to be removed it will be necessary to remove the transmission unit from the car so that the link can be withdrawn rearwards.

6   Refit in the reverse order, lubricating the housing prior to fitting.

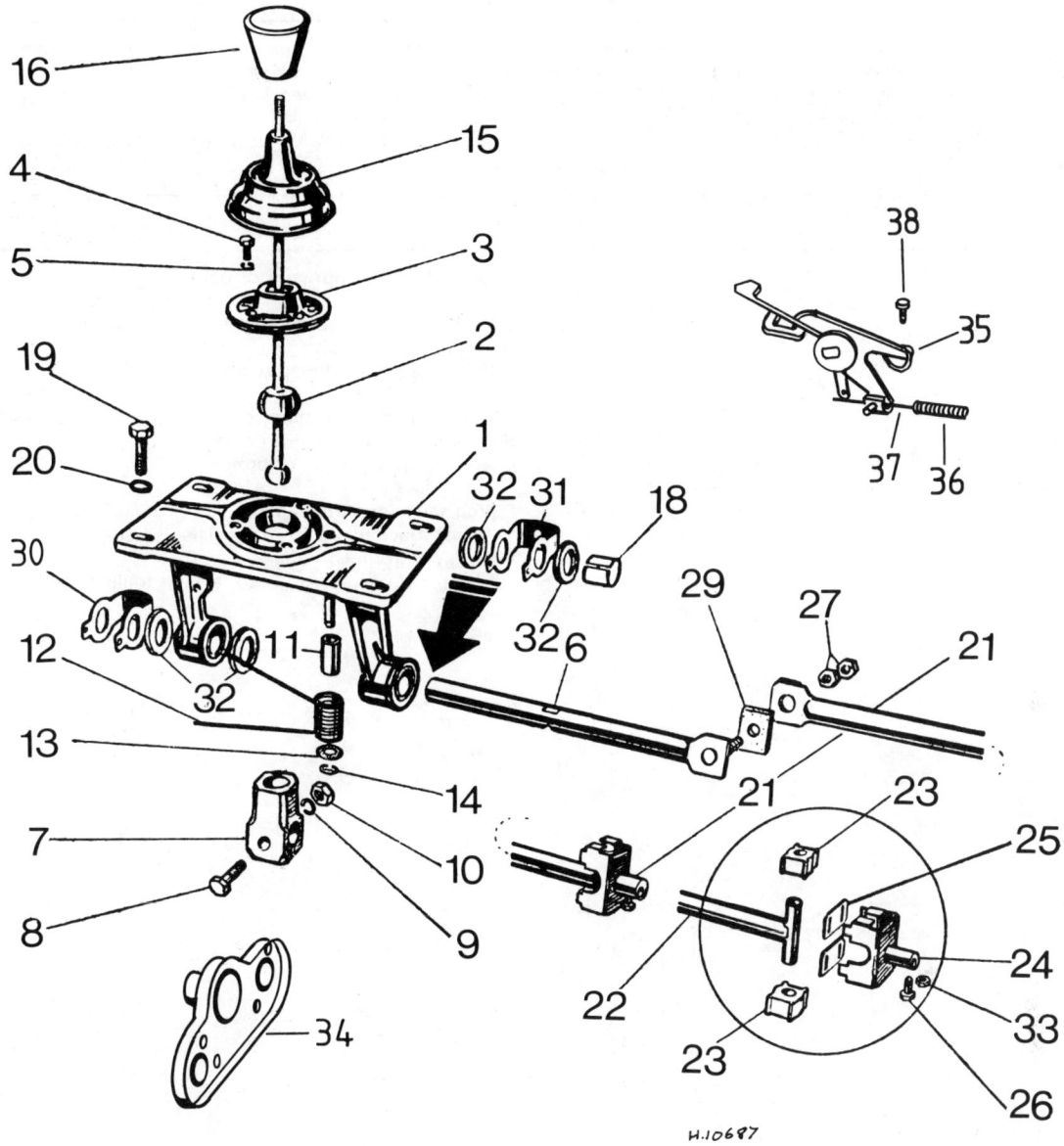

Fig. 6.7 Gearchange linkage components (Sec 21)

1 Gearlever housing	10 Nut	20 Washer	30 Clip
2 Gearlever	11 Guide tube	21 Tie-rod and joint	31 Clip
3 Cover plate	12 Spring	22 Tie-rod	32 Sealing ring
4 Screw	13 Washer	23 Rubber bushes	33 Locknut
5 Washer	14 Ring	24 Joint housing	34 Air duct cowling
6 Shift rod	15 Rubber boot	25 Joint plate	35 Choke lever
7 Sleeve	16 Knob	26 Lockscrew	36 Choke cable outer
8 Bolt	18 Rear bush	27 Nut	37 Choke cable inner
9 Washer	19 Screw	29 Clip	38 Screw

The felt rings on the links must be soaked in engine oil. Lubricate the gearlever housing (having removed the rubber boot).

7   Reattach the link to the shift rod, using a rubber washer placed under the nut, and tighten the nut with a locknut.

8   With the link connected, locate the gearlever housing into position with the lever in neutral and vertical. Tighten the housing retaining screws fitted with flat washers.

22 Speedometer cable – general

1   This is attached to the gearbox front cover by a bolted clamp.

2   The drivegear unit is driven by a small gear located on its own shaft, which is fully splined and fits into the rear end of the pinion shaft.

3   The cable is routed along the underneath of the car in the same channel as the gearshift, clutch and brake systems run. It finally passes through the floor at the front into the car below the dashboard. The cable then screws into the back of the speedometer.

4   The cable rarely needs attention, but it sometimes may need removing if in need of lubrication, when it will make a squeaking noise depending on the speed of the car.

5   The remedy is to liberally coat the inner cable with thick oil or grease before refitting into the outer cable.

23 Fault diagnosis – transmission

Note: *It is sometimes difficult to decide whether it is worthwhile removing and dismantling the gearbox for a fault which may be nothing more than a minor irritant. Gearboxes which howl, or where the synchromesh can be 'beaten' by a quick gear change, may continue to perform for a long time in this state. A worn gearbox usually needs a complete rebuild to eliminate noise because the various gears, if re-aligned on new bearings, will continue to howl when different wearing surfaces are presented to each other.*

The decision to overhaul, therefore, must be considered with regard to time and money available, relative to the degree of noise or malfunction that the driver can tolerate.

Symptom	Reason(s)
Excessive noise in one gear	Gear and/or bearing worn or damaged
Excessive noise in all gears	Low oil level or incorrect grade General wear or damage Differential worn or incorrectly set up
Jumping out of gear	Selector mechanism worn or maladjusted Synchromesh units worn or damaged Detent spring(s) weak or broken
Difficulty in engaging gear	Clutch fault (see Chapter 5) Selector mechanism worn or maladjusted Worn synchromesh units Oil level plug screwed in too far and fouling 1st/2nd selector fork

Chapter 7 Driveshafts, rear hubs, wheels and tyres

For modifications, and information applicable to later models, see Supplement at end of manual

Contents

Specifications

Driveshafts .... Enclosed, sliding joint at differential end, taper and thread at hub end

Wheels
Type .... Pressed steel disc or alloy 4-stud fixing
Wheel rim .... $4\frac{1}{2}$J x 14, $4\frac{1}{2}$J x 13, 5J x 13 or $5\frac{1}{2}$J x 13

Tyres
Tyre size (radial) .... 155 x 14 or 165 SR 13
Tyre pressures:
    Front .... 22 lbf/in² (1.5 kgf/cm²)
    Rear .... 27 lbf/in² (1.9 kgf/cm²)
For high speeds or heavy loads add 3 lbf/in² (0.2 kgf/cm²)

Torque wrench settings

	Nm	lbf ft
Wheel nuts	60 to 70	44 to 52
Axleshaft balljoint nut/bolt	20 to 25	15 to 18
Axleshaft nut	220*	165*
Brake backplate bolt	23	17
Brake wheel cylinder bolt	40 to 80	29.5 to 37

Then tighten further to nearest split pin hole

1 General description and maintenance

Drive is transmitted from the differential unit to the rear wheels by means of driveshafts, enclosed in their respective casings which incorporate the wheel bearing hub carrier flange and differential housing swivel flange.

The axial movement of the half axles is controlled by radius arms which are located round the half axle tubes and the underbody just forward of the rear wheel arches in rubber-mounted swivel joints.

Telescopic shock absorbers are located to the rear of the half axles between the radius arms and body mounting and are enclosed within the coil springs.

Routine maintenance

1 A weekly check should be made on the tyre pressures (including the spare) and tyre treads. Any small stones lodged between the treads must be removed. Look for signs of uneven tyre wear and scuffing, and if these are apparent the suspension and steering must be checked for misalignment. Ensure that the tread depths meet the legal requirements.

2 Every 30 000 miles (50 000 km) remove the hub grease caps and refill with a wheel bearing grease of suitable type. Check the endfloat and adjust if necessary (see Chapter 8).

2 Special precautions and notes

1 Never remove the radius arm connection from the half axle as this is preset to give the correct rear wheel alignment. If removal is ever necessary, it should be left for your Skoda dealer to do.

2 Similarly if the rear tyres are wearing unevenly and the rear wheels are suspected of being out of track, have them checked and if necessary adjusted by a Skoda dealer. The rear wheel toe-in can be checked in the same manner as that for the front wheels.

3 It is not possible to extract an axle driveshaft from the differential through the casing, due to the locating pin guide blocks on its inner end, within the axle housing. These can be removed after the withdrawal of the driveshaft from the casing. Therefore, the half axle assembly complete must be removed when required.

4 We found it virtually impossible to remove the rear brake drum/hub on either side, even with a substantial universal type puller. It is therefore suggested that if any work is to be carried out on the rear half axle units, it is best left to your Skoda agent. However, it may be possible to borrow the Skoda special tool required to remove the brake drum (Jig No MPS – 111). If the special tool is available then the brake drum should be removed prior to removing the half axle unit from the car. Do not try to force the brake drum off by hitting with a hammer!

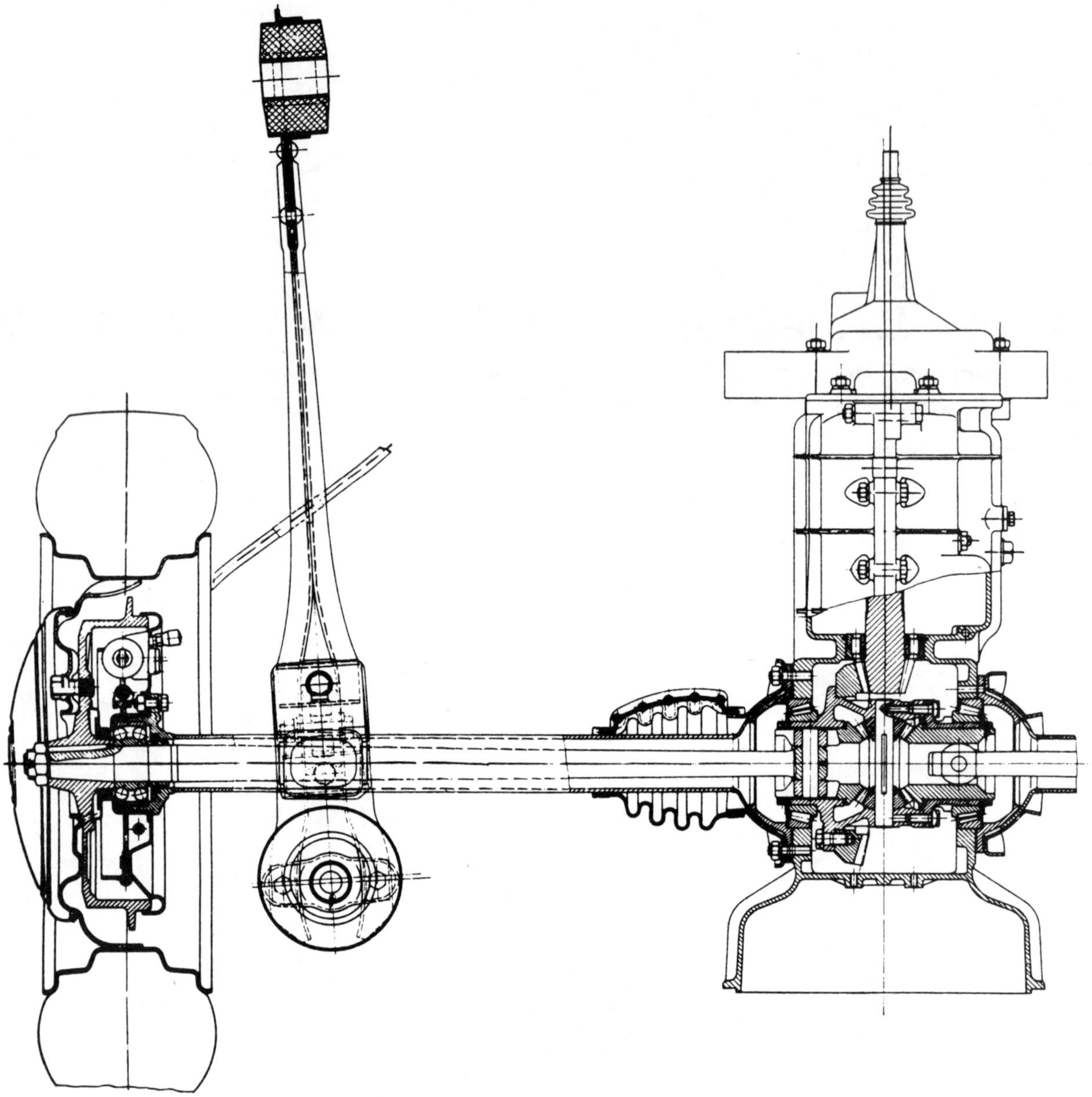

Fig. 7.1 Sectional view of wheel hub, half axle and differential assembly (Sec 1)

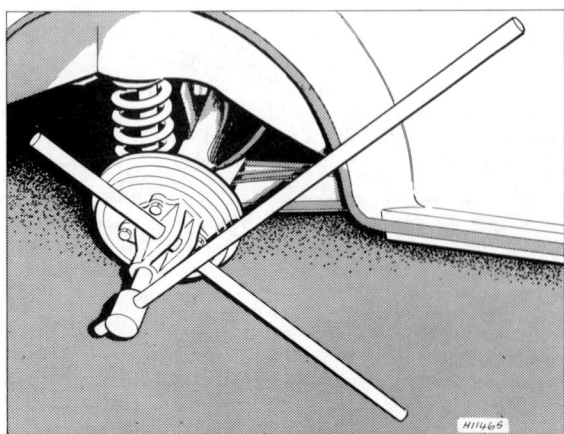

Fig. 7.2 Special tool MPS-111 required to withdraw the rear brake
drum/hub assembly (Sec 2)

3 Half axle units – removal and refitting (transmission in car)

1   Jack up the rear of the car and support the body on firmly based
axle stands or blocks. The front wheels should be chocked to prevent
any possible movement of the car.

2   From inside the car, disconnect the handbrake cable(s) by undoing
the cable adjusting nuts, on the handbrake linkage, located at the rear
end of the central tunnel in front of the rear seats. Pull the cable(s)
through the guide holes in the body to hang free under the car.

3   Remove the roadwheel and place a jack under the brake drum to
support.

4   Disconnect and remove the telescopic shock absorber as described in Chapter 8. Insert a 12 mm open-ended spanner through the
coil spring and locate on the nut on the base of the shock absorber
body to prevent it from turning whilst undoing the retaining nut.

5   Disconnect the rear brake hydraulic pipe unions.

6   Remove the yoke limiting strap(s) for the driveshaft.

7   Unscrew and remove the radius arm pivot bolt nut. Withdraw the
bolt and remove the special spacer washers and bush. Carefully lower
the arm from its forward location, then lower the jack under the brake
drum. The coil spring can now be removed.

8   Place a container under the differential housing and drain the oil.

3.9a Unscrew the driveshaft-to-axle housing flange nuts

3.9b Retain the respective guide blocks on their pegs

3.10 Fit gasket with breather hole at the top

9   Support the half axle in line with the differential housing and remove the axle housing flange bolts (photo) and withdraw the half axle unit complete. Do not disconnect the half axle and strut arm. The guide blocks must be kept in their respective positions (photo); this is best achieved by retaining them on their pegs with a rubber band round them. Oversize guide blocks are available to compensate for wear. Note the flange gasket/shim requirement of each half axle if they are both being removed.
10   Refitting is the reverse sequence of the above. When refitting the half axle to the differential housing, be sure to fit the same number and thickness of taper bearing preload shims as were originally fitted! A new gasket must be used. The gaskets differ in thickness according to requirements. If on assembly the half axle radial movement is stiff, a thicker, or additional, gasket is required. The gasket should be fitted so that the breather hole in the top of the differential housing flange face is not obstructed (photo).
11   If a new protective rubber boot is being fitted ensure that the joint flange is positioned facing upwards and approximately 45° from the half axle. The old flange faces may have been retained by rivets. However, as a special riveting tool is required, these may be replaced by bolts, flat washers and nuts, but do not overtighten. If a dust boot is being fitted to the axleshaft when removed from the car, leave the final tightening of these nuts until the half axle is relocated in order to prevent the possibility of the rubber boot twisting.
12   Top up the transmission oil level, and bleed the brakes. Adjust the hand and foot brakes (see Chapter 9).

4   Half axle unit – dismantling, inspection and reassembly

1   As previously mentioned, the half axle can only be dismantled if the brake drum is removed and this can prove difficult without the use of special tools. However, the procedure for brake drum removal is described in Section 5.
2   With the brake drum removed, withdraw the Woodruff key from the axleshaft.
3   Remove the brake shoes and actuating mechanism, as described in Chapter 9.
4   Unscrew the four nuts and bolts securing the hub cover to the backplate/bearing housing, and remove the cover.
5   If it is just the outer seal or O-ring that has to be renewed, these can now be removed.
6   If the inner seal or bearing has to be renewed then the halfshaft will have to be pressed into the housing approximately 0.40 in (10 mm) and then reverse pressed out of the housing complete with bearing. This will enable a puller to be located with its jaws behind the bearing to pull it off the shaft.
7   The inner seal can now be removed and the various components cleaned and inspected. Do not withdraw the axleshaft any more than is necessary, ie bearing thrust ring flush with half axle socket, otherwise the shaft may become disengaged from the differential unit, necessitating the detaching of the complete half axle housing from the transaxle unit for re-engagement.
8   Bearing shim(s) 0.3 mm thick are used to take up excessive shaft play. Up to three shims may be used for this purpose, but take care to avoid excessive preload of the bearing. Always fit at least one shim when renewing the hub bearing, even if none was fitted previously.
9   Having dismantled to this stage, always renew the oil seals and O-ring. Check the oil seal support ring on the axleshaft. If damaged or marked, so as to affect the seal, remove from the shaft and fit a new one – ensure that the new seal is located in exactly the same position as the old one. If the bearing is suspect, this should also be renewed.
10   Reassembly is the reverse procedure of dismantling, but be sure to refit the oil seals facing the correct way round. The inner seal must have its sealing edge and spring facing towards the axle. Lubricate the seals prior to assembly and smear the shaft and housing aperture with grease prior to fitting the bearing. Also lightly smear the tapered face of the shaft before fitting the brake drum/hub. Ensure that the retaining nut is tightened to the specified torque and a new split pin is used to retain it. It will probably be easiest to leave the final tightening of this nut until after the half axle assembly has been refitted to the car.

5   Wheel hub/brake drum unit – removal and refitting

1   To inspect the wheel hub unit only it is not necessary to remove

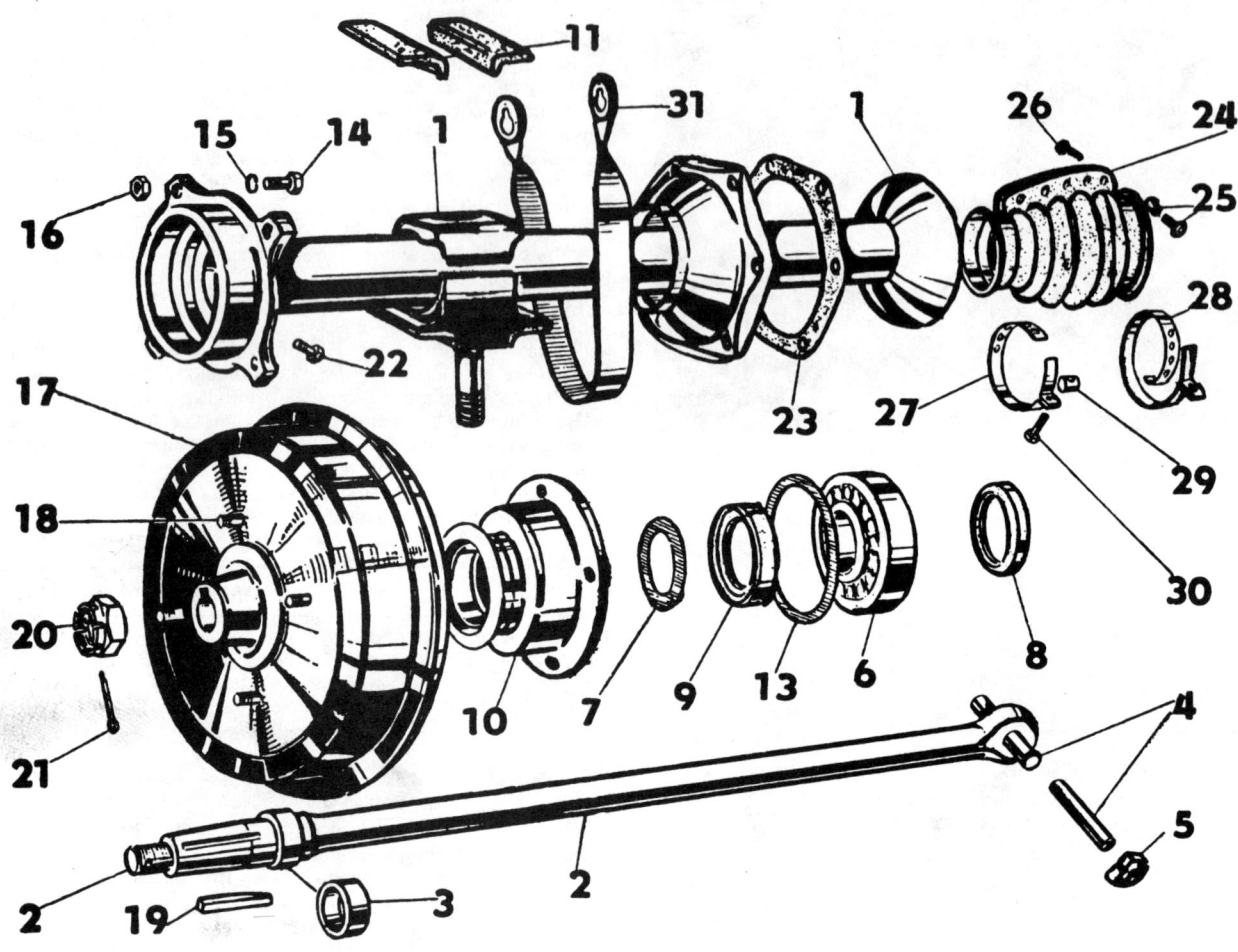

Fig. 7.3 Half axle components (Sec 4)

1	Half axle housing	9	Oil seal
2	Halfshaft assembly	10	Cover assembly
3	Support ring	11	Rubber bush
4	Pin	13	Rubber O-ring
5	Guide block	14	Bolt
6	Ball bearing (self-aligning)	15	Spring washer
7	Shim	16	Nut
8	Oil seal	17	Hub/brake drum assembly

18	Wheel stud	25	Rivet/nut
19	Key	26	Screw/washer/nut
20	Nut	27	Clip
21	Split pin	28	Clip
22	Bolt	29	Nut
23	Gasket	30	Screw
24	Rubber protection boot	31	Axle retaining strap

the complete half axle shaft from the car. However, a special puller will probably be required to remove the brake drum/hub, as mentioned in Section 2.

2   If a puller is available then jack up the car and remove the wheel. Back off the brake adjusting mechanism as described in Chapter 9.

3   Place on axle stand or blocks under the half axle to support, and chock the front wheels to prevent movement of the car.

4   Remove the split pin and undo the castle nut.

5   The brake drum/hub can now be removed from the tapered axle shaft, using the special puller. To remove the bearing cover and seals assembly, refer to Section 4.

6   Refitting is the reverse of the above procedure, but fit a new split pin after tightening the hub nut to the specified torque.

6   Wheels – general

Because of the design of the suspension of the car the strength and trueness of the roadwheels is critical. A great deal of excessive wear on the wheel bearings and driveshaft joints can be attributed to buckled and deformed wheels. Check, whenever there is a sudden difference in the feel at the steering wheel, that the wheels are not buckled or dented. Check also that the wheels are balanced, statically and dynamically; most garages and tyre specialists have balancing equipment. If any deformity is noticed the wheel should be renewed. Do not attempt to repair wheel rims.

Alloy wheels, when fitted, must be inspected regularly for signs of corrosion; they are also more vulnerable to impact damage.

7 Fault diagnosis – driveshafts, rear hub, wheels and tyres

Symptom	Reason(s)
Clonking noise from rear	Suspension unit(s) loose or defective Driveshaft guide blocks worn
Grinding or rumbling noise when cornering	Wheel bearing(s) worn Differential unit defective
Wheel wobble and vibration	Wheel nuts loose Wheel(s) unbalanced Wheel bearing(s) worn Wheel rim or tyre damaged
Excessive or uneven tyre wear	Incorrect tyre pressures Wheel bearing(s) worn Incorrect wheel alignment Suspension unit(s) loose, defective or misaligned Impact damage

Chapter 8 Front hubs, suspension and steering

For modifications, and information applicable to later models, see Supplement at end of manual

Contents

Specifications

Suspension

Front suspension	Independant, wishbone and coil spring
Rear suspension	Independant, swinging half axles with coil springs and radius arms
Shock absorbers	Telescopic front and rear
Coil springs free length:	
Front	276 or 284 mm, depending on model and year
Rear	310, 316 or 331 mm, depending on model and year

Steering

Type	Screw and nut
Ratio	17.3 : 1
Steering wheel turns lock-to-lock	2.5

Wheel alignment

Front wheel camber	1° 15'
Front wheel castor (full load)	6° 30'
Kingpin inclination	7° 30'
Toe-in:	
Front wheels	$2 {}^{+2}_{-1}$ mm ($0.079 {}^{+0.079}_{-0.039}$ in)
Rear wheels	$0 {}^{+2}_{-1}$ mm ($0 {}^{+0.079}_{-0.039}$ in)

Torque wrench settings

	Nm	lbf ft
Lower wishbone bracket-to-body nut	65 to 70	48 to 52
Lower wishbone fulcrum bracket nut – inner	45 to 60	33 to 44
Lower wishbone fulcrum bracket nut – outer	70 to 90	52 to 66
Upper wishbone fulcrum bracket nut – inner	45 to 60	33 to 44
Upper wishbone fulcrum bracket nut – outer	70 to 90	52 to 66
Upper wishbone pin nut (to steering knuckle)	70*	52*
Lower wishbone pin nut (to steering knuckle)	70*	52*
Front hub bearing nut	See text (Section 2)	
Steering knuckle pivot (kingpin) nut	See text (Section 16)	
Lower wishbone bracket bolt nut	40 to 50	30 to 37
Shock absorber-to-bracket nut	50 to 55	37 to 41
Shock absorber-to-body nut	12 to 14	9 to 10
Wheel nuts	60 to 70	44 to 52
Front axle-to-body bolt	40 to 45	30 to 33
Anti-roll bar bracket bolt	12 to 16	9 to 12
Upper wishbone bracket bolt	19 to 25	14 to 18
Shock absorber anchor bracket bolt	20 to 25	15 to 18
Brake disc bolts	48 to 60	35 to 44
Brake disc stirrup bolt	70 to 95	52 to 70

	Nm	lbf ft
Brake stirrup bracket bolt	19 to 25	14 to 18
Steering rocker shaft nut	10*	7*
Idler arm spindle nut (14 mm)	60*	44*
Idler arm spindle nut (10 mm)	40*	30*
Ballpin nuts	40*	30*
Drop arm nut	70*	52*
Track rod end locknut	50 to 60	37 to 44
Track rod connector locknut	50 to 60	37 to 44
Rocker shaft play adjustment screw nut	25 to 30	18 to 22
Steering wheel shaft joint nut	25 to 30	18 to 22
Steering box bearing cap bolt	7	5
Steering box cover bolt	15 to 17	11 to 13
Steering box retaining bolt	45 to 50	33 to 37
Steering wheel nut	25 to 30	18 to 22

Further tighten to nearest split pin hole

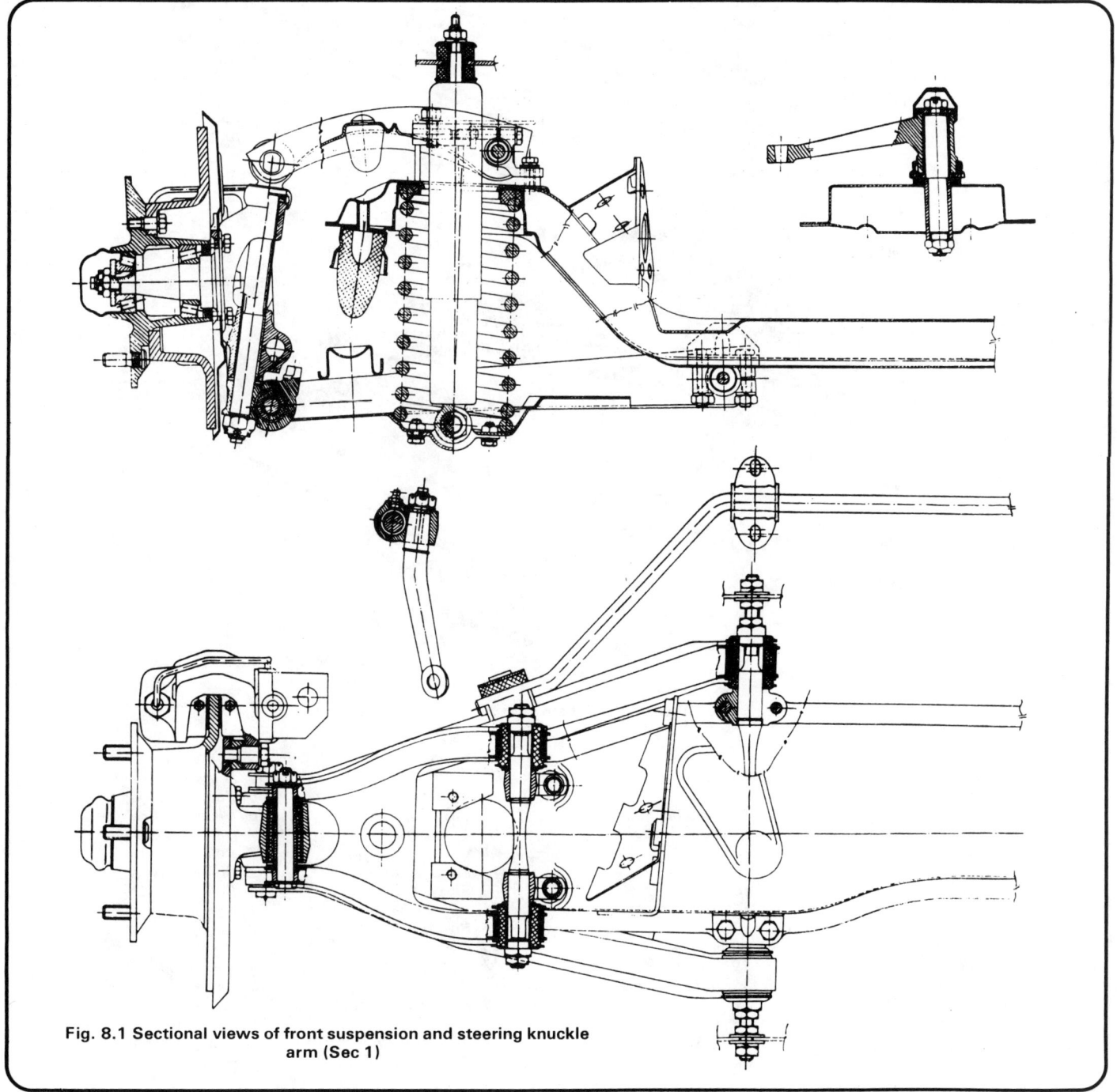

Fig. 8.1 Sectional views of front suspension and steering knuckle arm (Sec 1)

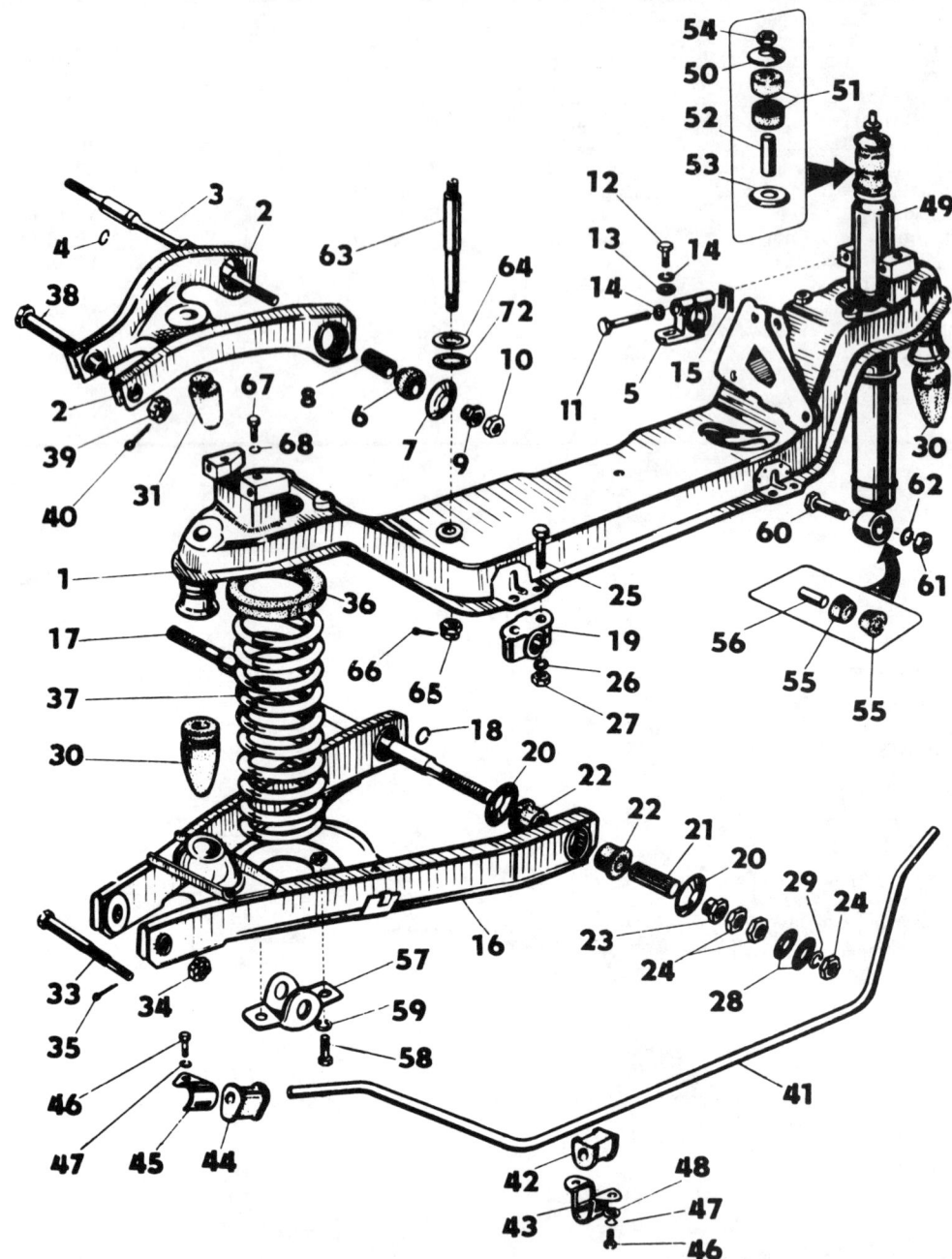

Fig. 8.2 Exploded view of front suspension components (Sec 1)

1	Crossmember	18	Circlip	36	Rubber washer	53	Cup washer
2	Top wishbone	19	Lower pivot pin holder	37	Front axle spring	54	Nut/spring washer
3	Pin	20	Cap	38	Upper wishbone pin	55	Rubber bushes
4	Circlip	21	Distance tube	39	Castellated nut	56	Distance tube
5	Top wishbone support	22	Rubber bushes	40	Split pin	57	Damper holder
6	Rubber bush	23	Nut	41	Anti-roll bar	58	Bolt
7	Cup washer	24	Nuts	42	Rubber bush	59	Spring washer
8	Distance tube	25	Bolt	43	Bracket	60	Bolt
9	Nut	26	Spring washer	44	Rubber bush	61	Nut
10	Nut	27	Nut	45	Bracket	62	Spring washer
11	Bolt	28	Washers	46	Bolts	63	Idler pin
12	Bolt	29	Spring washers	47	Spring washers	64	Idler thrust washer
13	Washer	30	Rubber bump stops	48	Washer	65	Castellated nut
14	Spring washers	31	Rubber stop	49	Hydraulic damper	66	Split pin
15	Camber adjustment shim	33	Eccentric bolt	50	Cup washer	67	Bolt
16	Lower wishbone	34	Castellated nut	51	Rubber bushes	68	Spring washer
17	Lower pivot pin	35	Split pin	52	Distance tube	72	Rubber washer

1 General description and routine maintenance

The independent front suspension is of the double-wishbone type, having coil springs controlled by double-acting telescopic shock absorbers. The steering box is of the worm and nut type.

The rear suspension is also independent, having swinging half axles pivoting from the transaxle unit. Coil springs and double-acting shock absorbers are fitted and strut rods located on the half axle casings at the rear, are located under the body just forward of the rear wheel arches, and are flexibly mounted.

Routine maintenance

It is essential to maintain the suspension and steering in good order if the safety of your car is to be preserved. Even small amounts of wear in the suspension joints and steering mechanism will affect the handling of the car to a dangerous extent. It is for that reason that the Department of Transport (DoT) test examines the condition and serviceability of the suspension and steering particularly, as well as the more obvious components such as the lights, tyres and chassis.

Regular checks should be made therefore to discover slackness and wear in the suspension and steering at the earliest moment. The components most likely to wear are:

Steering control rod balljoints
Stub axle knuckle bushes and kingpin bushes
Upper and lower wishbone pivot pin bushes
Front and rear hydraulic shock absorbers

All of those points should be tested with a tyre lever or screwdriver to see whether there is any movement between them and the fixed component. The tests should also be carried out with the front or back of the car jacked up so as to remove the imposed loads on the suspension assemblies. It will then be easier to detect small amounts of movement.

Together with the mechanical tests on the suspension and steering joints, the components themselves should be examined for serviceability particularly:

(a) Steering box mounting bolts for looseness
(b) Steering column to steering box coupling
(c) Anti-roll bar bushes
(d) Front and rear wheel hub bearings
(e) Front shock absorbers

There should be no play – or failure – in any single part of the aforementioned components. It is dangerous to use a vehicle in a doubtful condition.

Lubricate the kingpins and the front wheel bearings, and top up the steering box oil level if necessary, at the specified intervals. The stub axle turning force should be checked at 6000 – mile intervals as described in Section 16, paragraphs 4 to 9.

2 Front hub – endfloat adjustment

1 To check for excessive play in the front bearings, jack up and support the front of the car so that a front wheel is clear of the ground. Grasp the wheel at top and bottom and try to rock it (photo); no play should be felt. Do not confuse bearing play with worn kingpins or steering joints.
2 If adjustment is necessary, prise off the grease cap and remove the split pin from the hub nut. Slacken the nut a little, then tighten it to 15 Nm (11 lbf ft), rotating the wheel at the same time. Tap the hub to settle the bearings.
3 Back off the nut 180°, then retighten it to 5 Nm (3.6 lbf ft), still rotating the wheel. Back off the nut if necessary to the nearest split pin hole (no more than 30°) and secure with the split pin. **Do not** tighten the nut to align the split pin holes.
4 Spin the wheel and check that play has been taken up. If it is impossible to remove play by the above method, or if there are noises suggestive of bearing failure, it will be necessary to dismantle the hub for inspection as described in Section 3.
5 Fill the cap with wheel bearing grease of the correct type and refit it, carefully tapping it home if necessary.

3 Front wheel hub – dismantling, inspection and reassembly

1 Jack up the front of the car and chock the rear wheels to prevent movement of the car.
2 Remove the relevant roadwheel.
3 Prise the hub cap from the hub (photo), using a screwdriver.
4 Remove the split pin and undo the castle nut and the special washer.
5 Refer to Chapter 9 and remove the front disc brake caliper unit.
6 The outer bearing cone and cup may now be extracted from the hub for inspection.
7 The inner bearing cone and cup may be withdrawn after the oil seal is removed (note which way round it is fitted). If the inner bearing cone has remained on the stub axle it will have to be removed with a suitable puller. The bearing cups can be knocked out of their respective housings using a narrow drift or suitable puller.
8 All parts of the hub should now be washed in clean paraffin and inspected.
9 Check the bearings for excessive looseness in their cages, and the bearing cups for marks or scratches. If any part is in doubtful condition it should be renewed. The seal must be renewed regardless of condition.
10 Reassembly commences by packing the hubs with wheel grease of the correct type.

2.1 Checking the front wheel hub for excessive play

3.3 Grease cap removed to show hub nut and split pin

Fig. 8.3 Front wheel hub and bearing assembly (Sec 3)

1   Hub
2   Bolt
3   Packing ring
4   Bearing (inner)
5   Bearing (outer)
7   Washer
8   Nut
9   Split pin
10 Hub cap

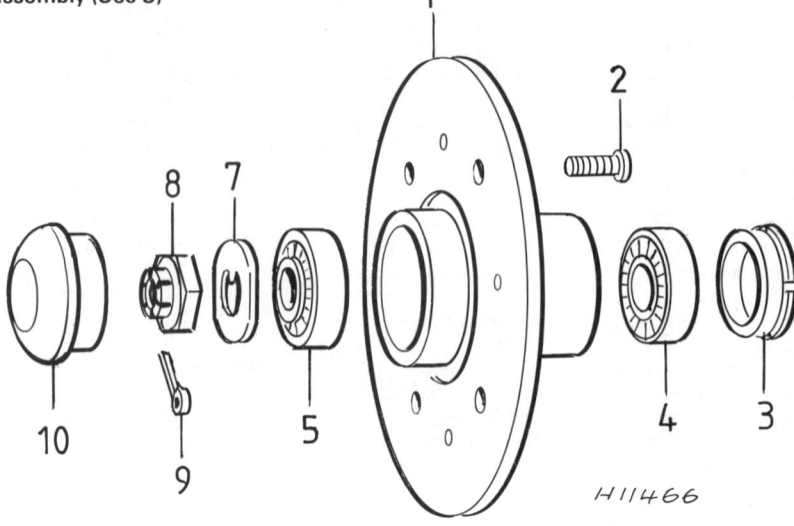

H11466

11 To refit the bearing cups place the housing onto a firm surface and place the cup squarely over its aperture. Place a block of wood over the cup and tap with a hammer until the cup is full home in its housing.
12 The remaining reassembly is a reversal of the dismantling procedure. Once reassembly is complete, the hub can be refitted to the stub axle and the hub endfloat adjustment made as described in Section 2. Refit and bleed the brakes.

4   Front axle and suspension unit – removal and refitting

1   If a comprehensive inspection and rebuild of the front axle and suspension unit is to be carried out is advisable, in the interest of working comfort, to remove the complete unit from the car. This can be achieved fairly easily and without any specialised tools. Proceed as follows, referring to Fig. 8.2 as necessary.
2   Jack up the front of the car and support, on the underside of the body, with blocks or axle stands so that no part of the suspension will be obstructed during dismantling or reassembly. Remove the road-wheels.
3   From inside the forward luggage compartment, unscrew completely the two retaining nuts for the right and left-hand shock absorbers.
4   Refer to Section 12 and disconnect and partially withdraw the steering wheel and column within the car.
5   From underneath the car, undo the wishbone arm pin retaining nuts just sufficiently to release the washers on the brackets of the stiffener panel (front) and underbody (rear) (photo).
6   Disconnect the anti-roll bar brackets from the body.
7   Disconnect the hydraulic brake hoses, place a polythene bag over the hose ends and retain with a rubber band to prevent the ingress of dirt into the pipes.
8   Support the axle centrally with a trolley jack, and remove the four retaining bolts (two on each side of the telescopic shock absorbers).
9   Compress the respective telescopic shock absorber piston rods though their apertures in the body and then carefully lower the axle unit complete, and remove from under the car.
10 Refitting of the axle unit is the reversal of removal procedure, however, the following points should be noted:

(a) Renew, if necessary, the rubber boot and, when fitting, smear with grease round its location on the shaft
(b) Before connecting the steering box to column coupling, ensure that the wheels are pointing straight-ahead and the steering wheel is in the corresponding position. Prior to tightening the coupling bolts, turn the steering wheel to full lock to the right and left to ensure that the steering lock is limited by the kingpin socket stops

4.5 Lower wishbone swivel pin mounting points (A), lower shock absorber mounting plate bolts (B) and anti-roll bar mounting bolts (C)

(c) Ensure that the wheels are correctly aligned (see Section 11)
(d) Refer to Section 16 for information on checking the steering adjustments

5   Front axle and suspension unit – dismantling and reassembly (general)

1   If the front axle and suspension unit is removed from the car for dismantling, it can be cleaned with a water-soluble grease solvent and hosed off, but be sure to cover the brake connections first to prevent dirt and water entering the hydraulic system.
2   No special tools are absolutely necessary, but a ballpin extractor and selection of drifts will be needed.
3   If required, the brakes can be removed as described in Chapter 9, and the hubs as described in Section 3.
4   If only minor work is to be carried out then, obviously, it will not be necessary to remove the complete axle unit from the car, generally the instructions in the following Sections for dismantling the various sub-assemblies will be the same.

5   If the same shims and spacing washers are used on reassembly as were originally found in the steering and suspension joints, then the camber and castor angles should be good enough to drive the car to your Skoda dealer for checking.

6   Anti-roll bar – removal and refitting

1   The anti-roll bar is located in rubber bushes which are retained in clamps to the lower wishbones on the outside (photo), and within brackets attached to the underside of the body.
2   The first action in the task of removing the anti-roll bar is to jack up the front of the car and to place axle stands under the two coil spring locations in the wishbone.
3   With the underside of the front of the car now accessible, the necessary clamp retaining bolts can be removed, and the anti-roll bar disconnected.
4   Clean and inspect the rubber bushes: if perished, split or generally worn, they should be replaced with a new set.
5   Refit the anti-roll bar to the suspension in the reverse sequence of removal. Do not fully tighten the retaining bolts to the specified torque settings until after the car has been lowered and is free standing.

7   Front shock absorbers – removal and refitting

1   To remove the front shock absorber, first unscrew the retaining nut of the piston rod which is located in the front luggage compartment (photo), by one complete turn to relieve the pressure.
2   From underneath unscrew the shock absorber lower retaining bracket bolts from the wishbone.
3   Unscrew the top retaining nut completely and remove the shock absorber through the wishbone aperture.
4   If there are signs of oil leakage and/or the compression resistance is low, then the shock absorber should either be repaired or exchanged by your local Skoda agent.
5   Refitting is the reversal of removal.

8   Front coil springs – removal and refitting

1   Before commencing work on dismantling the coil springs, a suitable coil spring compressor should be at hand. Various proprietary types are now available from most good accessory shops and tool factors.
2   Remove the shock absorber as described in Section 7.
3   Have an assistant sit on the front wing and whilst the spring is compressed, fit the spring compressor clips over two or three adjacent coils, ensuring that it is firmly located.
4   With the spring compressed, jack up the front of the vehicle and support the bodyframe and crossmember adequately on axle stands. Remove the roadwheel.
5   Withdraw the spring complete with compressor. With certain types of spring compressor it may be necessary to lower the wishbone in order to withdraw the spring.
6   Whenever springs are being renewed, get replacements of the correct type as there are two grades of spring available. The heavier

grade is identifiable by the ground flat section on the outside of the spring near its end (Fig. 8.4). Always renew a pair of springs. If only one is renewed the chances are that the original on the other side will be weaker and upset the balance of the suspension.
7   It is also advisable to renew the rubber washer located of the top of the spring within the axle housing.
8   Refitting of the front springs is a reversal of the removal procedure.

9   Stub axle, kingpin and wishbones – removal, inspection and refitting

1   See Fig. 8.5. If the axle asssembly is still on the car, jack up at the front and support with stands. Chock the rear wheels to prevent car movement.
2   Refer to Chapter 9 and remove the front brake caliper units.
3   Refer to Sections 7 and 8 and remove the front shock absorber and coil spring on the side concerned.
4   Disconnect the track rod and anti-roll bar.
5   Withdraw the split pin from the steering rod castle nut and loosen the nut. To remove the steering rod (located in the stub axle on a taper and Woodruff key) hit the nut with a soft-headed mallet. When the tapered joint is free, remove the nut and withdraw the steering rod. Remove the Woodruff key.
6   Remove the upper wishbone from the axle and stub axle by removing the respective split pin and castle nut and locking nuts from the wishbone pins. Remove the dust cap and rubber bush from the axle pin and disconnect the circlips from the groove within the wishbone.
7   With a soft drift and hammer, drive the pins through the wishbone, stub axle and axle locations, and remove the upper wishbone, noting the thickness of the horseshoe washers between the bracket and axle body.
8   Remove the lower wishbone by removing from the axle pivot pin the retaining nuts, washers, rubber bush and cap, and from within the wishbone, the circlips from their grooves (photo). Clean and keep the respective adjustment washers in order, for reassembly. Remove the split pin and castle nut from the eccentric bolt, and with a soft drift and hammer, drive the pin and bolt through the wishbone and stub axle to remove.
9   To dismantle the stub axle and kingpin unit, remove the castle nut and split pin from the kingpin at the bottom. Prise the Woodruff key from its groove.
10   Remove the steering knuckle and then withdraw the kingpin from the stub axle.
11   Clean all parts throughly and inspect for excessive wear of the kingpin and bushes.
12   If the bushes and kingpin are to be renewed, it is a task for your Skoda dealer as the new bushes will have to be reamed to suit the new kingpin. The dealer will also have the equipment to remove and refit the bushes. The steering knuckle bush will also have to be renewed, and this should be taken for attention at the same time. If the eccentric bush and eccentric bolt are to be renewed, this task should be entrusted to your Skoda dealer. This is because the bush setting is critical in terms of its effect on camber angle; the dealer will also have advice on the shim thickness requirements.

6.1 Anti-roll bar bush and retaining plate on the wishbone arm

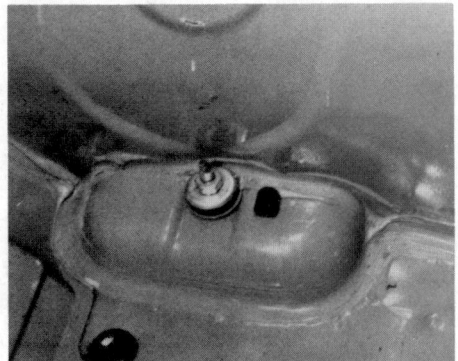

7.1 Front shock absorber upper retaining nut and washer/bush assembly in luggage compartment. Note protective rubber boot

Fig. 8.4 Heavy duty spring is identified by a flat section (arrowed) (Sec 8)

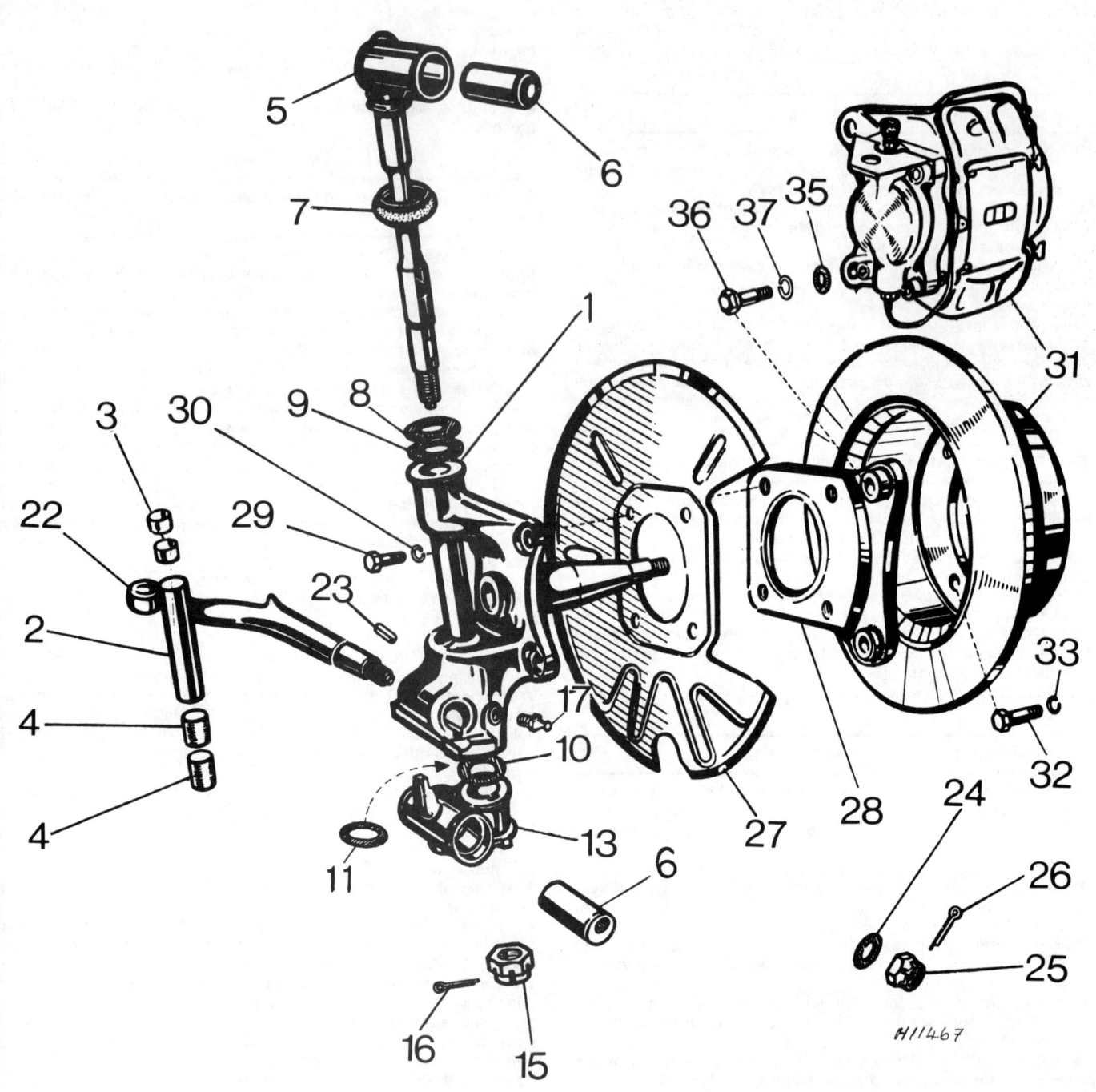

Fig. 8.5 Exploded view of stub axle and kingpin components (Sec 9)

1 Steering knuckle	9 Thrust washer	23 Key	30 Washer
2 Spacer	10 Thrust washer	24 Washer	31 Brake unit
3 Upper bush	11 Sealing ring	25 Nut	32 Bolt
4 Lower bushes	13 Trunnion	26 Split pin	33 Washer
5 Kingpin	15 Nut	27 Brake backplate	35 Shim
6 Rubber bushes	16 Split pin	28 Brake yoke	36 Bolt
7 Dust cap	17 Grease nipple	29 Screw	37 Washer
8 Friction washer	22 Steering lever		

9.8 Lower wishbone-to-axle pivot assembly

(a) Always lubricate with a good quality multi-purpose grease, the swivel pins, bushes and kingpin prior to assembly

(b) When fitting the bush to the upper wishbone, insert the bushes into hot, soapy water first, to ease entry into the wishbone arm 'eyes'. When fitted the bushes should protude equally each side of the eye. Any wet soapy solution remaining should be wiped or blown off with compressed air

(c) Always renew the circlips and ensure that they are correctly fitted in their respective grooves

(d) Connect the wishbone to the axle first and then insert the coil spring and rubber washer. It is advisable to smear the top of the coil spring and the washer joint faces with a rubber solution to ensure correct final location within the wishbone arm and axle. Having located the coil spring, compress it so that when the lower wishbone arm is raised the gap between the stop rubber in the axle and the wishbone stop is 0.79 in (20 mm), then refit the stub axle unit

(e) When fitting the steering knuckles, do not interchange the right or left-hand knuckles

(f) Refit the wheel hub and brakes, as described in Section 3 and Chapter 9 respectively. Bleed the brakes prior to using the car on the road

(g) When the track rods are reconnected, check the toe-in, as described in Section 11

(h) After the repair of any unit from the front suspension or steering assembly, it is most important that an alignment check should be made by your Skoda agent. He is fully equipped to do this, and for the comparatively small cost involved, it will save you money on tyre wear and ensure the correct handling and safety of your car

13 Remove the knuckle and stub axle grease nipples and clean out the oilways to ensure good lubrication of the new bushes.

14 The kingpin top wishbone location bolt should be renewed at this stage, also a job for your Skoda dealer.

15 Fit new seals and dust caps as required, and always use new split pins on assembly.

16 Reassembly of the stub axle and wishbones is a reversal of dismantling, but the following points should be noted:

10 Track rods – removal, inspection and refitting

1 If the track rods or joints are being removed for cleaning and inspection only, be extra careful not to damage the rubber boots during dismantling.

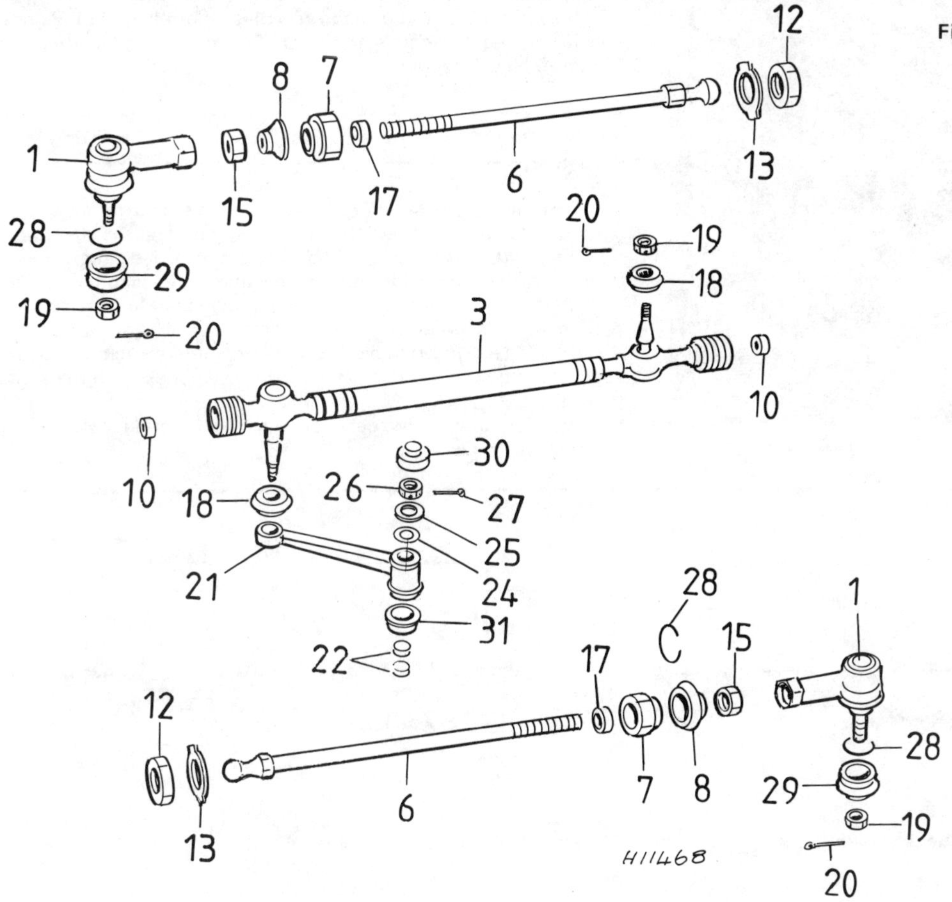

Fig. 8.6 Exploded view of track rod and tie-rod assemblies (Sec 10)

1   Track rod ends
3   Tie-rod
6   Track rods
7   Connectors
8   Dust caps
10 Sockets
12 Locknuts (connectors)
13 Lockwashers
15 Locknuts (track rod ends)
17 Bushes
18 Dust cap
19 Nuts
20 Split pins
21 Idler arm
22 Bushes
24 Shim
25 Washer
26 Nut
27 Split pin
28 Circlips
29 Dust caps
30 Cover plate
31 Cover ring

H11468

2   Remove the split pins from the steering arm and idler arm castle nuts and then unscrew the nuts. If a balljoint separator is available, remove the nuts and separate the joints. If a separator is not available, slightly loosen the nut and then strike it with a soft-faced mallet, supporting the steering arm or idler arm with a lump hammer on the other side. Take care not to damage the threads of the ballpin or the nut. Use the same technique to separate the outboard track rod end balljoints from the stub axle arms (photo).

3   The tie-rod and track rod assembly can now be withdrawn from the car and the respective joints cleaned and inspected. The balljoints should not show any signs of ovality or slackness: if they do, they should be renewed. The rubber boots and their retaining rings must also be inspected for signs of deterioration and renewed if necessary.

4   If the bushes in the tie-rod have to be renewed, drive the old bushes out with a suitable drift. Press the new ones in squarely, ensuring that they enter their location without binding. Pack all joints with multi-purpose grease on reassembly.

5   If the track rod ends have to be removed, note their relative positions before unscrewing them. If the new ends are fitted in the same positions, front wheel alignment will be sufficiantly correct for the car to be driven to a dealer for accurate setting. Refer to Fig. 8.7 if the basic setting is lost.

6   Reassembly of the track rods is the reverse of the removal procedure. Tighten the castle nuts to the specified torque and use new split pins to lock them.

7   The track rod connectors must be tightened to the point where the force required to move the track rod concerned is approximately 2 kg (4.6 lb), measured at the inboard end of the threaded portion. When this has been achieved, tighten the locknut to the specified torque and secure with the lockwasher.

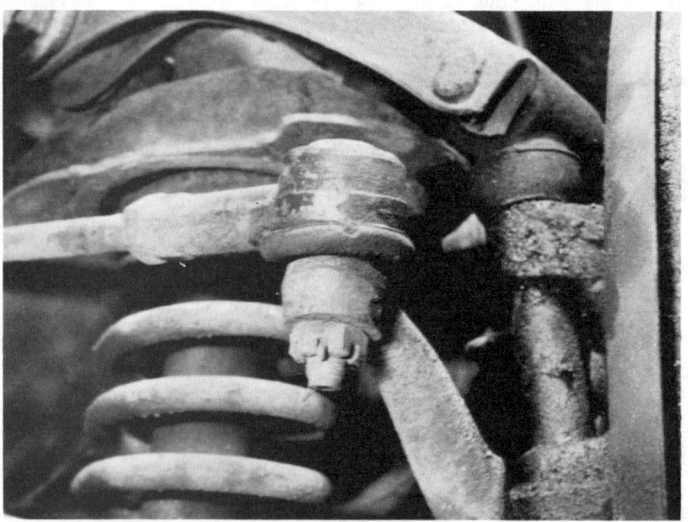

10.2 Track rod-to-stub axle arm joint

11 Wheel alignment – general

1   Provided that reassembly of the steering and suspension system involved only renewal of joints and/or bushes and not disturbance of the lengths of any of the steering rods or trackrods, then you should be able to drive carefully to your nearest Skoda dealer, where the wheels may be aligned with the specialized equipment that is absolutely necessary for this task.

2   If on reassembly steering rods or suspension arms have been renewed, then it will be necessary to check the alignment with simple equipment, before the car is driven to the local Skoda dealer for the final accurate alignment.

3   The settings are given in the Specifications Section of this Chapter.

4   Of all the settings to be considered, only the toe-in is likely to be seriously affected during repair work on the car.

5   The toe-in setting of the wheels is checked as follows. The car should be positioned on a flat level area and be unladen. The tyres should be at their correct pressures and the car should be level on the suspension.

6   The front wheels are correctly aligned when they are turning in by the specified amount. This toe-in figure is the difference in distance between the middle of the two front wheel rims when measured at hub level on the most forward tip and the most rearward tip of the wheel rims (Fig. 8.8).

7   Adjustment to the front wheel alignment is made by slackening the nuts locking the track rod relative to the balljoint sockets and screwing the track rod into, or out of, the balljoint socket, as necessary. Retighten the locknuts when the correct adjustment is made. If the adjustment required is considerable, distribute the adjustment equally between both track rods.

8   Mark the position checked with a piece of chalk and then move the car forwards so that the wheels are turned through 180° and recheck the alignment.

9   If incorrect, it may be that a wheel, or both wheels, are buckled, in which case get the adjustment as near as possible to the correct setting and have the alignment rechecked by your Skoda agent.

10   No attempt must be made to adjust the rear wheel alignment as specialised equipment is required. Entrust this adjustment to your Skoda dealer if needed.

12 Steering wheel and column – removal and refitting

1   Disconnect the battery earth lead.

2   To remove the steering wheel, unscrew and remove the spoke shroud retaining screws. Unscrew and remove the steering wheel retaining nut, but before withdrawing the wheel, mark its relative position on the shaft for correct relocation on assembly (photo).

3   Unscrew and remove the lower cowling retaining screws, then withdraw the cowling from the column.

4   Disconnect and remove the upper column cluster switch which is secured by two bolts. Detach leads and switches from the switch box (photo).

5   Working under the car, remove the steering column shaft-to-steering box coupling bolt.

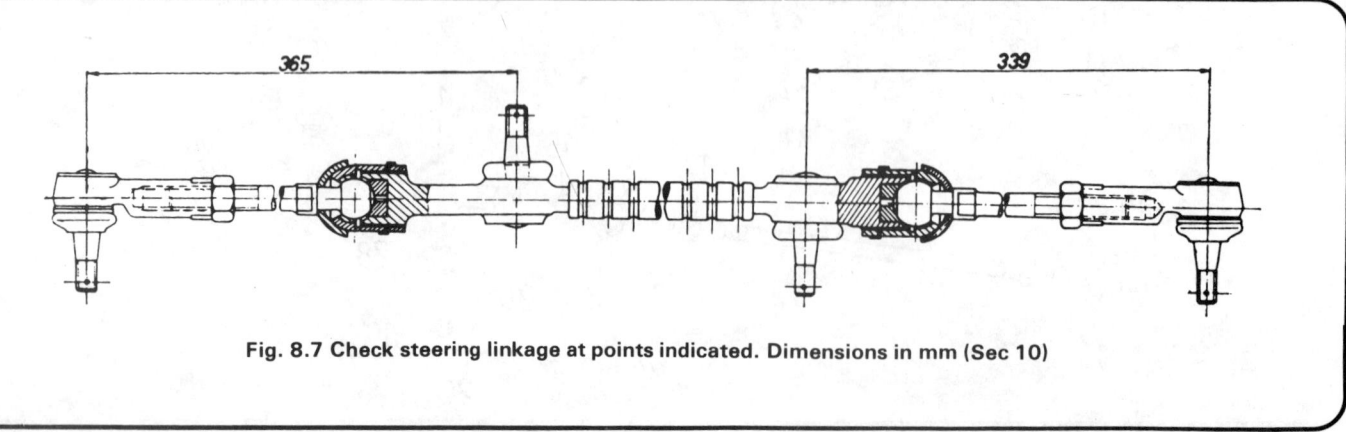

365   339

Fig. 8.7 Check steering linkage at points indicated. Dimensions in mm (Sec 10)

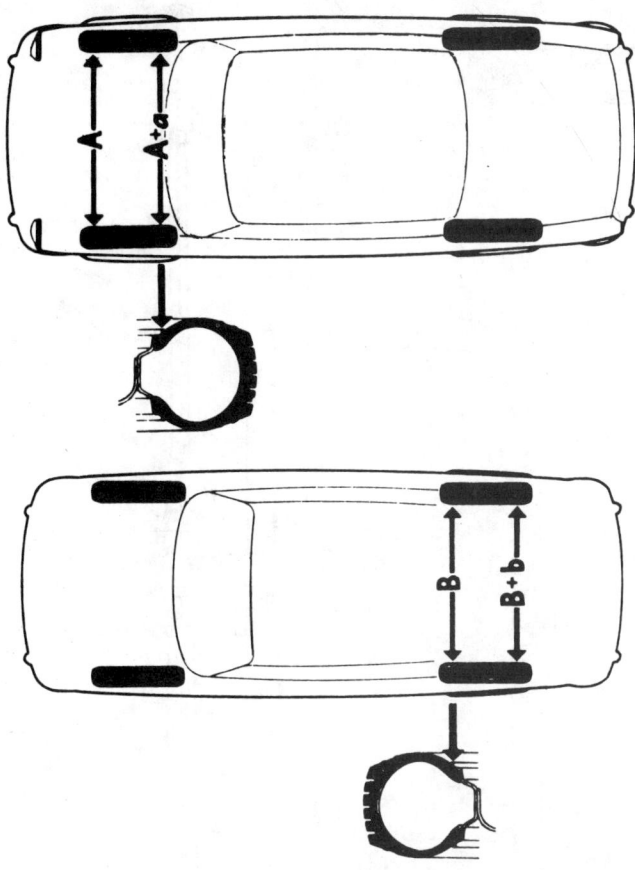

Fig. 8.8 Toe-in checking points (Sec 11)

A   Front wheels
B   Rear wheels
a and b = specified toe-in

12.2 Steering wheel spoke pad removed for access to retaining nut

12.4 The upper column switches shown with cover removed

6   Prise back the dust boot from the floor and remove the shaft bearing bolts (under shaft) and the steering lock bolts (front of shaft) which fastens the shaft to the body. Extract the shaft.
7   On removal the shafts can be separated by removing the crosspin joint bolt. The lower column crosspin joint cannot be dismantled and therefore if worn the unit must be renewed.
8   To check the upper column, remove the fastening sleeve and check that the shaft can rotate freely in its tube. If not, unlock the steering lock and press the shaft out (from its splined end).
9   Extract the shaft circlip and remove the upper bearing. To remove the lower bearing drive it out carefully through the tube cut-outs.
10 To remove the steering lock refer to Section 13.
11 Reassembly of the shaft components is a reversal of the removal procedure, but note the following.
12 Lubricate the bearings prior to fitting as they cannot be lubricated once in position. The bearing can now be dismantled for cleaning and inspection by removing its retaining circlip. Pack with grease on reassembly.
13 With the upper bearing in position, relocate the wedge-shaped ring with the tapered part facing the bearing, then retain with the circlip. Press the shaft into the tube and then install the bearing in the other end.
14 Smear the column shaft dust boot with oil prior to fitting to case assembly.
15 When reconnecting the shafts fit the fastening sleeve onto the tube with the shaft, lubricate the ring with oil and locate on the shaft end (wedge section to bearing). Fit the spring and joint socket, then tighten the joint to the specified torque. If a new sleeve has been fitted check that the sleeve does not clamp the tube tightly when fitted.
16 Tighten all fastenings to the specified torque and ensure that the steering wheel is correctly relocated onto its shaft.
17 Reconnect all electrical wires and attachments and check the respective circuits for correct operation to complete.

13 Steering lock – removal and refitting

1   Disconnect the battery earth lead, then referring to Section 12, disconnect and lower the steering column without actually detaching it from the steering box shaft.
2   To remove the steering lock, lubricate the shaft end with oil and rocking the steering lock and bracket, pull it from the shaft. The steering must be unlocked when removing. If the lock is stuck, then disconnect the upper shaft and remove the crosspin bolt to separate the upper and lower shaft sections. You will now need to drill out the shear bolt retaining the lock in position but take care not to damage the housing thread. The use of a suitable screw extractor is useful here.
3   The steering lock and ignition switch can be removed by loosening the two housing capscrews from the locations shown in Fig. 8.10.
4   Reassembly is the reversal of the removal sequence but particular attention should be paid to the following.
5   When reassembling the lock and switch, the key must be turned to the left-hand (stop) position.
6   The special lock retaining bolt is tightened until its head shears off.
7   Reassemble the column referring to Section 12 and check the column switch circuits and steering lock for correct operation before using the vehicle.

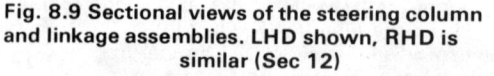

Fig. 8.9 Sectional views of the steering column
and linkage assemblies. LHD shown, RHD is
similar (Sec 12)

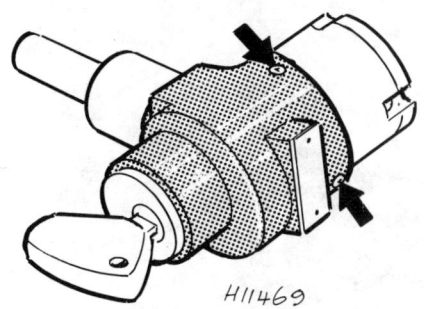

Fig. 8.10 Steering lock/ignition switch securing screw positions (arrowed) (Sec 13)

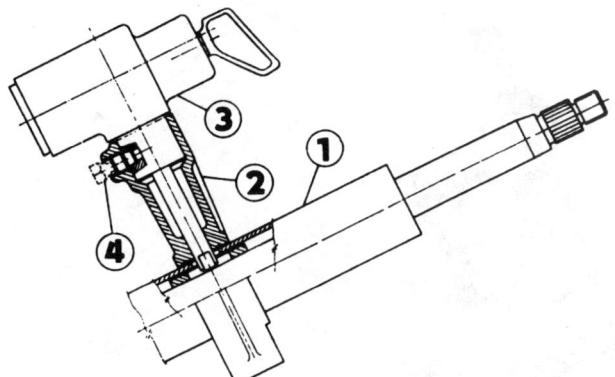

Fig. 8.11 Steering lock and bracket (Sec 13)

1	Column tube	3	Lock and switch
2	Lock bracket	4	Shear head bolt

14 Steering box – removal and dismantling

1   Remove the spare wheel.
2   Disconnect the steering linkage to the drop arm, removing the split pin and castle nut. Use a balljoint separator or the method described in Section 10 to separate the joint.
3   Unscrew and remove the steering column shaft to steering box through bolt.
4   Remove the steering box retaining bolts (photo) and lift the box clear. It may be necessary to disconnect the steering column assembly in order to withdraw the column shaft sufficiently to disengage it from the steering box. This being the case, refer to Section 12.

14.4 The steering box in position viewed from underneath. The filler/level plug is arrowed

5   Commence the dismantling of the steering box by cleaning its external surfaces.
6   Remove the tapered plug from its location in the steering box top cover and drain out the oil.
7   Remove the column coupling from the splines of the steering worm.
8   Extract the split pin and unscrew the retaining nut to remove the drop arm and its locating Woodruff key from the rocker arm shaft. It may be necessary to use a universal puller.
9   Loosen the nut and setscrews in the steering box cover and then remove the retaining bolts and lift the cover clear.
10 Now lift the rocker arm shaft out of the box, complete with the special worm actuating nut.
11 If the bearings are to be removed, unscrew the end cap retaining bolts and withdraw the bearings, complete with worm, by drifting out.
12 Remove the bearings from the shaft with a puller.
13 Clean all parts of the steering box thoroughly, and inspect for excessive wear in the worm and nut. Test the rocker arm fit in its locating bush and if required, drift out the bush and replace with a new one. The bearings do not normally wear to any extent, but they should also be checked. Always renew the O-rings and cover gaskets.

15 Steering box – reassembly and refitting

1   Assuming the rocker arm bush to have been renewed and pressed into position, refit the O-ring and dust cap into their aperture.
2   Press fit the bottom bearing into position in the box.
3   Smear both sides of the bottom cover gasket with a sealing compound, refit with the cover and retain with bolts and spring washers.
4   Fit the bearing washer onto the top of the shaft, and then press fit the top bearing into position on the end of the worm shaft. Insert the shaft into position in the box and press into the bottom bearing, then fit the top bearing into position within its orifice in the box.
5   Measure the thickness of the bearing protrusion from the box, and fit the appropriate number of washers required to offset this thickness; smear with sealing compound. Refit the top cover, the O-ring and the cover plate and tighten to the specified torque.
6   Check the worm shaft for smooth rotation, endfloat and axial play.
7   Now reassemble the rocker arm and nut into the box and also the spring and pin to the arm shaft. Coat the joint faces with sealer and fit the gasket and cover, securing with retaining bolts and washers.
8   Refit the drop arm and Woodruff key, then tighten the retaining castle nut firmly to the nearest split pin hole. Insert and divide the split pin to lock the nut.
9   Now insert the adjustment screw into the top cover and turn the drop arm to its limit. With the drop arm in this position, first tighten the adjustment screw fully and then unscrew it by 95° to 120° to ensure the correct amount of free play in the steering. Lock in position with the locknut.
10 Fit the column coupling to the worm shaft and retain with clamp bolt.
11 Try the steering action, which should be quite smooth. If tight, unscrew the adjustment screw to suit, and then lock with the nut. The maximum force required to turn the input shaft should not exceed 1.16 lbf ft (1.6 Nm).
12 Refit the steering box to the car and refill with oil to the brim of the filler hole.
13 Reconnect the track rod balljoint to the drop arm.

16 Steering adjustment checks

1   If the action of the steering should become stiff, a check should be made on the steering components concerned in the manner described below. The following checks should also be made (and where possible adjustments made if necessary), when a particular steering component assembly is overhauled or detached. Stiff steering can also be caused by under-inflated tyres and wheel and suspension misalignment, so check these first.
2   The following checks must be made with the wheels fitted and clear of the ground, so commence by raising and supporting the car at the front.

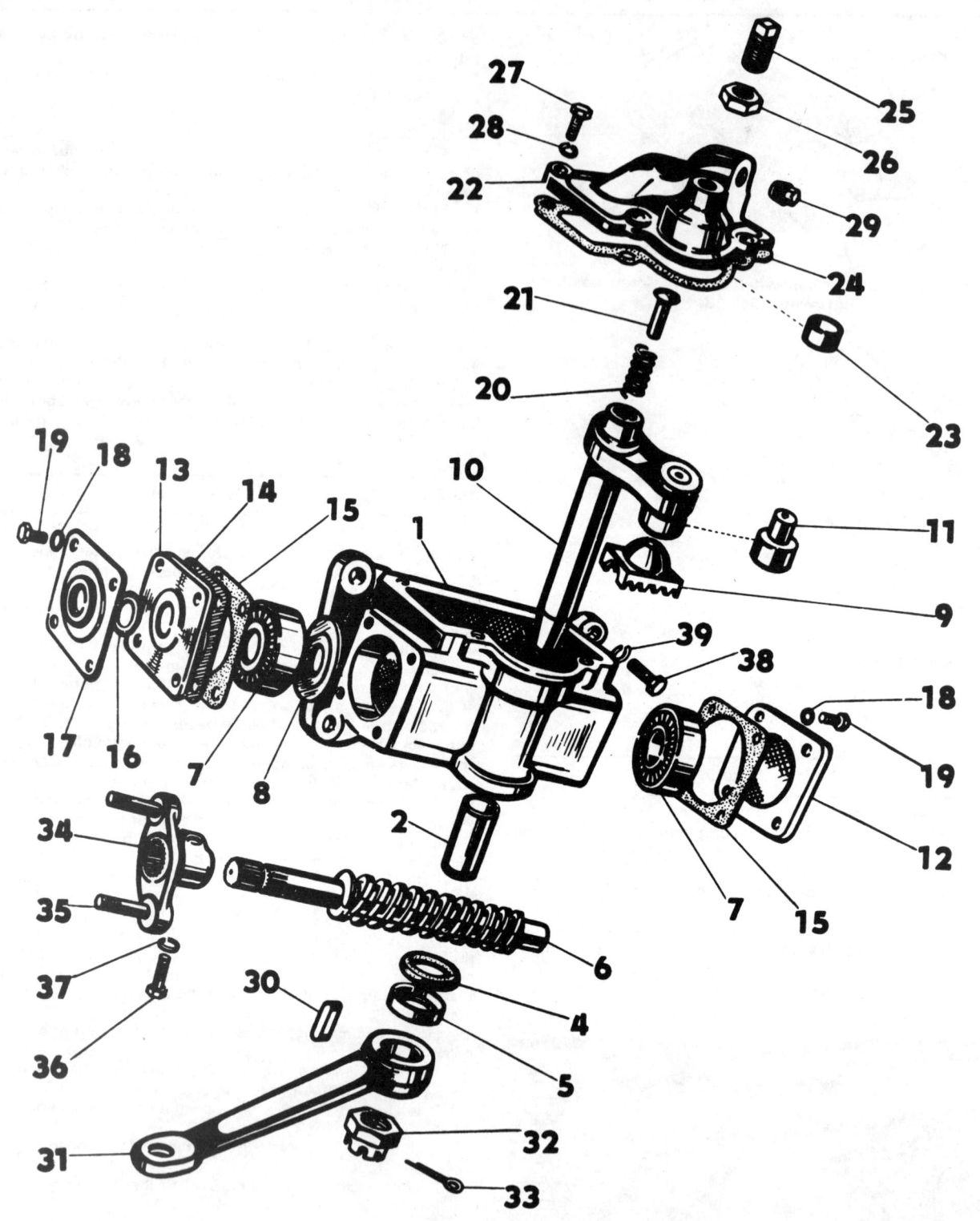

Fig. 8.12 Exploded view of steering box (Sec 14)

1	Steering box	11	Rocker shaft pin	21	Spring pin	31	Drop arm
2	Bush	12	Bottom box cover	22	Steering box top	32	Castellated nut
4	O-ring	13	Top box cover	23	Cover bush	33	Split pin
5	Dust cap	14	Preload adjustment shim	24	Cover gasket	34	Input shaft coupling
6	Steering worm	15	Preload adjustment gasket	25	Setscrew	35	Stud
7	Ball bearings	16	O-ring	26	Nut	36	Screw
8	Bearing washer	17	Cover plate	27	Bolt	37	Washer
9	Steering nut	18	Fan washer	28	Washer	38	Bolt
10	Rocker shaft	19	Bolt	29	Taper filler plug	39	Spring washer
		20	Rocker shaft spring	30	Key		

3 The following tools will be required:

Spring balance (0 to 4 kg – 0 to 8 lb)
Feeler gauges
Balljoint separator

Stub axle turning force

4 Detach the track rod end from the stub axle.

5 Extract the split pin from the kingpin securing nut and slacken the nut 3 turns. Check that the trunnion slides down the kingpin.

6 Lubricate the kingpin with a molybdenum disulphide (MS2) grease via the grease nipple; check that grease comes out at the top and bottom thrust washers.

7 Insert a 0.002 in (0.05 mm) feeler gauge between the kingpin head and the top thrust washer. Tighten the lower nut until the feeler gauge is just nipped, then remove the feeler and tighten a further 1 to $1\frac{3}{4}$ flats.

8 Hook the spring balance on the stub axle at the track rod attachment point and check the force required to move the axle. Pull at 90° to the arm. The force required must not exceed 4 lb (1.8 kg). If a greater force is necessary, repeat the procedure and try again; ultimately, consult your dealer if unable to achieve the required figure.

9 Insert a new split pin to secure the nut on completion.

Steering column, box and idler turning force

10 With the track rods still disconnected from the stub axles, hook the spring balance in the steering wheel spoke at its junction with the rim and check the force required to move the wheel when pulling at 90° to the spoke. The force required must not exceed 2.8 lb (1.27 kg) over $1\frac{1}{2}$ turns of the wheel. A small additional force may be needed to set the wheel turning; this can be disregarded.

11 Top up the oil level in the steering box, using a molybdenum disulphide additive. If the force required to turn the steering wheel is within the limits quoted above, refit the track rod ends and lower the vehicle to the ground. If the force exceeds that permitted, proceed with the checks below to isolate the cause of the trouble.

Steering idler check

12 Disconnect the balljoint from the steering idler arm, hook the spring balance into the end of the idler arm and check the force required to move the idler, pulling at 90° to the arm. The force must not exceed 2 lb (0.9 kg). If it does, proceed as follows.

13 Remove the idler and the large rubber washer underneath it, then refit the idler without the washer.

14 Measure the idler endfloat using feeler gauges. Permissible endfloat is between 0.0008 and 0.005 in (0.02 and 0.12 mm); add or remove shims as necessary under the small steel washer on the idler bolt head.

15 When satisfied, remove the idler, lubricate with gear oil and refit with the large rubber washer.

16 Before reconnecting the steering idler, carry out the check below.

Steering column and box turning force

17 With the steering idler disconnected, proceed as described in paragraph 10. The force required now must not exceed 2.6 lb (1.20 kg), again ignoring any small excess required to set the steering wheel moving. If there is excessive resistance to motion, the steering box will have to be removed and dismantled for checking.

18 The source of any excessive stiffness in the steering should now have been identified. Reconnect any steering joints which have been disconnected and lower the car to the ground to complete.

---

17 Rear suspension – general

1 Each side of the rear suspension basically consists of a coil spring and telescopic shock absorber, which are located between the car body and the half axle radius arms. The radius arms are located on the half axle casings at one end, and the forward end hinges in a flexible mounting bolted to the underbody, just forward of the rear wheel arches.

2 As previously mentioned, *on no account must the radius arm be disconnected or relocated, on its half axle mounting, as this will affect the rear wheel alignment.* Should it ever be necessary to remove the radius arms, work beyond this point should be left to your Skoda dealer.

3 Note that the rear coil springs are a heavier gauge than those of the front and they should never be interchanged.

---

18 Coil springs and shock absorbers (rear) – removal and refitting

1 Jack up the rear of the car until the half axle is lowered into the suspension yoke limiting strap. Further support the underbody with blocks or axle stands as a safety measure.

2 Remove the relevant roadwheel.

3 Working inside the car, fold back the rear wheel arch carpet in the rear luggage compartment on the side concerned and prise free the rubber bung from the aperture giving access to the upper shock absorber mounting (photo).

4 Grip the flat section on the top of the shock absorber with a self-grip wrench to prevent the shaft turning and unscrew and remove the retaining nut with damper washers and bushes, taking note of their order of fitting.

5 Working underneath the car, unscrew and remove the lower shock absorber retaining plate-to-radius arm mounting nuts.

6 Lower and remove the shock absorber (photo).

7 To remove the coil spring either compress it with a spring compressor and extract it, or remove by disconnecting at its forward end and lowering the radius arm (photo). Do not detach the radius arm from the half axle.

8 If on removal the upper and lower coil spring rubbers locating washers are perished, or worn, they should be renewed on assembly.

9 Refitting the coil springs and shock absorbers is a reversal of the removal procedure. Tighten all fastenings to their specified torque values.

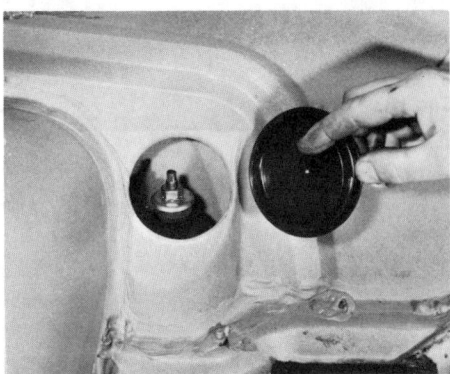
18.3 Rear shock absorber upper mounting location

18.6 Removing a rear shock absorber

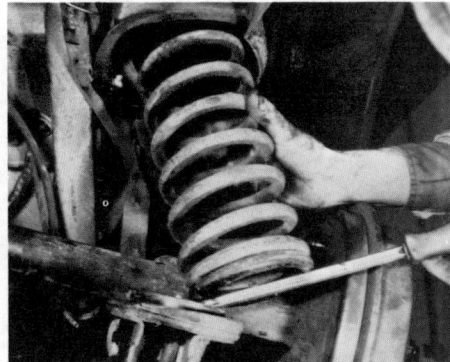
18.7 Removing a rear coil spring

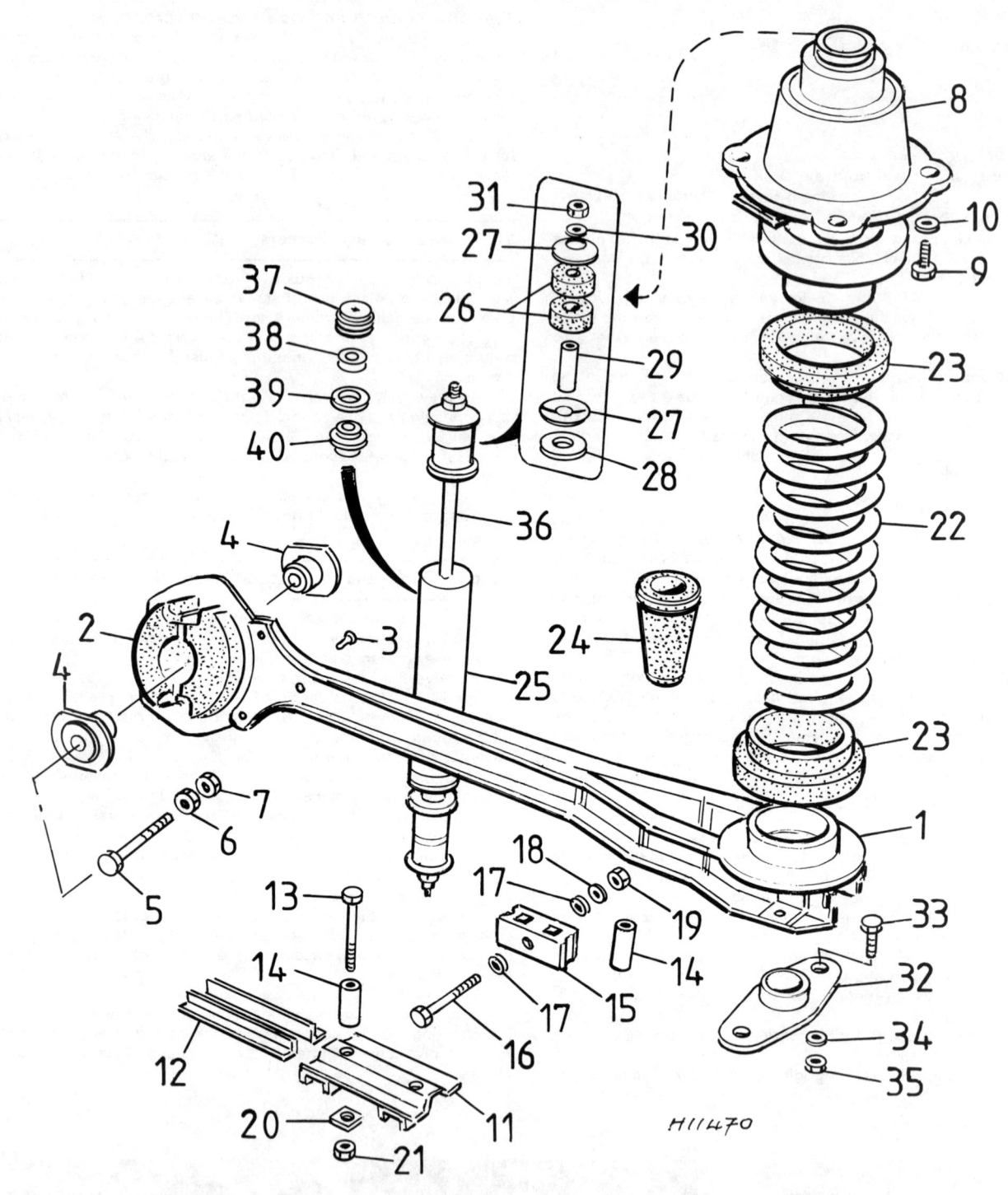

Fig. 8.13 Exploded view of rear suspension components (Sec 18)

1	Radius arm	11	Lug shim	21	Nut	31	Nut
2	Rubber bush	12	Rubber insert	22	Spring	32	Bracket
3	Rivet	13	Screw	23	Rubber washers	33	Bolt
4	Packing	14	Spacers	24	Bump stop	34	Washer
5	Bolt	15	Spacer	25	Shock absorber	35	Nut
6	Nut	16	Bolt	26	Rubber inserts	36	Piston rod
7	Nut	17	Washer	27	Washers	37	Plug
8	Upper mounting	18	Washer	28	Packing	38	Seal
9	Screw	19	Nut	29	Spacer	39	Seal
10	Washer	20	Lockwasher	30	Washer	40	Guide

19 Radius arms – general

1   The radius arms are attached to the half axle at the rear and pivot on a bolt at the front mounting to the underbody. The radius arms can only be removed complete with half axle (see Chapter 7). It is not permissible to detach the arms from the half axle as this would alter the rear axle/suspension geometry.

2   Should it be absolutely necessary to separate the two, then this should be entrusted to your Skoda dealer who will be able to realign the axle and arm using the specialised equipment necessary.

3   The front pivot bolt and washer/bush can be removed for renewal without lowering the arm providing it is supported by a jack underneath (photo).

19.3 Removing the radius arm forward pivot bolt

20 Fault diagnosis – front hubs, suspension and steering

Before diagnosing faults from the following chart, check that any irregularities are not caused by:
1 *Binding brakes*
2 *Incorrect 'mix' of radial and crossply tyres*
3 *Incorrect tyre presures*
4 *Misalignment of the bodyframe or rear axle*

Symptom	Reason(s)
Steering vague, car wanders and floats at speed	Front wheel alignment incorrect Steering joints worn Steering box maladjusted or worn Front wheel bearings maladjusted or worn
Steering heavy and stiff (refer to Section 16)	Front wheel alignment incorrect Steering joint(s) or kingpin seized Steering box or idler inadequately lubricated
Excessive pitch or roll when cornering or braking	Shock absorber(s) defective or loose Coil spring(s) weak or broken Anti-roll bar damaged or loose
Rattles or knocks	Rubber bushes deteriorated Shock absorber(s) defective or loose Steering joints worn Steering box or idler loose Spring(s) weak or broken
Car sits low at one corner	Spring weak or broken Incorrect replacement spring fitted Shock absorber defective

Chapter 9 Braking system

For modifications, and information applicable to later models, see Supplement at end of manual

Contents

Specifications

System type .... Disc brakes at front, drums at rear. Dual circuit hydraulic operation. Handbrake mechanical to rear wheels

Disc brakes
Disc diameter .... 252.5 mm (9.9 in)
Disc thickness:
    New .... 9 mm (0.354 in)
    Minimum after regrinding .... 7.5 mm (0.295 in)
    Minimum due to wear .... 6.5 mm (0.256 in)
Maximum disc run-out .... 0.15 mm (0.006 in)
Pad thickness:
    New .... 15 mm (0.59 in)
    Minimum allowable .... 7.5 mm (0.295 in)

Drum brakes
Drum internal diameter:
    New .... 230 mm (9.06 in)
    Maximum after regrinding .... 231 mm (9.10 in)
    Maximum due to wear .... 232 mm (9.13 in)
Brake shoe lining thickness:
    New .... 5 mm (0.197 in)
    Minimum allowable .... 1 mm (0.039 in)

Brake pedal free travel .... 3 to 5 mm (0.12 to 0.20 in)

Torque wrench settings

	Nm	lbf ft
Brake disc bolts	48 to 60	35 to 44
Caliper yoke bolts	70 to 95	52 to 70
Caliper yoke bracket bolt	19 to 25	14 to 18
Rear brake wheel cylinder bolts	40 to 50	30 to 37
Brake backplate bolts	23	17
Axleshaft nut*	220	165

* Tighten further if necessary to align nearest split pin hole

1 General description and maintenance

Both the front disc brakes and the rear drum brakes are hydraulically actuated. The hydraulic circuit is shown in Figure 9.1, where it can be seen that the principal components in the system are the brake fluid reservoir and master cylinder unit, the respective circuit lines to each brake unit and the caliper units (front) and wheel cylinder units (rear).

The hydraulic circuit operates when pressure on the foot brake pedal moves a piston in the master cylinder. The moving piston pumps the fluid in the cylinder into the pipe lines under pressure, and thus forces the wheel cylinder or caliper pistons to move out, pushing the shoes or pads against the brake drums or disc as they do so.

When the brake pedal pressure is released the brake shoes or pads retract under spring tension and the fluid displaced from the master cylinder is returned.

The master cylinder is of tandem type, incorporating two pistons and seal assemblies, which operate simultaneously. The front piston operates the forward brakes and the rear piston the rear brakes. The

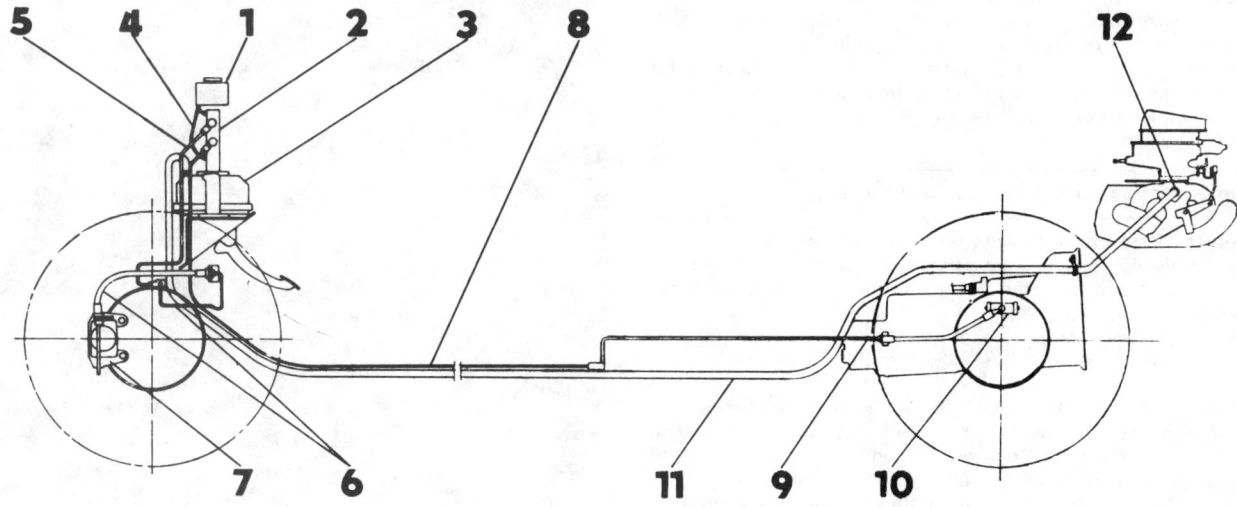

Fig. 9.1 Braking system layout (Sec 1)

1 Fluid reservoir	5 Front brake line	9 Rear brake line
2 Master cylinder	6 Front brake line and flexible hose	10 Wheel cylinder
3 Servo (if fitted)	7 Disc caliper unit	11 Servo vacuum line (if fitted)
4 Supply line	8 Rear brake line	12 Servo manifold connection (if fitted)

advantage of this type of braking unit is that if the front circuit should fail for any reason, the rear circuit will still operate and vice versa.

On some models the brake system is power-assisted by a servo unit (brake booster) attached to the master cylinder. The servo draws its vacuum from the inlet manifold of the engine.

The handbrake lever is located between the front seats and this actuates the rear brakes only, by means of cables.

Brake adjustment both front and rear is automatic, whilst the handbrake cable can be adjusted independently.

Routine maintenance

1 Maintenance procedures on the brake system are minimal, but it is essential that the following checks be made at the prescribed intervals.

2 Make a weekly check on the brake fluid reservoir to ensure that the fluid is at the specified level which is 5 mm (0.2 in) below the tank upper wall.

If the fluid is below this level, top up the reservoir with the correct type of brake fluid. It is vital that no other type of brake fluid is used. Use of a non-standard fluid will result in brake failure caused by the perishing of the special seals in the master and brake cylinders. If topping up becomes frequent then check the metal piping and flexible hose for leaks, and check for worn brake or master cylinders which will also cause loss of fluid. Take great care not to spill hydraulic fluid on the paintwork when topping up the reservoir, as the fluid will damage any paintwork it comes into contact with.

3 Every 12 000 miles (20 000 km) check the brake disc pads and linings for wear. If worn to the minimum allowable thickness they must be renewed.

4 An occasional check must be made to ensure that the hydraulic pipes and connections are in good condition and secure. If there are signs of leakage or corrosion, renew the section(s) concerned.

2 Disc brake pads – removal, inspection and refitting

1 Jack up the front of the car and remove the relevant roadwheel.

2 Unscrew the filler cap of the hydraulic fluid reservoir and stretch a piece of thin polythene over the top of the neck and replace the cap. This prevents excessive leakage of brake fluid when the flexible hose connecting the front brake is removed.

3 Remove the disc pad cover by withdrawing the two R-clips (photo) and extracting the cover retaining pins (photo).

4 Now remove the disc pads by simply pulling out, noting from which side each pad came if they are to be reinserted (photo).

5 The pads should be renewed when any one is worn to the minimum thickness specified, or if they will be before the next inspection.

6 Disc pads must be renewed in whole axle sets, even if only one is worn to the limit. Do not interchange pads in an attempt to equalise wear.

7 Refitting the pads is a reversal of removal. However, if new pads are being fitted in place of worn ones it may be necessary to push the

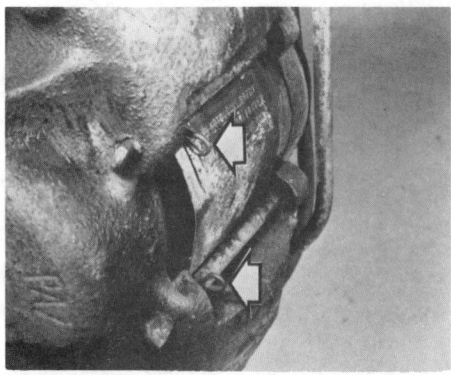

2.3a Withdraw the R-clips (arrowed) ...

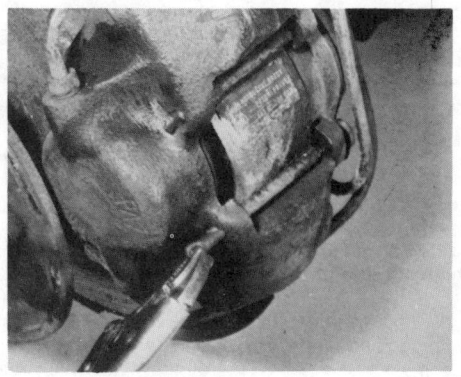

2.3b ... and extract the pins and retaining plate

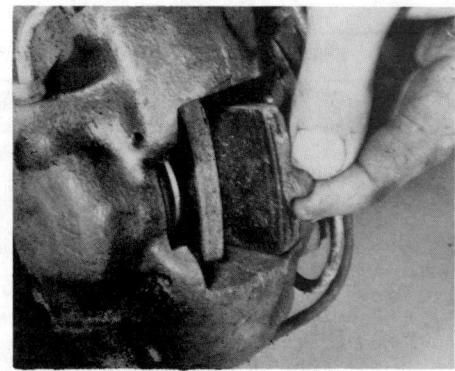

2.4 Withdraw the pads

caliper pistons into their bores to allow sufficient clearance. This action can cause the brake fluid reservoir to overflow, so remove its cap and wrap a rag around the reservoir to catch spilt fluid.

8   Disc brakes are self-adjusting. However, it may be necessary to pump the brake pedal a few times to bring the pads into contact with the disc after work has been carried out.

3   Disc brake caliper unit – removal and refitting

1   Jack up the front of the car and remove the front wheel(s).
2   Clamp the flexible hose to the caliper unit at the brake end (to prevent excess fluid spillage), then disconnect the hydraulic pipe at the caliper bracket (photo).
3   Plug the hydraulic connection in the caliper and the pipe to prevent the ingress of dirt – cleanliness is essential when working the hydraulics.
4   Unscrew and remove the caliper retaining bolts and lift the caliper clear of the disc. As the caliper is removed, note the thickness of packing shims used for correct caliper location.
5   To dismantle and overhaul the caliper refer to Section 4.
6   Refit the caliper in the reverse order to removal. If the original caliper is being refitted, be sure to fit it using the same number of packing shims between the caliper and location lugs. When bolted in position the distance between the lug and the disc must be as shown in Fig. 9.2.
7   If a new or replacement caliper unit is being fitted, select suitable shims to set the caliper position as specified.
8   On completion bleed the brakes and top up the hydraulic reservoir as given in Section 12.

4   Disc brake caliper unit – overhaul

1   Having removed the caliper unit (see Section 3), clean it externally.
2   Remove the brake pads as given in Section 2.
3   Remove the interconnecting hydraulic pipe.
4   Unscrew and remove the four screws and detach the yoke cylinder from the flange cylinder.
5   Remove the dust boot.
6   To extract the piston from its cylinder, connect a foot pump to the hydraulic inlet and inject some air into the orifice to eject the piston. Catch the piston as it is ejected to prevent it being damaged.
7   Remove the seal and, if required, the bleed nipple.
8   Do not under any circumstances remove the brake pad guide abutments as these are preset at the factory.
9   Clean the respective components in methylated spirit and wipe dry with a clean lint-free cloth for inspection.
10   Check the piston and cylinder bore for signs of scratches, wear or damage. Renew if necessary.
11   The seal must automatically be renewed, and a new dust boot also fitted on assembly.
12   Reassembly is a reversal of the dismantling procedure, but when fitting the piston and seal, smear them with some clean hydraulic fluid to ease entry and fitting. Check that the dust boot and retaining ring are securely fitted. Do not overtighten the retaining screws of the caliper or the interconnecting hydraulic pipe retainers, or distortion and leakage may occur.

5   Brake disc – removal, inspection and refitting

1   To remove the brake disc, follow the instructions given in Section 3. Remove the brake caliper unit, but leave its hydraulic connections intact.
2   Then undo the hub nut as described in Chapter 8.
3   Undo the four retaining bolts and remove the disc from the hub.
4   If the disc is badly scored it should be renewed, but it is sometimes possible to have the disc re-machined in an engineering machine shop to remove normal wear marks. The minimum possible disc thickness is given in the Specifications.
5   If the disc is machined the amount of metal removed must be equal on each face. Run-out must not exceed that specified. This can be checked with a dial gauge.
6   Refitting the disc is a reversal of the removal procedure.

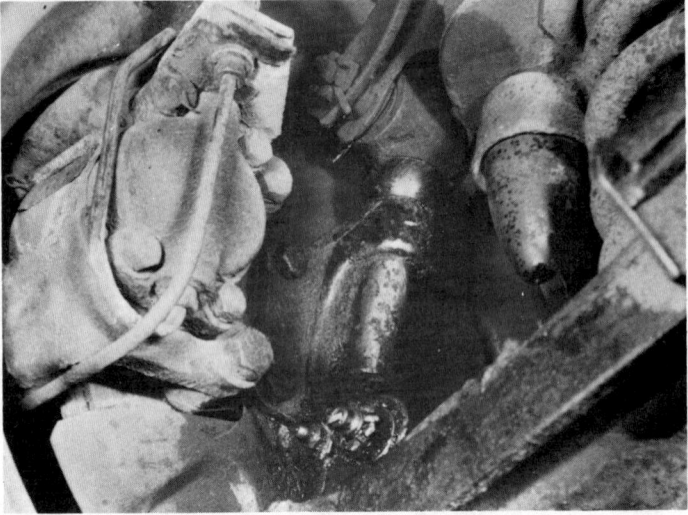

3.2 Caliper and hydraulic pipe connections

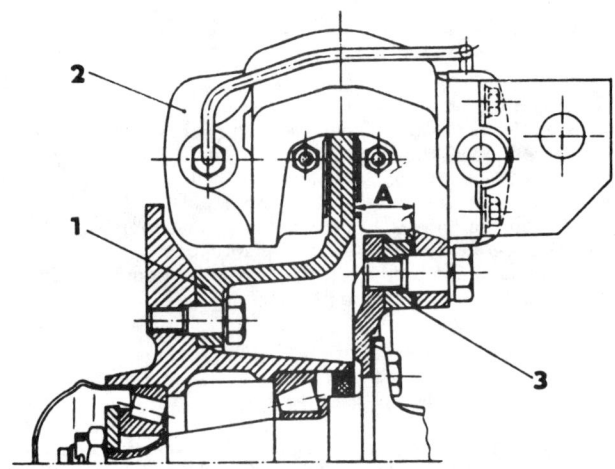

Fig. 9.2 Sectional view of caliper and disc (Sec 3)

1 Disc	2 Caliper	3 Shims

$A = 18.7 \pm 0.2$ mm (0.736 ± 0.008 in)

6   Rear brake drums and shoes – removal, inspection and refitting

1   The brake drums at the rear also serve as the hubs. As mentioned in Chapter 7, Section 5, a special puller is required to remove the drums before any work may be carried out on the brakes or hubs. If the puller is available proceed as follows.
2   Jack up the rear of the car, support firmly on axle stands and remove the roadwheel. Release the handbrake. Remove the upper plug in the brake backplate and use a screwdriver to back off the swinging arm of the self-adjusting mechanism.
3   Withdraw the split pin and unscrew the hub nut.
4   With the special puller, remove the brake drum/hub. The brake shoes and wheel cylinder are now exposed.
5   The brake linings should be renewed if they are worn down to, or near, the specified thickness. As the linings are bonded in position on the brake shoes they will have to be exchanged complete or new linings put on by a brake specialist.
6   To remove the brake shoes, first remove the shoe location washer and spring by rotating the washer with a pair of pliers, so that the slot aligns with the head of the pin, and then withdraw the whole assembly.

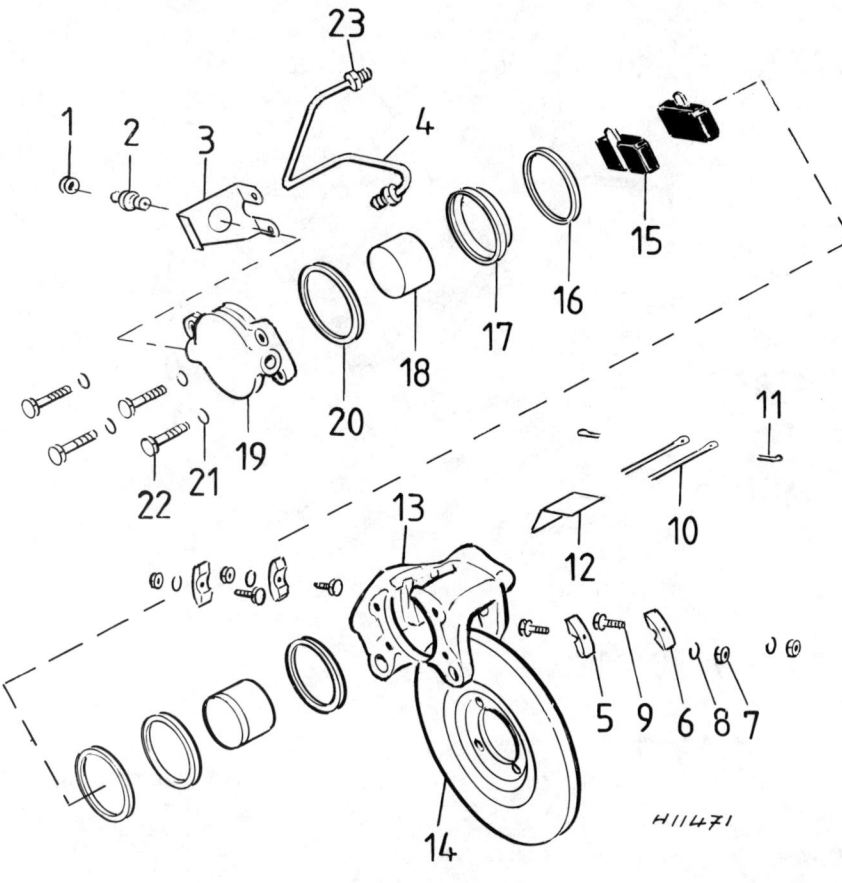

Fig. 9.3 Front brake components (Sec 4)

1	Dust cap
2	Bleed nipple
3	Bracket
4	Pipe
5	Pad bracket
6	Pad bracket
7	Nut
8	Washer
9	Bolt
10	Guide pin
11	Pin retainer
12	Cover
13	Yoke
14	Disc
15	Pad
16	Lockring
17	Dust boot
18	Piston
19	Cylinder
20	Seal
21	Washer
22	Bolt
23	Union

10 Tie a piece of string or place an elastic band around the wheel cylinder to prevent piston movement. Do not apply pressure to the brake pedal while the shoes are removed, as this will eject the pistons, necessitating brake bleeding.

11 Thoroughly clean all traces of dust from the brake shoes, backplate, and brake drums, using a dry paintbrush. Do not inhale the dust as it is harmful.

12 Check that the rubber dust covers are in good order on the wheel cylinders, and that there are no hydraulic fluid leaks.

13 Before reassembly, smear a trace of brake grease to the sliding surfaces.

14 Refitting is a straightforward reversal of the removal procedure, but note the following points:

  (a) Do not omit to replace the shoe steady pins and springs.
  (b) Ensure that the return springs are in their correct holes. To fit the springs locate one end in its location hole and engage a screwdriver into the hooked end of the spring still disengaged. Use the screwdriver as a lever to stretch and locate it spring end
  (c) Refit the hub unit, referring to Chapter 7
  (d) Adjust the handbrake as given in Section 13

Fig. 9.4 Sectional views of brake assembly (Sec 6)

7 Unhook the retractor spring which connects the two shoes at the top by prising with a screwdriver, and then unhook the lower spring in a similar fashion.

8 Detach the handbrake cable from the rear brake shoe lever.

9 Now remove the brake shoes complete with the distance lever.

7 Rear wheel cylinder – removal, overhaul and refitting

1 To inspect, remove or replace the rear wheel slave cylinder, it is necessary to remove the rear wheels, brake drums and brake shoes, as described in Section 6.

2 Before disconnecting the hydraulic hose connection from the backplate, remove the hydraulic fluid reservoir filler cap and place a piece of polythene over the seal and replace the cap. This restricts the flow of the fluid from the disconnected pipe.

3 Now remove the connecting pipe from the backplate. Note the pipe angle and be sure to refit at this angle to prevent chafing of the hose of the radius arm. Temporarily tie the hose out of the way and plug the end to prevent the ingress of dirt.

4 Remove the brake bleed nipple and disconnect the cylinder from the backplate by undoing the two bolts (photo).

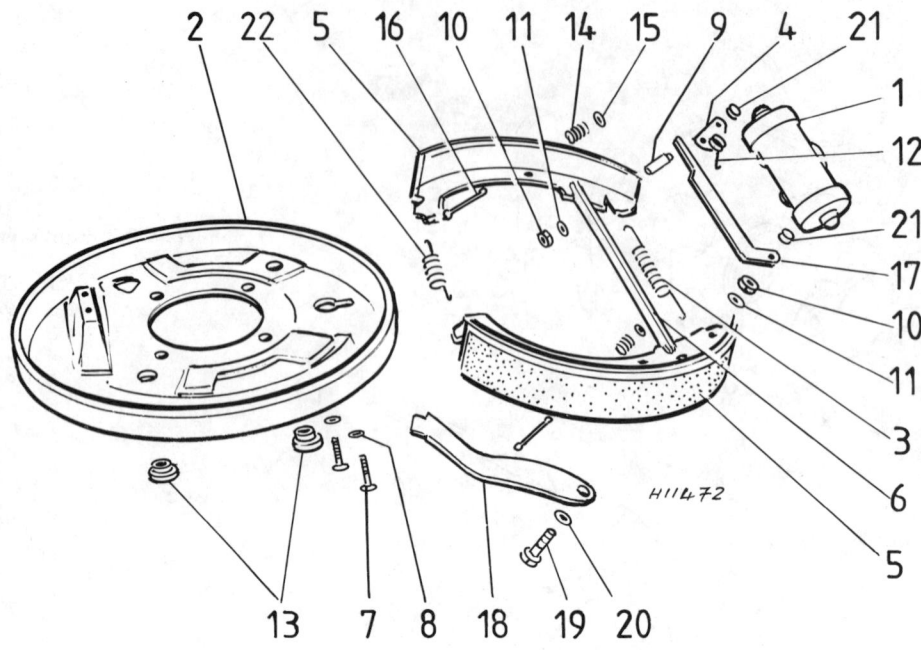

Fig. 9.5 Rear brake components (Sec 6)

1	Wheel cylinder	7	Screw	13	Plugs	18	Handbrake lever
2	Backplate	8	Washer	14	Spring	19	Pin
3	Spring	9	Pin	15	Location washer	20	Washer
4	Swinging arm	10	Nut	16	Location pin	21	Ring
5	Shoe	11	Washer	17	Self-adjuster lever	22	Spring
6	Lever	12	Spring				

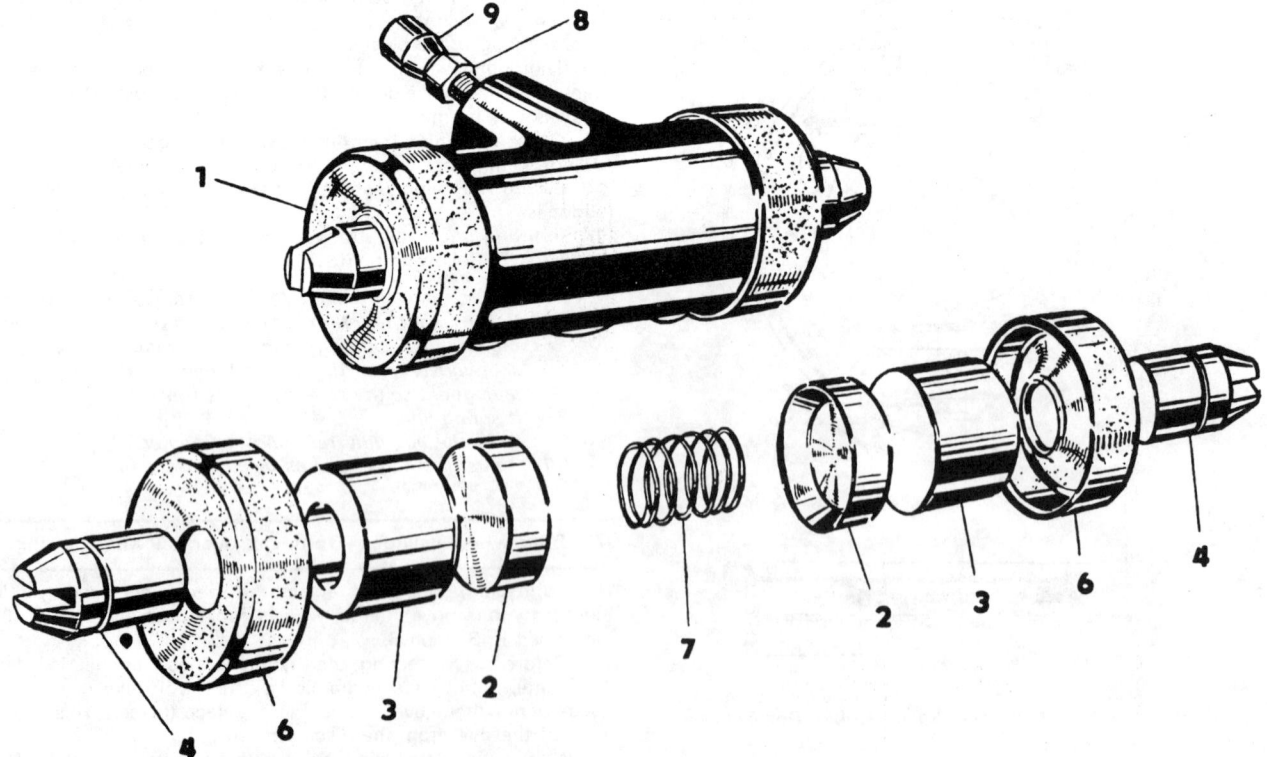

Fig. 9.6 Wheel cylinder components (Sec 7)

1	Wheel cylinder	3	Pistons	6	Dust covers	8	Bleed nipple
2	Seals	4	Pushrods	7	Spring	9	Dust cap

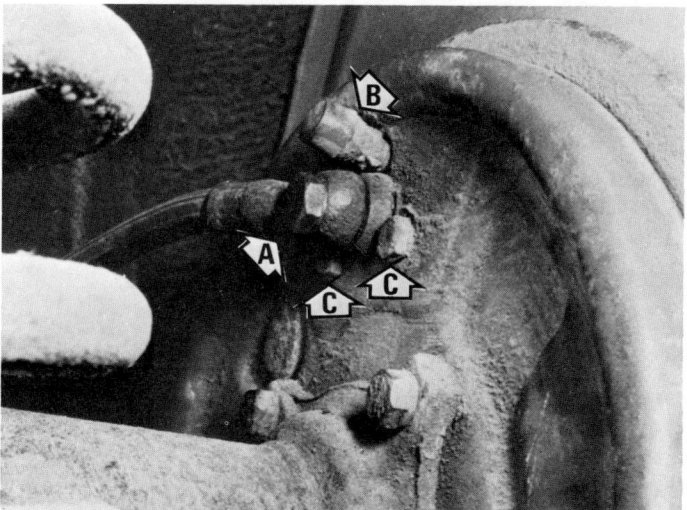

7.4 Rear brake hydraulic connection (A), bleed nipple (B) and wheel cylinder retaining bolts (C)

8.3 The feed pipes (arrowd) to the brake master cylinder

5   Thoroughly clean off the outside of the cylinder and remove to the workbench, where it may be stripped down on a sheet of clean paper. Cleanliness during dismantling, inspection and reassembly is essential.

6   To strip for inspection, remove from each end of the cylinder, the two dust seal rubbers, then remove the pistons and slotted rods and finally the inner seals and spring.

7   Clean all parts thoroughly and inspect the seals for signs of wear or perishing, and the pistons and cylinder bore for scratches or pitting – renew as required. Replacement seals are usually readily available and are relatively inexpensive.

8   Reassembly of the cylinder unit is a straight reversal of dismantling, but when fitting the seals, smear with some hydraulic fluid to ease entry into the bore. The lip of the seal should face away from the piston.

9   On refitting the cylinders to the backplate, reconnect the hydraulic pipe, brake shoes, drum/hub and wheel and then bleed the hydraulic system, as described in Section 12.

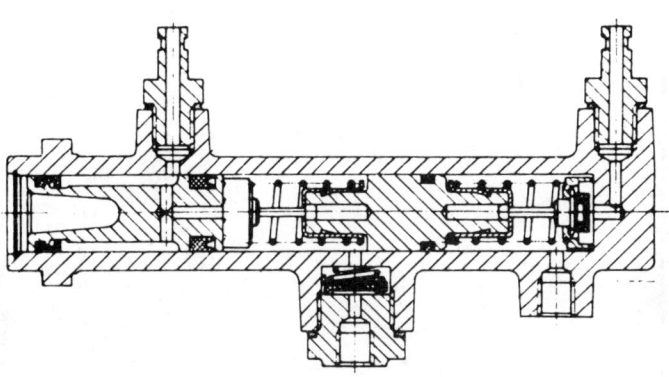

Fig. 9.7 Sectional view of brake master cylinder (Sec 8)

8   Master cylinder – removal and refitting

1   The brake system incorporates a dual hydraulic circuit in which there are effectively two control cylinders in line with each other. Each piston within its respective part of the cylinder moves simultaneously. The front piston operates the front wheel disc brakes and the rear piston the rear drum brakes. If one circuit fails the other still operates.

2   It will be noted on dismantling the hydraulic pipe unions that two types of valve are used. The rear circuit valve does not have a hole in it, unlike the front circuit valve which has. **The two valves must not be interchanged.**

3   Remove and refit the unit as follows, having detached the plastic cover. It is first necessary to drain the reservoir fluid into a clean container. This can be done by siphoning out through the filler neck or by undoing the feed pipe to the master cylinder (photo). Be careful not to spill any brake fluid onto the car bodywork. On servo-equipped models, do not allow fluid to spill onto the rubber seal of the operating rod.

4   Unscrew the remaining hydraulic pipe connections to the cylinder body.

5   Unscrew and remove the cylinder flange retaining nuts and then carefully withdraw the cylinder unit, taking care not to spill any remaining fluid.

6   Refit in the reverse order and when all the pipes are reconnected, top up and bleed the system as described in Section 12. Then check and adjust the pedal rod-to-piston clearance and adjust if necessary as given in Section 17. On servo-equipped models refer to Section 10 and adjust the servo operating rod-to-master cylinder piston clearance.

9   Master cylinder – dismantling, overhaul and reassembly

1   Refer to Fig 9.7 and 9.8. Thoroughly clean the outside of the cylinder unit before dismantling.

2   Remove the rubber boot from the rear of the cylinder and take out the circlip from the bore of the cylinder.

3   The two pistons and their respective components may then be extracted from the cylinder. Do this carefully, taking note of the order of dismantling and the relative positions of all components as they are withdrawn.

4   Having dismantled, lay the parts out in order on a clean surface after cleaning them thoroughly with hydraulic fluid. Inspect the cylinder bore and pistons for pitting or general wear, renew as necessary. Piston seals should be renewed as a matter of course.

5   Reassembly is the reverse order to dismantling, but note the following points:

(a)   *Special care should be taken not to overstretch the new seals when fitting to the pistons*

(b)   *Ensure that the valves and stems are correctly located and do not distort the piston cups when fitting*

(c)   *Lubricate all parts in clean hydraulic fluid prior to assembly*

6   Note that the master cylinders differ in internal diameter, depending on whether a servo is fitted, and although they are similar in construction the two cylinders are not interchangeable.

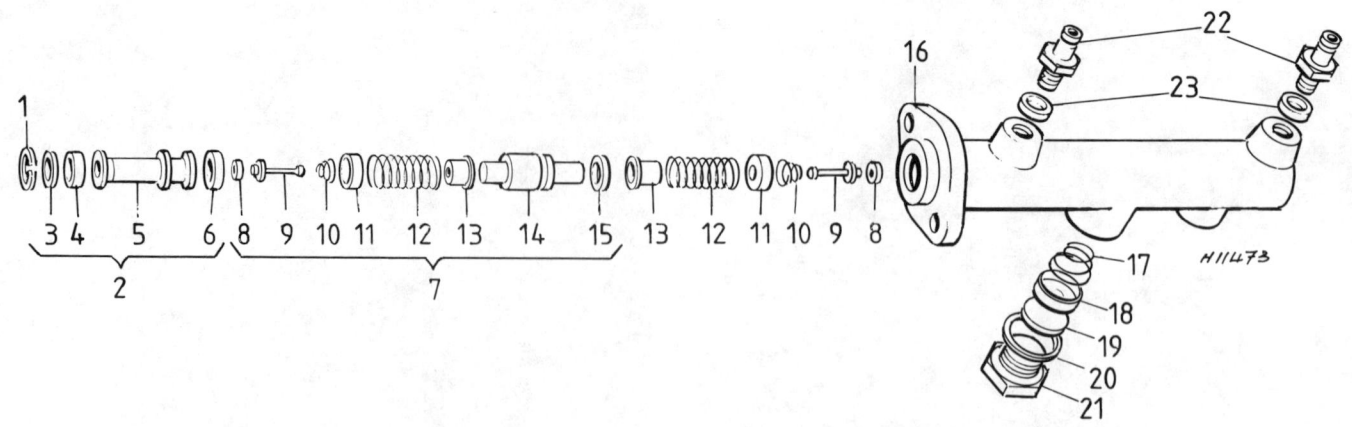

Fig. 9.8 Brake master cylinder components (Sec 8)

1 Circlip	7 Secondary piston assembly	13 Retaining plates	19 Valve packing
2 Primary piston assembly	8 Valves	14 Secondary piston	20 Sealing ring
3 Cap ring	9 Shanks	15 Sealing ring	21 Outlet union
4 Seal	10 Springs	16 Body	22 Inlet unions
5 Primary piston	11 Bushes	17 Spring	23 Sealing rings
6 Cup	12 Springs	18 Valve body	

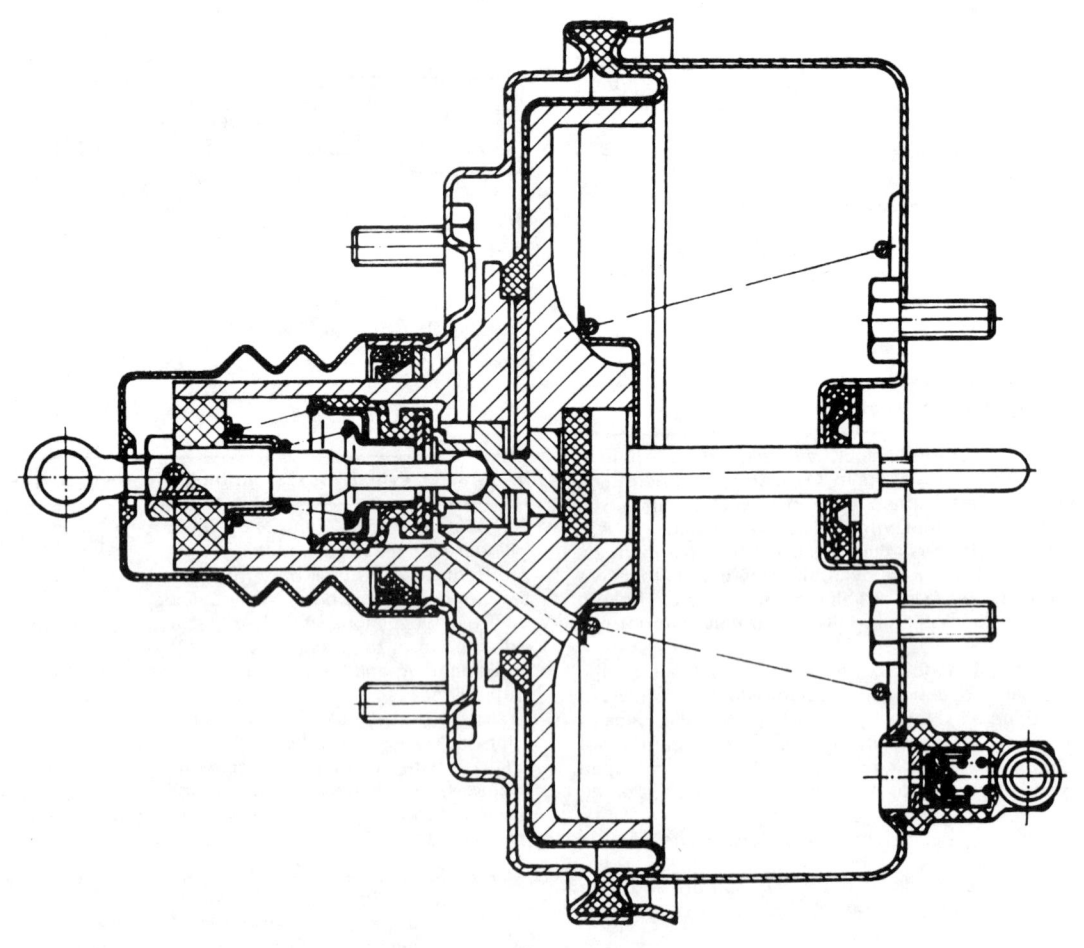

Fig. 9.9 Sectional view of the brake servo unit fitted to some models (Sec 10)

10 Brake servo unit – removal and refitting

1   A sectional view of the servo unit is shown in Fig. 9.9. The servo (brake booster) unit is fitted to some 120 models. It does not normally give any trouble and requires only the minimum of maintenance, which consists of checking the unit for security and the condition of the vacuum hose to the inlet manifold.

2   If the servo unit is defective there is little that the home mechanic can do to repair it and it should therefore be removed and either exchanged for a new replacement or entrusted to your Skoda dealer for repair.

3   The servo unit is located between the master cylinder and pedal bracket. To remove the unit first detach the master cylinder as described in Section 8.

4   Disconnect the brake pedal from the piston rod.

5   Detach the vacuum hose from the servo unit.

6   Remove the vacuum unit retaining nuts from the pedal bracket and withdraw the servo complete.

7   Refitting is a reversal of the removal process, but the clearance between the servo operating rod and the master cylinder piston must be checked and adjusted if necessary. To do this, calculate the clearance between the cylinder bottom recess and the cylinder flange mating surface. Measure the length of the servo operating rod protruding beyond the servo mating flange surface. Compare the measurements and if necessary adjust accordingly to give a clearance of 0.5 to 1 mm (0.019 to 0.039 in) between the piston and the press button.

8   If on assembly the brake and clutch pedals are not level, readjust the length of the servo operating rod by removing the servo unit, detaching the collar and refitting the servo temporarily to the pedal. Now adjust the rod by rotating the hexagon to level up the pedal positions. Remove the servo, refit the collar and relocate the servo.

9   It is emphasised that even if the servo unit fails completely, brake position is not affected. Higher pedal pressure will be needed to achieve the same braking effect, as will also be the case if the brakes are used when the engine is not running (eg when being towed).

11 Hydraulic fluid pipes and fittings – inspection, removal and refitting

1   Periodically and certainly well in advance of the DoT Test, if due, all brake pipes, connections and unions, should be completely and carefully examined.

2   Examine first all the unions for signs of leaks. Then look at the flexible hoses for signs of fraying and chafing (as well as for leaks). This is only a preliminary inspection of the flexible hoses, as exterior condition does not necessarily indicate interior condition which will be considered later.

3   The metal pipes must be examined equally carefully. They must be thoroughly cleaned and examined for signs of dents or other percussive damage, rust and corrosion. Rust and corrosion should be scraped off, and, if the depth of pitting in the pipes is significant, they will need renewal. This is most likely in those areas underneath the body and near the rear suspension arms where the pipes are exposed to the full force of road and weather conditions. Also check the pipe connections at the three-way joint junctions at the front and rear.

4   In particular inspect the front feed pipe to the disc brake caliper flexible hose joint. The metal pipe must be close fitting to the inner wing panel to avoid the tyre rubbing against it when on full lock. Also check this pipe to ensure it is not being fouled by the wishbone arm and, if necessary, reposition the pipe by bending out of the way. The loop pipe over the disc brake caliper unit has also been known to rub against the disc and there should therefore be a clearance of at least 0.25 in (6 mm).

5   At the rear, check that the flexible pipes are not rubbing against the radius arms when the suspension is compressed.

6   If any section of pipe is to be removed, first take off the fluid reservoir cap, line it with a piece of polythene film to make it airtight and screw it back on. This will minimise the amount of fluid dripping out of the system when the pipes are removed.

7   Rigid pipe removal is usually quite straightforward. The unions at each end are undone and the pipe drawn out of the connection. The clips which hold it to the car body are bent back and it is then removed. Underneath the car the exposed union can be particularly

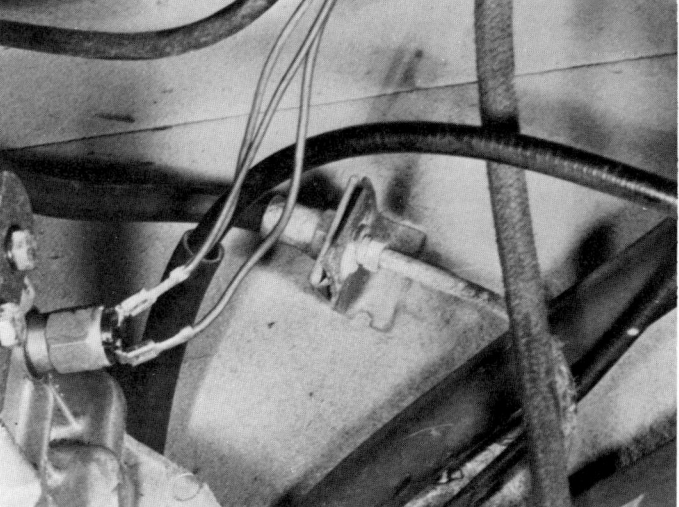

11.8 Typical flexible-to-rigid hydraulic pipe bracket

stubborn, defying the efforts of an open-ended spanner. As few people will have the special split ring spanner required, a self-grip wrench is the only answer. If the pipe is being renewed, new unions will be provided. If not, then one will have to put up with the possibility of burring over the flats on the union and of using a self-grip wrench for refitting also.

8   Flexible hoses are always fitted to a rigid support bracket where they join a rigid pipe (photo). The rigid pipe unions must first be removed from the flexible union, releasing the end of the pipe from the bracket. As these connections are usually exposed they are, more often than not, rusted up and a penetrating fluid is virtually essential to aid removal. When undoing them, both halves must be supported as the bracket is not strong enough to support the torque required to undo the nut and can be snapped off easily.

9   Once the flexible hose is removed, examine the internal bore. If clear of fluid it should be possible to see through it. Any specks of rubber which come out, or signs of restriction in the bore, mean that the inner lining is breaking up and the pipe must be renewed.

10   Rigid pipes which need renewal can usally be purchased at your local garage where they have the pipe, unions and special tools to make them up. All that they need to know is the pipe length required and the type of flare used at the ends of the pipe. These may be different at each end of the same pipe.

11   Refitment of pipes is a straightforward reversal of the removal procedure. It is best to get all the sets (bends) in the pipe made preparatory to installation. Also any acute bends should be put in by the garage on a bending maching, otherwise there is the possibility of kinking them and restricting the bore area and fluid flow.

12   Rigid brake pipes are now available made of copper or copper alloy. Whilst such pipes are obviously immune from rusting, it must be remembered that copper may fatigue and break up subject to vibration. Follow the maker's instructions carefully if such pipes are used; extra pipe support clips may be necessary.

12 Hydraulic system – bleeding

1   If any of the hydraulic components in the braking system have been removed or disconnected, or if the fluid level in the master cylinder has been allowed to fall appreciably, it is inevitable that air will have been introduced into the system. The removal of air from the hydraulic system is essential if the brakes are to function correctly, and the process of removing it is known as bleeding.

2   There are a number of one-man, do-it-yourself, brake bleeding kits currently available from motor accessory shops. It is recommended that one of these kits should be used wherever possible as they greatly simplify the bleeding operation and also reduce the risk of expelled air or fluid being drawn back into the system.

3   If one of these kits is not available then it will be necessary to gather a clean jar and a suitable length of clear plastic tubing which is

a tight fit over the bleed screw, and also to engage the help of an assistant.

4   Before commencing the bleeding operation, check that all rigid pipes and flexible hoses are in good condition and that all hydraulic unions are tight. Take great care not to allow hydraulic fluid to come into contact with the vehicle paintwork, otherwise the finish will be seriously damaged. Wash off any spilled fluid immediately with cold water.

5   If hydraulic fluid has been lost from the master cylinder, due to a leak in the system, ensure that the cause is traced and rectified before proceeding further or a serious malfunction of the braking system may occur.

6   To bleed the system, clean the area around the bleed screw at the wheel cylinder to be bled. If the hydraulic system has only been partially disconnected and suitable precautions were taken to prevent further loss of fluid, it should only be necessary to bleed that part of the system. However, if the entire system is to be bled, start at the wheel furthest away from the master cylinder.

7   Remove the master cylinder filler cap and top up the reservoir. Periodically check the fluid level during the bleeding operation and top up as necessary, using only new brake fluid of the specified type.

8   If a one-man brake bleeding kit is being used, connect the outlet tube to the bleed screw (photo) and then open the screw half a turn. If possible position the unit so that it can be viewed from the car, then depress the brake pedal to the floor and slowly release it. The one-way valve in the kit will prevent dispelled air from returning to the system at the end of each stroke. Repeat this operation until clean hydraulic fluid, free from air bubbles, can be seen coming through the tube. Now tighten the bleed screw and remove the outlet tube.

9   If a one-man brake bleeding kit is not available, connect one end of the plastic tubing to the bleed screw and immerse the other end in the jar containing sufficient clean hydraulic fluid to keep the end of the tube submerged. Open the bleed screw half a turn and have your assistant depress the brake pedal to the floor and then slowly release it. Tighten the bleed screw at the end of each downstroke to prevent expelled air and fluid from being drawn back into the system. Repeat this operation until clean hydraulic fluid, free from air bubbles, can be seen coming through the tube. Now tighten the bleed screw and remove the plastic tube.

10   If the entire system is being bled the procedures described above should now be repeated at each wheel, finishing at the wheel nearest to the master cylinder. Do not forget to recheck the fluid level in the master cylinder at regular intervals and top up as necessary.

11   When completed, recheck the fluid level in the reservoir, top up if necessary and refit the cap. Check the feel of the brake pedal which should be firm and free from any sponginess which would indicate air still present in the system.

12   Discard any expelled hydraulic fluid as it is likely to be contaminated with moisture, air and dirt which makes it unsuitable for further use.

13 Handbrake – adjustment

1   The handbrake does not normally require adjustment as it is automatically adjusted by the rear brake/self-adjusting mechanism. However, if there is play in the handbrake mechanism proceed as follows.

2   Jack up the rear of the car so that the rear wheels clear the ground, and place chocks in front of and behind the front wheels.

3   From inside the car, fold forward the carpet over the central tunnel just in front of the rear seat, and remove the cover plate to reveal the handbrake tie-rod and cable mechanism (photo).

4   Position the handbrake in the fully off position, and then apply it so that it is located on its second notch.

5   The cables to each rear brake can now be adjusted in turn by tightening the regulating nuts as required to take up any slack in either cable.

6   When the adjustment has been made, release the handbrake to the fully off position and spin the wheels to ensure that the handbrake is fully released.

14 Handbrake cables – removal and refitting

1   Disengage the front end of the cable concerned from the rocker arm by unscrewing and removing the adjuster nut.

2   Detach the cable retainer from the rear axle radius arm.

3   Prise free the rubber plug from the brake backplate and working through the exposed hole, detach the cable from the relay lever of the brake mechanism within the drum. Extract the cable retaining ring from the rear of the sheath and withdraw the cable.

4   Fitting is a reversal of the removal procedure, but adjust the cable to complete (Section 13).

15 Handbrake lever – removal and refitting

1   Little attention is ever needed by the handbrake lever unit apart from occasionally lubricating the lever hinge pin and ratchet. If it is to be removed, proceed as follows.

2   Remove the floor covering from the central tunnel to reveal the handbrake mounting point and handbrake cable adjustment access just forward of the rear seats.

3   Unscrew the regulating nuts from the cables.

4   Undo the handbrake ratchet plate bolts.

5   Remove the split pin and disconnect the pivot pin of the handbrake lever, and lift the lever clear.

6   Disconnect the handbrake lever from the ratchet plate by removing the split pin and withdrawing the locating pin. The tie-rod, spring and press button may also be removed, if required.

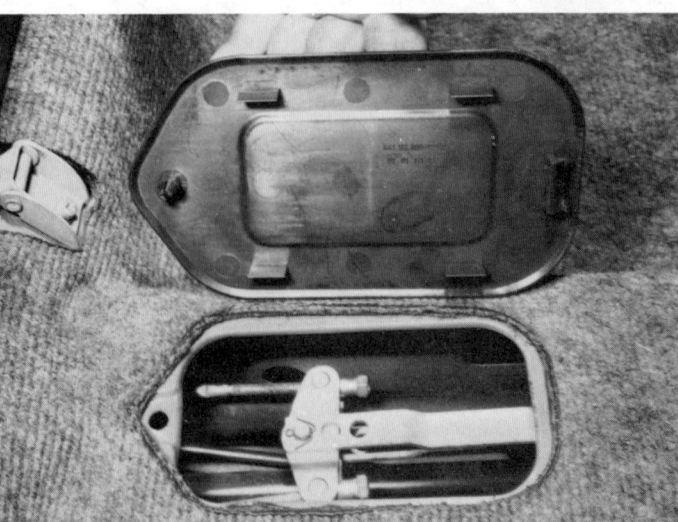

12.8 A one-man brake bleeding kit connected to a front disc brake caliper unit

13.3 Handbrake cable adjusters

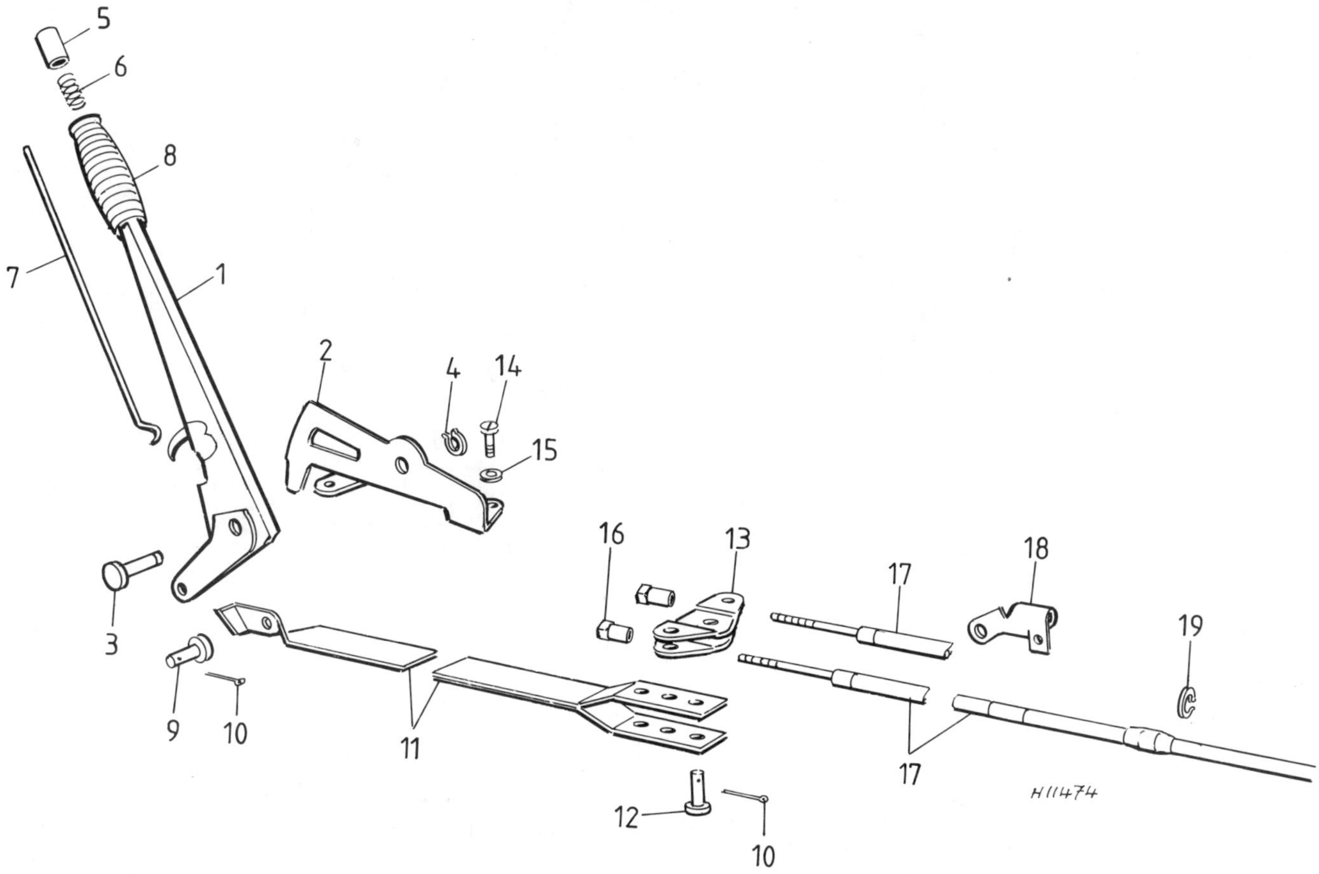

Fig. 9.10 Handbrake lever and linkage components (Sec 15)

1	Lever	6	Spring	11	Yoke	16	Nuts
2	Ratchet	7	Pawl link	12	Pin	17	Cables
3	Pivot pin	8	Grip	13	Rocker arm	18	Clip
4	Circlip	9	Pin	14	Screw	19	Circlip
5	Push button	10	Split pins	15	Washer		

7   Refitting is a reversal of removal, but the handbrake must be readjusted, as described in Section 13, on completion.

16 Brake switches

1   Two switches are fitted to the brake pedal bracket, being the stoplight switch and the pedal travel warning switch (photo).
2   Both switches are retained by screws and can easily be removed if necessary once these screws are extracted. Disconnect the battery earth lead and detach the switch wires at the connectors for complete removal from the car. Note the packing piece under the pedal travel warning switch.
3   Refit in the reverse order but adjust (if necessary) the stoplight switch so that it is activated after a pedal travel of 10 to 15 mm (0.39 to 0.59 in).
4   The pedal travel warning switch must be adjusted to release the side push button after a pedal travel of 100 to 110 mm (3.9 to 4.3 in). When this adjustment is complete the push button is set by pushing it into the switch.
5   Check the stoplight switch and lights for satisfactory operation on completion.

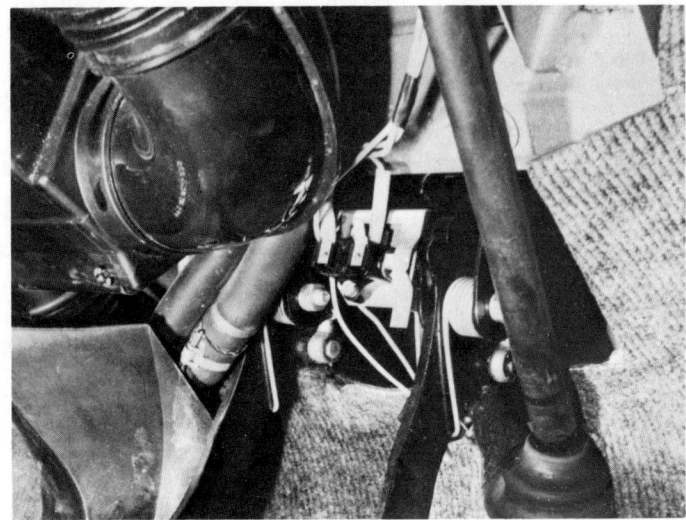

16.1 The brake stoplight and pedal travel warning switch positions

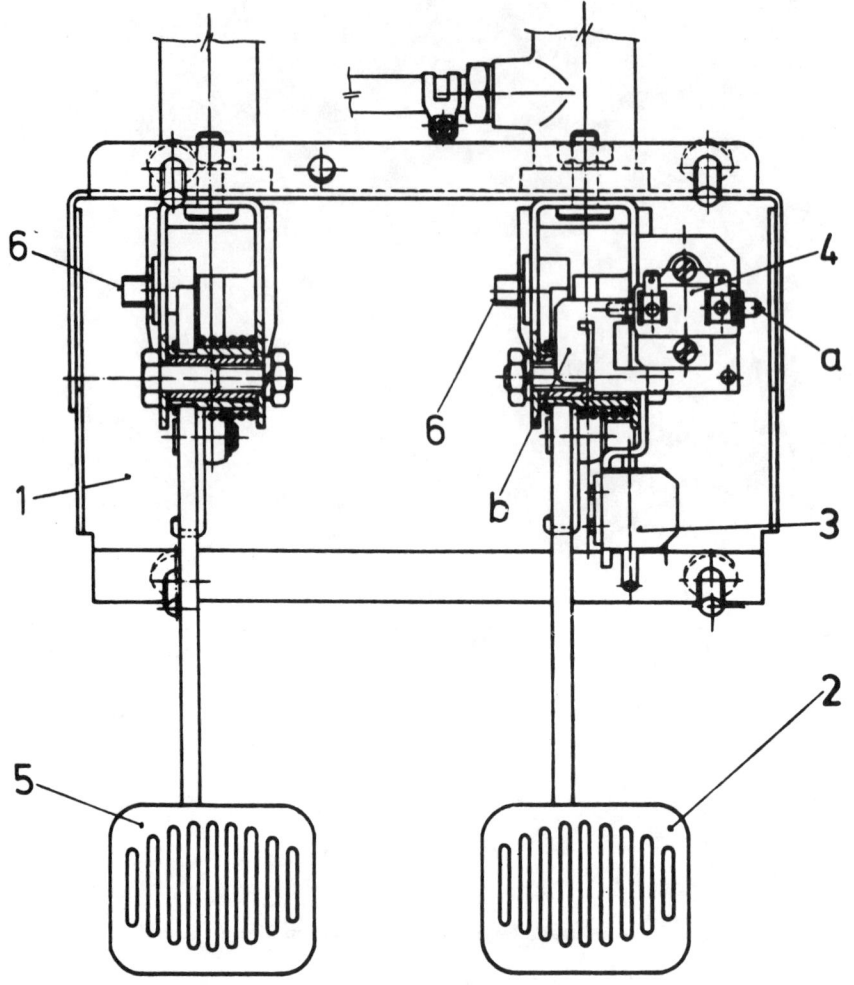

Fig. 9.11 Brake and clutch pedal mechanisms (Sec 17)

1 Bracket	4 Brake pedal travel warning	6 Adjuster pins (not fitted to	a Push button
2 Brake pedal	switch	models with servo)	b Push button pawl
3 Stoplight switch	5 Clutch pedal		

17 Brake and clutch pedals – removal and refitting

1   The brake and clutch pedals are mounted on a common bracket. Both are removed in a similar manner as follows.

2   Disconnect the battery earth lead, followed by the stoplight switch and brake pedal warning switch wires.

3   Unscrew and remove the nuts and spring washers retaining the master cylinders to the bracket or servo unit (as applicable).

4   Working inside the car, remove the bracket retaining nuts and carefully withdraw the bracket and pedals.

5   Refit in the reverse order and check the operation of the brake and pedal warning light switches. If a new pedal assembly is being fitted, or if the pedals have been disconnected, then the pedal free play will have to be checked and adjusted as necessary.

6   The pedals can be removed separately if desired by unscrewing the pivot screw and disengaging the return spring. It is not necessary to disconnect the pedal switches in this instance.

7   Refit is the reverse order, lubricating the pedal bush with a medium grease.

8   On models without a brake servo, the brake pedal free travel is adjusted by rotating the eccentric cam on the left-hand side (Fig. 9.11) to give a clearnace of 0.019 to 0.039 in (0.5 to 1 mm) between the pedal piston rod and the piston in the master cylinder. The pedal free travel must then be as given in the Specifications.

9   On servo equipped models, refer to Section 10 and adjust the servo operating rod-to-master cylinder piston clearance as described.

18 Fault diagnosis – braking system

Symptom	Reason(s)
Brake pedal travels almost to floor before brakes operate	Low fluid level Pads and/or shoes worn Self-adjusting mechanism seized or defective Air in hydraulic system Master cylinder seals defective
Brake pedal feels hard and springy	New pads and/or shoes not yet bedded in or incorrect grade Discs and/or drums excessively worn Brake backplate bolts loose Master cylinder bolts loose
Brake pedal feels spongy and soggy	Air in hydraulic system Brake calipers and/or wheel cylinders leaking Master cylinder seals defective
Car pulls to one side when brakes applied	Tyre pressures uneven Pads and/or shoes contaminated on one side Pads and/or shoes renewed on one side only Suspension or steering defect Caliper or wheel cylinder loose or defective
Brakes binding	Handbrake over-adjusted or cable seized Rear brake self-adjusting mechanism faulty Caliper or wheel cylinder seized
Brake judder	Excessive disc run-out or drum ovality Disc, caliper, backplate and/or wheel cylinder loose Wheel nuts loose Wheel bearings defective Steering or suspension components loose or defective
Excessive effort required to brake car	Friction linings contaminated, worn, or incorrect grade Servo defective or vacuum line disconnected (if applicable) Discs and/or drums badly worn

Chapter 10 Electrical system

For modifications, and information applicable to later models, see Supplement at end of manual

Contents

Specifications

Battery
Type	12 volt, negative earth
Capacity	37 amp hr

Alternator
Type:	
105S, 105L and 120L and LE models	Pal Magneton 443.113.516.021
120 LS and LSE models	Pal Magneton 443.113.516.121
Service voltage	14V
Maximum current:	
Pal Magneton 443.113.516.021	35 amp
Pal Magneton 443.113.516.121	42 amp
Current at 2600 rpm (engine warm):	
Pal Magneton 443.113.516.021	26 amp
Pal Magneton 443.113.516.121	31 amp

Starter motor
Type	Pal Magneton 443.115 – 142.070
Output	0.66 kilowatts (0.9 hp)
Direction of rotation	Anti-clockwise

Windscreen wiper motor
Type	Pal 443.122 – 0.76.071
Current	4 amp (high speed), 2.50 amp (low speed)

Radiator fan
Type	Pal Magneton 443.132 – 097.045
Current	7.50 amp
Output	55 watts
Direction of rotation	Clockwise (viewed from front end of the shaft)

Heater fan
Type	Pal Magneton 443.132 – 084.025
Output	60 watts

Windscreen washer
Type .... ME2 MM 2004
Minimum pump discharge .... 15cc at a pressure of 1 kg/cm^2

Bulbs
Headlights:

All except 105 S models	12V, 60/55W H4 (halogen)
105S models	12V, 45/40W (twin filament)
120LS and LSE models (auxiliary lamps)	12V, 55W H1 (halogen, single filament)
Sidelights and parking lights	12V 4W T8/4
Direction indicators	12V, 21W P25-1
Tail lights	12V, 5W R19/5
Stoplights	12V, 21W P25-1
Reversing lights	12V, 21W P25-1
Number plate lights	12V, 5W R19/5
Instrument lights	12V, 2W Blue
Warning lights	12V, 2W
Interior lights	12V, 5W C11

1 General description and maintenance

The electrical system is of 12 volt type and the major components comprise a 12 volt battery with a negative earth, a regulator relay unit, an alternator driven by a V-belt from the crankshaft pulley and a starter motor which is located on the engine/transaxle bellhousing.

The potential power output of the alternator or battery is sufficient to severely damage the electrical wiring if a short circuit occurs, most therefore, are protected by fuses.

Systems not protected by fuses are associated with the engine and include the ignition and starter motor circuits.

Maintenance of the electrical system is minimal but what little there is should not be neglected. A weekly check should be made to ensure that all lights and indicators front and rear are fully operational. Check that the alternator drivebelt is in good condition and correctly adjusted for tension. Check battery electrolyte level and terminals for security. Make an occasional inspection of the wiring to ensure that it is in good condition, correctly located, and that the respective connections are clean and secure.

2 Battery – removal and refitting

1   The battery is located in a recess to the rear of the rear passenger seat under the luggage compartment (photo). It is important to remember that the battery cables must not be disconnected whilst the engine is running or serious damage may occur in the alternator.

2   To inspect or remove the battery, tilt the rear seat backrest forwards and remove the compartment floor covering, to reveal the battery recess lid on the left-hand side (viewed from the rear). Unclip the lid and remove the battery by undoing and disconnecting the positive and negative terminals.

3   Note which way round the battery is situated and lift it clear of the recess. Keep it the correct way up to prevent spillage of the highly corrosive electrolyte.

4   Refitting is a reversal of the removal procedure, but it is advisable, prior to connection of the two terminals, to smear them with petroleum jelly (not grease) to prevent future corrosion.

3 Battery – maintenance and inspection

1   Normal weekly battery maintenance consists of checking the electrolyte level of each cell to ensure that the separators are covered by up to 4 mm (0.15 in) of electrolyte. If the level has fallen, top up the battery using distilled water only (photo). Do not overfill. If a battery is over-filled, or any electrolyte spilled, immediately wipe away the excess; electrolyte attacks and corrodes any metal it comes into contact with very rapidly.

2   As well as keeping the terminals clean and covered with petroleum jelly, the top of the battery, and especially the top of the cells, should be kept clean and dry. This helps prevent corrosion (photo) and ensures that the battery does not become partially discharged by leakage through dampness and dirt.

3   Once every three months, remove the battery and inspect the battery tray, and battery leads for corrosion (white fluffy deposits on the metal which are brittle to touch). If any corrosion is found, clean off the deposits with ammonia and paint over the clean metal with an anti-rust/anti-acid paint.

4   At the same time inspect the battery case for cracks. If a crack is found, clean and plug it with one of the proprietary compounds for this

3.1 Topping-up the battery

3.2 A badly corroded battery terminal

purpose. If leakage through the crack has been excessive, it will be necessary to refill the appropriate cell with fresh electrolyte as detailed later. Cracks are frequently caused to the top of the battery case by pouring in distilled water in the middle of winter *after* instead of *before* a run. This gives the water no chance to mix with the electrolyte and so the former freezes and splits the battery case.

5   If topping-up the battery becomes excessive and the case has been inspected for cracks that could cause leakage, but none are found, the battery is being overcharged and the voltage regulator will have to be checked and reset.

6   With the battery on the bench at the three monthly interval check, measure its specific gravity with a hydrometer to determine the state of charge and condition of the electrolyte. There should be very little variation between the different cells and if a variation in excess of 0.025 is present it will be due to:

(a)   *Loss of electrolyte from the battery at some time caused by spillage or a leak resulting in a drop in the specific gravity of the electrolyte when the deficiency was replaced with distilled water instead of fresh electrolyte*

(b)   *An internal short circuit caused by buckling of the plates or a similar malady pointing to the likelihood of total battery failure in the near future*

7   The specific gravity of the electrolyte for various conditions at the electrolyte temperature indicated, is listed below.

8   Specific gravity is measured by drawing up into the body of a hydrometer sufficient electrolyte to allow the indicator to float freely. The level at which the indicator floats indicates the specific gravity.

Reading at a temperature of + 25°C (77°F).
Cell fully charged	*1.28*
Cell half charged	*1.22*
Cell fully discharged	*1.15*

4   Battery – charging

1   During the winter months a heavier demand is placed upon the battery, such as when starting from cold, and additional electrical equipment is used more continually. It is therefore a good idea, especially with an older battery, to occasionally charge the battery from an external source. Several types of proprietary battery chargers are available from good accessory shops. Alternatively, your local garage will charge a battery for you at a nominal cost. The charging rate required is 3.5 amp.

2   Continue to charge the battery at this rate until no further rise in specific gravity is noted over a four hour period.

3   Alternatively a trickle charger of 1.5 to 2 amps output can be safely used overnight.

4   Special rapid 'boost' charges which claim to restore the battery power in 1 to 2 hours are not advised as they can seriously damage the battery plates through overheating.

5   *Do not allow the electrolyte temperature to exceed +40°C (104°F).* Should this temperature be reached, disconnect the charger leads and allow the electrolyte to cool before continuing the charge (if needed).

6   Always disconnect the positive and negative leads from the battery terminals when charging the battery. This is to protect the diodes of the alternator during high voltage peaks.

5   Alternator drivebelt – removal, refitting and adjustment

1   Loosen the alternator mounting bolts and pivot the alternator inwards towards the engine to slacken off the belt tension.

2   Remove the drivebelt from the drive pulleys of the alternator, water pump and crankshaft.

3   The belt must be renewed if it shows signs of excessive wear or cracks.

4   Refit the belt in the reverse order to removal, looping it over the respective pulleys; then pivot the alternator outwards from the engine to the point where the correct drivebelt tension is attained.

5   To check the tension, apply a firm thumb pressure at the midpoint position of the belt between pulleys. There should be a deflection of 10 to 15 mm (0.39 to 0.59 in). If necessary, adjust the alternator mounting position to suit, then retighten the mounting and pivot bolts to secure in the set position (photo).

5.5 Checking and adjusting the drivebelt tension

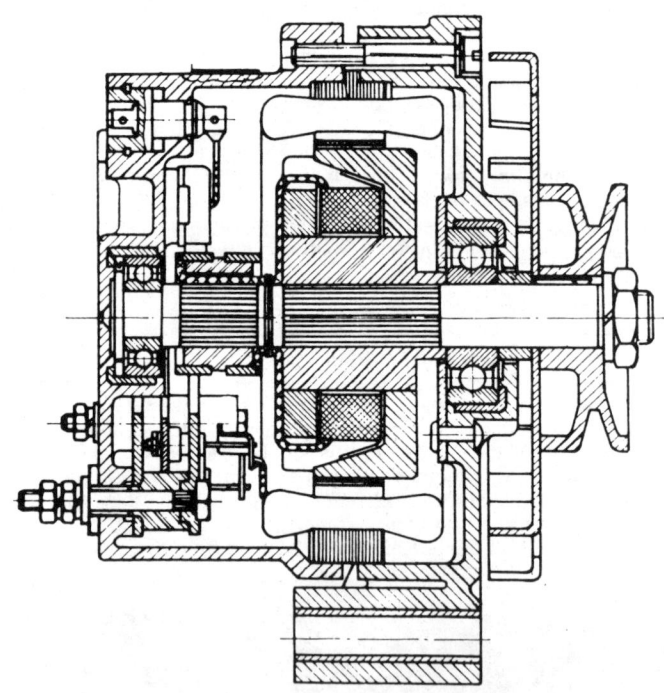

Fig. 10.1 Sectional view of alternator (Sec 6)

6   If a new belt has been fitted, recheck the tension after an initial mileage has been covered as it is quite possible that the belt may have stretched and need retensioning.

6   Alternator – general information and precautions

1   The alternator is a three phase type having semi conductor rectifiers.

2   The alternator must be treated with the utmost respect as it is comparatively delicate. The following points must be observed if an alternator is fitted to the car:

(a)   Never arc-weld any part of the car structure without first disconnecting the alternator and battery

(b)   If using an additional battery with jump leads to start the car, ensure the two batteries are connected positive-to-positive and negative-to-negative and that the bodywork of the two cars is not in contact

(c)   If charging the battery from an external source, disconnect the battery terminals completely first

(d)   Never run the engine with the battery or alternator leads disconnected

(e)   Do not disconnect the battery with the engine running

(f)   Always renew a defective ignition warning light as soon as is possible. The voltage control of the alternator depends on this circuit

3   No maintenance is required on the alternator, apart from checking the electrical connections for security and cleanliness and checking the drivebelt condition and tension periodically. Also, the alternator mounting bolts should be checked for security at fairly regular intervals.

7   Alternator – testing in the car

1   If a fault is suspected in the alternator, first check that the battery is fully charged and that all charge circuit wiring is in good condition and securely connected (see Fig. 10.2).

2   Obtain a suitable voltmeter and disconnect the 'R' terminal wire (red insulator) and the 'M' terminal wire (black insulator) from the rear face of the alternator, noting their respective positions.

3   Bridge the terminals (shown in Fig. 10.3) with an auxiliary conductor. Connect up the voltmeter to terminal +B and to the alternator frame for earth (-).

4   Start the engine and allow it to idle but do not accelerate it. Now connect the third (free wire) of the auxiliary conductor to the '+B' terminal for a few seconds. If no voltmeter reading is visible, the alternator is defective.

5   Where a reading is visible, slowly increase the engine speed and observe whether the alternator output increases accordingly, but do not increase the engine speed in excess of a 20 volt output reading. A 15 volt reading should be all that is necessary to check for satisfactory alternator operation.

6   Finally, check the difference in voltage between the terminals marked '+B' and 'R'. The difference should not exceed 0.40 volts.

7   Where the above tests prove that the alternator is working in a satisfactory manner, the problem must be elsewhere in the charging circuit, probably the regulator unit. Checking of the regulator should be entrusted to an auto electrician or your Skoda dealer.

8   If the alternator is found to be faulty, it is generally recommended that you take it to your Skoda dealer or auto electrician for inspection and repair (where possible); specialised knowledge and equipment is required to fully check and repair an alternator.

9   The alternator can be dismantled for inspection (if you feel yourself to be sufficiently competent!) and this is described in Section 9.

8   Alternator – removal and refitting

1   Disconnect the battery terminals.

2   Note the terminal connections at the rear of the alternator and disconnect the electrical leads.

3   Undo and remove the adjustment arm bolts and slacken the alternator mounting bolts and then hinge the alternator towards the engine. Disconnect the drivebelt from the pulley.

4   Remove the mounting bolts and lift the alternator clear.

5   Refitting the alternator is the reverse sequence to removal.

6   When the alternator is in position, do not fully tighten the mounting bolts until the drivebelt has been relocated onto the pulleys and tensioned correctly, as given in Section 5.

9   Alternator – dismantling and assembly

1   Unscrew and remove the drivebelt pulley nut. Withdraw the pulley and fan.

2   Use two pieces of hooked wire; poke them through the 3 mm

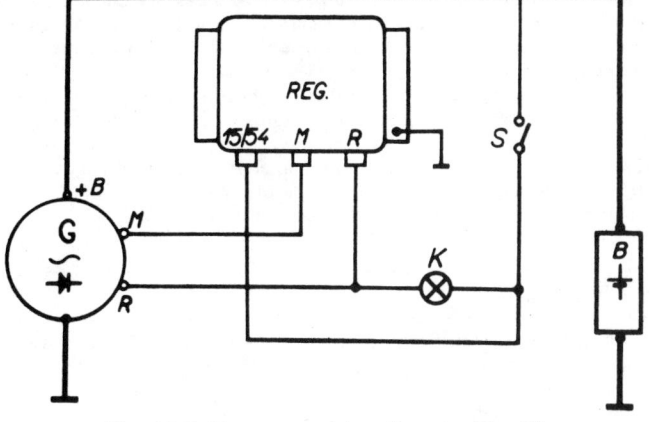

Fig. 10.2 Alternator wiring diagram (Sec 7)

G	Alternator	S	Switch
REG	Voltage regulator	K	Warning lamp
B	Battery		

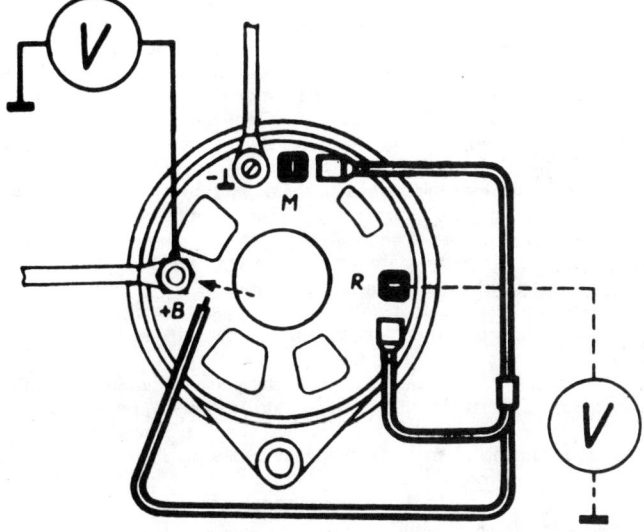

Fig. 10.3 Alternator test circuit diagram (Sec 7)

(0.12 in) holes in the rear face and lift the brushes from the slip rings.

3   Index mark the relative positions of the end shields.

4   Unscrew and remove the retaining bolts and separate the two assemblies. Do not attempt to detach the drive end shield from the stator.

5   The respective parts can now be inspected. Check the bearings for signs of wear or damage. The bearings can be removed using a suitable puller if necessary. The drive end shield bearing is removed after the flanged rivet heads have been drilled out.

6   If the brushes are obviously worn down, they should also be renewed at this stage.

7   Although the diodes are now accessible, they require special equipment to test them fully.

8   Reassemble the alternator in the reverse order and take care not to overtighten the fastenings. Align the relative mark positions made on dismantling and if new bearings are being used, fit them with a suitable drift whilst supporting the housing.

9   The bearings are pre-lubricated for life during manufacture and therefore once assembled require no further attention; they are sealed.

10   Withdraw the two wires used to raise the brushes during dismantling and reassembly.

10   Regulator relay unit – description, removal and refitting

1   A regulator relay unit, to control the alternator voltage, is fitted to the right-hand rear chassis member in the engine compartment.

Together with the alternator, it supplies the necessary current to the battery and electric circuits in the car. No maintenance is required, apart from occasionally checking its electrical terminals for cleanliness and secure fitting.

2   To remove the regulator unit, disconnect the battery terminals and then the respective wires to the regulator unit, noting where they are fitted.

3   Unscrew the regulator unit retaining screws and remove the unit, but handle with care – it should not be dropped.

4   Refitting is the reversal of the removal procedure.

11 Fault diagnosis – regulator relay unit

As with the alternator, specialist knowledge and equipment is required to test or service the regulator unit. Therefore if it is suspected of being defective, it should be left to an auto electrician who will have the necessary facilities. Prior to taking this course of action, however, check the following.

   (a) Check the regulator unit wiring connections, they should be clean and secure, and the earth connection good
   (b) Check that the warning lamp is not defective

12 Starter motor – general description and maintenance

The starter motor is mounted to the transaxle bellhousing on two studs and is situated directly over the right-hand half-axle. It is an electrically operated, pre-engaged type starter motor.

The method of engagement is that when the ignition is switched on, current flows from the battery to the solenoid which is fitted to the starter motor body. The plunger in the solenoid moves inward, in turn moving the pivoted lever in such a manner that the forked end engages a clutch, thus transmitting movement to the flywheel.

When the flywheel solenoid plunger reaches the end of its travel, it closes an internal contact and full current flows to the starter field coils. The armature is then able to rotate the crankshaft to start the engine.

A one-way clutch device is fitted to the starter drive pinion so that the engine, on starting, does not continue to drive the starter motor.

Very little maintenance is required as the bearings are self lubricating, and apart from occasionally checking the cable connections, the starter motor should not need attention.

However, it is not a bad idea to remove the starter motor every other year to check the following:

   (a) Carbon brushes
   (b) Carbon brush springs
   (c) The pinion and idler condition

13 Fault diagnosis – starter motor

1   If the starter motor fails to turn the engine when the switch is operated there are four possible reasons why:

   (a) The battery is flat
   (b) The electrical connections between switch, solenoid, battery and starter motor are somewhere failing to pass the necessary current from the battery to the starter
   (c) The solenoid switch is defective
   (d) The starter motor is either jammed or electrically defective

2   To check the battery, switch on the headlights. If they go dim after a few seconds, the battery is in a low state of charge. If the lamps glow brightly, next operate the starter switch and see what happens to the lights. If they go dim, power is reaching the starter motor but failing to turn it. Therefore, check that it is not jammed by placing the car in gear and rocking it to and fro. If it is not jammed, the starter will have to come out for examination. If the starter should turn very slowly, go on to the next check.

3   If, when the starter switch is operated, the lights stay bright, the power is not reaching the starter motor. Check all connections from battery to solenoid switch and starter for perfect cleanliness and tightness. With a good battery, this is the most usual cause of starter motor problems. Check that the earth link cable between the engine and

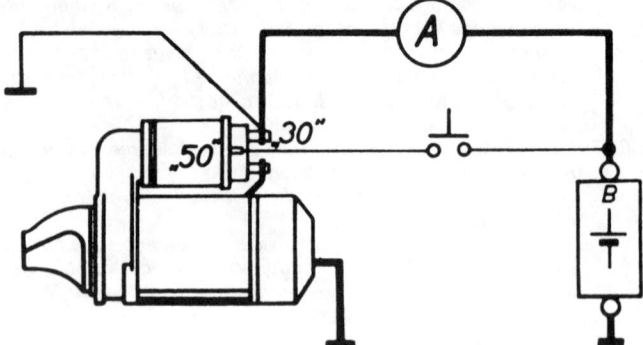

Fig. 10.4 Starter motor test circuit diagram (Sec 13)

frame is also intact and cleanly connected. This can sometimes be overlooked when the engine has been taken out.

4   If no results have yet been achieved, turn off the headlights, otherwise the battery will go flat. You will possibly have heard a clicking noise each time the switch was operated. This is the solenoid switch operating but it does not necessarily follow that the main contact is closing properly. (**Note:** *If no clicking has been heard from the solenoid it is certainly defective*). The solenoid contact can be checked by putting a voltmeter or bulb across the main cable connection on the starter side of the solenoid and earth. When the switch is operated, there should be a reading or lighted bulb.

5   If not, the solenoid switch is no good. If, finally, it is established that the solenoid is not faulty and 12 volts are getting to the starter, the starter motor must be the culprit and should be removed for inspection.

6   Refer to next Section for removal, then check the following.

7   If a large size ammeter is available, connect it up to the starter motor circuit as shown in Fig. 10.4. The light running current must not exceed 65 amps (apart from the initial start peak).

8   The starter motor must run quietly and the pinion action be smooth when engaging and disengaging.

9   When switching off the starter motor, ensure that it does not run on for more than eight seconds.

10   Check and, if necessary, renew the brushes as given in Section 15.

14 Starter motor – removal and refitting

1   Remove the rear seat backrest and fold the rear luggage compartment floor covering out of the way. Remove the central inspection cover from the floor, and also the battery panel.

2   Disconnect the battery.

3   Disconnect the cables from their terminals on the solenoid (photo) after noting how they are fitted.

4   Undo the flange mounting nuts and withdraw the starter motor unit from the location studs.

5   Refitting is a reversal of the removal process.

15 Starter motor brushes – removal and refitting

1   Dismantling the starter motor completely is not a job for the home mechanic. Although not too difficult to dismantle, the reassembly and adjustments required before refitting are beyond his scope, due to the specialised equipment necessary. It is, therefore, preferable to have the starter motor or solenoid checked or overhauled by a specialist auto electrician.

2   The exception to the above note is the removal and refitting of the commutator brushes. Remove these as follows.

3   Unscrew the small retaining bolt in the end cover and prise the cover off with a screwdriver.

4   To remove the brush for inspection, prise the retaining spring back with a small screwdriver and withdraw the brush from its guide (photo).

5   If the brushes are badly worn, remove them after unscrewing the connecting lead screw and replace with new brushes. Whilst the brushes are removed, inspect their contact faces and if badly worn, the

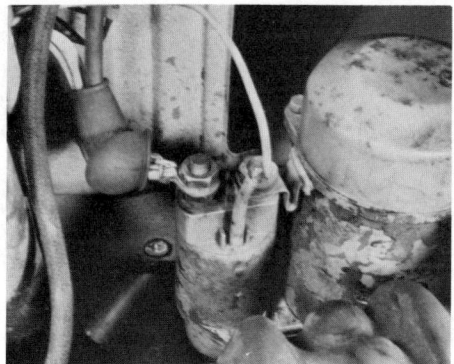

14.3 Disconnect the starter motor leads at the solenoid

15.4 Starter motor brush removed for inspection whilst holding back retaining spring

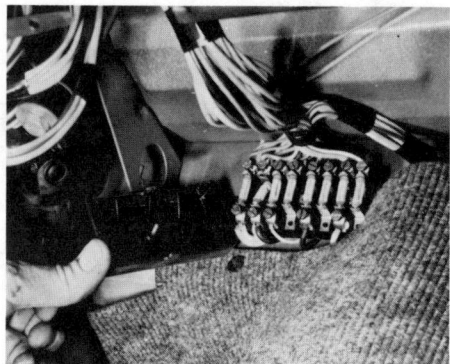

16.2 Remove cover to inspect fuses

starter motor should preferably be checked by an auto electrician — there is little point in fitting new brushes to a worn out starter motor.
6   Reassembly of the starter motor brushes and end cover is the reversal of dismantling, but check that the brushes are free to move in their guides before retaining with the springs.

16 Fuses – general

1   The electrical circuits are protected against overloading by fuses which are located in a common block under the dashboard.
2   To inspect the fuses, unscrew the cover retaining bolt and remove the cover (photo).
3   To remove a fuse simply prise it from its holder.
4   All fuses are 15 amp rating, and their positions are numbered accordingly, as follows:

(1) Interior light, horn, radiator fan motor, stoplights, stoplight pilot light, and warning flash signal
(2) Direction indicators and pilot light, windscreen wiper, heater fan, reversing lamps, battery charge and oil pressure warning lights, temperature gauge and fuel gauge and fuel reserve warning light
(3) Left-hand tail light and left-hand clearance light
(4) Right-hand tail light and right-hand clearance light, instrument panel light and number plate light
(5) Headlamp left-hand dip
(6) Headlamp right-hand dip
(7) Headlamp left-hand main beam and main beam warning light; auxiliary lights
(8) Headlamp right-hand main beam

5   Never substitute tin foil, or similar, for blown fuses. A fuse blows for a reason and if the fault is not located and rectified immediately, serious damage to the wiring circuit will result.
6   A fuse failure is easily identified as all the systems it protects will be inoperative.

17 Headlights – bulb and unit removal and refitting

1   Remove the screws retaining the radiator outer cover grille in position, and push the cover outwards to remove it. The headlight unit adjustment and retaining screws are now accessible.
2   Referring to Fig. 10.5, loosen off the three headlight unit retaining screws, rotate the light unit and withdraw it (photo).
3   To disconnect the wiring to the unit, lift the packing away, then rotate the retainer anti-clockwise to remove it (photos). The bulb can now be withdrawn, but take care not to handle the glass with the fingers if it is a halogen type bulb. Wash it clean with alcohol if you do.
4   Detach the sidelight bulb and socket from the headlight unit if it is to be removed completely.
5   Refitting is a direct reversal of the removal procedure, but be sure to make good wiring connections and on completion, check the operation of all lights. If the adjustment has for any reason been disturbed, refer to the next Section and realign the headlights.

18 Headlights – adjustment

1   It is always advisable to have the headlamps aligned on proper optical beam setting equipment but if this is not available, the following procedure may be used.

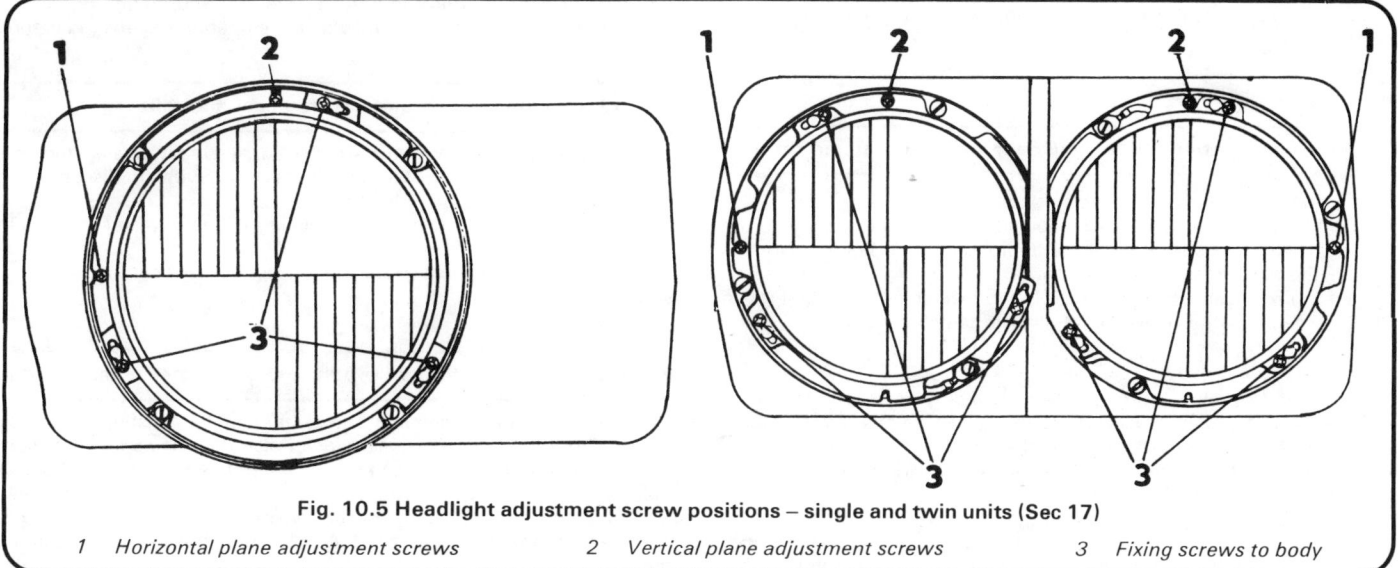

Fig. 10.5 Headlight adjustment screw positions – single and twin units (Sec 17)

1   Horizontal plane adjustment screws   2   Vertical plane adjustment screws   3   Fixing screws to body

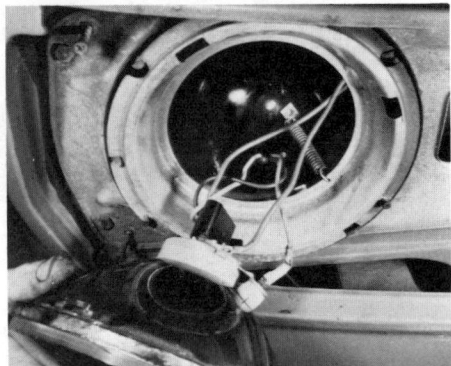

17.2 Withdrawing a headlight unit

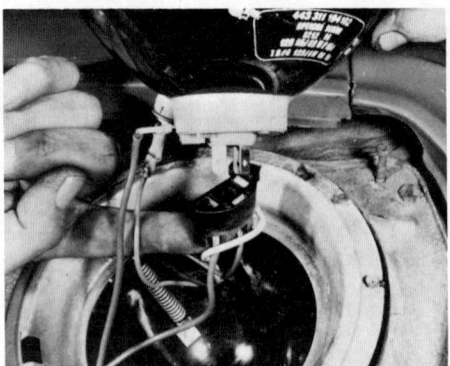

17.3a Detach wiring block connector

17.3b Unscrew holder and remove bulb. Note sidelight bulb holder is also contained in reflector

2   Position the car on level ground 16.4ft (5 metres) in front of a dark wall or board. The wall or board must be at right angles to the centre line of the car.
3   Draw a vertical line on the board in line with the centre line of te car.
4   Bounce the car on its suspension to ensure correct settlement and then measure the height between the ground and the centre of the headlamps. (C in Fig. 10.6).
5   Draw a horizontal line across the board at this measured height, less 2.36 in (60 mm).
6   On this horizontal line, mark a cross on either side of, and equidistant from, the vertical line. The distance between the two crosses must be equal to the distance between the headlamp centres (A), and auxiliary lights (B).
7   Switch the headlamps to *dipped* beam.
8   Cover the right-hand headlamp and, by carefully adjusting the horizontal adjusting screws, align the lamp so that the intersection of the horizontal and angled light pattern coincides with the vertical line on the aiming board.
9   Similarly adjust the vertical screw so that the light/dark intersection of the beam pattern coincides with the 15° line on the aiming board.
10   Cover the left-hand headlamp and adjust the right-hand lamp horizontal and vertical alignment in the same way as for the left-hand lamp. Switch off the headlamps.

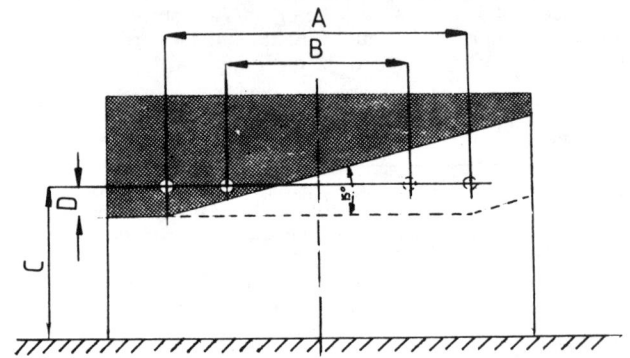

Fig. 10.6 Headlight beam adjustment (Sec 18)

A   *Headlight beam centre*
B   *Auxiliary beam centre*
C   *Height of beam centre from ground*
D   *Low beam deviation from high is 60 mm (2.36 in)*

19 Sidelights – bulb renewal

The front sidelight units are contained in the reflector of the headlight unit; therefore refer to Section 17 for the removal of the headlight, sidelight bulb holder and bulb.

20 Rear combination lights – bulb and unit removal and refitting

Bulb renewal
1   To renew a defective combination light bulb at the rear, raise the bonnet, then twist and remove the appropriate bulb holder from the rear of the combination unit (photo).
2   Fit the replacement bulb holder in the reverse order to that given above and check the operation of all rear lights/indicators.

Unit removal
3   The tail lamp cluster unit can be removed by unscrewing the nuts and removing the plain washers and bolts which secure it to the body. Note that the top bolt retains the earth cable.
4   Disconnect the respective bulb holders and wiring, then withdraw the unit from the panel.
5   Refit in the reverse order to that given above and on completion, check the operation of the respective rear lights and indicators; from the top they are: tail lights, stoplights, indicators, reverse lights.

21 Front indicators – bulb and unit removal and refitting

1   To remove the bulb, twist and pull the holder from the rear of the unit (on the inner face) (photo). Remove the bulb from the holder.
2   To remove the unit complete, unscrew the retaining bracket nut to the bumper and withdraw the unit to the rear and down.
3   Refit in the reverse order and check the operation of the indicators.

22 Interior lights – bulb and unit removal and refitting

1   The interior lights are easily removed by simply prising the unit from its location in the roof (photo). Detach the wires to disconnect it completely.
2   The bulb is removed by simple pulling it free from the holders in the unit cavity.
3   Refit in the reverse order and check the operation is now satisfactory.

23 Rear number plate light – bulb and unit removal and refitting

1   The bulbs are removable from the unit by twisting free their holders from the light unit inside face (raise the engine compartment lid for access). The bulbs can then be removed from their holders (photo).
2   To remove the unit, unscrew the two retaining nuts and detach the earth lead. If not disconnected, detach the bulb holders, and withdraw the unit.

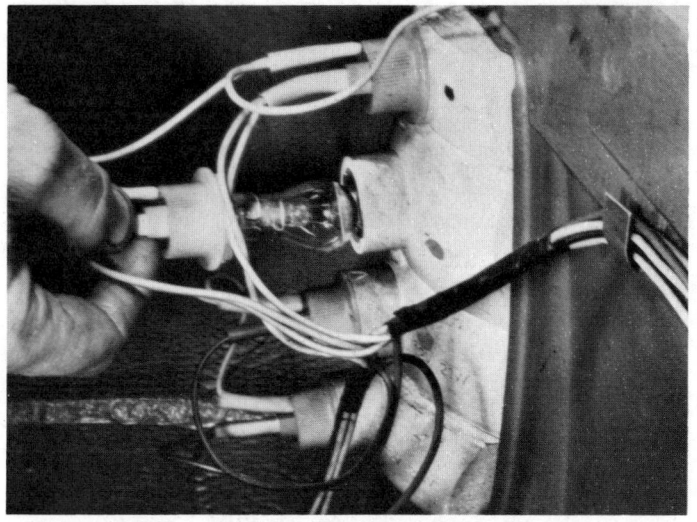

20.1 Rear combination lights, bulb and holder removal

21.1 Front indicator bulb and holder removed for inspection

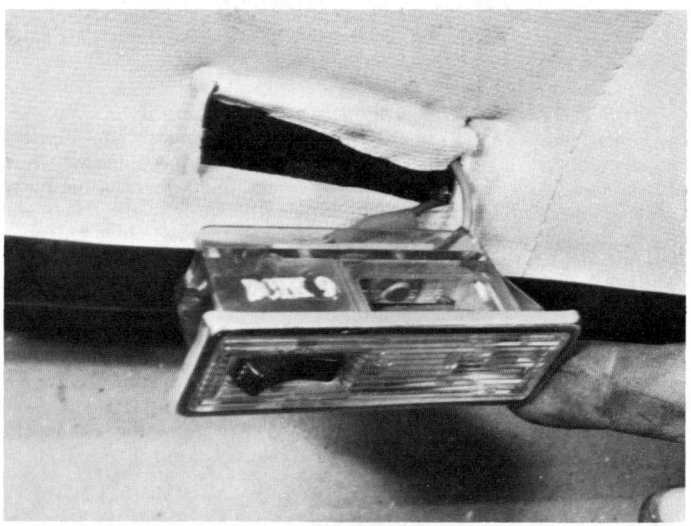

22.1 Interior light unit removed for bulb inspection

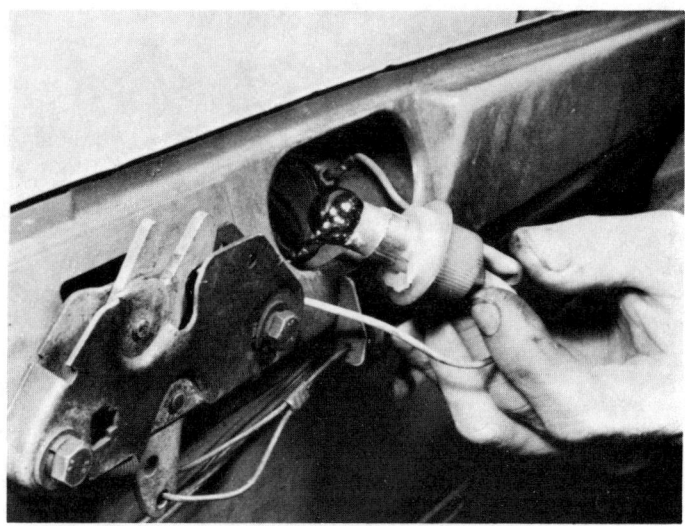

23.1 Rear number plate bulb and holder removed for inspection

3   Refit in the reverse order and check the operation is now satisfactory.

24 Horn – removal, refitting and adjustment

1   The horn is located on the left-hand side of the front bumper (photo). To remove the horn, detach the leads, unscrew the retaining bracket bolt and withdraw the horn.
2   Refit in the reverse order and check for satisfactory operation.
3   To adjust the horn, first ensure that the retaining nuts are tight. Adjust the horn by rotating the central adjuster screw in the back of the horn whilst an assistant presses the operating button. Screw in the required direction until the required pitch is achieved (Fig. 10.7).

25 Combination switches – removal and refitting

1   Before removing the combination switch, detach the battery earth lead.
2   Refer to Chapter 8 and remove the steering wheel (although this is not necessary if the switch is only to be inspected).
3   Unscrew the retaining screws and detach the lower column cover (the shroud). The switch and wiring can now be inspected (photo).

24.1 Horn location under front bumper

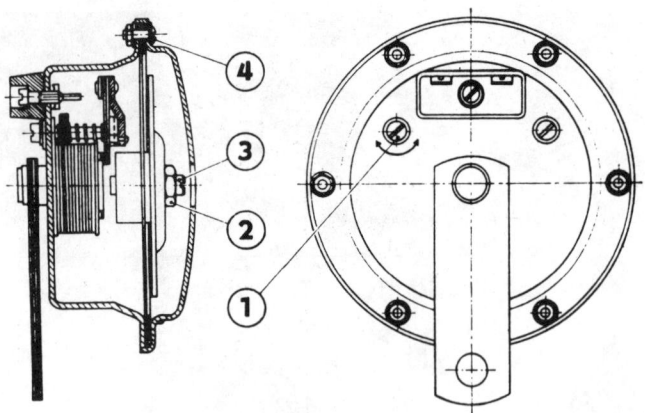

Fig. 10.7 Horn adjustment screw (3), locknut (2), armature points adjustment screw (1) and front cover screw (4) (Sec 24)

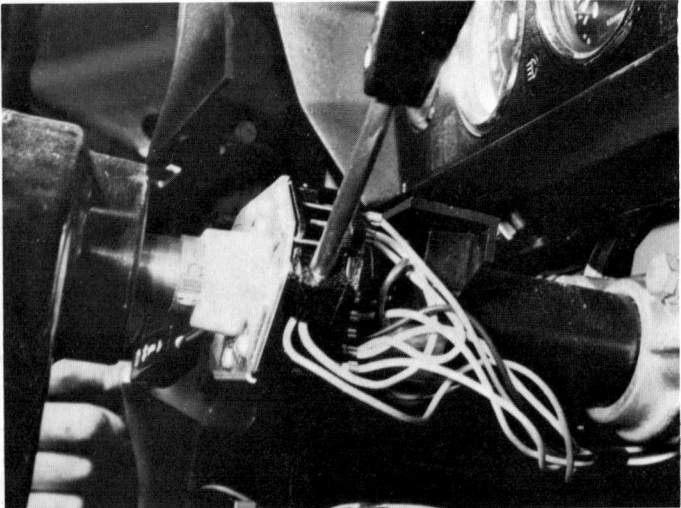

25.3 General view of combination switches with shrouds removed

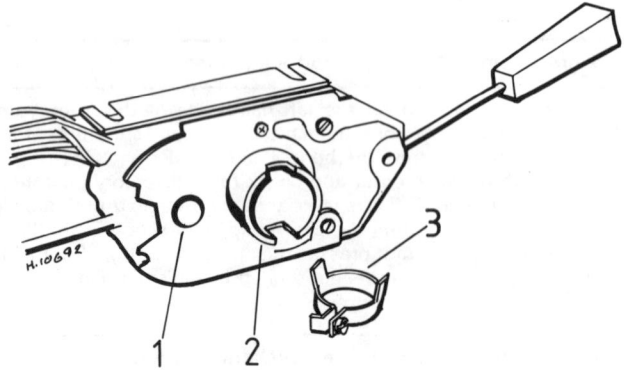

Fig. 10.8 Direction indicator switch (Sec 25)

1   *Centering pin*
2   *Boss*
3   *Driver*

4   To remove the switch from the shaft, loosen the screw retaining the driver (see Fig. 10.8) and remove the driver.
5   Loosen the switch yoke screw (bottom right-hand side).
6   Loosen and remove the upper column cover retaining screws and remove the cover.
7   If the steering gear is to be removed, loosen the screw on the left-hand side of the switch (*not* the bottom right-hand side), then lift the switch and reducer sleeve clear.
8   To refit the switch, reverse the removal instructions. Adjust the automatic cancel position for the indicator by turning the front wheels to the straight-ahead position, then turning the outer bush, with the boss, towards the centre-line of the centering pin of the switch (left-hand side). Refit the driver and tighten its retaining screw.
9   Check the operation of the various switch functions on completion.

26 Switches – removal and refitting

1   Whenever any switches are being removed, always disconnect the battery earth lead first as a safety precaution.
2   Defective switches will have to be renewed as they are not repairable. Note wire connections as they are disconnected.

Parking lights/headlights switch
3   Unscrew the retaining nut and remove the switch from the instrument panel. Remove the pushbutton by simply pulling free. The switch is refitted by turning it so that it is engaged in the lock slots. Press the pushbutton into position if removed.

Heater switch/hazard warning switch/auxiliary switch
4   These are mounted in the central heater control panel and the panel must first be detached to gain access to the rear of the switches. To remove the panel, unscrew the two retaining screws at the panel base (photo), pull the heater control lever knobs from the levers and withdraw the panel sufficiently to remove the switch in question (photo). Detach the switch wires, the nut and washer then remove the switch. Refit in the reverse sequence to that given above, but test the switch operation before refitting the panel.

Auxiliary headlight switch
5   Located under the facia on the auxiliary panel, this switch is removed by detaching the wires, unscrewing the retaining nut and withdrawing the washer. Remove the switch from the panel. The pushbutton can be unscrewed, if required, for removal. Refit in the reverse sequence to that given above.

Light relay switch
6   This is located in the front luggage compartment and is situated on the partition between the brake/clutch master cylinders and side panel. Disconnect the wires, unscrew the retaining screws and remove the unit.

Indicator flasher
7   The flasher unit is located on the rear wall of the ashtray in the facia panel; the facia panel must therefore be removed for access (see paragraph 4). Before removing the unit, note that the contacts face downwards and a new unit must therefore be fitted in the same manner. Before assuming that the flasher unit is defective, check that the electrical and earth connections to each light unit are secure and clean. The flasher unit should give 60 ± 30 flashes per minute. On some models, an adjuster screw is fitted and is accessible on removing the seal in the contact plate. Note that the 'P' terminal is for the hazard warning lights (where fitted).

Door courtesy light switches
8   This switch is located in the door frame (photo) and is automatically actuated by the door when opened or closed. The switch is retained by a single screw which when removed enables the switch to be withdrawn and the wires disconnected. Refit in reverse and ensure that the rubber seal is correctly located.

Reversing light switch
9   This is located in the right-hand side of the gearbox and is removed from underneath the vehicle. Detach the wires from the

26.4a Remove central panel retaining screws at base ...

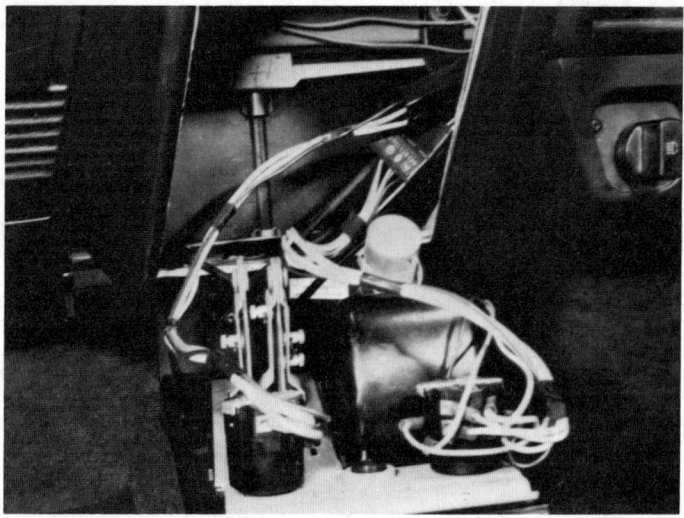

26.4b ... and withdraw the panel

26.8 Door courtesy light switch location in door pillar

26.10 Engine oil pressure switch position

switch terminals and unscrew the switch to remove it. Refit in the reverse order and check for satisfactory operation by selecting reverse gear with the ignition switched on.

Engine oil pressure switch
10 This is located on the right-hand side of the cylinder block near the clutch housing, and is screwed into the pressure/oil cooler pipes connection (photo). To remove the switch, place a drain can underneath to collect spilled oil. Pull off the leads and unscrew the switch, whilst supporting the oil return pipe (into which the switch is fitted) with a spanner, to prevent it being loosened. Refitting is the reverse procedure, but ensure the switch is clean before fitting, and top up the engine oil level, as required.

Brake light switch and pedal travel switch
11 Refer to Chapter 9, Section 16.

Fuel gauge sender unit switch
12 Refer to Chapter 3, Section 11 for removal and refitting instructions. Particular care must be taken here; when removing and disconnecting the switch, ensure that:

(a) the battery earth lead is detached
(b) no smoking or presence of naked flame in any form is permitted within the car

27 Instrument panel – removal and refitting

1 Disconnect the battery earth lead.
2 Unscrew and remove the four instrument panel retaining screws – one in each corner.
3 Working underneath and on the rear side of the panel, disconnect the speedometer drive cable from the rear of the speedometer.
4 Carefully, push the instrument panel through the facia from the underside, then disconnect the terminal blocks. On the 105 S model, the earth cable will also have to be detached. Remove the panel completely.
5 The respective instruments can now be removed from the panel by extracting their retaining clips, the speedometer nut, and the six screws retaining the fuel and temperature gauges, having first detached the lamp housings.
6 The repair of instruments should either be left to a specialist or they should be renewed. The bulbs are easily renewed if required, but be sure to get a replacement bulb of the correct rating. Where wires are disconnected, note their respective locations for correct refitting.

7   Refit in the reverse order to that given above, ensuring that all connections are securely made; check for satisfactory operation of all panel components on completion.

28 Radiator fan – removal, dismantling and reassembly

1   The electrically operated radiator fan can only be removed together with the radiator as described in Chapter 2, Section 4.
2   The fan unit is mounted to the radiator by means of a rim and retaining screws.
3   To disconnect the motor from the impeller, support the fan hub and press out the motor unit. Do not hit the motor or use undue force.
4   Unscrew and remove the clamp bolts, support the grooved shaft end and lift the commutator end shield and stator clear.
5   Pull the brushes partly out from their holders, and with the compression springs held against them, withdraw the rotor. The brushes can be detached by unsoldering the leads, but note the respective lead colours and positions.
6   Inspect and renew defective components as necessary. It may be cheaper to renew the motor as a unit; this should be considered, depending on the extent of the problem .
7   Reassemble in the reverse order noting the following:

   (a) On relocating the oil thrower ring onto the rotor of the commutator, fit the three washers with the felt one between the rubberised types, the thin one fitted first. This is 0.5 mm (0.019 in) thick
   (b) When fitting new brushes, solder their leads on, then partially locate the brushes and adjust the conductor outlets and rubber grommets when in position
   (c) When the rotor is fitted and the brushes fully located, bend the cables over to enable the brushes freedom of movement and to prevent the possibility of short circuiting
   (d) When fitting the stator, align its slotted line with the commutator end shield index line
   (e) When assembled, lightly tap the end shields to seat the rotor and bearings, then test run the motor by connecting it temporarily to a suitable power supply. Should the motor run in the reverse direction, the commutator end shield must be rotated by 180°

29 Windscreen washer reservoir – removal and refitting

1   Unscrew and remove the reservoir cover band retaining screws, then remove the band.
2   Detach the reservoir hose connections and cap and lift the reservoir clear.
3   To remove the pump unit, unscrew and remove the retaining screws with their flat washers. Disconnect the pipes and the wires from terminals, noting their colours. Remove the unit.
4   Refitting the washer reservoir/pump unit is a direct reversal of the removal procedure.
5   To remove the washer nozzles, push them up through their bushes in the body. Refit by pressing them down into the bushes and adjust by swivelling the nozzle head to the desired angle and direction.
6   When refilling the reservoir in the winter months, use a washer liquid with an antifreeze solution specially for windscreens – **not** cooling system antifreeze; this will harm the paintwork.

30 Fault diagnosis – windscreen wiper mechanism

1   If the wipers fail to operate, check first that the current is reaching the motor. This can be done by switching on and using a voltmeter or 12 volt bulb and two wires placed between the (+) terminal on the motor and earth (the car body adjacent to motor).
2   If no current is reaching the motor, check whether there is any at the switch. If there is, then a break has occurred in the wiring between switch and motor.
3   If there is no current at the switch, go back to the ignition switch and so isolate the area of the fault.
4   If current is reaching the motor but the wipers do not operate, switch on and give the wiper arms a push – they or the motor could

31.3 Windscreen wiper arm removed from shaft

be jammed. Switch off immediately if nothing happens otherwise further damage to the motor may occur. If the wipers now run, the reason for them jamming must be found. It will almost certainly be due to wear in either the linkage of the wiper mechanism or the mechanism in the motor gearbox.
5   If the wipers run too slowly it will be due to something restricting the free operation of the linkage or a fault in the motor. In such cases, it is well to check the current being used by connecting an ammeter in the circuit. If it exceeds three amps at slow speed, something is restricting free movement. If less, then the commutator and brush gear in the motor are suspect. The shafts to which the wipers are attached run in brushes and often suffer from lack of lubrication. Regular application to each shaft of a few drops of light penetrating oil, preferably graphited, helps to prevent partial or total seizure. First pull outwards the rubber grommets; afterwards, wipe off any excess.
6   If wear is obviously causing malfunction, or there is a fault in the motor, it is best to remove the motor or wiper mechanism for further examination and repairs.

31 Windscreen wiper blades and arms – removal and refitting

1   The wiper blades should be renewed every year or whenever they fail to wipe the windscreen cleanly.
2   To remove the blades, lift the arm and blade away from the screen and pull the rubber blade from the bridged retaining clamps.
3   If the arm is to be removed also, unscrew the pivot shaft nut on each wiper arm and pull clear (photo).
4   When refitting the arms, operate the wiper motor and stop it so that it is in the extreme rest position. Fit the wiper arms so that the blades are 0.4 in (10 mm) from the windscreen channel and tighten.
5   Operate the motor and check the action of the blades and readjust to suit if necessary.

32 Windscreen wiper linkage – removal and refitting

1   Remove the windscreen wiper arms, as described in Section 31.
2   From the wiper arm shafts, remove the washers, seals and nuts on the outer body.
3   Then push the shafts into the body for removal of the linkage unit.
4   Check all the pivots, bearings and levers of the mechanism in your hands, to locate wear or troublesome mechanical interference.
5   It will soon be obvious if anything has broken, and if the whole mechanism is worn, it would be wise to renew it as a whole rather than mend the worst individul faults.
6   It is worth noting too that wiper spindles should be renewed as pairs and lubricated with graphite oil.
7   Assembling the mechanism and motor is an exact reversal of dismantling.

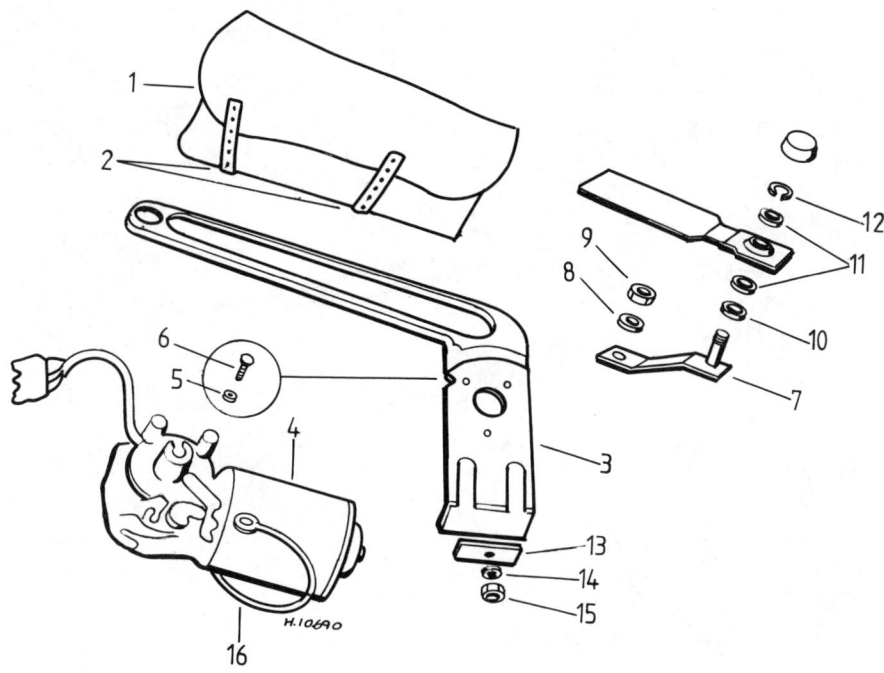

Fig. 10.9 Windscreen wiper components (Sec 30)

1	Cover	5	Washer	9	Nut	13	Washer
2	Retaining band	6	Capscrew	10	Washer	14	Washer
3	Bracket	7	Quadrant	11	Washers	15	Nut
4	Wiper motor	8	Washer	12	Ring	16	Connecting wire

33 Windscreen wiper motor – removal and refitting

1   Detach the battery earth lead.
2   The wiper motor is located within the trough between the bulkhead and luggage compartment (photo).
3   Unclip and detach the tie-rod from the motor pivot.
4   Unbolt the relay arm and detach it from the top of the motor.
5   Remove the motor retaining bolts (noting the earth lead) and withdraw the motor.
6   Refit in the reverse sequence to that given above. Check motor operation and wiper park angle on completion.

34 Windscreen wiper motor – dismantling and reassembly

1   Having removed the wiper motor from the car, it can be dismantled for inspection and if possible, repair.
2   Unscrew the wiper motor clamp bolt nuts, then remove the commutator end shield and stator. Lift the rotor clear, holding it in position initially, to enable it to be separated from the stator.
3   Check the brushes; they may simply by stuck in their holders or worn down. If they are worn, unsolder the connecting wires (or cut them free if a crimped connection is used). Note the colour of the leads to each brush.
4   To reassemble the motor, first locate the oil thrower ring onto the commutator and the three washers each side, the felt fitting between the two rubber washers. The thinnest washer – measuring 0.5 mm (0.02 in) – must be fitted first.
5   When fitting new brushes, solder them to the cables, noting that the third brush is located offset and has a slot in it. When fitted, check that the brushes can move freely in their holders.
6   Pull the rotor partially out, to locate the thrust washer into the gearcase. Loosen off the adjuster screw, then fit the stator, aligning the mating marks.
7   Fit the rear cover and secure it with the bolts and spring washers of the commutator end shield. The rotor axial play is adjusted by turning the adjustment screw to give 0.2 to 0.3 mm (0.007 to 0.011 in) play, then tighten the locknut whilst holding the screw in the set position.

33.2 The windscreen wiper motor and linkage location

Gearcase

8   To dismantle the gearcase, unscrew and remove the cover retaining screws (three) then lift the cover clear.
9   To remove the gear train, press the primary driveshaft. The planet wheel assemblies can be removed after disengaging the double gear from the shaft.
10   Renew any defective or worn gears. A new set is generally advised in this instance.
11   The planet wheels can be removed from the shaft carrier pins by prising the lockrings free.
12   Reassembly is a reversal of the removal procedure. Smear the carrier pins and gears with grease, prior to fitting, and apply grease into the packing in the casing.
13   On reassembly, check the self-parking action and if adjustment is necessary, remove the cover to press out the lid over the adjuster

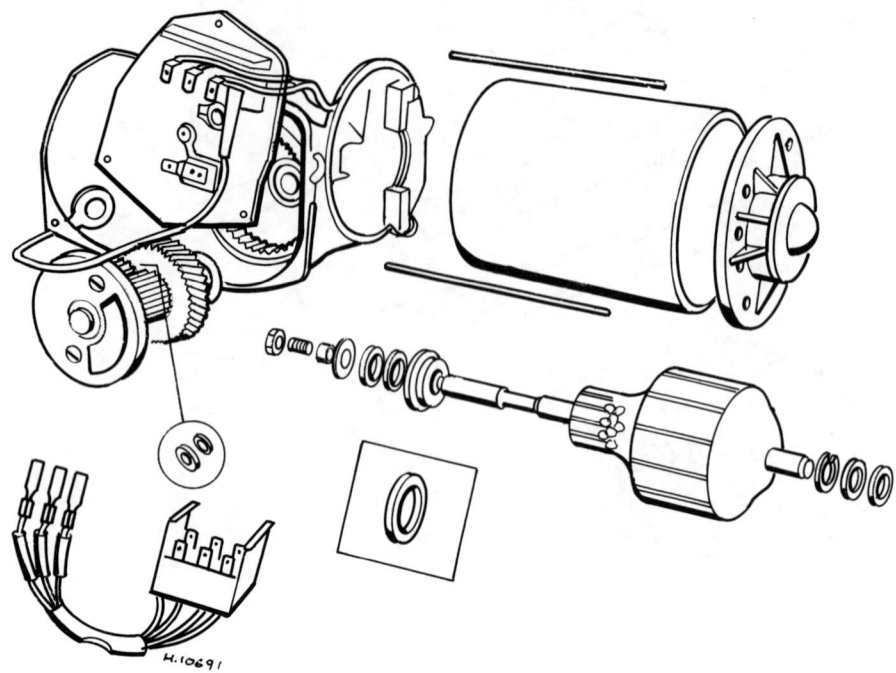

Fig. 10.10 Exploded view of windscreen wiper motor (Sec 34)

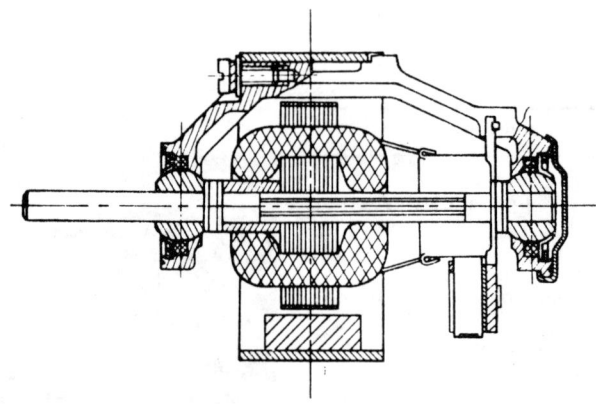

Fig. 10.11 Sectional view of the heater fan motor (Sec 35)

screw. Rotate the screw accordingly to adjust the self-parking, then refit the cover and lid.

35 Heater fan motor – dismantling and assembly

1   With the heater fan motor removed from the heater unit (as described in Chapter 2), clean off the external surfaces and proceed as follows.
2   Prise free the lockring from the impeller whilst supporting the shaft.
3   Unscrew and remove the clamp bolt from the bracket. Lift the motor clear, then remove the motor clamp bolt to extract the stator and brush assembly. **Note:** *Do not attempt to dismantle the motor further.*
4   Inspect the various components, particularly the brushes and bearings for wear; renew them as applicable.
5   Reassemble in the reverse order, noting that the stator slot fits towards the frame bosses and the index lines corresponding. Check that the brush cables are positioned so that they are not likely to short out by rubbing against adjacent components. Lubricate the bearings

prior to assembly.
6   Before refitting the motor into the fan unit, test it for satisfactory running and ensure that it rotates in the required direction. If it rotates in reverse, rotate the frame through 180° to correct this. When fitted, the impeller-to-bracket clearance must be 1.5 to 2.0 mm (0.059 to 0.078 in).

36 Fault diagnosis – electrical system (general)

Faults occurring in the major electrical components have been dealt with elsewhere in this Chapter. Electrical failures generally can be attributed to one of the following causes:

(a) *Failure of current supply (blown fuse, disconnected wire, defective switch)*
(b) *Failure of earth return (loose, dirty or corroded component mounting)*
(c) *Failure of the component in question*

Always check that current and earth return are satisfactory before condemning the component.

See overleaf for Wiring Diagrams

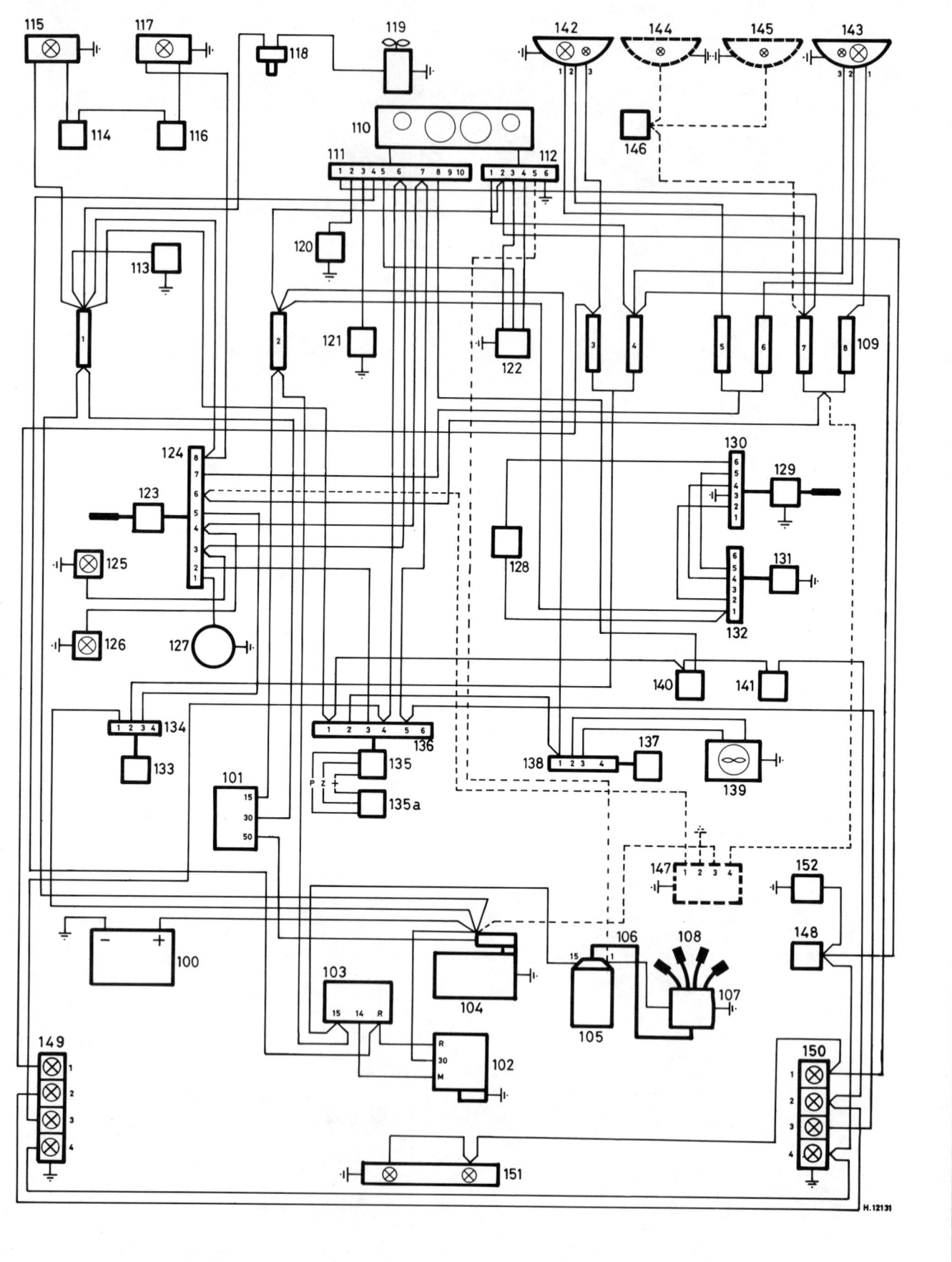

H.12131

Fig. 10.12 Wiring diagram (models up to 1980)

100 Battery
101 Switch box
102 Alternator
103 Voltage regulator
104 Starter motor
105 Ignition coil
106 Ignition cable
107 Distributor
108 Ignition harness and sparking plug interference suppressing resistors
109 Fuses
110 Instrument panel
111 Instrument panel terminal board:
   1 High beam warning light
   2 Lubrication warning light
   3 Telethermometer
   4 Alternator (charging) warning light
   5 Fuel reserve warning light
   6 LH indicators warning light
   7 RH indicators warning light
   8 Brake system warning light
   9 Fog lamp warning light (optional extra)
   10 Unoccupied
112 Instrument panel terminal board:
   1 Instrument illumination
   2 Lead-in from fuse No 2
   3 Fuel gauge (yellow)
   4 Fuel gauge (blue)
   5 Tachometer
   6 Earthing
113 Receptacle
114 LH door switch
115 LH interior lamp
116 RH door switch
117 RH interior lamp
118 Radiator fan motor switch (automatic thermoswitch)
119 Radiator fan motor
120 Oil pressure warning lamp switch
121 Telethermometer primary element
122 Fuel reserve warning lamp switch
123 Direction indicator and horn switch, dipswitch
124 Terminal board:
   1 Horn
   2 Direction indicator ticker feeder
   3 LH direction indicators
   4 RH direction indicators
   5 Dipswitch (bunched conductors "56")
   6 High beam
   7 Low beam
   8 Lead-in from fuse No 1
125 LH front indicator
126 RH front indicator
127 Horn
128 Windscreen washer motor

129 Windscreen washer and wiper motor switch
130 Terminal board:
   1 Unoccupied
   2 Windscreen wiper motor (bunched conductors "2")
   3 Earthing
   4 Wiper motor (bunched conductors "4")
   5 Wiper motor (bunched conductors "5")
   6 Windscreen washer motor
131 Windscreen wiper motor
132 Terminal board:
   1 Lead in from fuse No 2
   2 To switch
   4 To switch
   5 To switch
133 Parking light switch and high beam feeder
134 Terminal board:
   1 Feeder
   2 Clearance (sidelights)
   3 High beam
135 Hazard warning flasher
136 Terminal board:
   1 Lead-in from fuse No 1
   2 Lead-in from fuse No 2
   3 Feeder of indicator circuit breaker
   4 LH indicators
   5 RH indicators
137 Heater motor switch
138 Terminal board:
   1 Lead-in from fuse No 2
   2 Heater motor (high speed)
   3 Heater motor (low speed)
139 Heater motor
140 Brake system warning light switch
141 Stop light switch
142 LH headlight
143 RH headlight:
   1 Full beam
   2 Dipped beam
   3 Parking light
144 LH auxiliary headlight
145 RH auxiliary headlight
146 Auxiliary headlight switch
147 Auxiliary headlight switching relay
148 Reversing light switch
149 LH tail light cluster
150 RH tail light cluster:
   1 Tail lights
   2 Stop lights
   3 Indicators
   4 Reversing lights
151 Number plate light
152 Carburettor solenoid valve

Note: A universal wiring diagram is shown, with bunched conductor leads, illustrating the basic (ie standard) equipment layout. Wiring for the various models differs slightly, dependent upon the fittings offered with these cars.

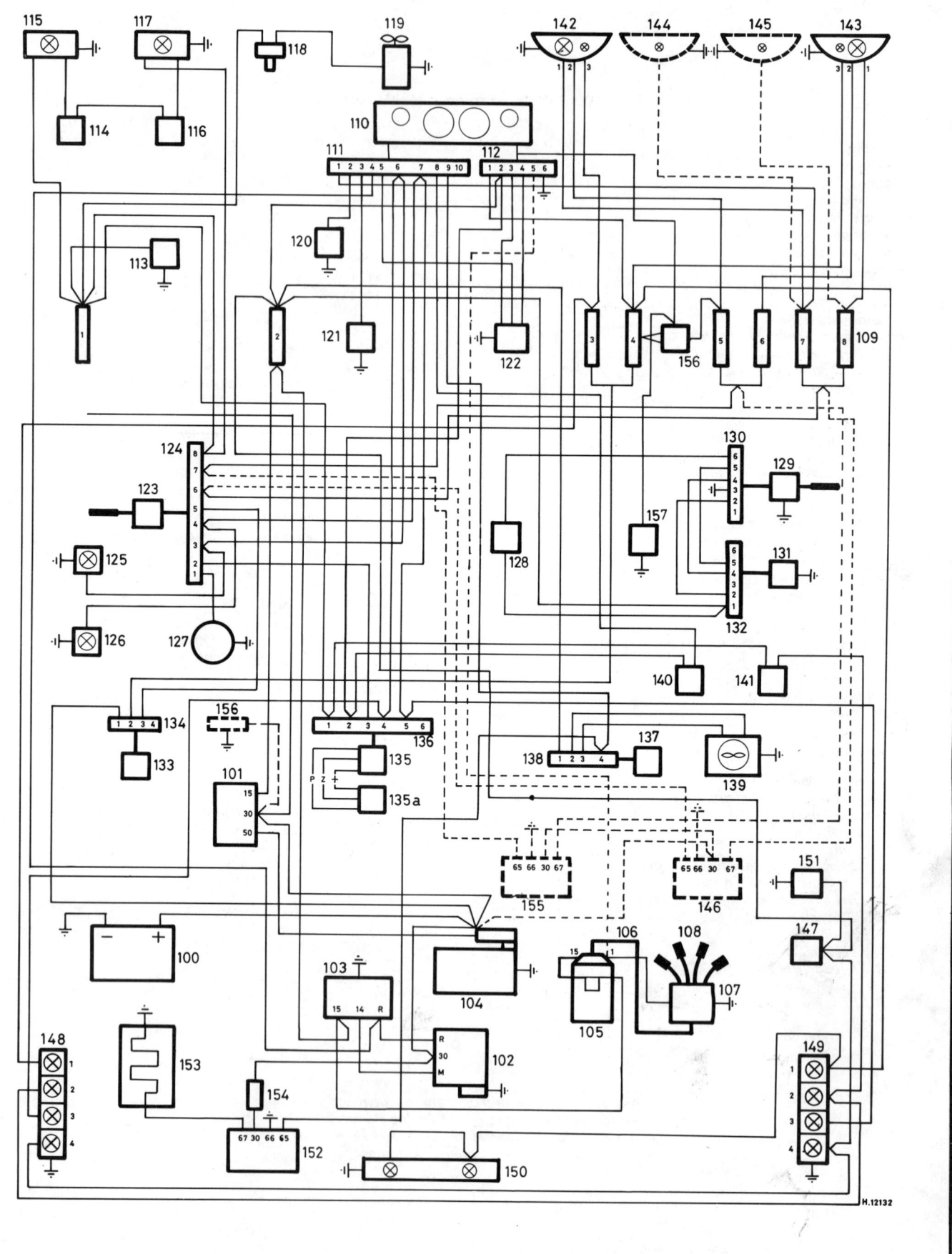

H.12132

Fig. 10.13 Wiring diagram (1980 models)

100 Battery
101 Switchbox
102 Alternator
103 Voltage Regulator
104 Starter Motor
105 Ignition coil
106 Coil ignition cable
107 Distributor
108 Ignition cables and sparking plug interference suppressing
     resistors
109 Fuses
110 Instrument Panel
111 Instrument panel terminal board:
     1   High beam warning light
     2   Lubrication warning light
     3   Thermometer
     4   Alternator operation warning light
     5   Fuel reserve warning light
     6   LH indicators warning light
     7   RH indicators warning light
     8   Brake system warning light
     9   Heated rear screen
     10 Unoccupied
112 Instrument panel terminal board
113 Inspection lamp socket
114 LH door switch (courtesy light)
115 LH courtesy light
116 RH door switch (courtesy light)
117 RH courtesy light
118 Radiator fan switch
119 Radiator fan motor
120 Oil pressure warning light switch
121 Thermocouple element
122 Fuel reserve warning light switch
123 Indicators/horn/dipped beam switch
124 Terminal board:
     1   Horn
     2   Feeder of indicator flasher
     3   LH indicators
     4   RH indicators
     5   Headlamp dipswitch (bunched leads No 56)
     6   High beam
     7   Dipped beam
     8   Lead-in from fuse No 1
125 LH front indicator
126 RH front indicator
127 Horn
128 Washer motor
129 Windscreen wiper and washer motor switch

130 Terminal board:
     1   Unoccupied
     2   Wiper motor (bunched leads No 2)
     3   Earthing
     4   Wiper motor (bunched leads No 4)
     5   Windscreen washer motor
131 Wiper motor
132 Terminal board:
     1   Lead-in from fuses Nos 2, 4 and 5 (bunched leads 2,
     4 and 5)
133 Parking light switch and headlight feeder
134 Terminal board:
     1   Current supply
     2   Clearance lights
     3   Headlights
135 Hazard warning lights switch
136 Terminal board:
     1   Lead-in from fuse No 1
     2   Lead-in from fuse No 2
     3   Indicator flasher feeder
     4   LH indicators
     5   RH indicators
137 Heater motor/heated rear screen switch
138 Terminal board:
     1   Lead-in from fuse No 2
     2   Heater motor (high speed)
     3   Heater motor (low speed)
     4   Heated rear screen
139 Heater motor
140 Brake system warning light switch
141 Stoplight switch
142 LH headlight
143 RH headlight:
     1   High beam
     2   Dipped beam
     3   Parking light
144 LH auxiliary headlight
145 RH auxiliary headlight
146 Switching relay for main beam (LS models)
147 Reversing light switch
148 LH tail light cluster
149 RH tail light cluster:
     1   Tail lights
     2   Stoplights
     3   Indicators
     4   Reversing lights
150 Number plate light
151 Carburettor solenoid valve
152 Heated rear screen relay
153 Heated rear screen
154 Fuse
155 Dipped beam relay (120 GLS models only)
156 Rear fog lamp switch
157 Rear fog lamp

Chapter 11 Bodywork and fittings

For modifications, and information applicable to later models, see Supplement at end of manual

Contents

1 General description

The all metal body is of monocoque construction, has four doors, four seats and the main luggage compartment is at the front, the engine being rear mounted.

All wing panels are of the bolt-on type, as are the front and rear panels. The boot and engine compartment lids have internal hinges and are retained by cable operated locks. The operating lever for the engine compartment lid is located in the rear door pillar and the luggage compartment lid release is operated from under the dashboard.

The spare wheel is carried under the luggage compartment floor panel at the front of the car. The fuel tank is also located under the rear passenger seat floor.

As well as providing the essential strong points for seat belts, seats and jacking, the floor structure also contributes significantly to the strength and stiffness of the bodyshell, therefore, it cannot be emphasised too much that it is as necessary to keep the floor structure clean and free from corrosion, as it is to keep the upper structure and coachwork clean and corrosion free.

2 Maintenance – bodywork and underframe

1   The general condition of a car's bodywork is the thing that significantly affects its value. Maintenance is easy but needs to be regular. Neglect, particularly after minor damage, can lead quickly to further deterioration and costly repair bills. It is important also to keep watch on those parts of the car not immediately visible, for instance the underside, inside all the wheel arches and the lower part of the engine compartment.

2   The basic maintenance routine for the bodywork is washing – preferably with a lot of water, from a hose. This will remove all the loose solids which may have stuck to the car. It is important to flush these off in such a way as to prevent grit from scratching the finish. The wheel arches and underframe need washing in the same way to remove any accumulated mud which will retain moisture and tend to encourage rust. Paradoxically enough, the best time to clean the underframe and wheel arches is in wet weather when the mud is thoroughly wet and soft. In very wet weather the underframe is usually cleaned of large accumulations automatically and this is a good time for inspection.

3   Periodically, it is a good idea to have the whole of the underframe of the car steam cleaned, engine compartment included, so that a thorough inspection can be carried out to see what minor repairs and renovations are necessary. Steam cleaning is available at many garages and is necessary for removal of the accumulation of oily grime which sometimes is allowed to become thick in certain areas. If steam cleaning facilities are not available, there are one or two excellent grease solvents available which can be brush applied. The dirt can then be simply hosed off.

4   After washing paintwork, wipe off with a chamois leather to give an unspotted clear finish. A coat of clear protective wax polish will give added protection against chemical pollutants in the air. If the paintwork sheen has dulled or oxidised, use a cleaner/polisher combination to restore the brilliance of the shine. This requires a little effort, but such dulling is usually caused because regular washing has been neglected. Always check that the door and ventilator opening drain holes and pipes are completely clear so that water can be drained out. Bright work should be treated in the same way as paintwork. Windscreens and windows can be kept clear of the smeary film which often appears, by adding a little ammonia to the water. If they are scratched, a good rub with a proprietary metal polish will often clear them. Never use any form of wax or other body or chromium polish on glass.

3 Maintenance – upholstery and carpets

1   Mats and carpets should be brushed or vacuum cleaned regularly to keep them free of grit. If they are badly stained remove them from the car for scrubbing or sponging and make quite sure they are dry before refitting. Seats and interior trim panels can be kept clean by a wipe over with a damp cloth. If they do become stained (which can be more apparent on light coloured upholstery) use a little liquid detergent and a soft nail brush to scour the grime out of the grain of the material. Do not forget to keep the head lining clean in the same way as the upholstery. When using liquid cleaners inside the car do not over-wet the surfaces being cleaned. Excessive damp could get into the seams and padded interior causing stains, offensive odours or even rot. If the inside of the car gets wet accidentally it is worthwhile taking some trouble to dry it out properly, particularly where carpets are involved. *Do not leave oil or electric heaters inside the car for this purpose.*

4 Minor body damage – repair

The photographic sequences on pages 150 and 151 illustrate the operations detailed in the following sub-sections.

Repair of minor scratches in the vehicle's bodywork

If the scratch is very superficial, and does not penetrate to the metal of the bodywork, repair is very simple. Lightly rub the area of the scratch with a paintwork renovator, or a very fine cutting paste, to remove loose paint from the scratch and to clear the surrounding bodywork of wax polish. Rinse the area with clean water.

Apply touch-up paint to the scratch using a thin paint brush; continue to apply thin layers of paint until the surface of the paint in

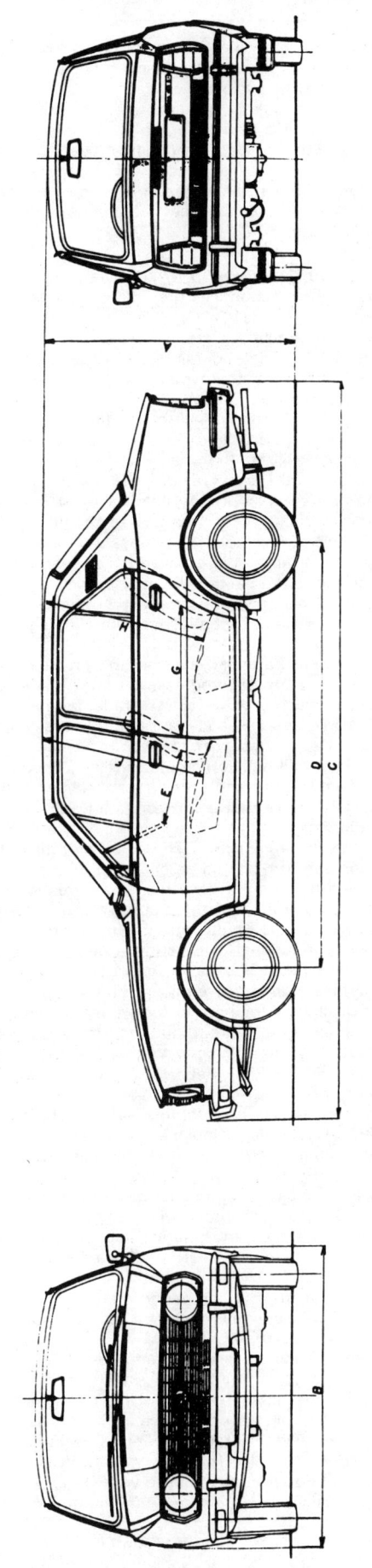

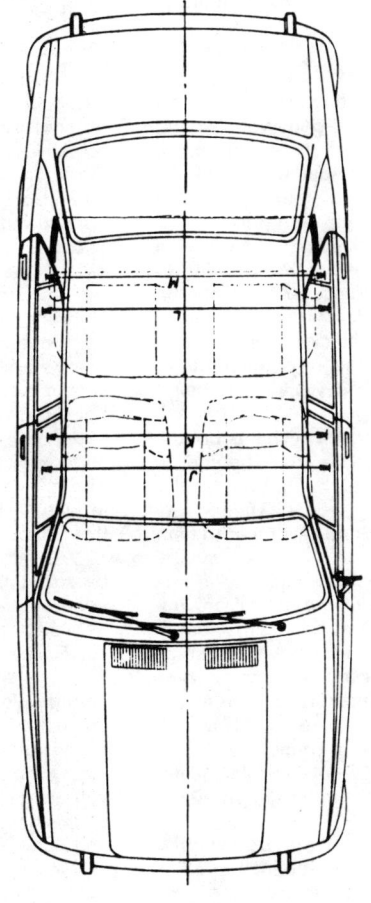

Fig. 11.1 Dimensional drawing of body (Sec 1)

A   Overall height = 1400 mm
B   Overall width = 1595 mm
C   Overall length = 4160 mm
D   Wheelbase = 2400 mm
E   Steering wheel to seat backrest = 400 mm (+ 50 – 100 mm)
F   Seat to roof = 900 mm
G   Seat to seat backrest = 7 mm (+ 100 – 500 mm)
H   Seat to roof = 870 mm
J and L Elbow height width = 1350 mm
K and M Shoulder height width = 1320 mm

the scratch is level with the surrounding paintwork. Allow the new paint at least two weeks to harden: then blend it into the surrounding paintwork by rubbing the paintwork, in the scratch area, with a paintwork renovator or a very fine cutting paste. Finally, apply wax polish.

Where the scratch has penetrated right through to the metal of the bodywork, causing the metal to rust, a different repair technique is required. Remove any loose rust from the bottom of the scratch with a penknife, then apply rust inhibiting paint to prevent the formation of rust in the future. Using a rubber or nylon applicator fill the scratch with bodystopper paste. If required, this paste can be mixed with cellulose thinners to provide a very thin paste which is ideal for filling narrow scratches. Before the stopper-paste in the scratch hardens, wrap a piece of smooth cotton rag around the top of a finger. Dip the finger in cellulose thinners and then quickly sweep it across the surface of the stopper-paste in the scratch; this will ensure that the surface of the stopper-paste is slightly hollowed. The scratch can now be painted over as described earlier in this Section.

Repair of dents in the vehicle's bodywork

When deep denting of the vehicle's bodywork has taken place, the first task is to pull the dent out, until the affected bodywork almost attains its original shape. There is little point in trying to restore the original shape completely, as the metal in the damaged area will have stretched on impact and cannot be reshaped fully to its original contour. It is better to bring the level of the dent up to a point which is about $\frac{1}{8}$ in (3 mm) below the level of the surrounding bodywork. In cases where the dent is very shallow anyway, it is not worth trying to pull it out at all. If the underside of the dent is accessible, it can be hammered out gently from behind, using a mallet with a wooden or plastic head. Whilst doing this, hold a suitable block of wood firmly against the outside of the panel to absorb the impact from the hammer blows and thus prevent a large area of the bodywork from being 'belled-out'.

Should the dent be in a section of the bodywork which has double skin or some other factor making it inaccessible from behind, a different technique is called for. Drill several small holes through the metal inside the area – particularly in the deeper section. Then screw long self-tapping screws into the holes just sufficiently for them to gain a good purchase in the metal. Now the dent can be pulled out by pulling on the protruding heads of the screws with a pair of pliers.

The next stage of the repair is the removal of the paint from the damaged area, and from an inch or so of the surrounding 'sound' bodywork. This is accomplished most easily by using a wire brush or abrasive pad on a power drill, although it can be done just as effectively by hand using sheets of abrasive paper. To complete the preparation for filling, score the surface of the bare metal with a screwdriver or the tang of a file, or alternatively, drill small holes in the affected area. This will provide a really good 'key' for the filler paste.

To complete the repair see the Section on filling and re-spraying.

Repair of rust holes or gashes in the vehicle's bodywork

Remove all paint from the affected area and from an inch or so of the surrounding 'sound' bodywork, using an abrasive pad or a wire brush on a power drill. If these are not available a few sheets of abrasive paper will do the job just as effectively. With the paint removed you will be able to gauge the severity of the corrosion and therefore decide whether to renew the whole panel (if this is possible) or to repair the affected area. New body panels are not as expensive as most people think and it is often quicker and more satisfactory to fit a new panel than to attempt to repair large areas of corrosion.

Remove all fittings from the affected area except those which will act as a guide to the original shape of the damaged bodywork (eg headlamp shells etc). Then, using tin snips or a hacksaw blade, remove all loose metal and any other metal badly affected by corrosion. Hammer the edges of the hole inwards in order to create a slight depression for the filler paste.

Wire brush the affected area to remove the powdery rust from the surface of the remaining metal. Paint the affected area with rust inhibiting paint; if the back of the rusted area is accessible treat this also.

Before filling can take place it will be necessary to block the hole in some way. This can be achieved by the use of Zinc gauze or Aluminium tape.

Zinc gauze is probably the best material to use for a large hole. Cut a piece to the approximate size and shape of the hole to be filled, then position it in the hole so that its edges are below the level of the surrounding bodywork. It can be retained in position by several blobs of filler paste around its periphery.

Aluminium tape should be used for small or very narrow holes. Pull a piece off the roll and trim it to the approximate size and shape required, then pull off the backing paper (if used) and stick the tape over the hole; it can be overlapped if the thickness of one piece is insufficient. Burnish down the edges of the tape with the handle of a screwdriver or similar, to ensure that the tape is securely attached to the metal underneath.

Bodywork repairs – filling and re-spraying

Before using this Section, see the Sections on dent, deep scratch, rust holes and gash repairs.

Many types of bodyfiller are available, but generally speaking those proprietary kits which contain a tin of filler paste and a tube of resin hardener are best for this type of repair. A wide, flexible plastic or nylon applicator will be found invaluable for imparting a smooth and well contoured finish to the surface of the filler.

Mix up a little filler on a clean piece of card or board – measure the hardener carefully (follow the maker's instructions on the pack) otherwise the filler will set too rapidly or too slowly.

Using the applicator apply the filler paste to the prepared area; draw the applicator across the surface of the filler to achieve the correct contour and to level the filler surface. As soon as a contour that approximates the correct one is achieved, stop working the paste – if you carry on too long the paste will become sticky and begin to 'pick up' on the applicator. Continue to add thin layers of filler paste at twenty-minute intervals until the level of the filler is just proud of the surrounding bodywork.

Once the filler has hardened, excess can be removed using a metal plane or file. From then on, progressively finer grades of sandpaper should be used, starting with a 40 grade production paper and finishing with 400 grade wet-and-dry paper. Always wrap the abrasive paper around a flat rubber, cork, or wooden block – otherwise the surface of the filler will not be completely flat. During the smoothing of the filler surface the wet-and-dry paper should be periodically rinsed in water. This will ensure that a very smooth finish is imparted to the filler at the final stage.

At this stage the 'repair area' should be surrounded by a ring of bare metal, which in turn should be encircled by the finely 'feathered' edge of the good paintwork. Rinse the repair area with clean water, until all of the dust produced by the rubbing-down operation has gone.

Spray the whole repair area with a light coat of primer – this will show up any imperfections in the surface of the filler. Repair these imperfections with fresh filler paste or bodystopper, and once more smooth the surface with abrasive paper. If bodystopper is used, it can be mixed with cellulose thinners to form a really thin paste which is ideal for filling small holes. Repeat this spray and repair procedure until you are satisfied that the surface of the filler, and the feathered edge of the paintwork are perfect. Clean the repair area with clean water and allow to dry fully.

The repair area is now ready for final spraying. Paint spraying must be carried out in warm, dry, windless and dust free atmosphere. This condition can be created artificially if you have access to a large indoor working area, but if you are forced to work in the open, you will have to pick your day very carefully. If you are working indoors, dousing the floor in the work area with water will help to settle the dust which would otherwise be in the atmosphere. If the repair area is confined to one body panel, mask off the surrounding panels; this will help to minimise the effects of a slight mis-match in paint colours. Bodywork fittings (eg chrome strips, door handles etc) will also need to be masked off. Use genuine masking tape and several thicknesses of newspaper for the masking operations.

Before commencing to spray, agitate the aerosol can thoroughly, then spray a test area (an old tin, or similar) until the technique is mastered. Cover the repair area with a thick coat of primer; the thickness should be built up using several thin layers of paint rather than one thick one. Using 400 grade wet-and-dry paper, rub down the surface of the primer until it is really smooth. While doing this, the work area should be thoroughly doused with water, and the wet-and-dry paper periodically rinsed in water. Allow to dry before spraying on more paint.

Spray on the top coat, again building up the thickness by using several thin layers of paint. Start spraying in the centre of the repair area and then, using a circular motion, work outwards until the whole repair area and about 2 inches of the surrounding original paintwork is covered. Remove all masking material 10 to 15 minutes after spraying on the final coat of paint.

Allow the new paint at least two weeks to harden, then, using a paintwork renovator or a very fine cutting paste, blend the edges of the paint into the existing paintwork. Finally, apply wax polish.

5 Major body damage – repair

Major chassis and body repair work cannot be successfully undertaken by the average owner. Work of this nature should be entrusted to a competent body repair specialist who should have the necessary jigs, welding and hydraulic straightening equipment as well as skilled panel beaters to ensure a proper job is done.

6 Maintenance – hinges and locks

Once every six months the door, rear window, bonnet and boot hinges should be oiled with a few drops of engine oil from an oil can. The door striker plates can be given a thin smear of grease to reduce wear and ensure free movement.

7 Door trim panels and handles – removal and refitting

1 Remove the armrest/door pull by unscrewing the retaining screws (105 S models) (photo).
2 Prise back the window winder plastic section (photo) and remove the screw and handle (photo).
3 Prise free and withdraw the door catch release handle trim (photo).
4 The door panel can now be removed by prising between the door and panel edges, to release it from the clips around its periphery.
5 Refitting is a reversal of the removal procedure for any of the above.

8 Door locks – removal and refitting

1 Wind the window completely up.
2 Remove the door handle, window winder and armrest. Remove the door panel as described in Section 7.
3 Disconnect the pullrods from the control levers (photo).
4 Unscrew the inner door lock retaining screws and withdraw the lock from the door (photo).

7.1 Remove arm rest retaining screws

7.2a Prise back winder handle plastic strip ...

7.2b ... and remove exposed screw and handle

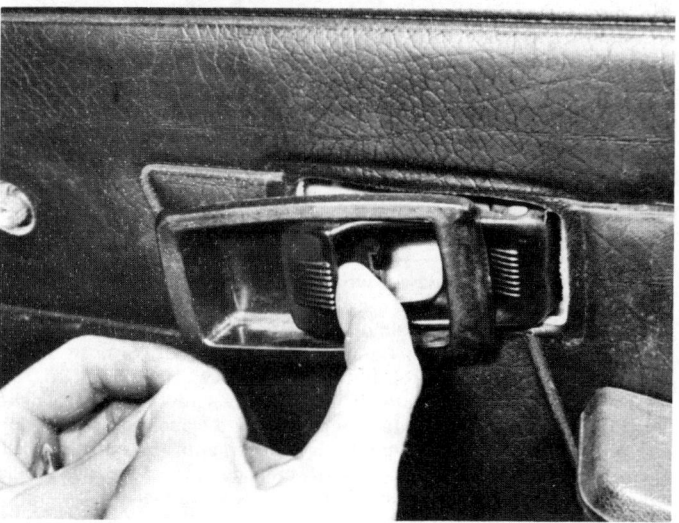

7.3 Remove handle surround trim

8.3 Front door with trim removed   B   *Handle pullrod*
A   *Latch control*   C   *Centre post retaining nut*

8.4 Door lock retaining screws

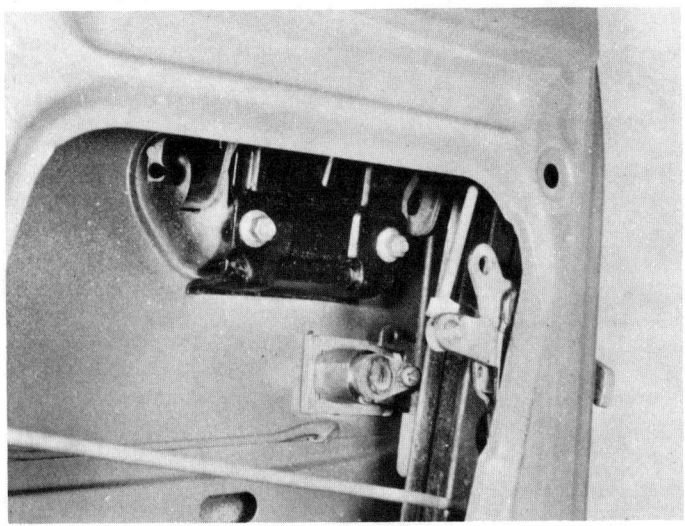

8.5 Door outer lock retaining bolts

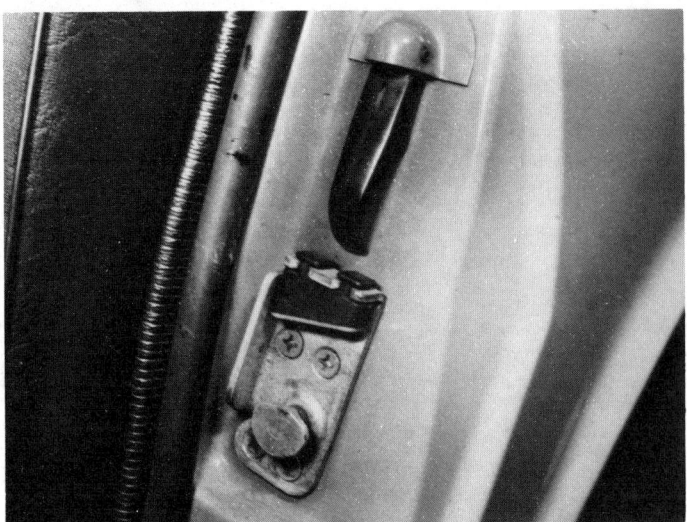

9.2 Rear door striker plate. The engine compartment lid catch release is shown above it

5   Remove the outer lock bolts, also the relay lever bolt, and remove the outer lock (photo).
6   Refitting is the reverse procedure, but be sure to refit with the levers and mechanism suitably lubricated. Renew the plastic pullrod (control lever) clips, if worn.
7   Before trying the refitted door lock in the closed position, wind the window down to ensure freedom of movement and also as a safety precaution unlock the passenger door!

9   Door striker plate – removal, refitting and adjustment

1   If it is wished to renew a worn striker plate, mark its position on the door pillar so a new plate can be fitted in the same position.
2   To remove the plate, simply undo the crosshead screws which hold the plate in position. Remove the plate and take note of any packing shims fitted (photo). Refitting is equally straightforward.
3   To adjust the striker plate, first slacken the screws and remove the striker plate slightly. Retighten the screws and close the door, noting the position of the door. Repeat this process until the door is 'flush' with the adjacent rear body panel. The crease in the door panel should be level with the crease in the rear body panel as well.
4   Check that the door closes easily without lifting or dropping and that on the road it does not rattle.

10   Door and door hinge – removal and refitting

1   Remove the door handle, armrest and panel trim (see Section 7).
2   From inside the door, unscrew the door tie-rod retaining nut to remove the rubber grommet and washer.
3   From the door hinge, unclip the snap-ring retaining the hinge pin.
4   Get an assistant to support the weight of the door and withdraw the hinge pin to remove the door.
5   The door hinges are retained by countersunk screws. If the hinges are to be removed, it is advisable to mark around the outside of the hinge so that it may be correctly repositioned on refitment.
6   Unscrew the screws to remove the hinges. It may be necessary to apply some penetrating oil to assist removal.
7   Refitting is the reversal of the removal process. If the door has dropped, it can be adjusted by inserting some packing shims under the lower hinge.

11   Door window and winder mechanism – removal and refitting

1   Wind the window fully up, then remove the door trim panel as given in Section 7.
2   Remove the short guide rail retaining screw, then carefully press

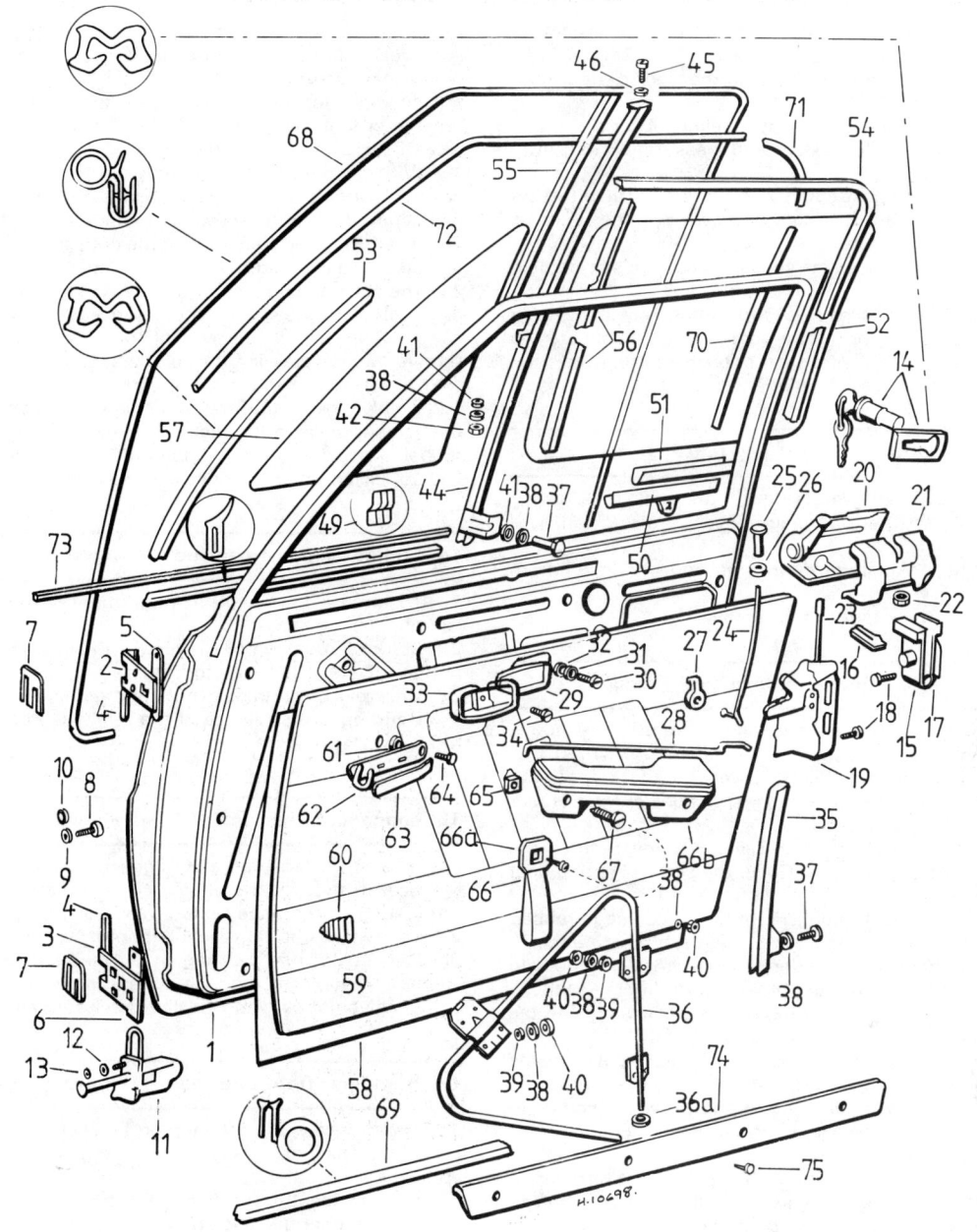

Fig. 11.2 Front door components (Sec 11)

1 Door	37 Bolt
2 Fixed hinge arm (upper)	38 Washer
3 Fixed hinge arm (lower)	39 Washer
4 Distance pin	41 Washer
5 Weatherstrip (upper)	42 Nut
6 Weatherstrip (lower)	44 Centre post
7 Shim	45 Capscrew
8 Capscrew	46 Washer
9 Washer	47 Weatherstrip
10 Washer	49 Clip
11 Door check	50 Window channel
12 Special nut	51 Channel weatherstrip
13 Pin	52 Window
14 Lock insert	53 Weatherstrip
15 Lock latch	54 Weatherstrip – front
16 Guide plate	55 Centre post weatherstrip
17 Latch support plate	56 Centre post weatherstrip
18 Fastening screw	57 Fixed window
19 Lock	58 Door protective cover
20 Outer door handle	59 Door panel (trim)
21 Handle grip	60 Door trim clip
22 Special nut	61 Cup (window winder)
23 Outer handle link	62 Crank
24 Safety catch link	63 Crank shield
25 Safety catch link	64 Bolt
extension	65 Nut
26 Extension ring	66 Door pull strap
27 Lock link clamp	66a Cover
28 Inner handle link	66b Armrest
29 Inner lock handle	67 Screw
30 Capscrew	68 Weatherstrip
31 Washer	69 Door sill weatherstrip
32 Washer	70 Trim frame
33 Inner handle bush	71 Connecting piece
34 Setscrew	72 Trim frame
35 Guide bar	73 Door trim moulding
36 Window winder mechanism	74 Panel
36a End piece	75 Screw

free the window weatherstrip. Lift the guide rail clear. The shorter guide rail is only removed from the front doors.

3   Remove the centre post bolts and nut (in the door cavity), then lower the window (see Fig. 11.2).

4   Detach the winder from the glass support channel.

5   Lower the window to its fullest extent and press it from its centre post guide rail.

6   Remove the upper centre post frame weatherstrip, then withdraw the centre post. The glass can now be withdrawn together with its support channel from the door.

7   To remove the window winder mechanism, unscrew its retaining nuts.

8   Refitting is a reversal of the removal procedure. Any lateral play can be corrected by adjusting the centre post position. Lubricate the window winder and door lock mechanism prior to refitting the trim; check the operation of the locks and winder.

12 Rear door fixed window – removal and refitting

1   Refer to Section 7 and remove the door trim panel.

2   Remove the holder and packing piece, which are retained by a bolt.

3   Manoeuvre the glass through the door cavity and withdraw it from the door frame.

4   Refit in the reverse procedure to the removal.

13 Windscreen and rear window – removal and fitting

1   Should it be necessary to remove the windscreen or rear window, it is generally recommended that the task be left to a glass replacement specialist or experienced fitter. However, for the owner who wishes to do the job himself, the following instructions apply. For rear screen operations, ignore paragraph 2.

2   Remove the wiper arms from their spindles, then remove the interior rear view mirror and the visors. Cover the screen heating duct aperture and upper dash panel.

3   Next, extract the trim from the outside of the screen edge rubber. This trim locks the rubber extrusion around the glass screen edge.

4   Place a blanket or suitable protection on the car bonnet/boot to prevent scoring the paintwork with the broken glass (if applicable).

5   Move to the inside of the car and have an assistant, outside the car, ready to catch the screen as it is released.

6   Wearing leather gloves or similar hand protection, push on the glass screen as near to the edge as possible, beginning at the top corners. The rubber extrusion should deform and allow the screen to move outwards out of the screen aperture. This, of course, is not applicable if the screen has shattered.

7   Remove the rubber surround from the glass or alternatively, carefully pick out the remains of the glass. Use a vacuum cleaner to extract as much of the screen debris as possible.

8   Carefully, inspect the rubber extrusion surround for signs of pitting and deterioration. Offer up the new glass to the screen aperture and check that the shape and curvature of the screen conforms to that of the aperture. A screen will break quite soon again if the aperture and glass do not suit, typically if the vehicle has been involved in an accident during which the screen broke. A car bodyshell can be

deformed easily in such instances to an extent when the aperture will need reshaping by a competent body repairer to ensure conformity with a new screen.

9   Position the new glass into the rubber extrusion surround; remember that the groove for the metal trim needs to be on the outer side of the screen assembly.

10   With the rubber now correctly positioned around the glass, a long piece of strong cord should be inserted in the slot in the rubber extrusion which is to accept the flange of the screen aperture in the bodyshell. The two free ends of the cord should finish at either the top or bottom centre and overlap each other.

11   The screen is now offered up to the aperture, and an assistant will be required to press the rubber surround hard against the bodyshell flange. Slowly, pull one end of the cord, moving around the windscreen, thereby drawing the lip of the rubber extrusion screen surround over the flange of the screen aperture.

12   Finally, ensure that the rubber surround is correctly seated around the screen; press in the metal trim strip which locks the screen in the rubber. Once the glass has been fitted satisfactorily, the windscreen wipers, visors and interior mirror may be refitted.

14 Engine compartment lid – removal and refitting

1   To remove the engine compartment lid first open it to its fullest extent.

2   Mark the position of the hinges to ensure correct alignment upon refitting. Detach the stay rod at one end (photo).

3   Unscrew the retaining nuts and remove the lid from the car.

4   Refitting is the reverse of the removal procedure. Renew the stay rod bush if it is worn.

15 Luggage compartment lid – removal and refitting

1   The procedure for the luggage compartment lid removal is identical to that for the engine compartment lid except that the stay rod is located by hinge bolts at each end (photo).

2   To remove the lid catches (photo), unscrew their retaining bolts, drive the pin from the handle (inside) and withdraw the rod and catches through the luggage compartment. Refit in the reverse order to that given above, and finally, check for satisfactory operation.

16 Bumpers (front and rear) – removal and refitting

1   The bumpers are retained on brackets secured to the main body structure. The corner sections of each bumper are attached to the adjacent wing panel.

2   If removing the front bumper, first disconnect the battery earth lead. Disconnect the leads of the horn, also the indicator lights on each side.

3   Unscrew and detach the bumper-to-body and bracket bolts, then carefully lift away the bumper.

4   Refit in the reverse order to that given above, but do not tighten the respective retaining bolts until they are all fitted and the bumper is aligned correctly. Check the indicator and horn operation to complete.

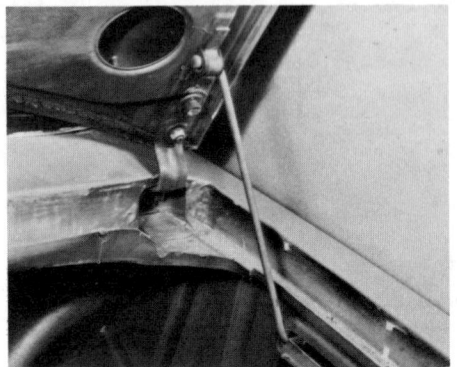

14.2 Engine compartment lid hinge and stay rod, showing rubber bush location at lid end

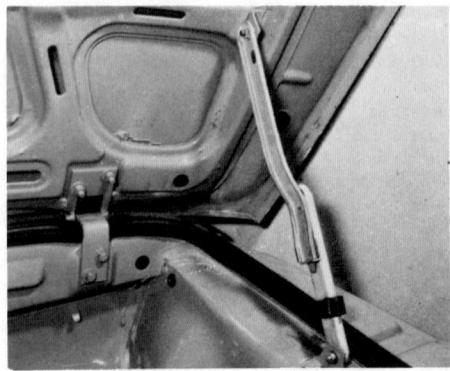

15.1 Luggage compartment lid hinge and stay rod

15.2 Luggage lid catch

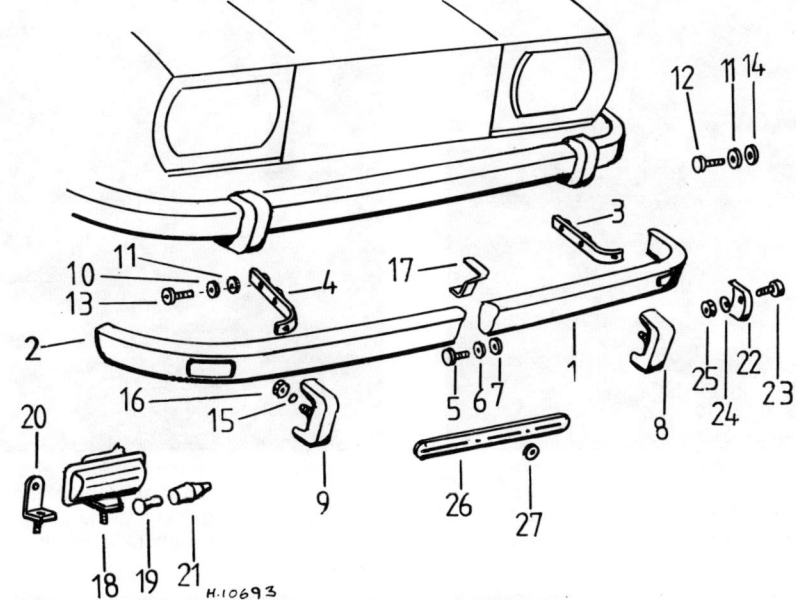

Fig. 11.3 Front bumper and indicator assembly (Sec 15)

1	Bumper (LH)	8	LH overrider	15	Washer	22	Horn bracket
2	Bumper (RH)	9	RH overrider	16	Nut	23	Bolt
3	Bracket (LH)	10	Washer	17	Joint cover	24	Washer
4	Bracket (RH)	11	Washer	18	Indicator (LH)	25	Nut
5	Bolt	12	Screw	19	Bulb	26	Number plate bracket
6	Washer	13	Screw	20	Bulb holder	27	Packing
7	Nut	14	Packing	21	Bulb holder		

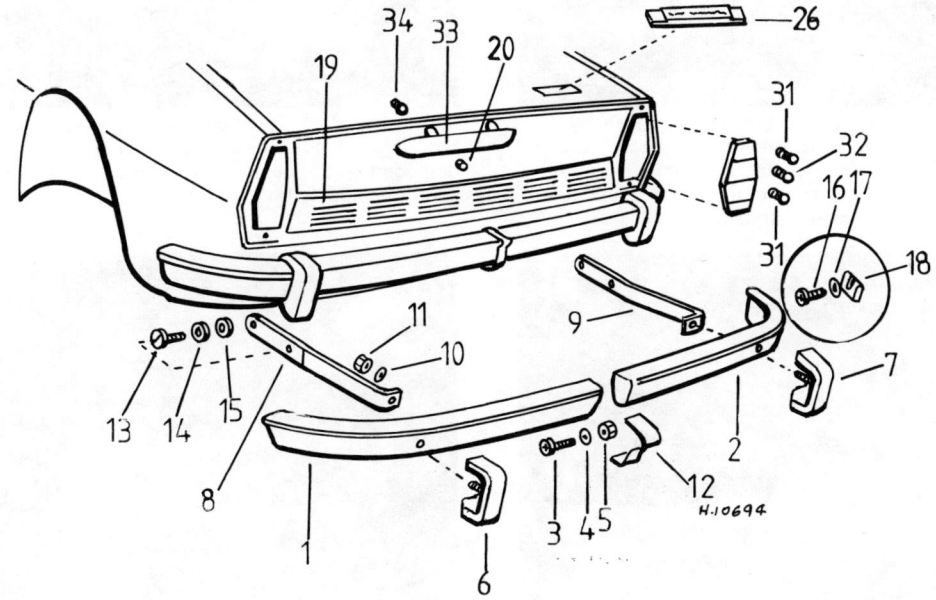

Fig. 11.4 Rear bumper and combination light assembly (Sec 16)

1	Bumper (LH)	8	Bracket (LH)	15	Washer	26	Motif
2	Bumper (RH)	9	Bracket (RH)	16	Screw	30	Rear combustion light unit
3	Bolt	10	Washer	17	Washer	31	Bulb
4	Washer	11	Nut	18	Retainer packing	32	Bulb
5	Nut	12	Joint plate	19	Rear grille panel	33	Number plate light
6	Overrider (LH)	13	Screw	20	Rubber cap	34	Soffit lamp
7	Overrider (RH)	14	Washer				

This sequence of photographs deals with the repair of the dent and paintwork damage shown in this photo. The procedure will be similar for the repair of a hole. It should be noted that the procedures given here are simplified — more explicit instructions will be found in the text

In the case of a dent the first job — after removing surrounding trim — is to hammer out the dent where access is possible. This will minimise filling. Here, the large dent having been hammered out, the damaged area is being made slightly concave

Now all paint must be removed from the damaged area, by rubbing with coarse abrasive paper. Alternatively, a wire brush or abrasive pad can be used in a power drill. Where the repair area meets good paintwork, the edge of the paintwork should be 'feathered', using a finer grade of abrasive paper

In the case of a hole caused by rusting, all damaged sheet-metal should be cut away before proceeding to this stage. Here, the damaged area is being treated with rust remover and inhibitor before being filled

Mix the body filler according to its manufacturer's instructions. In the case of corrosion damage, it will be necessary to block off any large holes before filling — this can be done with aluminium or plastic mesh, or aluminium tape. Make sure the area is absolutely clean before ...

... applying the filler. Filler should be applied with a flexible applicator, as shown, for best results; the wooden spatula being used for confined areas. Apply thin layers of filler at 20-minute intervals, until the surface of the filler is slightly proud of the surrounding bodywork

Initial shaping can be done with a Surform plane or Dreadnought file. Then, using progressively finer grades of wet-and-dry paper, wrapped around a sanding block, and copious amounts of clean water, rub down the filler until really smooth and flat. Again, feather the edges of adjoining paintwork

The whole repair area can now be sprayed or brush-painted with primer. If spraying, ensure adjoining areas are protected from over-spray. Note that at least one inch of the surrounding sound paintwork should be coated with primer. Primer has a 'thick' consistency, so will find small imperfections

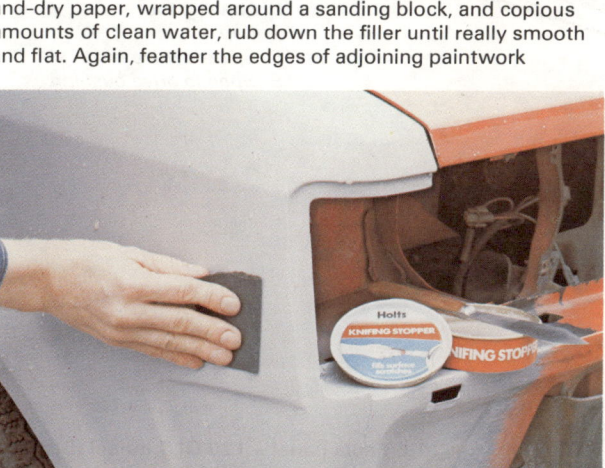

Again, using plenty of water, rub down the primer with a fine grade wet-and-dry paper (400 grade is probably best) until it is really smooth and well blended into the surrounding paintwork. Any remaining imperfections can now be filled by carefully applied knifing stopper paste

When the stopper has hardened, rub down the repair area again before applying the final coat of primer. Before rubbing down this last coat of primer, ensure the repair area is blemish-free — use more stopper if necessary. To ensure that the surface of the primer is really smooth use some finishing compound

The top coat can now be applied. When working out of doors, pick a dry, warm and wind-free day. Ensure surrounding areas are protected from over-spray. Agitate the aerosol thoroughly, then spray the centre of the repair area, working outwards with a circular motion. Apply the paint as several thin coats

After a period of about two weeks, which the paint needs to harden fully, the surface of the repaired area can be 'cut' with a mild cutting compound prior to wax polishing. When carrying out bodywork repairs, remember that the quality of the finished job is proportional to the time and effort expended

Fig. 11.5 Facia panel components (Sec 20)

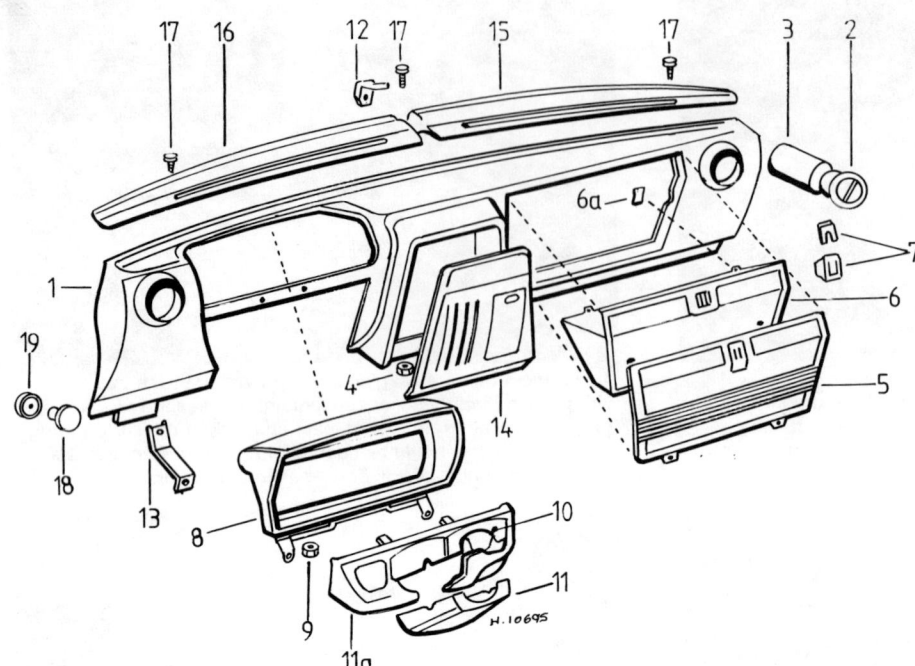

1 Panel
2 Side window demister vent
3 Vent hose
4 Nut
5 Lid
6 Glovebox
7 Fastening latch
8 Instrument panel surround
9 Nut
10 Steering column – upper shroud
11 Steering column – lower shroud
12 Centre bracket
13 Lower bracket
14 Centre panel
15 RH lower panel
16 Lower panel
17 Clip
18 Speedo drive bush
19 Speedo drive bushing

Fig. 11.6 Facia panel – 120 GLS model (Sec 20)

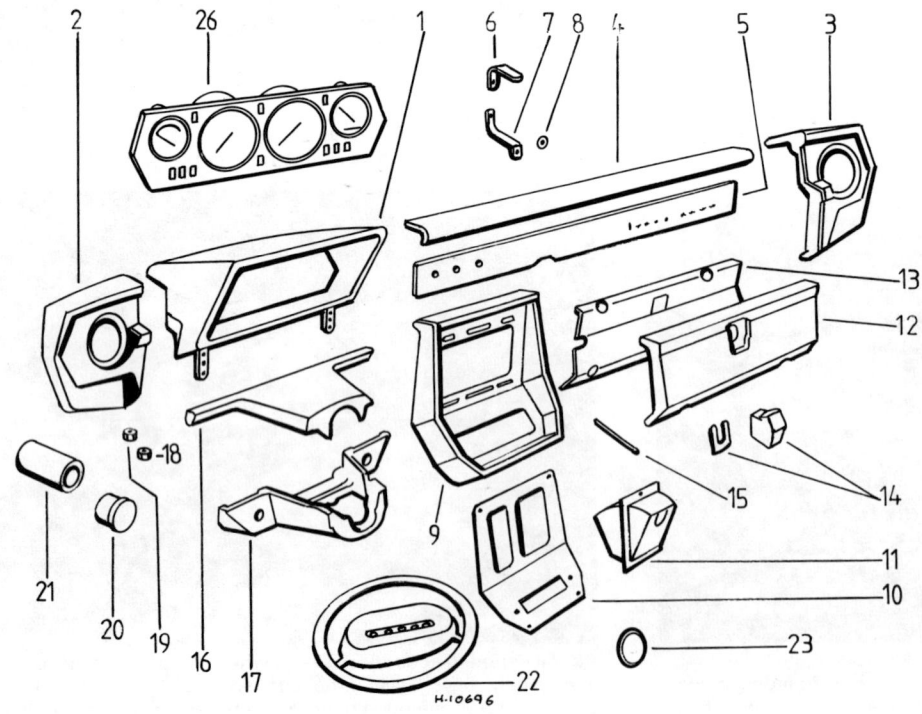

1 Instrument panel
2 LH side panel
3 RH side panel
4 Front panel
5 Cover moulding
6 Upper bracket
7 Lower bracket
8 Rubber packing
9 Centre panel
10 Centre panel cover
11 Ashtray
12 Cover panel lid
13 Lid cover
14 Lid lock
15 Link
16 Column panel upper
17 Column panel lower
18 Nut
19 Nut
20 Side window demister vent
21 Hose
22 Steering wheel (sports)
23 Emblem
26 Instrument panel

17 Front wing panel – removal and refitting

1   Refer to the previous Section and remove the bumper. If the left-hand wing panel is to be removed, detach and remove the boot lid (see Section 15).
2   Remove any trim moulding from the door sill.
3   Remove the screw holding the wing panel to the body under the sill; working from underneath, remove the three wing-to-body/door pillar post bolts, and from the boot lid-to-wing drain channel surface, remove the five retaining bolts. Just two bolts remain; these are in the front panel, directly underneath the headlight units. Get an assistant to support the wing panel whilst you remove these last two bolts. Lift the panel clear.
4   Fit a new wing-to-body seal strip.
5   Locate the wing panel and secure it with the respective bolts and screw; do not tighten them fully until the wing is aligned correctly.

18 Front body panel – removal and refitting

1   Remove the front bumper as described in Section 16.
2   Unscrew and remove the front end panel-to-wheel arch retaining bolts (located under the headlights) and the lower edge behind the bumper.
3   Remove the grille retaining bolts and lift the assembly clear. Remove the outer grille first, followed by the central panel.
4   Refit in the reverse order to that given above, but do not tighten the retaining bolts fully until all fasteners are in position and the panels are aligned.

19 Rear body panel – removal and refitting

1   Refer to Section 16 and remove the rear bumper.
2   Disconnect the engine compartment lid release cable from the catch on the panel.
3   Disconnect the battery earth cable, then detach the respective rear combination light leads on each side and the number plate light in the middle.

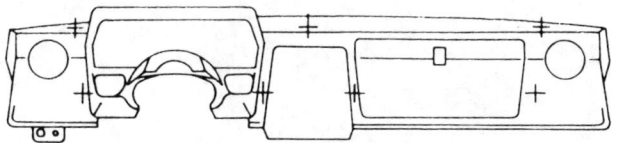

Fig. 11.7 Facia panel fastening points marked with cross (Sec 20)

4   Unscrew and remove the panel-to-body retaining bolts on each side; carefully, withdraw the panel rearwards. If necessary, give it no more than a light blow with the hand on each side to free it, but take care not to damage the panel.
5   Refitting is the reverse of the removal procedure. Do not fully tighten the retaining bolts until after the panel is correctly aligned. Reattach the rear lights and check their operation. Don't forget to reattach the engine lid release cable before shutting the lid!

20 Facia panel – removal and refitting

1   Disconnect the battery earth lead.
2   Refer to Chapter 10, Section 27 and remove the instrument panel.
3   Refer to Chapter 8, Section 12 and remove the steering wheel, then unscrew and remove the retaining screws of the upper and lower steering column shrouds.
4   Pull the heater control knobs from the levers, remove the control panel retaining screws and withdraw the panel.
5   Detach and remove the glovebox which is retained by stop screws inside.
6   The panel should now be ready for removal. Disconnect any auxiliary switches which may have been fitted and then, referring to Fig. 11.7, unscrew and remove the facia retaining bolts from the panel underside. Withdraw the panel.
7   Refit in the reverse order to that given above, ensuring that all electrical connections are securely made. On completion, check that the functions of the various instrument panel and facia switches are operational.

Skoda 120 LSE

Chapter 12 Supplement:
Revisions and information on later models

Contents

1 Introduction

This supplement contains information which is a revision of, or supplementary to, that given in the preceding eleven Chapters. It deals mainly with the modifications and improvements to the Estelle range. It is therefore recommended that, before any work starts, the relevant Sections of this Supplement are read so that any changes to servicing procedure or components may be verified.

The Sections of this Supplement follow the same order as the Chapters to which they relate, and although the Specifications are all grouped together for convenience they follow Chapter order too.

2 Specifications

The Specifications listed here are supplementary to, or revisions of, those given in earlier Chapters.

Fuel system
Jikov 32 EDSR carburettor – models from 1979
Main petrol jet:
    120L and LE models – Stage 1 110
    120 LS and LSE models:
        Stage 1 110
        Stage 2 125

Choke petrol jet (120L, LE, LS and LSE)	90		
Choke air jet diameter (all models)	5.5 mm		
Pump bypass orifice (all models)	45		
Accelerator pump discharge (all models)	6 to 8 cc per 10 strokes		

Jikov 32 EDSR carburettor – models from 1981

Main air jet – Stage 1 (all models)	185

Jikov 32 SEDR carburettor

105S and L models:

	Stage 1		Stage 2
Atomizer core diameter	20 mm		20 mm
Main petrol jet	108		125
Main air jet	190		140
Pilot jet	50		50
Pilot air jet	130		120
Auxiliary pilot jet		90	
Choke petrol jet		130	
Choke air jet diameter		7 mm	
Diaphragm control air valve	130		80
Pump bypass orifice		60	
Injector	50		–
Needle valve diameter		1.5 mm	
Suction connection diameter		1.2 mm	
Accelerator pump discharge	5 to 7 cc per 10 strokes		
Float weight	16.5 to 18.5 g		

120L models:

	Stage 1		Stage 2
Atomizer core diameter	20 mm		24 mm
Main petrol jet	108		130
Main air jet	190		140
Pilot jet	50		50
Pilot air jet	130		120
Auxiliary pilot jet		90	
Choke petrol jet		130	
Choke air jet diameter		7 mm	
Diaphragm control air valve	160		80
Pump bypass orifice		60	
Injector	50		–
Needle valve diameter		1.5 mm	
Suction connection diameter		1.2 mm	
Accelerator pump discharge	5 to 7 per 10 strokes		
Float weight	16.5 to 18.5 g		

120LS, LSE and Rapid:

	Stage 1		Stage 2
Atomizer cone diameter	20 mm		24 mm
Main petrol jet	110		135
Main air jet	190		140
Pilot jet	50		50
Pilot air jet	130		120
Auxiliary pilot jet		90	
Choke petrol jet		130	
Choke air jet diameter		7 mm	
Diaphragm control air valve	160		80
Pump bypass orifice		60	
Injector	50		–
Needle valve diameter		1.5 mm	
Suction connection diameter		1.2 mm	
Accelerator pump discharge	5 to 7 cc per 10 strokes		
Float weight	16.5 to 18.5 g		

Driveshafts – Rapid with trailing arm suspension
Torque wrench settings

	Nm	lbf ft
Set bolts – outboard flange	32 to 35	24 to 26

Suspension and steering
Front spring dimensions

Wire diameter:	
Saloon from 1979	12.5 mm
Rapid	12 mm
Coil outer diameter:	
Saloon from 1979	103 mm
Rapid	102 mm
Free length:	
Saloon 1979 to 1983	276 mm
Saloon from 1983	284 mm
Rapid	304 mm

Rear suspension

Type (Rapid from 1984 on)	Trailing arm, swinging half axle and independently sprung wheels with coil springs and telescopic shock absorbers

Spring dimensions:
   Wire diameter:

Saloon October 1979 to July 1983	13.6 mm
Saloon from July 1983	13.5 mm
Rapid	12.5 mm

   Coil outer diameter:

Saloon October 1979 to July 1983	114.6 mm
Saloon from July 1983	114 mm
Rapid	113.5 mm

   Free length:

Saloon October 1979 to July 1983	316 mm
Saloon from July 1983	325.5 mm
Rapid 1982 to 1984	412 mm
Rapid from 1984 (trailing arm)	436 mm

Wheel alignment – 13 in wheels

Front wheel toe-in	1 ± 2 mm (0.039 ± 0.079 in)
Front wheel camber	1° ± 30'
Front wheel castor angle*	4°45' to 6°30'
Kingpin inclination	8°30'

*A 1° difference between left and right wheels is permissible
Note: All settings are with the vehicle in a semi laden condition

Rack and pinion steering

Axial force required to move rack	10 to 12 kgf (22.5 to 27 lbf)

Torque wrench settings

	Nm	lbf ft
Rear suspension/axle		
Wheel hub drive flange nut (outer)	300	220
Wheel hub shaft flange nut (inner)	100	74
Oblique arm mounting block bolt	60	44
Rack and pinion steering		
Pinion cover-to-housing bolts	7	5
Reducing sleeve to rack	50 to 60	37 to 44
Reducing sleeve ro rack locknut	50 to 60	37 to 44

Braking system
Disc brakes – Rapid

Disc:

Diameter	247 mm (9.633 in)

   Thickness:

Early models	9 mm (0.351 in)
Late models	9.5 mm (0.371 in)

   Minimum thickness:

Due to regrinding	8 mm (0.312 in)
Due to wear	7.5 mm (0.293 in)

Caliper-to-disc clearance:

Early models	17.4 to 17.6 mm (0.679 to 0.686 in)
Late models	17.15 to 17.35 mm (0.669 to 0.677 in)

Caliper piston:

Diameter	34 mm (1.326 in)
Length	29.6 mm (1.154 in)

Servo unit – Rapid and 1984 Saloon

Servo-to-master cylinder clearance	0.5 to 1 mm (0.0195 to 0.039 in)

Brake light switch

Pedal-to-switch clearance:

Saloons	10 mm (0.39 in)
Rapid	15 mm (0.58 in)

General dimensions and weights
Where different from the values given at the front of the book
Overall dimensions

Length:

Rapid up to October 1984	4175 mm (162.8 in)
All models from October 1984	4200 mm (163.8 in)

Width:

Rapid and all other models from October 1984	1610 mm (62.8 in)

Height (laden):

Rapid up to October 1984	1345 mm (52.5 in)
All models from October 1984	1400 mm (54.6 in)

Ground clearance (laden):
    Rapid up to October 1984 .... 116 mm (4.5 in)
    All models from October 1984 .... 110 mm (4.3 in)

Kerb weight
Rapid up to October 1984 .... 915 kg (2017 lb)

Underbody view of front end

1 Spare wheel and retainer	4 Steering balljoints	7 Track rod
2 Anti-roll bar	5 Lower wishbone	8 Steering rack housing
3 Front shock absorber lower mounting	6 Lower pivot pin	9 Steering pinion housing

Underbody view of rear end

1	Cooling system drain plugs	5	Shock absorber lower mounting	9	Gearbox oil drain plug
2	Brake hydraulic hose	6	Radius arm to half axle attachment point	10	Differential oil drain plug
3	Radius arm mounting block	7	Exhaust silencer	11	Engine oil sump
4	Radius arm	8	Driveshaft	12	Gearbox support crossmember

Engine compartment

1	Air cleaner	5	Oil filler cap (engine)	8	Exhaust downpipes
2	Ignition coil	6	Water pump	9	Coolant header tank
3	Alternator	7	Distributor/carburettor vacuum hose	10	Carburettor
4	Distributor				

3 Engine

General

1 Design changes have been made to various components, but these do not affect the procedures given in Chapter 1. Where changes are worthy of note, they will be given in the following paragraphs.

Full-flow lubrication

2 As from engine number 853575/9 (August 1983) all engines, including that fitted to the Rapid, have a full-flow oil system which is self-bleeding.

3 This system is similar to the older type except that the oil spray bolt for lubrication of the timing chain is deleted, and the lower gallery blanking plug inside the timing cover has a 1 mm bleed hole drilled in it.

4 Cooling system

Automatic hot air intake

1 Since October 1983, a revised carburettor air filter intake pipe assembly has been introduced, which incorporates air automatic changeover for hot/cold air intake.

2 A wax pellet type thermostat, housed in the air filter intake operates a flap valve via linkages.

3 When ambient air temperature is cold, hot air will be drawn through the duct from above the exhaust manifold. When warm, cool air will be drawn straight from the air intake.

4 The thermostat changeover temperature is set at about 32 to 35°C (90 to 95°F).

5 Fuel system

Jikov 32 EDSR carburettor – modifications

1 The Jikov 32 EDSR carburettor has been modified in various areas

over the years to improve performance and give better starting and fuel economy when running. The following paragraphs deal with these changes, and include some information which is not given in Chapter 3.

Secondary stage throtttle operation

2 The second stage throttle is operated by the diaphragm (item C in photo 3.0 of Chapter 3).

3 The purpose of the secondary throttle is to act as the main system for higher engine loads, incorporating a bypass when it is not in use, and provide an auxiliary idle run.

4 The Stage 1 throttle valve unlocks the second stage mechanically when it has opened through 43°. After which the diaphragm, operating by air taken from the narrow part of the atomizer cover, will, through mechanical linkage, operate the second stage throttle valve.

5 Early (pre 1980) diaphragm housings were cast, the diaphragm being retained on its shaft by a nut. If this nut is not tight, it can cause leakage and subsequent failure of the second stage.

6 From 1980 the lower casing was made of steel with the diaphragm riveted on to the pushrod.

Choke – improving control

7 On pre 1980 carburettors, the choke control was by means of a spring, piston and brass jet (see photo 6.9 in Chapter 3).

8 Post 1980, this control was replaced by drillings in the carburettor body, and led to a tendency for the engine to run excessively fast when on choke.

9 This can be overcome by drilling a 1 mm hole in the choke plate, as shown in Fig. 12.1

Jikov 32 SEDR carburettor
General description

10 The Jikov 32 SEDR fitted to 1984 models is very similar in operation to its predecessor being of the same downdraught, two stage principle of operation. Some minor changes in design are apparent but, in general, provided the servicing operations in Chapter 3 are followed, and attention given to the Specifications of this Chapter, no difficulty should be encountered on servicing the carburettor.

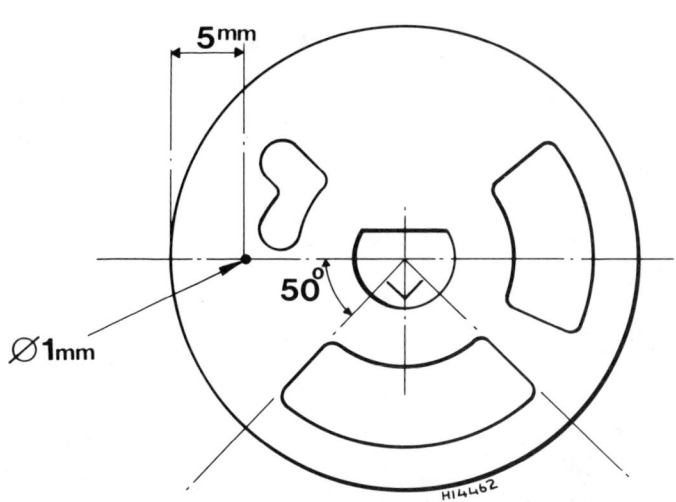

Fig. 12.1 Drill a 1 mm hole in the indicated position to reduce excessive engine speed when on choke (Sec 5)

Adjustment – slow running

11 The adjustment procedure for the 32 EDSR carburettor should be followed, except that the adjustment screws are in different positions (photo).

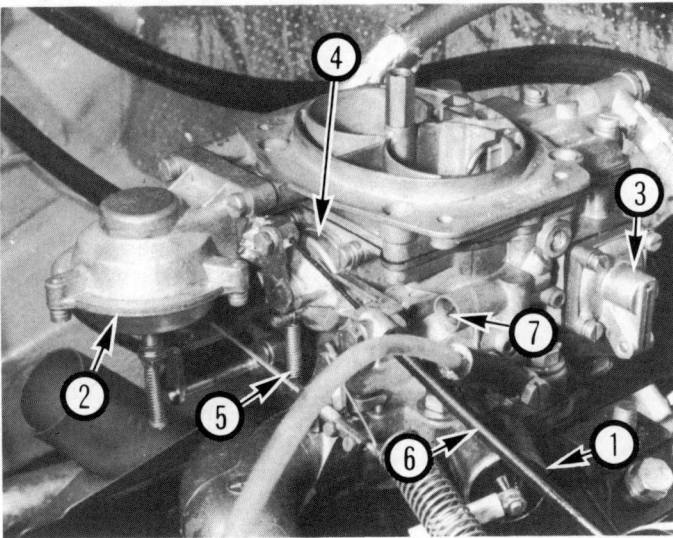

5.11 Jikov 32 SEDR carburettor

1 Anti-dieseling valve	5 Accelerator cable
2 Stage II diaphragm	6 Choke cable
3 Accelerator pump	7 Air correction screw
4 Choke housing	

The idle mixture screw is situated just below the air correction screw

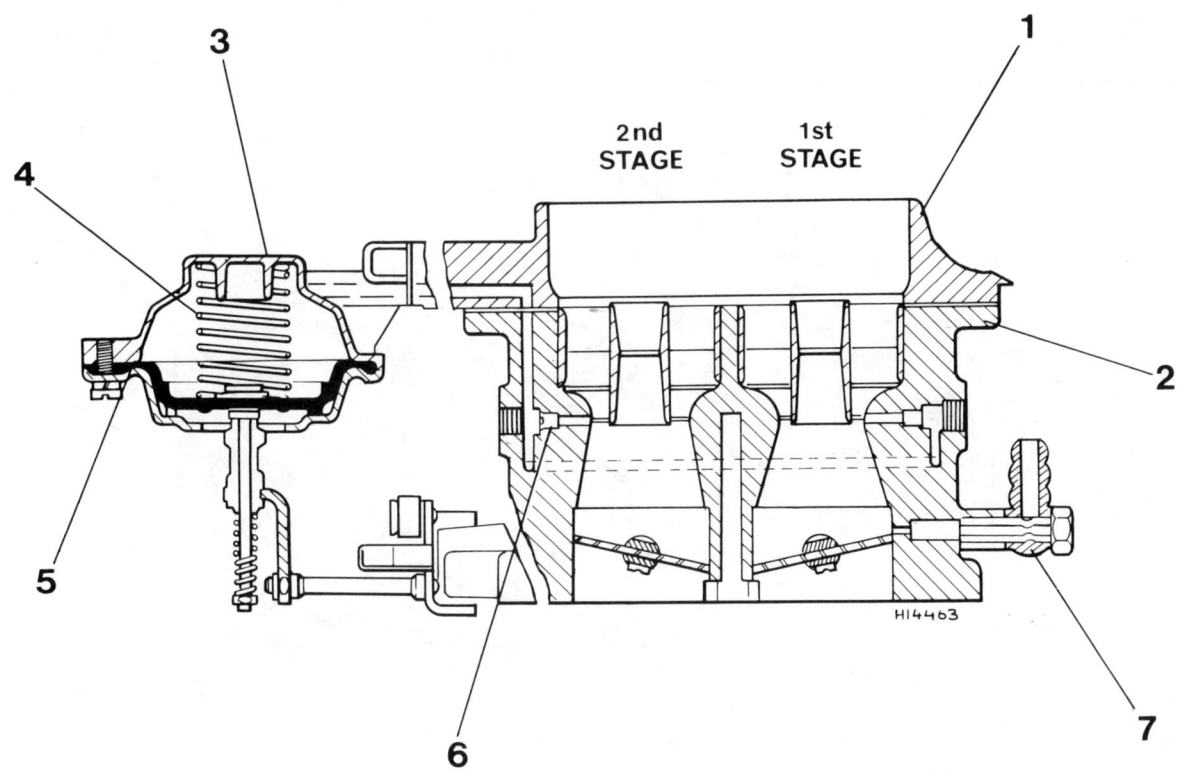

Fig. 12.2 Sectional view of Jikov 32 SEDR carburettor – Stage II control (Sec 5)

1 Float chamber cover	4 Spring	6 Diaphragm control air	7 Vacuum connection
2 Float chamber body	5 Diaphragm	valve	
3 Diaphragm housing			

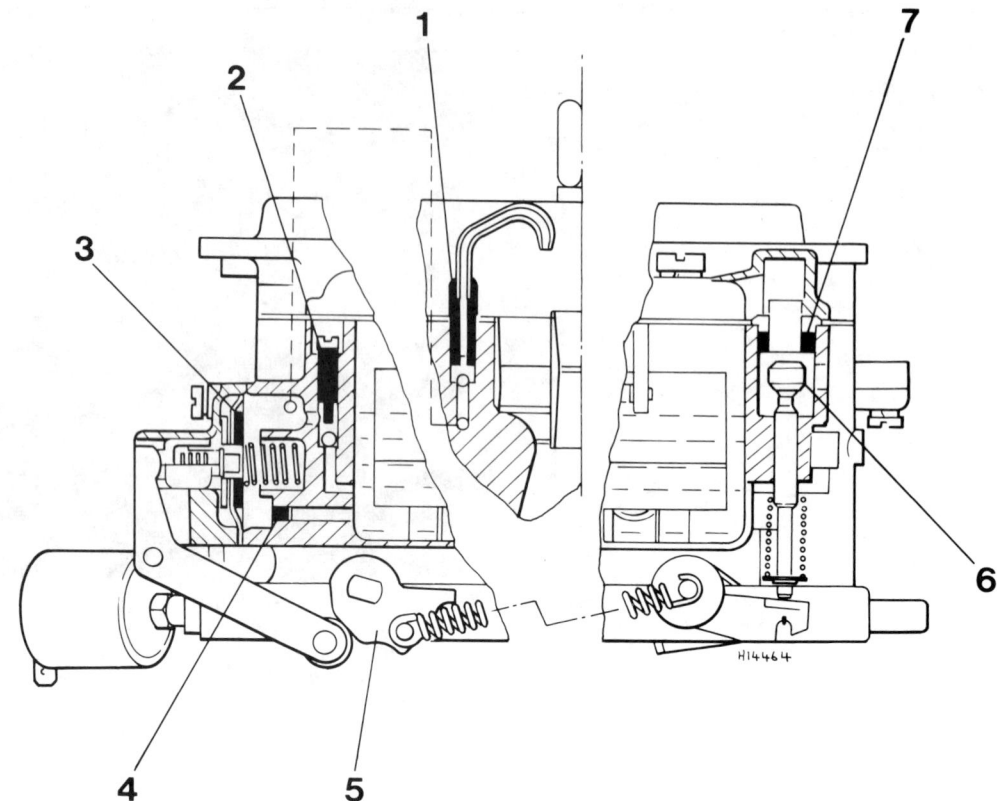

Fig. 12.3 Cutaway view of Jikov 32 SEDR carburettor – accelerator pump and float chamber air venting system (Sec 5)

1 Injector	3 Diaphragm	5 Accelerator pump actuating arm	6 Air venting valve
2 Stop screw	4 Pump bypass orifice		7 Air venting valve seat

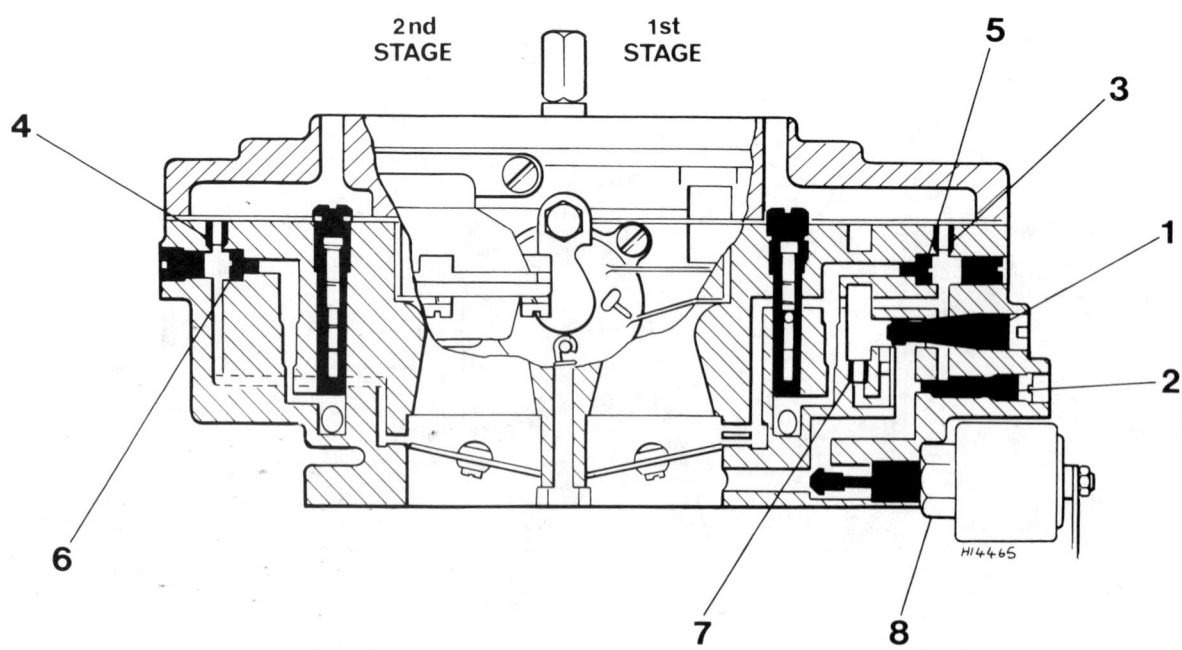

Fig. 12.4 Sectional view of Jikov 32 SEDR carburettor (Sec 5)

1 Air correction screw	4 Bypass air jet	7 Auxiliary air pilot jet (Stage I)	8 Electromagnetic separator (anti-dieseling valve)
2 Rich mixture screw (idle)	5 Pilot jet		
3 Pilot air jet	6 Bypass jet		

6 Clutch

Diaphragm clutch

1 Later Skoda models are fitted with a dipahragm type clutch, replacing the coil spring type originally fitted.
2 These diaphragm type clutches may be of differing manufacture, and although different in construction to the coil spring type, the servicing procedures in Chapter 5 should suffice to enable a clutch change to be carried out.

Clutch release bearings

3 Some replacement clutch release bearings may have the bearing shield (which rotates with the bearing) in contact with the release arm.
4 If this occurs, file the release arm at point of contact to give a 0.5 mm (0.02 in) clearance.

7 Transmission

Gearchange mechanism – modifications

1 The gearchange rod from the gear lever to the gearbox (the tie-rod item 22 in Fig. 6.7 of Chapter 6) has been manufactured in three different forms.
2 The basic servicing procedures in Chapter 6 remain unchanged but, for clarity, the differences are detailed in Fig. 12.5.
3 The overall lengths (Y) are identical and are interchangeable on all four-speed gearboxes.

Gearbox mountings – transmission noise

4 Some vehicles may develop a pronounced transmission noise which can be traced to the gearbox mounting bushes.
5 It is caused by the gearbox support beam cutting through the space

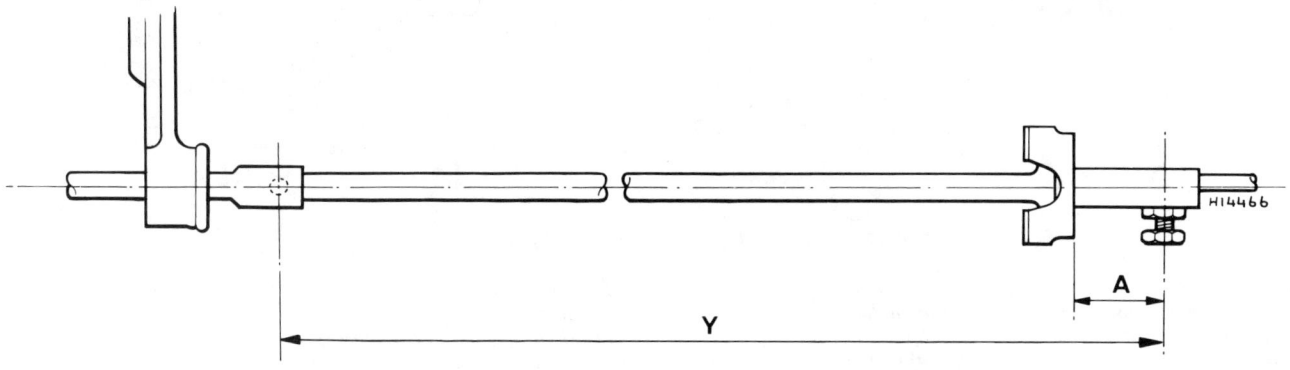

Fig. 12.5 Gearchange rod dimensions (Sec 7)

Models 1976 to May 1983 A = 12 mm (0.46 in)
Cage and bushes available separately
Models May 1983 to August 1984 A = 12 mm (0.46 in)
Cage and bushes integral part of rod

Models from August 1984 A = 77 mm (3 in)
Cage and bushes integral with rod
Dimension Y is the same for all models

tube rubber spigot; allowing metal-to-metal contact (Fig. 12.6).
6 The bushes should be renewed and checked for correct alignment on refitting.

8 Driveshafts – Rapid

Removal and refitting

1 Remove the bolts from the outer flange and lower the shaft away from the trailing axle assembly.
2 Using two broad-faced levers on the inner joint and gearbox case, lever out the shaft. A sharp jolt will disengage the circlip holding the driveshaft to the differential pinion. **Note:** *to replace either rubber gaiter, it is easier to remove the outboard joint.*
3 Refit the driveshafts by pressing the inboard end into the differential sun gear, ensuring the retaining clip is fully engaged.
4 Offer the outboard flange up to its position on the trailing axle and insert and tighten the bolts to the correct torque (see Specifications).

Dismantling and reassembly

5 The shaft should be kept scrupulously clean at all times. **Note:** *The constant velocity joint should never be dismantled beyond that stage given here for regreasing.*
Outboard joint
6 Hold the shaft in a soft-faced vice, remove the gaiter retaining clips, and pull back the gaiter.
7 Using a soft metal drift of block of wood, drive the constant velocity joint centre off the shaft. Keep the drift as close to the shaft as possible, and hold the shaft at a slight angle while driving the joint off. Be ready to catch the joint before it falls.
8 Remove the outer gaiter and carefully clean the joint and shaft.
Constant velocity joint
9 *Under no circumstances is the constant velocity joint to be dismantled.* It should be cleaned, and then repacked with a suitable lubricant (consult your dealer).

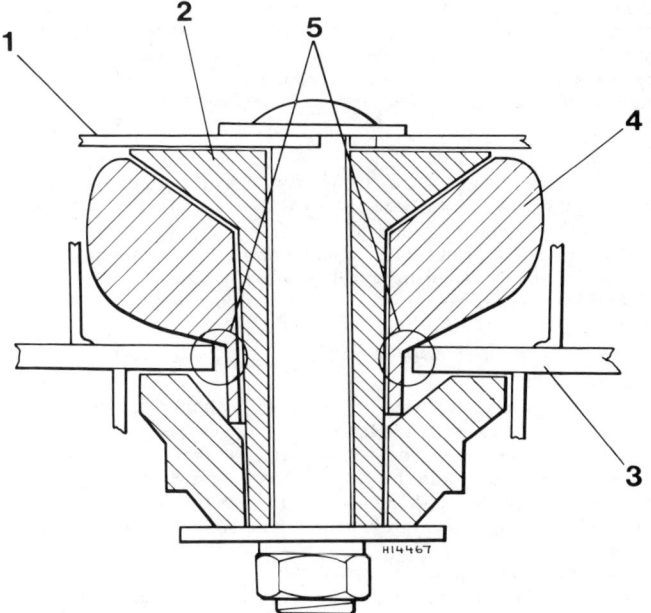

Fig. 12.6 Gearbox mounting (Sec 7)

1 *Gearbox bracket*
2 *Spacer tube*
3 *Gearbox support beam*
4 *Rubber spigot*
5 *Area of most wear*

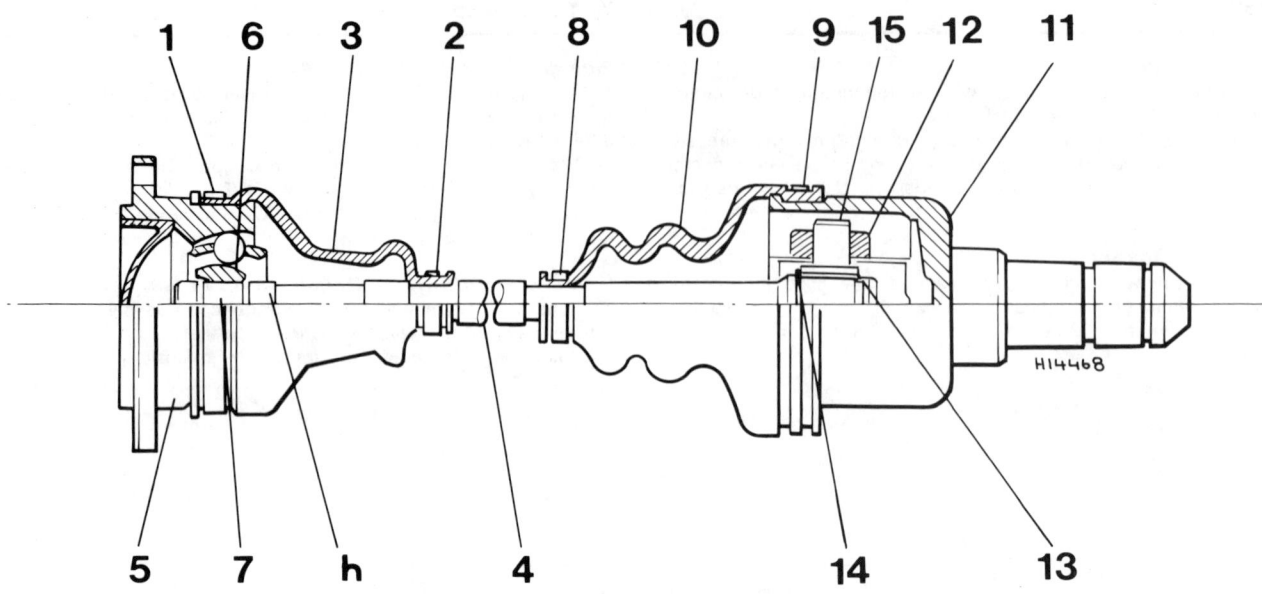

Fig. 12.7 Sectional view of Rapid driveshaft (Sec 8)

1	Gaiter retaining clip	5	Outboard flange
2	Gaiter retaining clip	6	Joint centre
3	Gaiter (outer)	7	Circlip
4	Driveshaft	8	Gaiter retaining clip

9	Gaiter retaining clip	12	Drive blocks
10	Gaiter (inner)	13	Circlip
11	Inner flange and splined	14	Circlip
	shaft	15	Spider

Inner joint
10 Remove the inner gaiter clips and gaiter. **Note:** *this will allow the inner flange with splined shaft and drive blocks to become disengaged.*
11 Mark all components relative to one another before disengaging the splined shaft and drive blocks.
12 To remove a spider joint from the shaft, remove its circlip and mark the joint's position relative to the shaft. Using a press suitably arranged, push the shaft out of the spider.
13 Refitting a spider is a reversal of this procedure, but it should be pointed out that it is really a specialist job; requiring pressures in the order of 2.5 tonnes, and is best left to a suitably equipped garage.
Reassembly
14 Lubricate the spider, drive blocks and housing using 100g of plastic lubricant (always use the full 100g).
15 Assemble the components in their relative marked positions.
16 Fit the small end of the gaiter into its recess and over the carrier. Move the joint over its full extent of travel several times.
17 Centralise the joint and lift the gaiter to allow any air pressure to dissipate. Refit the retaining cups.
18 Fit the circlip and gaiter to the shaft and fill the constant velocity joint with a suitable lubricant.
19 Hold the driveshaft vertically in a vice, and position the constant velocity joint centrally on the shaft. Compress the circlip and push the joint on to the shaft.
20 Using a block of wood to protect the joint, drive it onto the shaft until the circlip engages with its retaining groove.
21 With the joint assembled this far, complete the lubrication by packing a further 80g of lubricant into the joint.
22 Fit the gaiter over the joint and refit the retaining clips.
23 Fit the shaft(s) back into the vehicle, as described in the preceding paragraphs.

9 Suspension and steering

General
1 The front suspension has undergone some minor changes, but remains basically the same as described in Chapter 8. The main changes are of a dimensional nature, later models having a wider track, and uprated springs. Refer to the Specifications for details.
2 The rear suspension has undergone dimensional changes, and uprated springs are fitted on some models. On Rapid models the rear

suspension is completely different, being of the semi-trailing arm type and this is discussed later in this Supplement.
3 On models produced after November 1981 rack and pinion steering is used, and this will be dealt with in this Supplement.

Front axle – servicing
4 As previously mentioned, the front axle generally remains the same as before except for dimensional changes to the tie-rods. The torsion bars and some bushes may be slightly different.
5 In the case of those vehicles fitted with rack and pinion steering, the front axle beam has a slightly different profile. Provided the instructions for dismantling and reassembly in Chapter 8 are followed, no problems should occur during servicing of these items.

Steering box oil level
6 Previously it has been stated that the oil level should reach the brim of the filler hole (Chapter 8, Section 15), but it has been found that this can lead to an increase in oil leaks.
7 The correct oil level can be determined by manufacturing a dipstick from stiff wire to the dimensions shown in Fig. 12.8.
8 As can be seen, the full mark is 15 mm from the end of the dipstick.

Rack and pinion steering
General
9 The rack and pinion steering assembly is bolted to the front axle beam by two brackets. The track rods complete the connection to the front wheels, via a ball and socket joints at their inboard ends and balljoints, where they join the wheels. The pinion shaft is connected to the steering column shaft by a bolted coupling. The track rods are adjustable, meaning the front wheels can be set to the desired toe-in or toe-out.
Removal from vehicle
10 Remove the spare wheel and, from inside the vehicle, pull back the carpet and disconnect the lower coupling on the steering wheel shaft (photo).
11 Referring to Chapter 8, remove the two outer track rod balljoints.
12 Remove the four bolts securing the two brackets which hold the steering rack to the front axle beam (photo).
13 Remove the rack, complete with track rod, from the vehicle.
Dismantling and inspection
14 With the pinion shaft suitably protected, clamp the assembly in a vice

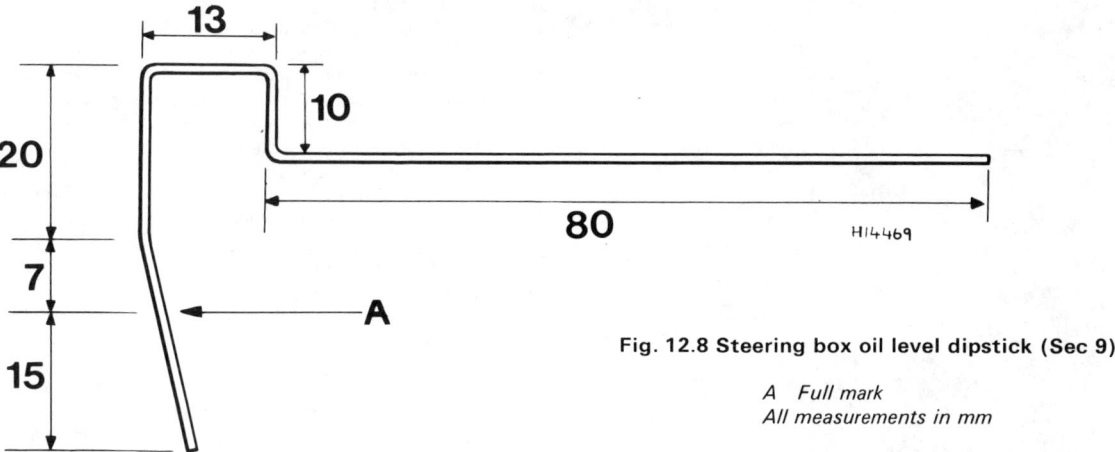

Fig. 12.8 Steering box oil level dipstick (Sec 9)

A   Full mark
All measurements in mm

9.10 Steering shaft lower coupling securing bolt (arrowed)

with soft jaws, so both track rod ends may be worked on.

15 Loosen the locknuts on the balljoints and then unscrew them from the track rod. Inspect them for excessive wear and renew as necessary.

16 Remove the clips securing the rubber gaiters to the rack assembly and remove them (photo). Be prepared to catch any oil spillage. If the rubber gaiters are spilt, or show signs of cracking, they should be renewed.

17 To remove the inner ball and socket joint, bend back the tabs of the locking washer, undo the locking nut and unscrew the coupling sleeve and reducing sleeve.

18 Alternatively, leave the locknut done up, and unscrew the coupling and secure as a unit, then remove the coupling from the sleeve.

19 The coupling and balljoint can now be inspected for pitting, scoring, cracks or excessive wear, and new parts obtained as necessary.

20 Remove the two bolts from the yoke cover on the pinion housing (carefully, as there is a spring under it) retrieve the spring and then remove the yoke and the O-ring seal from the pinion housing (photo).

21 Inspect the O-ring for condition, and the yoke for any scoring or deep wear marks in the area where it bears on the pinion shaft. Obtain new parts as necessary.

22 Remove the bolts securing the pinion cover and lift off the cover; retaining the distance washers and spacers.

9.12 Steering rack-to-front axle beam bolts (arrowed)

9.16 The steering rack rubber gaiters are secured by plastic clips (arrowed)

9.20 Steering rack yoke cover retaining bolts (arrowed)

23 Clamp the pinion housing in the vice by the pinion shaft and gently tap the pinion housing off the shaft. The top bearing will remain on the shaft.
24 Push the rack out of the pinion housing.
25 The two pinion shaft bearings can now be inspected, they are on the shaft and the outer still in the pinion housing. If they need replacing then some form of puller and or extractor will be required to remove them. If they are renewed, care should be exercised when pressing the bearings back into the housing or onto the shaft to avoid damage.
26 Inspect the toother rack for pitting, broken teeth or excessive wear and obtain new parts as necessary.

Reassembly
27 With new parts to hand, as required, press the bottom bearing into the housing after smearing it with oil. Ensure the outer face of the bearing contacts the housing bottom face.
28 Coat the steering rack with oil and re-install it in the housing.
29 Next reinstall the pinion, oil the top bearing, and push it over the end of the pinion shaft. A special tool (MP 7-109) should now be used to press the bearings fully home. If this is not available, careful use of a vice may suffice.
30 The bearings and shaft should be pressed together until the inner faces of the bearings are contacting the faces of the rack teeth.

31 Smear the pinion housing-to-pinion cover mating surfaces with oil, and locate a new gasket on the housing.
32 Measure the distance from the inner face of the bearing to the outer face of the gasket.
33 Assemble the spacer, with distance washers, so that their total thickness is within 1 mm of this measurement. Distance washers can be obtained which are 1 and 2 mm thick.
34 Place these assembled parts into the housing, the distance washers on the outer surface of the bearing, followed by the spacer ring.
35 Fit an O-ring seal in place on the pinion cover, smear with oil and bolt the cover in place on the pinion housing, tightening to the torque figures given in the Specifications.
36 Check that the pinion rotates freely and that there is no excessive backlash in the rack.
37 Oil the surface of the yoke bore in the pinion housing and the mating surface of the yoke cover.
38 Locate the yoke into the bore of the housing, press a sealing ring into the groove, and position the spring into the recess in the yoke.
39 Using a new gasket, bolt down the yoke cover.
40 Using a dynamometer (or a spring balance) check the axial force required to move the steering rack. Do this three times and use the average figure obtained. This should be within the figures shown in the Specifications.
41 If the figure is too high, reduce it by fitting distance washers between the yoke cover and pinion housing. Washers available are 0.2 mm thick; one washer will reduce the axial force by 2 kgf (4.5 lbf).
42 If the figure is too low, renew the pressure spring.
43 Screw the bolt and locknut into the centre of the yoke cover, set the rack at its central position and tighten the bolt to eliminate backlash between the rack and the pinion. Back off the bolt about one tenth of a turn (approximately 30°), coat the shank with sealing compound and tighten the locknut.
44 Screw **new** threaded reducing sleeves on to both ends of the rack, tightening to the torque figure given in the Specifications (to tighten use the coupling sleeve with the locknut screwed onto the reducing sleeve). The recommended tightening method is to clamp one coupling sleeve in a vice and induce the torque by tightening the other sleeve.
45 Using a suitable drift, stake the threaded reducing sleeve to the slot in the steering rack.
46 Remove the coupling sleeves used to tighten the reducing sleeves, grease the ball ends of the track rods (use a lithium based grease), insert the ball end into the cavity of the reducing sleeve and loosely assemble the coupling sleeve to the reducing sleeve; attaching the track rod to the the rack. Do the sleeves up finger tight.
47 Place the rubber dust boots on to the track rods and then screw the balljoints to the outer ends of the track rods.
48 These outer balljoints should be screwed down the track rod until the distance between the centre of the ball pin and the first reduced land on the inner track rod end as specified (see Fig. 12.9).

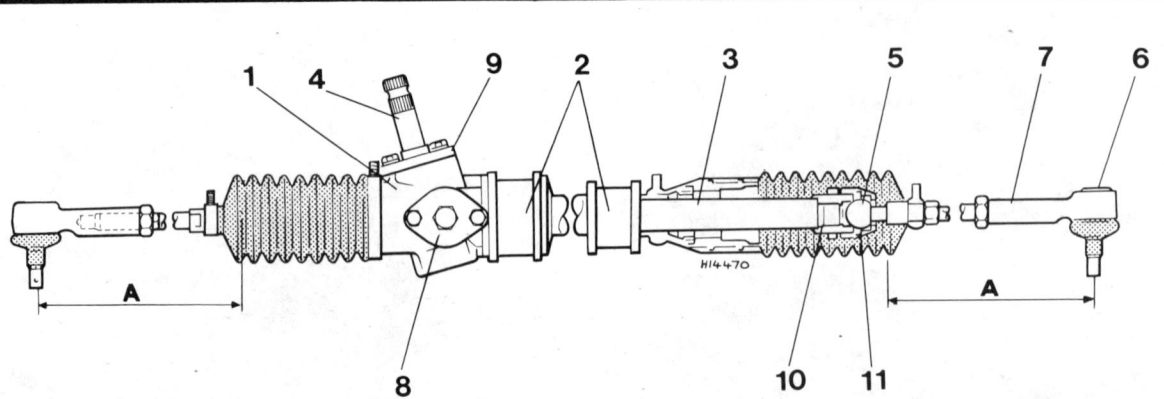

Fig. 12.9 Cutaway view of steering rack and pinion (Sec 9)

1 Rack housing	4 Pinion	6 Balljoint (outer)	9 Pinion cover
2 Crossmember bracket	5 Ball and socket connection	7 Track rod	10 Reducing sleeve
location	(inner)	8 Yoke cover	11 Coupling sleeve
3 Rack			

A = 268 mm (10.5 in): Initial setting

49 If it is necessary to adjust this dimension, then move each outer ball pin joint by an equal amount to preserve steering geometry. **Note:** *this is a basic setting only and final tracking operations will be done with the steering gear in the car.*

50 Tighten the coupling sleeve on the threaded reducing sleeve so that a force of 1.5 to 2.5 kgf m (3.3 to 5.5 lbf) is required to induce axial movement of the track rods.

51 When this condition has been obtained tighten the locknuts to the specified torque and then bend the tab washers to lock both the coupling sleeve and the locknut in position.

52 Slip the ends of the dust boots into their recesses on the track rods and fit and tighten their securing clips.

53 Fit and secure the clip to the rubber gaiter farthest from the pinion housing, then pour 150 cc of EP 90 oil into the housing through the remaining open end of the other gaiter, then fit and tighten the securing clip.

54 Fit new rubber bushes to the recesses in the steering rack housing. The unit is now ready for installation in the vehicle.

Refitting to vehicle

55 Offer the rack up to its position on the front axle beam, and ensure that the steering pinion enters the lower steering coupling inside the car.

56 Position the retaining brackets over the rubber bushes, fit and tighten the bolts.

57 Tighten the clamp bolt on the lower steering coupling, ensuring the split segment of the splined socket is perpendicular to the flat ground land on the upper shaft.

58 Refer to Chapter 8 and refit the outer balljoints. Chapter 8 also gives the detail for setting the tracking, which is best done by your Skoda dealer who has the necessary equipment.

Rear suspension/axle – Rapid

59 The rear suspension on Rapid models is different to that on Saloons in that it employs trailing arms, swinging half axles and independently-sprung wheels.

60 The rear suspension/axle unit can be removed after disconnecting the coil springs, shock absorbers, and all connection to the body and differential. **Note:** *When removing the rear suspension/axle unit* **do not**

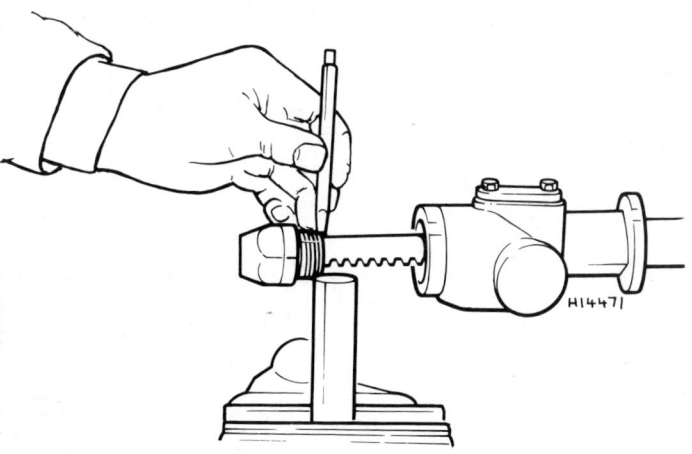

Fig. 12.10 Staking the threaded reducing sleeve to the rack (Sec 9)

separate the oblique and trailing arms as this will upset the axle geometry. If separation is absolutely necessary the job should be entrusted to your dealer.

61 The following tasks can be successfully undertaken with the suspension/axle unit *in situ*.

Removal and refitting of the brake mechanism
Removal and refitting of the driveshafts
Removal and refitting of the shock absorbers
Removal and refitting of the coil springs

Reference to Chapters 7, 8 and 9 will enable these operations to be carried out, as many trailing arm suspension components are the same as used for the older suspension.

62 The following tasks require the removal of the suspension/axle assembly.

Removal and refitting of the brake backing plate
Removal and refitting of the wheel hub flanges (inner and outer)
Removal and refitting of the wheel hub bearings

All these procedures are given in the next sub-section.

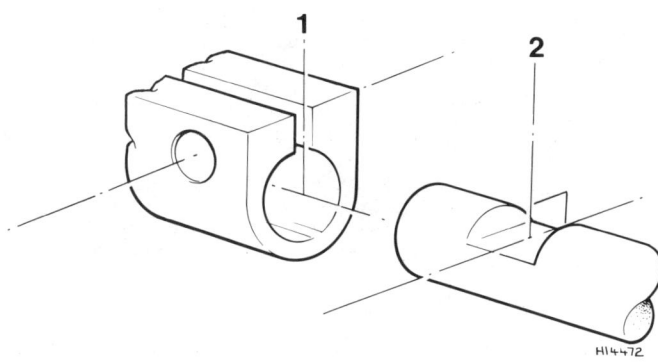

Fig. 12.11 Steering column lower coupling (Sec 9)

Ensure the split segment of the splined socket (1) is perpendicular to the flat ground land on the upper shaft (2)

Rear hub bearings – Rapid

Note: *special pullers, jigs, presses and drifts are used by Skoda dealers during the following operations. The home mechanic should be able to adapt standard tools if the Skoda equipment cannot be borrowed.*

Removal and refitting

63 Jack up the car and support it securely under the rear subframe.

64 Remove the roadwheel, shock absorber and coil spring (chapters 7 and 8). Detach the driveshaft from the wheel hub shaft flange and tie it up out of the way. Clean and cover the exposed joint to prevent the ingress of dirt.

65 Remove the elastic strip which forms the bottom stop of the trailing arm.

66 Detach the handbrake cable (Chapter 9).

67 Undo the bolt which secures the forward end of the oblique arm to the gearbox support frame.

68 Disconnect the trailing arm where it joins the vehicle subframe. The whole assembly can now be lifted clear. **Note:** *do not separate the oblique and trailing arms.*

69 Remove the brake drum and the nut securing the wheel hub drive flange to the wheel hub shaft.

70 Using a puller (or the special Skoda jig) remove the hub drive flange from the shaft splines. It will probably be necessary to use a suitable device to stop the shaft rotating.

71 Remove the complete brake mechanism, backing plate cover and backing plate.

72 Remove the nut of the wheel hub shaft flange from the inner side of the hub and pull the flange from the shaft.

73 Using a puller, remove the wheel hub shaft and bearing.

74 Remove the sealing ring from the inner side of the hub, using a hook. From the outer side, drift the inner, single new bearing out of the hub.

75 Refitting is a reversal of this procedure bearing in mind the following points.

76 Drive the inner bearing in as far as it will go, and reinstall the sealing ring with sealing lip and expander spring toward the bearing.

77 Use a press to fit the double row ball-bearings to the wheel hub shaft, and press it home until it bears against the shaft collar.

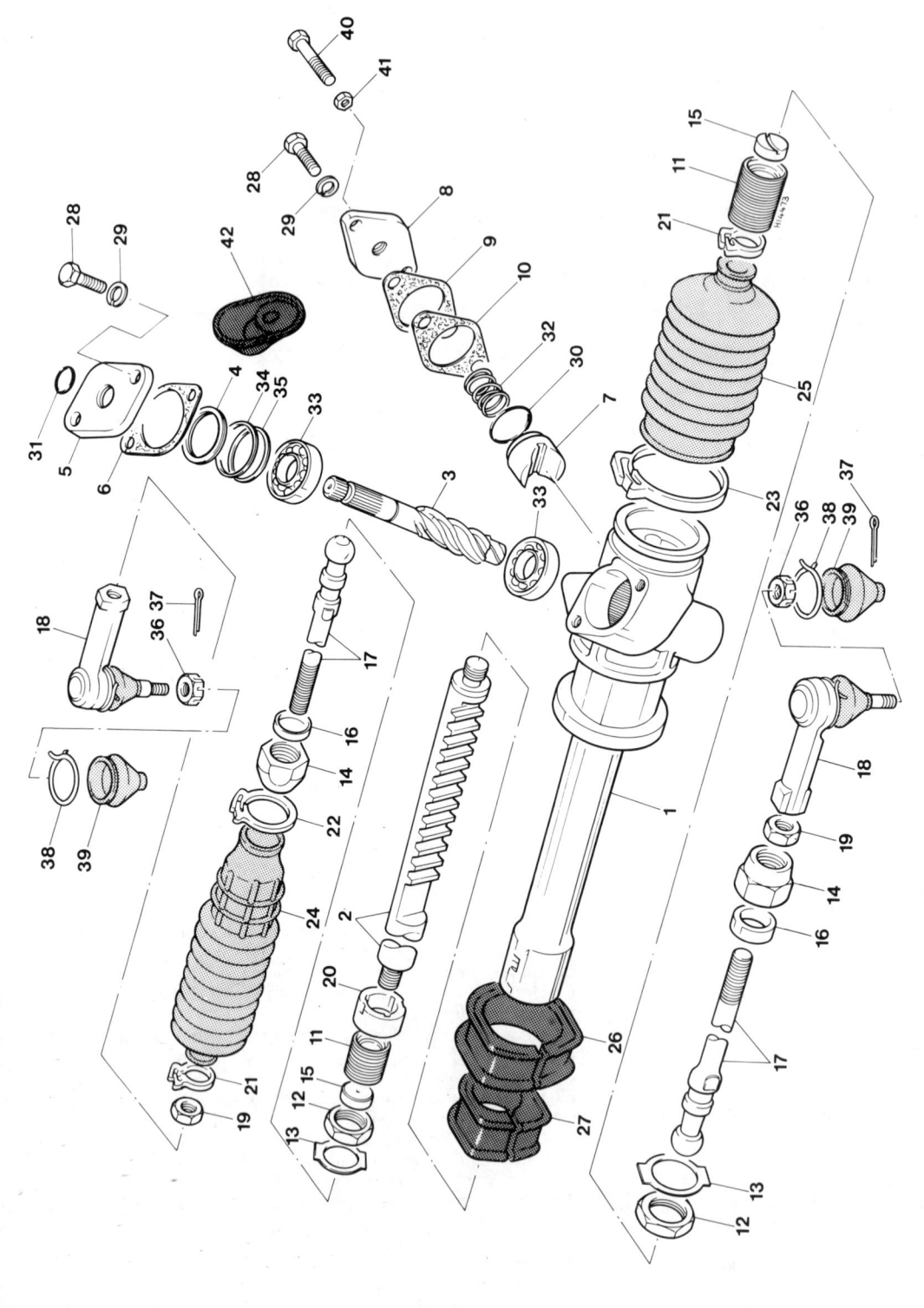

Fig. 12.12 Exploded view of the rack and pinion steering (Sec 9)

1 Steering housing
2 Rack
3 Pinion
4 Ring
5 Pinion cover
6 Cover gasket
7 Yoke
8 Yoke cover
9 Gasket

10 Shim (or distance washer)
11 Threaded reducing sleeve
12 Locknut
13 Locking washer
14 Coupling
15 Socket
16 Insert
17 Steering rod
18 Balljoint end

19 Nut
20 Bush
21 Clip
22 Clip
23 Clip
24 Rubber gaiter
25 Rubber gaiter
26 Rubber bush

27 Rubber bush
28 Bolt
29 Washer
30 Sealing ring
31 Sealing ring
32 Spring
33 Bearings
34 Shim

35 Shim
36 Nut
37 Split pin
38 Clip
39 Rubber gaiter
40 Bolt
41 Nut
42 Cover

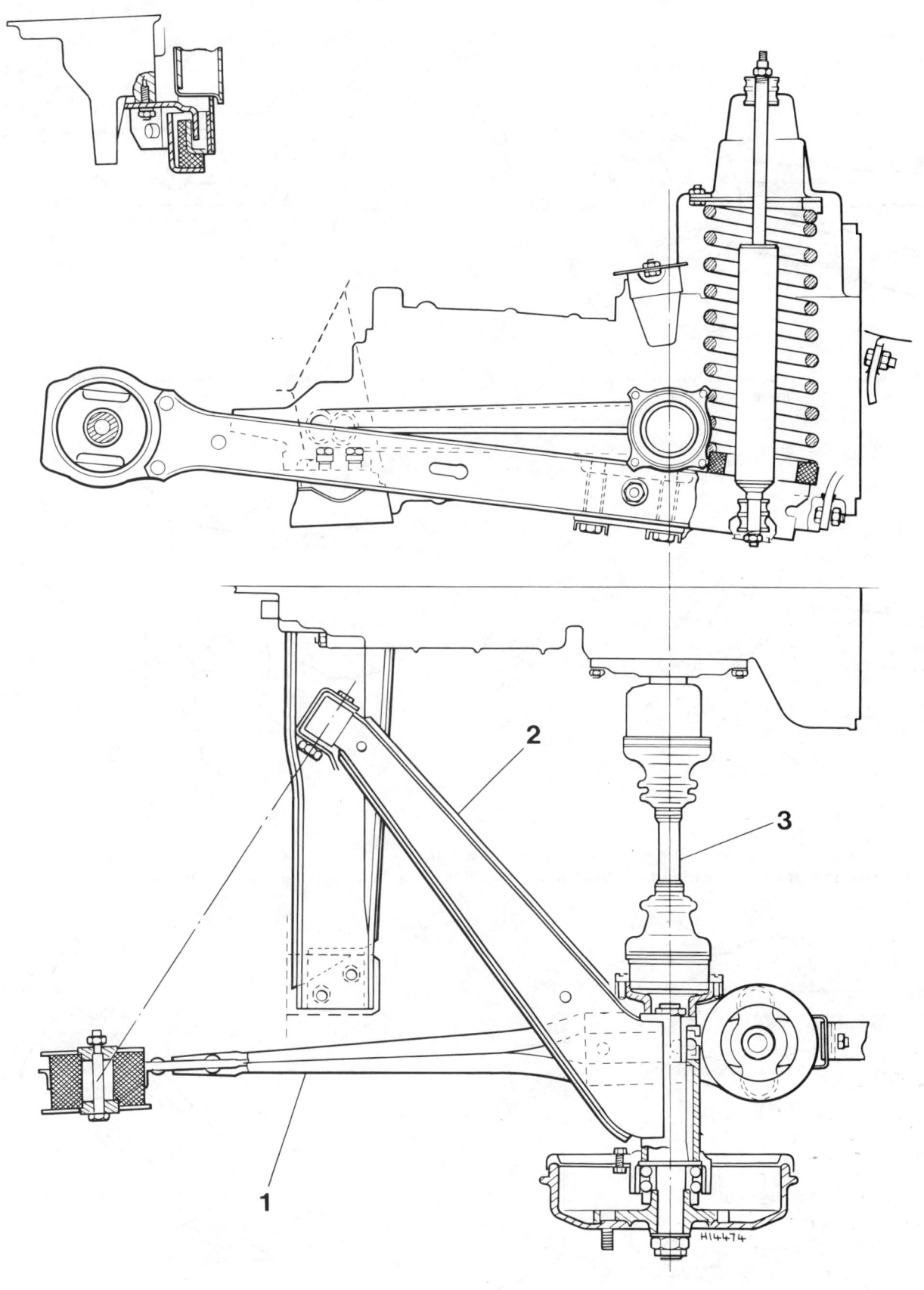

Fig. 12.13 Diagrammatic view of the rear trailing arm suspension/axle (Sec 9)

1 Radius arm
2 Oblique arm

3 Driveshaft

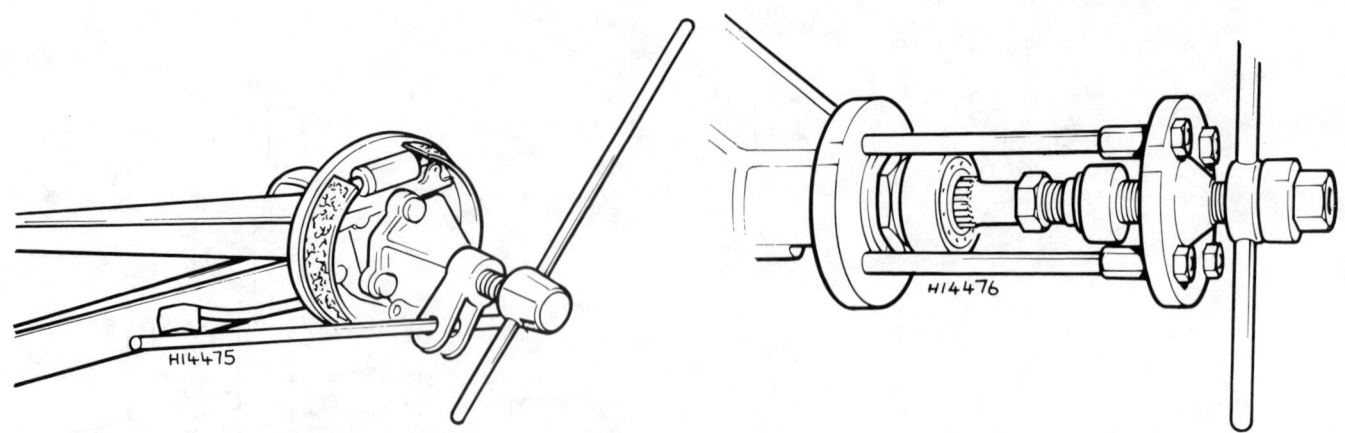

Fig. 12.14 Removing the wheel hub drive flange using the Skoda tools (Sec 9)

Fig. 12.15 Removing the wheel hub shaft using a Skoda tool (Sec 9)

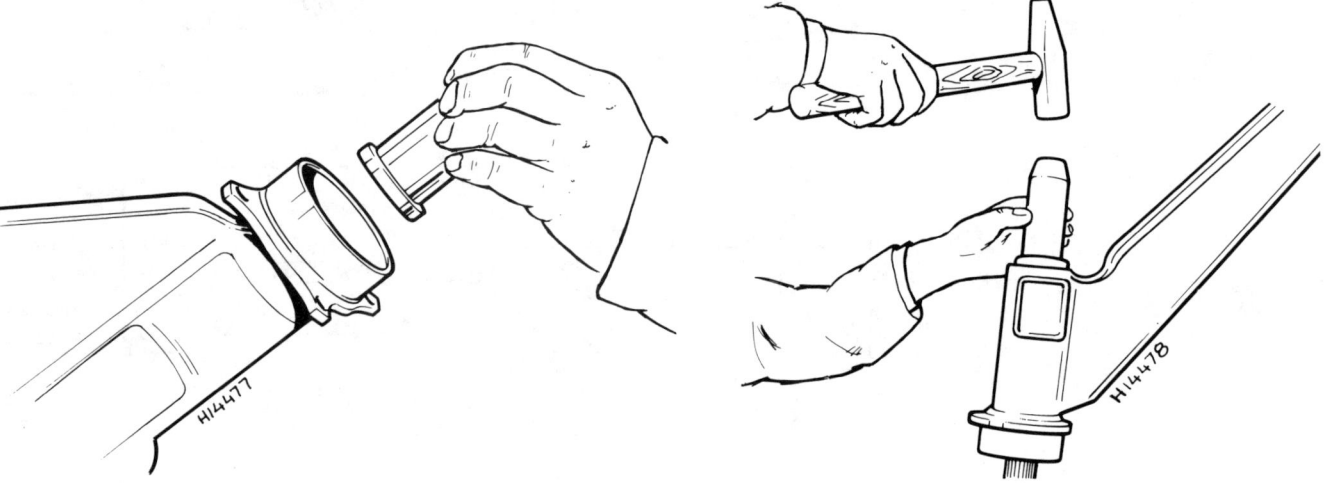

Fig. 12.16 Driving the inner bearing from the hub (Sec 9)

Fig. 12.17 Driving the inner bearing into the hub (Sec 9)

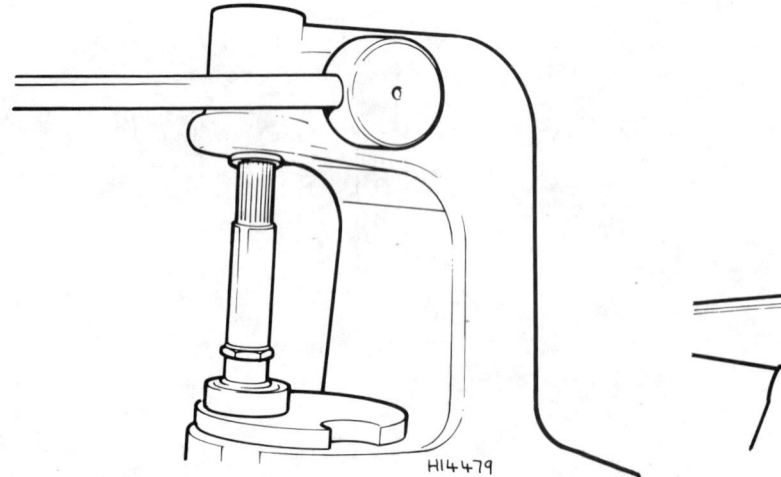

Fig. 12.18 Pressing in the double row ball-bearing (Sec 9)

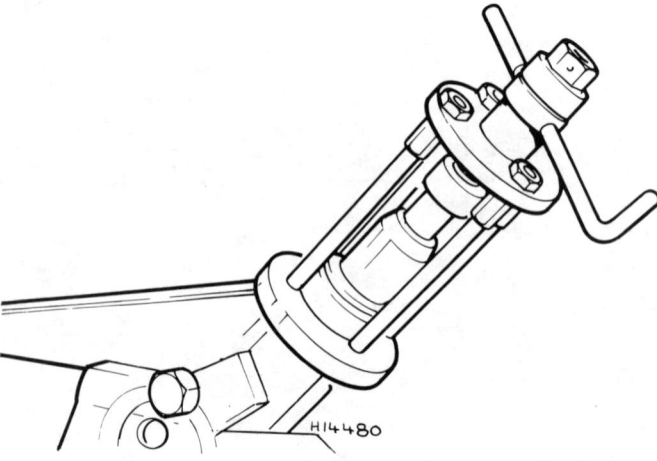

Fig. 12.19 Pressing the wheel hub shaft into the hub (Sec 9)

78 Insert the wheel hub shaft with the pressed on double row bearing into the hub from the outer side and press it home.
79 From the inner side of the hub, press the flange on to the wheel hub shaft, tighten the nut, and peen the nut into the slot on the shaft.
80 Refit the brake backing plate and mechanism before fitting the wheel hub drive flange to the outer end of the wheel hub shaft; pressing it home.
81 Tighten the wheel hub nut to the specified torque, and press it into the slot in the wheel hub shaft.
82 When reconnecting the wheel hub shaft flange to the driveshaft joint be careful not to damage the rubber sealing ring.

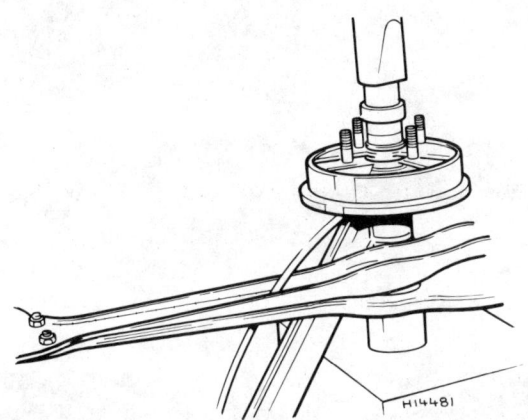

Fig. 12.20 Pressing the wheel hub drive flange onto the shaft
(Sec 9)

10 Braking system

General
1 Rapid and later Estelle models are fitted with slightly revised braking systems. The new system is not that different from the old one (Chapter 9) and the servicing procedures still apply.

Caliper and mounting
2 The Rapids use calipers with 4 pistons.
3 Rapid models no longer have spacing shims between the caliper and mounting bracket. The caliper-to-disc clearance is therefore reduced (see Specifications).

Discs
4 The discs used on Rapid models are smaller in diameter than those used on Saloons, to allow use of the 4 piston caliper on 13 inch wheels (see Specifications).
5 The later (thicker) Rapid discs can be used on early Rapid models as long as the caliper-to-disc clearance is set correctly.

Rear brakes – late Saloons and Rapids
6 The slave cylinders have new seals of ATE design and are of larger diameter on Rapid models.
7 The shoe return springs are slightly different.

Master cylinder – later Saloons and Rapids (with a servo)
8 The master cylinder has new seals of ATE design.
9 The braking circuit is split in the ratio 60:40. This is achieved by using floating piston rods of different lengths. When reassembling the cylinder, ensure the short rod is entered before the long one; seal end first.

Brake pedal – later models
10 The pedal assembly has been moved to the right, to allow for the repositioning of the steering column lower sections. It is now necessary to remove the brake pedal to gain access to the servo (Chapter 9, Section 17).

11 Electrical system

Part A: General

Alternator bracket – engine noise
1 It is possible that the bolt which secures the alternator bracket to the timing cover may be tightened correctly but still allows the bracket to vibrate, causing noise.
2 This can be overcome by fitting a suitable washer between the bracket and the timing cover case to eliminate any clearance and allow the bracket to be securely cramped.

Rectangular headlamps
Adjustment
3 The adjustment procedure given in Chapter 19 should be followed, using the adjustment points shown in Fig. 12.21.

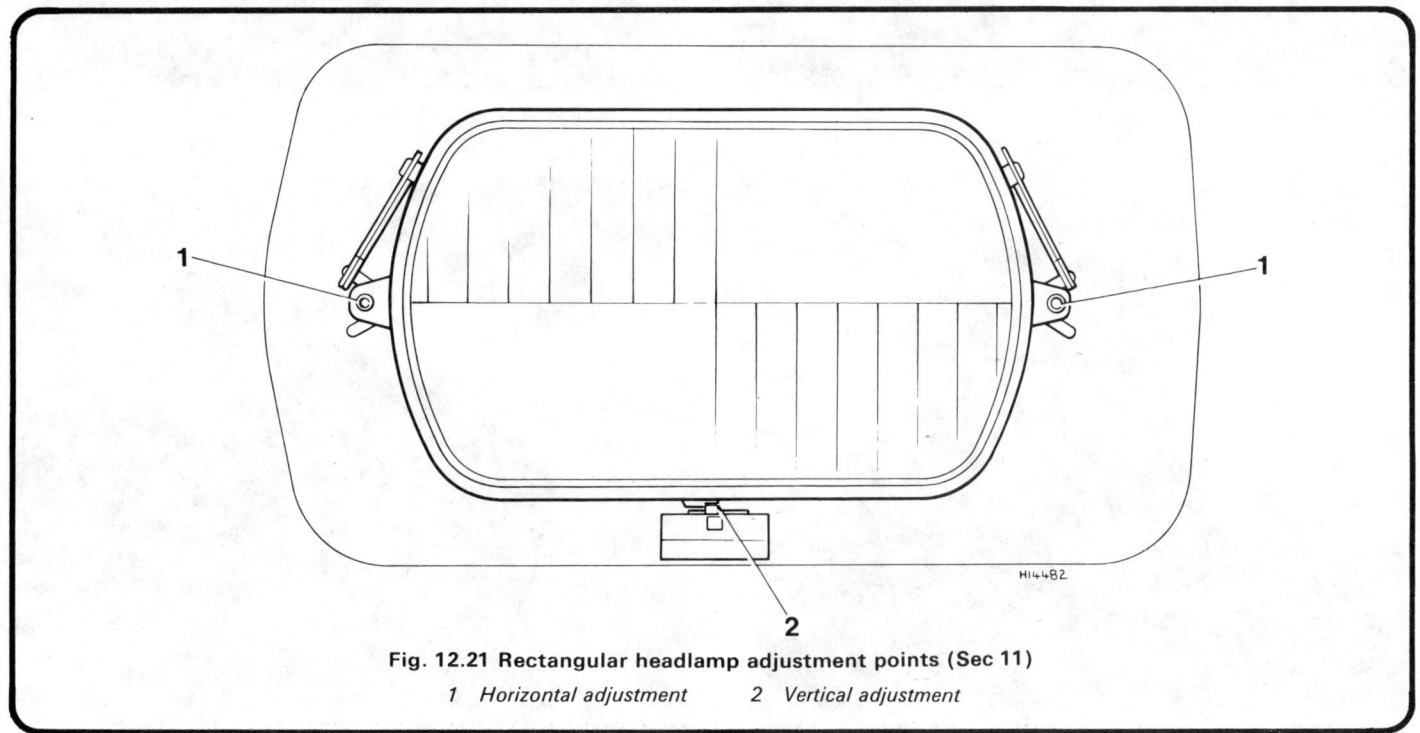

Fig. 12.21 Rectangular headlamp adjustment points (Sec 11)

1 Horizontal adjustment   2 Vertical adjustment

Load adjuster

4   Rectangular headlamps have an adjuster for load levelling.

5   Full left is for normal loads, central for loads of two persons and 40 kg luggage, and full right for access to the bulb.

Bulb and unit – removal and refitting

6   To change a headlamp bulb, lift the bonnet, pull off the connector block (photo) and release the bulb holder (photo).

7   Remove the bulb from its holder.

8   To remove the complete headlamp, remove the radiator grille (see Section on bodywork), undo the securing clip (photo) and pull the lamp unit forward out of its nylon holding lugs.

9   There are three of these lugs, which locate with spigots on the lamp unit.

Sidelights (later models) – bulb changing

10   The sidelight bulb is contained in its holder in the headlamp unit (photo).

11   Just pull out the holder to change the bulb.

Rear combination lights – later models

12   The rear combination light unit is held in place by three screws (photo).

11.8 Headlamp securing clip

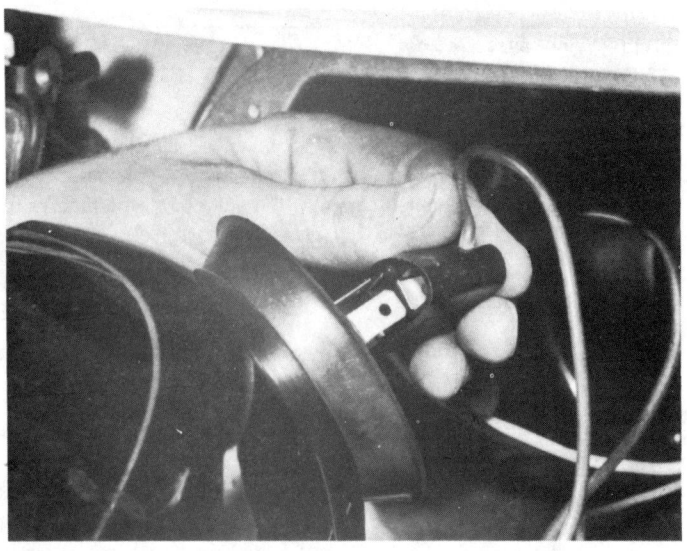

11.6A Headlamp connector block

11.10 Location of sidelight in headlamp

11.6B The headlamp bulb holder is a bayonet fit

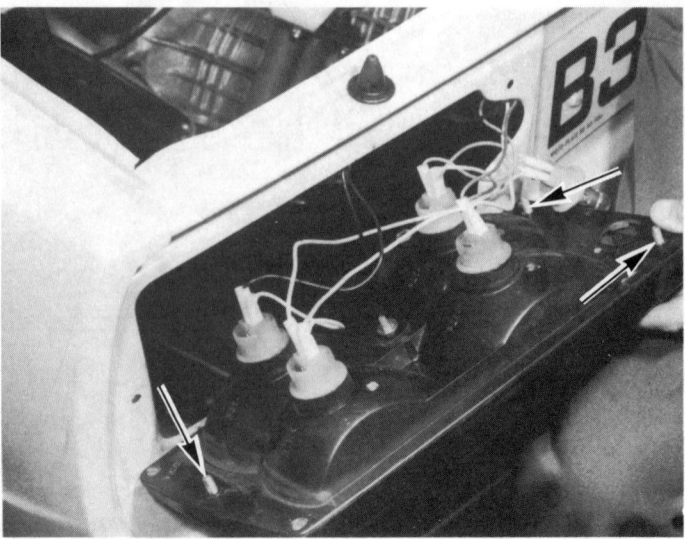

11.12 The rear combination light securing screws (arrowed)

13 Undo the three nuts on these screws from inside the engine bay and the unit will come away, revealing the bulb holders (photo). It is not necessary to remove the combination light assembly to renew the bulb(s).

14 To dismantle the unit further, for changing of lenses, undo the screws coloured red and the lens unit can be separated from the backlight. Note that the bulb holders are colour-coded to match the various wires to the unit.

15 Reassembly is a reversal of this procedure.

Front indicator lights – later models

16 To change the bulb in the indicator lights locate the rear of the unit under the front wheel arch (photo) and unscrew the holder. The bulb is a bayonet fit.

17 To remove the lens unit, undo the two retaining screws (photos). **Note:** *the bulbs may also be changed by this method which may be cleaner than going under the wheel arch! To remove the unit completely from the vehicle, undo the two securing nuts and screws.*

18 Refitting is a reversal of these procedures.

Side repeater lights – later models

19 Undo the two screws securing the unit to the wing and remove the lens unit (photo).

11.17A Undo the indicator lens retaining screws ...

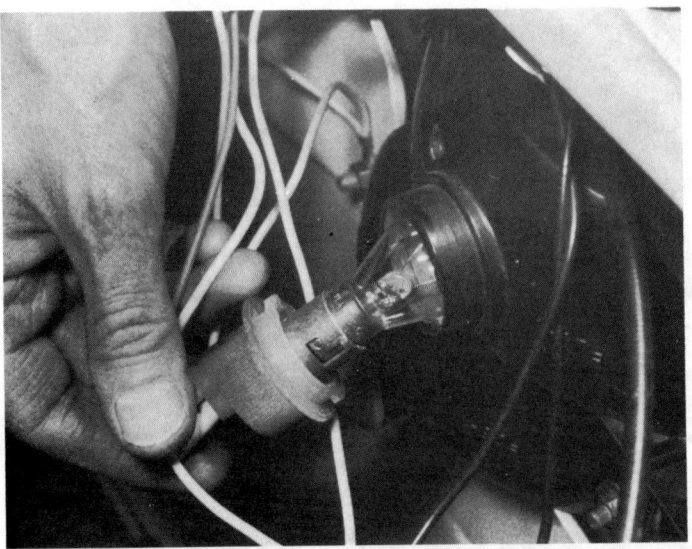

11.13 The bulbs are a bayonet fit in their holders

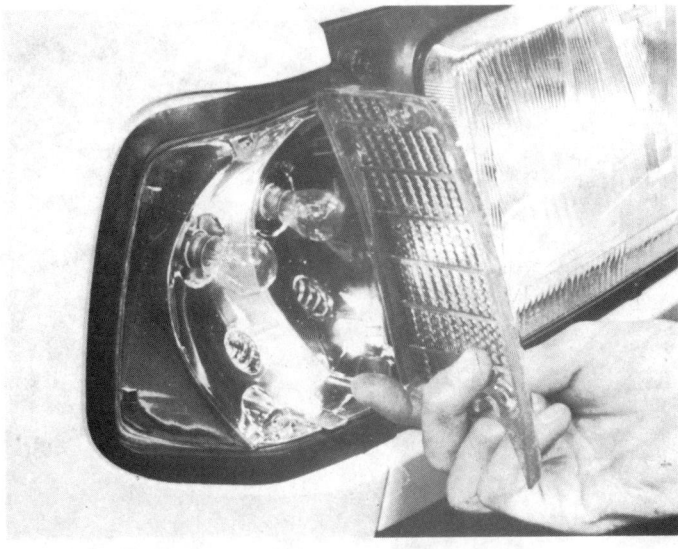

11.17B ... and remove the lens

11.16 Rear view of front indicator unit (from wheel arch)

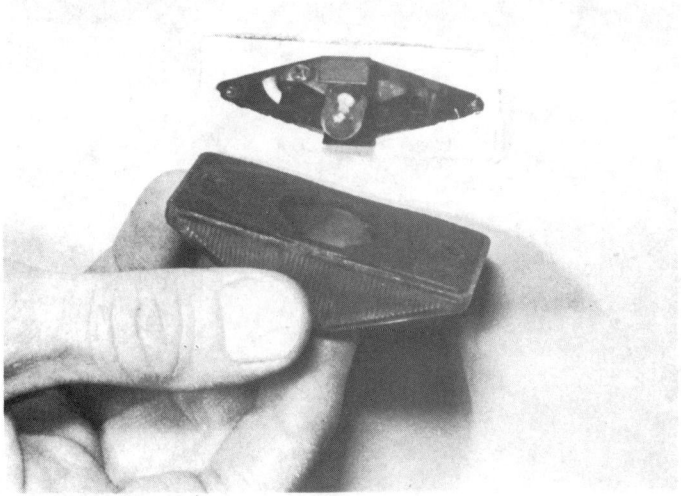

11.19 Side repeater light

20 The bulb is a bayonet fit in its holder.

21 To remove the holder, depress the two clips holding it in the wing aperture.

22 Reverse these procedures to refit.

Radio/cassette unit (standard fitment) removal and refiitting

23 The radio is housed in the center console and removal is made easier if the sides of the vinyl covered console are first removed. These are held in place by several screws.

24 Remove the control knobs on either side of the radio, and the plastic knobs underneath these (photo).

25 Using a box spanner, undo the two nuts securing the embellishers (photo).

26 Next, disconnect the electrical connectors and then remove the nut from the supportive metal strap on the back of the radio (photo).

27 The radio can now be eased backward and out of its housing in the console (photo).

28 The speakers are simply held to the bulkhead by two screws. Disconnect the speaker wires and the speakers and housings can be removed (photo). Four screws hold the speaker in the housing.

29 Installation is a reversal of the above, but refer to the following sub-sections on radio installation for any faults etc.

11.26 Disconnect the electrical leads and the supportive strap (arrowed) from the rear of the radio/cassette

11.24 Remove the radio/cassette control knobs ...

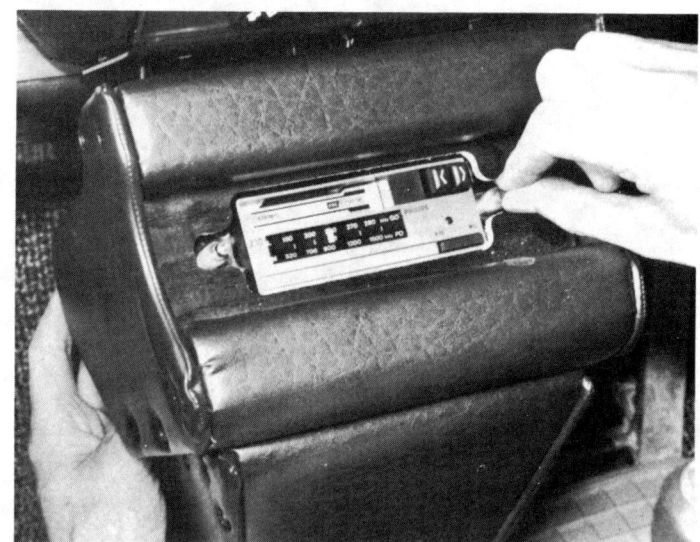

11.27 Ease the radio/cassette backwards out of its housing

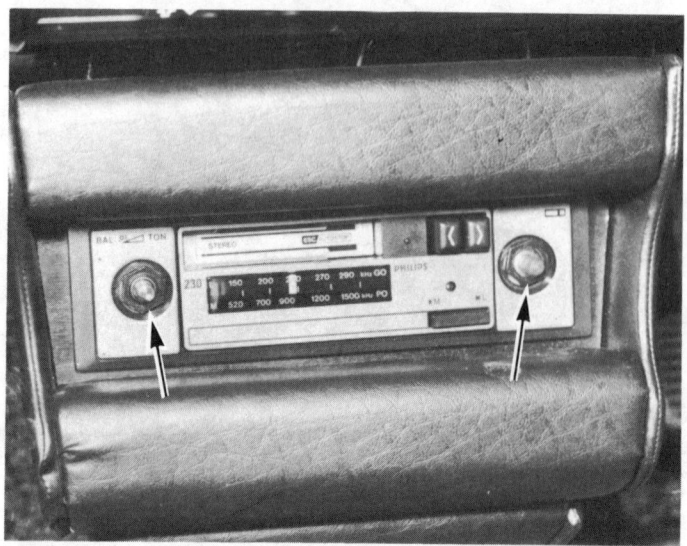

11.25 ... to reveal the embellisher retaining nuts (arrowed)

11.28 Speaker assembly

Part B: Mobile radio equipment – interference-free installation

Aerials – selection and fitting

The choice of aerials is now very wide. It should be realised that the quality has a profound effect on radio performance, and a poor, inefficient aerial can make suppression difficult.

A wing-mounted aerial is regarded as probably the most efficient for signal collection, but a roof aerial is usually better for suppression purposes because it is away from most interference fields. Stick-on wire aerials are available for attachment to the inside of the windscreen, but are not always free from the interference field of the engine and some accessories.

Motorised automatic aerials rise when the equipment is switched on and retract at switch-off. They require more fitting space and supply leads, and can be a source of trouble.

There is no merit in choosing a very long aerial as, for example, the type about three metres in length which hooks or clips on to the rear of the car, since part of this aerial will inevitably be located in an interference field. For VHF/FM radios the best length of aerial is about one metre. Active aerials have a transistor amplifier mounted at the base and this serves to boost the received signal. The aerial rod is sometimes rather shorter than normal passive types.

A large loss of signal can occur in the aerial feeder cable, especially over the Very High Frequency (VHF) bands. The design of feeder cable is invariably in the co-axial form, ie a centre conductor surrounded by a flexible copper braid forming the outer (earth) conductor. Between the inner and outer conductors is an insulator material which can be in solid or stranded form. Apart from insulation, its purpose is to maintain the correct spacing and concentricity. Loss of signal occurs in this insulator, the loss usually being greater in a poor quality cable. The quality of cable used is reflected in the price of the aerial with the attached feeder cable.

The capacitance of the feeder should be within the range 65 to 75 picofarads (pF) approximately (95 to 100 pF for Japanese and American equipment), otherwise the adjustment of the car radio aerial trimmer may not be possible. An extension cable is necessary for a long run between aerial and receiver. If this adds capacitance in excess of the above limits, a connector containing a series capacitor will be required, or an extension which is labelled as 'capacity-compensated'.

Fitting the aerial will normally involve making a ⅞ in (22 mm) diameter hole in the bodywork, but read the instructions that come with the aerial kit. Once the hole position has been selected, use a centre punch to guide the drill. Use sticky masking tape around the area for this helps with marking out and drill location, and gives protection to the paintwork should the drill slip. Three methods of making the hole are in use:

(a) Use a hole saw in the electric drill. This is, in effect, a circular hacksaw blade wrapped round a former with a centre pilot drill.

(b) Use a tank cutter which also has cutting teeth, but is made to shear the metal by tightening with an Allen key.

(c) The hard way of drilling out the circle is using a small drill, say ⅛ in (3 mm), so that the holes overlap. The centre metal drops out and the hole is finished with round and half-round files.

Whichever method is used, the burr is removed from the body metal and paint removed from the underside. The aerial is fitted tightly ensuring that the earth fixing, usually a serrated washer, ring or clamp, is making a solid connection. *This earth connection is important in reducing interference.* Cover any bare metal with primer paint and topcoat, and follow by underseal if desired.

Aerial feeder cable routing should avoid the engine compartment and areas where stress might occur, eg under the carpet where feet will be located. Roof aerials require that the headlining be pulled back and that a path is available down the door pillar. It is wise to check with the vehicle dealer whether roof aerial fitting is recommended.

Loudspeakers

Speakers should be matched to the output stage of the equipment, particularly as regards the recommended impedance. Power transistors used for driving speakers are sensitive to the loading placed on them.

Before choosing a mounting position for speakers, check whether the vehicle manufacturer has provided a location for them. Generally door-mounted speakers give good stereophonic reproduction, but not all doors are able to accept them. The next best position is the rear parcel shelf, and in this case speaker apertures can be cut into the shelf, or pod units may be mounted.

For door mounting, first remove the trim, which is often held on by 'poppers' or press studs, and then select a suitable gap in the inside door assembly. Check that the speaker would not obstruct glass or winder mechanism by winding the window up and down. A template is often provided for marking out the trim panel hole, and then the four fixing holes must be drilled through. Mark out with chalk and cut cleanly with a sharp knife or keyhole saw. Speaker leads are then threaded through the door and door pillar, if necessary drilling 10 mm diameter holes. Fit

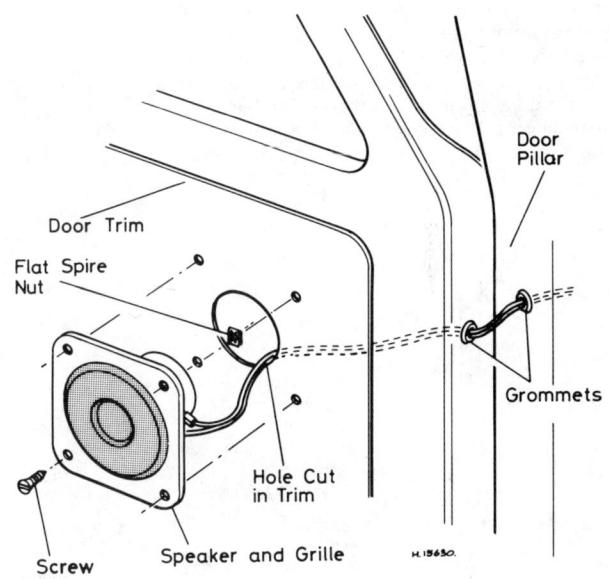

Fig. 12.23 Door-mounted speaker installation (Sec 11)

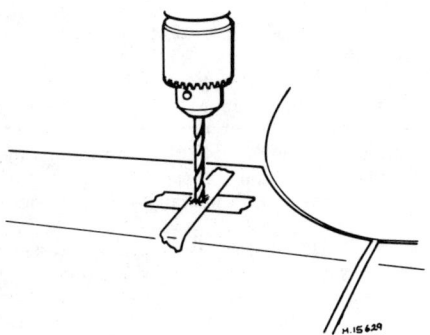

Fig. 12.22 Drilling the bodywork for aerial mounting (Sec 11)

grommets in the holes and connect to the radio or tape unit correctly. Do not omit a waterproofing cover, usually supplied with door speakers. If the speaker has to be fixed into the metal of the door itself, use self-tapping screws, and if the fixing is to the door trim use self-tapping screws and flat spire nuts.

Rear shelf mounting is somewhat simpler but it is necessary to find gaps in the metalwork underneath the parcel shelf. However, remember that the speakers should be as far apart as possible to give a good stereo effect. Pod-mounted speakers can be screwed into position through the parcel shelf material, but it is worth testing for the best position. Sometimes good results are found by reflecting sound off the rear window.

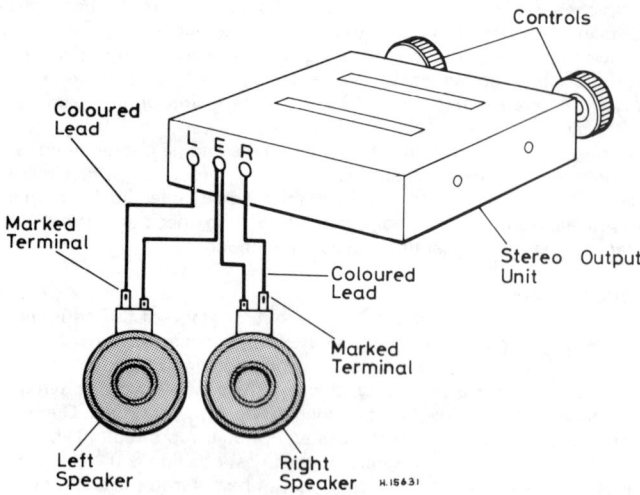

Fig. 12.24 Speaker connections must be correctly made (Sec 11)

Unit installation

Many vehicles have a dash panel aperture to take a radio/audio unit, a recognised international standard being 189.5 mm x 60 mm. Alternatively a console may be a feature of the car interior design and this, mounted below the dashboard, gives more room. If neither facility is available a unit may be mounted on the underside of the parcel shelf; these are frequently non-metallic and an earth wire from the case to a good earth point is necessary. A three-sided cover in the form of a cradle is obtainable from car radio dealers and this gives a professional appearance to the installation; in this case choose a position where the controls can be reached by a driver with his seat belt on.

Installation of the radio/audio unit is basically the same in all cases, and consists of offering it into the aperture after removal of the knobs

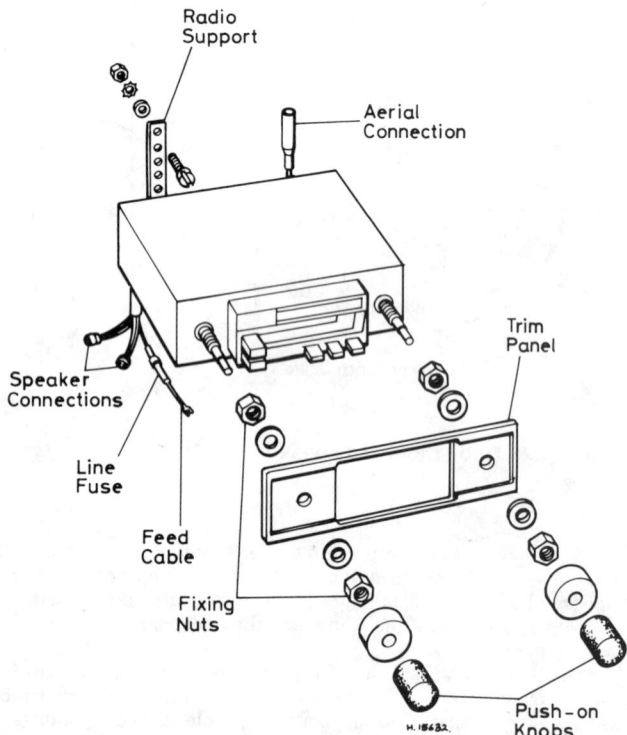

Fig. 12.25 Mounting component details for a radio/cassette unit (Sec 11)

(not push buttons) and the trim plate. In some cases a special mounting plate is required to which the unit is attached. It is worthwhile supporting the rear end in cases where sag or strain may occur, and it is usually possible to use a length of perforated metal strip attached between the unit and a good support point nearby. In general it is recommended that tape equipment should be installed at or nearly horizontal.

Connections to the aerial socket are simply by the standard plug terminating the aerial downlead or its extension cable. Speakers for a stereo system must be matched and correctly connected, as outlined previously.

Note: *While all work is carried out on the power side, it is wise to disconnect the battery earth lead.* Before connection is made to the vehicle electrical system, check that the polarity of the unit is correct. Most vehicles use a negative earth system, but radio/audio units often have a reversible plug to convert the set to either + or – earth. *Incorrect connection may cause serious damage.*

The power lead is often permanently connected inside the unit and terminates with one half of an in-line fuse carrier. The other half is fitted with a suitable fuse (3 or 5 amperes) and a wire which should go to a power point in the electrical system. This may be the accessory terminal on the ignition switch, giving the advantage of power feed with ignition or with the ignition key at the 'accessory' position. Power to the unit stops when the ignition key is removed. Alternatively, the lead may be taken to a live point at the fusebox with the consequence of having to remember to switch off at the unit before leaving the vehicle.

Before switching on for initial test, be sure that the speaker connections have been made, for running without load can damage the output transistors. Switch on next and tune through the bands to ensure that all sections are working, and check the tape unit if applicable. The aerial trimmer should be adjusted to give the strongest reception on a weak signal in the medium wave band, at say 200 metres.

Interference

In general, when electric current changes abruptly, unwanted electrical noise is produced. The motor vehicle is filled with electrical devices which change electric current rapidly, the most obvious being the contact breaker.

When the spark plugs operate, the sudden pulse of spark current causes the associated wiring to radiate. Since early radio transmitters used sparks as a basis of operation, it is not surprising that the car radio will pick up ignition spark noise unless steps are taken to reduce it to acceptable levels.

Interference reaches the car radio in two ways:

(a) by conduction through the wiring.
(b) by radiation to the receiving aerial.

Initial checks presuppose that the bonnet is down and fastened, the radio unit has a good earth connection (*not* through the aerial downlead outer), no fluorescent tubes are working near the car, the aerial trimmer has been adjusted, and the vehicle is in a position to receive radio signals, ie not in a metal-clad building.

Switch on the radio and tune it to the middle of the medium wave (MW) band off-station with the volume (gain) control set fairly high. Switch on the ignition (but do not start the engine) and wait to see if irregular clicks or hash noise occurs. Tapping the facia panel may also produce the effects. If so, this will be due to the voltage stabiliser, which is an on-off thermal switch to control instrument voltage. It is located usually on the back of the instrument panel, often attached to the speedometer. Correction is by attachment of a capacitor and, if still troublesome, chokes in the supply wires.

Switch on the engine and listen for interference on the MW band. Depending on the type of interference, the indications are as follows.

A harsh crackle that drops out abruptly at low engine speed or when the headlights are switched on is probably due to a voltage regulator.

A whine varying with engine speed is due to the dynamo or alternator. Try temporarily taking off the fan belt – if the noise goes this is confirmation.

Regular ticking or crackle that varies in rate with the engine speed is due to the ignition system. With this trouble in particular and others in general, check to see if the noise is entering the receiver from the wiring or by radiation. To do this, pull out the aerial plug, (preferably shorting out the input socket or connecting a 62 pF capacitor across it). If the noise disappears it is coming in through the aerial and is *radiation noise*. If the noise persists it is reaching the receiver through the wiring and is said to be *line-borne*.

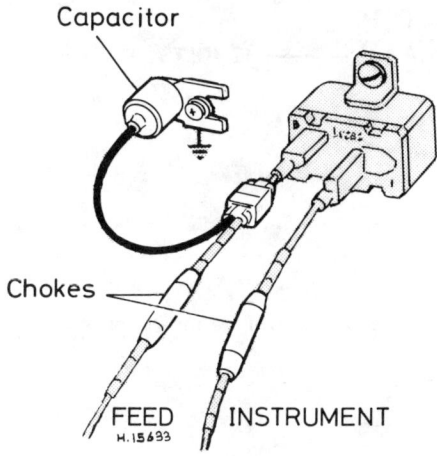

Fig. 12.26 Voltage stabiliser interference suppression (Sec 11)

Interference from wipers, washers, heater blowers, turn-indicators, stop lamps, etc is usually taken to the receiver by wiring, and simple treatment using capacitors and possibly chokes will solve the problem. Switch on each one in turn (wet the screen first for running wipers!) and listen for possible interference with the aerial plug in place and again when removed.

Electric petrol pumps are now finding application again and give rise to an irregular clicking, often giving a burst of clicks when the ignition is on but the engine has not yet been started. It is also possible to receive whining or crackling from the pump.

Note that if most of the vehicle accessories are found to be creating interference all together, the probability is that poor aerial earthing is to blame.

Component terminal markings

Throughout the following sub-sections reference will be found to various terminal markings. These will vary depending on the manufacturer of the relevant component. If terminal markings differ from those mentioned, reference should be made to the following table, where the most commonly encountered variations are listed.

Alternator	Alternator terminal (thick lead)	Exciting winding terminal
DIN/Bosch	B+	DF
Delco Remy	+	EXC
Ducellier	+	EXC
Ford (US)	+	DF
Lucas	+	F
Marelli	+B	F

Ignition coil	Ignition switch terminal	Contact breaker terminal
DIN/Bosch	15	1
Delco Remy	+	–
Ducellier	BAT	RUP
Ford (US)	B/+	CB/–
Lucas	SW/+	–
Marelli	BAT/+B	D

Voltage regulator	Voltage input terminal	Exciting winding terminal
DIN/Bosch	B+/D+	DF
Delco Remy	BAT/+	EXC
Ducellier	BOB/BAT	EXC
Ford (US)	BAT	DF
Lucas	+/A	F
Marelli		F

Suppression methods – ignition

Suppressed HT cables are supplied as original equipment by manufacturers and will meet regulations as far as interference to neighbouring equipment is concerned. It is illegal to remove such suppression unless an alternative is provided, and this may take the form of resistive spark plug caps in conjunction with plain copper HT cable. For VHF purposes, these and 'in-line' resistors may not be effective, and resistive HT cable is preferred. Check that suppressed cables are actually fitted by observing cable identity lettering, or measuring with an ohmmeter – the value of each plug lead should be 5000 to 10 000 ohms.

A 1 microfarad capacitor connected from the LT supply side of the ignition coil to a good nearby earth point will complete basic ignition interference treatment. *NEVER fit a capacitor to the coil terminal to the contact breaker – the result would be burnt out points in a short time.*

If ignition noise persists despite the treatment above, the following sequence should be followed:

(a) Check the earthing of the ignition coil; remove paint from fixing clamp.

(b) If this does not work, lift the bonnet. Should there be no change in interference level, this may indicate that the bonnet is not electrically connected to the car body. Use a proprietary braided strap across a bonnet hinge ensuring a first class electrical connection. If, however, lifting the bonnet increases the interference, then fit resistive HT cables of a higher ohms-per-metre value.

(c) If all these measures fail, it is probable that re-radiation from metallic components is taking place. Using a braided strap between metallic points, go round the vehicle systematically – try the following: engine to body, exhaust system to body, front suspension to engine and to body, steering column to body (especially French and Italian cars), gear lever to engine and to body (again especially French and Italian cars), Bowden cable to body, metal parcel shelf to body. When an offending component is located it should be bonded with the strap permanently.

(d) As a next step, the fitting of distributor suppressors to each lead at the distributor end may help.

(e) Beyond this point is involved the possible screening of the distributor and fitting resistive spark plugs, but such advanced treatment is not usually required for vehicles with entertainment equipment.

Electronic ignition systems have built-in suppression components, but this does not relieve the need for using suppressed HT leads. In some cases it is permitted to connect a capacitor on the low tension supply side of the ignition coil, but not in every case. Makers' instructions should be followed carefully, otherwise damage to the ignition semiconductors may result.

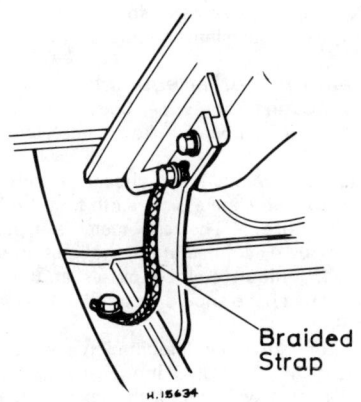

Fig. 12.27 Braided earth strap between bonnet and body (Sec 11)

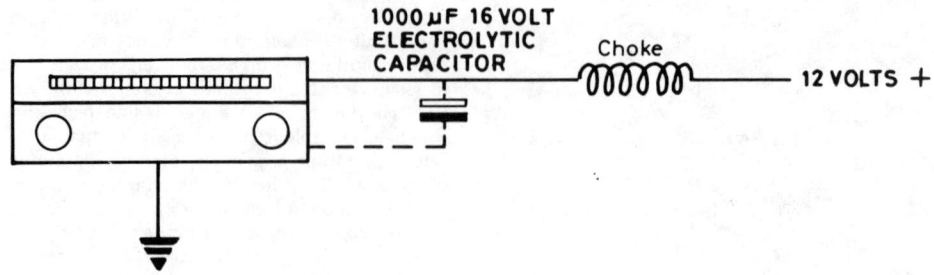

1000 μF 16 VOLT ELECTROLYTIC CAPACITOR   Choke   12 VOLTS +

Fig. 12.28 Line-borne interference suppression (Sec 11)

Suppression methods – generators

For older vehicles with dynamos a 1 microfarad capacitor from the D (larger) terminal to earth will usually cure dynamo whine. Alternators should be fitted with a 3 microfarad capacitor from the B + main output terminal (thick cable) to earth. Additional suppression may be obtained by the use of a filter in the supply line to the radio receiver.

It is most important that:

(a) Capacitors are never connected to the field terminals of either a dynamo or alternator.

(b) Alternators must not be run without connection to the battery.

Suppression methods – voltage regulators

Voltage regulators used with DC dynamos should be suppressed by connecting a 1 microfarad capacitor from the control box D terminal to earth.

Alternator regulators come in three types:

(a) Vibrating contact regulators separate from the alternator. Used extensively on continental vehicles.

(b) Electronic regulators separate from the alternator.

(c) Electronic regulators built-in to the alternator.

In case (a) interference may be generated on the AM and FM (VHF) bands. For some cars a replacement suppressed regulator is available. Filter boxes may be used with non-suppressed regulators. But if not available, then for AM equipment a 2 microfarad or 3 microfarad capacitor may be mounted at the voltage terminal marked D + or B + of the regulator. FM bands may be treated by a feed-through capacitor of 2 or 3 microfarad.

Electronic voltage regulators are not always troublesome, but where necessary, a 1 microfarad capacitor from the regulator + terminal will help.

Integral electronic voltage regulators do not normally generate much interference, but when encountered this is in combination with alternator noise. A 1 microfarad or 2 microfarad capacitor from the warning lamp (IND) terminal to earth for Lucas ACR alternators and Femsa, Delco and Bosch equivalents should cure the problem.

Suppression methods – other equipment

Wiper motors – Connect the wiper body to earth with a bonding strap. For all motors use a 7 ampere choke assembly inserted in the leads to the motor.

Heater motors – Fit 7 ampere line chokes in both leads, assisted if necessary by a 1 microfarad capacitor to earth from both leads.

Electronic tachometer – The tachometer is a possible source of ignition noise – check by disconnecting at the ignition coil CB terminal. It usually feeds from ignition coil LT pulses at the contact breaker terminal. A 3 ampere line choke should be fitted in the tachometer lead at the coil CB terminal.

Horn – A capacitor and choke combination is effective if the horn is directly connected to the 12 volt supply. The use of a relay is an alternative remedy, as this will reduce the length of the interference-carrying leads.

Electrostatic noise – Characteristics are erratic crackling at the receiver, with disappearance of symptoms in wet weather. Often shocks may be given when touching bodywork. Part of the problem is the build-up of static electricity in non-driven wheels and the acquisition of charge on the body shell. It is possible to fit spring-loaded contacts at the wheels to give good conduction between the rotary wheel parts and

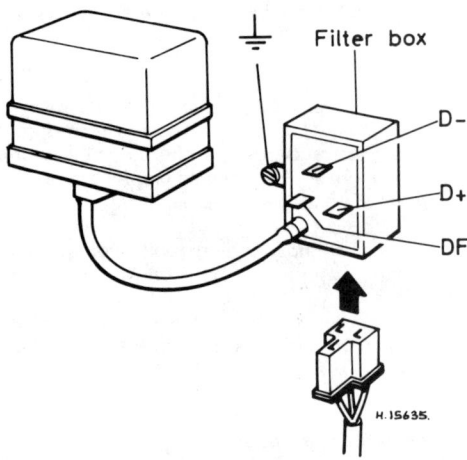

Filter box   D–   D+   DF

H.15635.

Fig. 12.29 Typical filter box for vibrating contact voltage regulator (alternator equipment) (Sec 11)

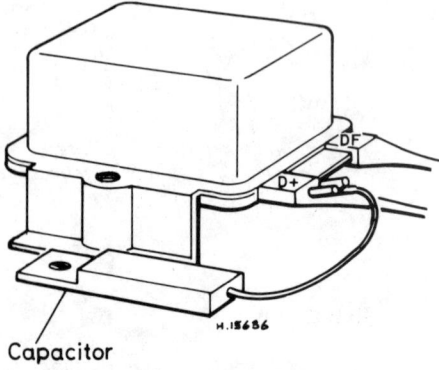

DF   D+

Capacitor   H.15636

Fig. 12.30 Suppression of AM interference by vibrating contact voltage regulator (alternator equipment) (Sec 11)

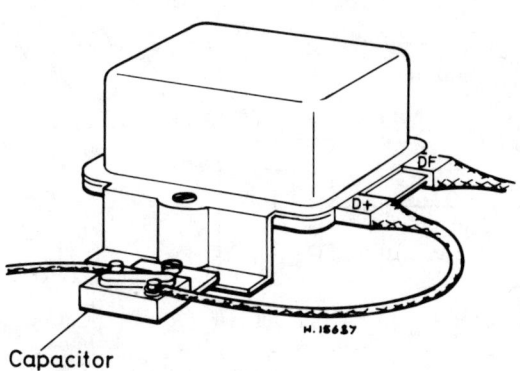

Fig. 12.31 Suppression of FM interference by vibrating contact voltage regulator (alternator equipment) (Sec 11)

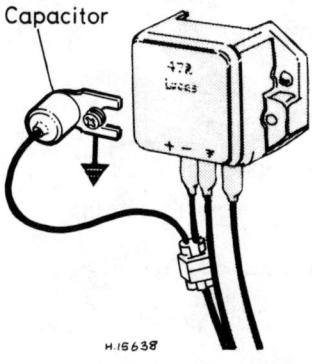

Fig. 12.32 Electronic voltage regulator suppression (Sec 11)

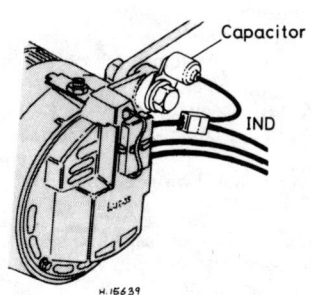

Fig. 12.33 Suppression of interference from electronic voltage regulator when integral with alternator (Sec 11)

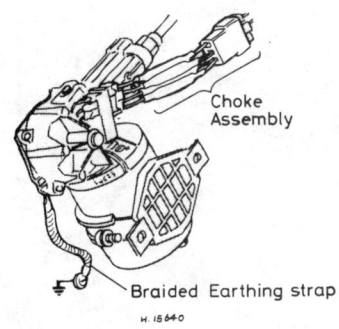

Fig. 12.34 Wiper motor suppression (Sec 11)

the vehicle frame. Changing a tyre sometimes helps – because of tyres' varying resistances. In difficult cases a trailing flex which touches the ground will cure the problem. If this is not acceptable it is worth trying conductive paint on the tyre walls.

Fuel pump – Suppression requires a 1 microfarad capacitor between the supply wire to the pump and a nearby earth point. If this is insufficient a 7 ampere line choke connected in the supply wire near the pump is required.

Fluorescent tubes – Vehicles used for camping/caravanning frequently have fluorescent tube lighting. These tubes require a relatively high voltage for operation and this is provided by an inverter (a form of oscillator) which steps up the vehicle supply voltage. This can give rise to serious interference to radio reception, and the tubes themselves can contribute to this interference by the pulsating nature of the lamp discharge. In such situations it is important to mount the aerial as far away from a fluorescent tube as possible. The interference problem may be alleviated by screening the tube with fine wire turns spaced an inch (25 cm) apart and earthed to the chassis. Suitable chokes should be fitted in both supply wires close to the inverter.

Radio/cassette case breakthrough

Magnetic radiation from dashboard wiring may be sufficiently intense to break through the metal case of the radio/cassette player. Often this is due to a particular cable routed too close and shows up as ignition interference on AM and cassette play and/or alternator whine on cassette play.

The first point to check is that the clips and/or screws are fixing all parts of the radio/cassette case together properly. Assuming good earthing of the case, see if it is possible to re-route the offending cable – the chances of this are not good, however, in most cars.

Next release the radio/cassette player and locate it in different positions with temporary leads. If a point of low interference is found, then if possible fix the equipment in that area. This also confirms that local radiation is causing the trouble. If re-location is not feasible, fit the radio/cassette player back in the original position.

Alternator interference on cassette play is now caused by radiation from the main charging cable which goes from the battery to the output terminal of the alternator, usually via the + terminal of the starter motor relay. In some vehicles this cable is routed under the dashboard, so the solution is to provide a direct cable route. Detach the original cable from the alternator output terminal and make up a new cable of at least 6 mm² cross-sectional area to go from alternator to battery with the shortest possible route. *Remember – do not run the engine with the alternator disconnected from the battery.*

Ignition breakthrough on AM and/or cassette play can be a difficult problem. It is worth wrapping earthed foil round the offending cable run near the equipment, or making up a deflector plate well screwed down to a good earth. Another possibility is the use of a suitable relay to switch on the ignition coil. The relay should be mounted close to the ignition coil; with this arrangement the ignition coil primary current is not taken into the dashboard area and does not flow through the ignition switch. A suitable diode should be used since it is possible that at ignition switch-off the output from the warning lamp alternator terminal could hold the relay on.

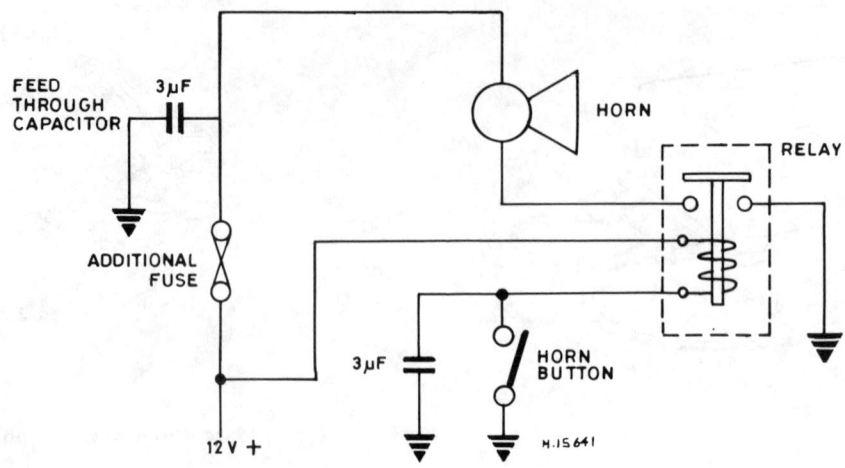

Fig. 12.35 Use of relay to reduce horn interference (Sec 11)

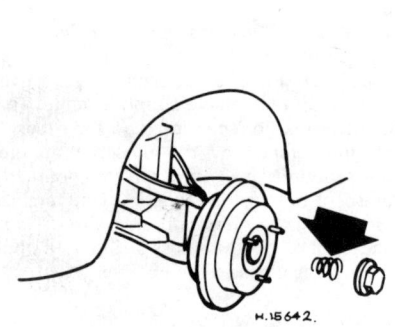

Fig. 12.36 Use of spring contacts at wheels (Sec 11)

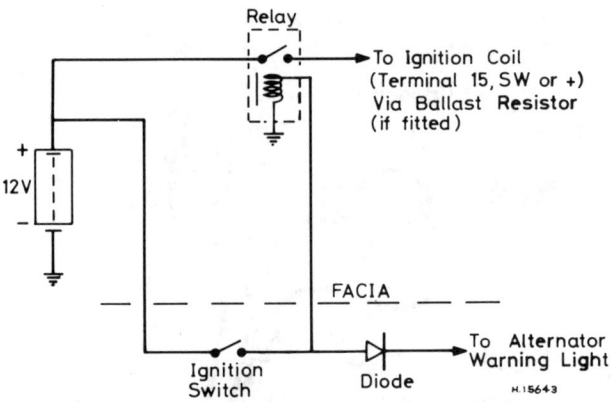

Fig. 12.37 Use of ignition coil relay to suppress case breakthrough (Sec 11)

Connectors for suppression components

Capacitors are usually supplied with tags on the end of the lead, while the capacitor body has a flange with a slot or hole to fit under a nut or screw with washer.

Connections to feed wires are best achieved by self-stripping connectors. These connectors employ a blade which, when squeezed down by pliers, cuts through cable insulation and makes connection to the copper conductors beneath.

Chokes sometimes come with bullet snap-in connectors fitted to the wires, and also with just bare copper wire. With connectors, suitable female cable connectors may be purchased from an auto-accessory shop together with any extra connectors required for the cable ends after being cut for the choke insertion. For chokes with bare wires, similar connectors may be employed together with insulation sleeving as required.

VHF/FM broadcasts

Reception of VHF/FM in an automobile is more prone to problems than the medium and long wavebands. Medium/long wave transmitters are capable of covering considerable distances, but VHF transmitters are restricted to line of sight, meaning ranges of 10 to 50 miles, depending upon the terrain, the effects of buildings and the transmitter power.

Because of the limited range it is necessary to retune on a long journey, and it may be better for those habitually travelling long distances or living in areas of poor provision of transmitters to use an AM radio working on medium/long wavebands.

When conditions are poor, interference can arise, and some of the suppression devices described previously fall off in performance at very high frequencies unless specifically designed for the VHF band. Available suppression devices include reactive HT cable, resistive distributor caps, screened plug caps, screened leads and resistive spark plugs.

For VHF/FM receiver installation the following points should be particularly noted:

(a) Earthing of the receiver chassis and the aerial mounting is important. Use a separate earthing wire at the radio, and scrape paint away at the aerial mounting.

(b) If possible, use a good quality roof aerial to obtain maximum height and distance from interference generating devices on the vehicle.

(c) Use of a high quality aerial downlead is important, since losses in cheap cable can be significant.

(d) The polarisation of FM transmissions may be horizontal, vertical, circular or slanted. Because of this the optimum mounting angle is at 45° to the vehicle roof.

Citizens' Band radio (CB)

In the UK, CB transmitter/receivers work within the 27 MHz and 934 MHz bands, using the FM mode. At present interest is concentrated on 27 MHz where the design and manufacture of equipment is less difficult. Maximum transmitted power is 4 watts, and 40 channels spaced 10 kHz apart within the range 27.60125 to 27.99125 MHz are available.

Aerials are the key to effective transmission and reception. Regulations limit the aerial length to 1.65 metres including the loading coil and any associated circuitry, so tuning the aerial is necessary to obtain optimum results. The choice of a CB aerial is dependent on whether it is to be permanently installed or removable, and the performance will hinge on correct tuning and the location point on the vehicle. Common practice is to clip the aerial to the roof gutter or to employ wing mounting where the aerial can be rapidly unscrewed. An alternative is to use the boot rim to render the aerial theftproof, but a popular solution is to use the 'magmount' – a type of mounting having a strong magnetic base clamping to the vehicle at any point, usually the roof.

Aerial location determines the signal distribution for both transmission and reception, but it is wise to choose a point away from the engine compartment to minimise interference from vehicle electrical equipment.

The aerial is subject to considerable wind and acceleration forces. Cheaper units will whip backwards and forwards and in so doing will alter the relationship with the metal surface of the vehicle with which it forms a ground plane aerial system. The radiation pattern will change correspondingly, giving rise to break-up of both incoming and outgoing signals.

Interference problems on the vehicle carrying CB equipment fall into two categories:

(a) Interference to nearby TV and radio receivers when transmitting.
(b) Interference to CB set reception due to electrical equipment on the vehicle.

Problems of break-through to TV and radio are not frequent, but can be difficult to solve. Mostly trouble is not detected or reported because the vehicle is moving and the symptoms rapidly disappear at the TV/radio receiver, but when the CB set is used as a base station any trouble with nearby receivers will soon result in a complaint.

It must not be assumed by the CB operator that his equipment is faultless, for much depends upon the design. Harmonics (that is, multiples) of 27 MHz may be transmitted unknowingly and these can fall into other user's bands. Where trouble of this nature occurs, low pass filters in the aerial or supply leads can help, and should be fitted in base station aerials as a matter of course. In stubborn cases it may be necessary to call for assistance from the licensing authority, or, if possible, to have the equipment checked by the manufacturers.

Interference received on the CB set from the vehicle equipment is, fortunately, not usually a severe problem. The precautions outlined previously for radio/cassette units apply, but there are some extra points worth noting.

It is common practice to use a slide-mount on CB equipment enabling the set to be easily removed for use as a base station, for example. Care must be taken that the slide mount fittings are properly earthed and that first class connection occurs between the set and slide-mount.

Vehicle manufacturers in the UK are required to provide suppression of electrical equipment to cover 40 to 250 MHz to protect TV and VHF radio bands. Such suppression appears to be adequately effective at 27 MHz, but suppression of individual items such as alternators/dynamos, clocks, stabilisers, flashers, wiper motors, etc, may still be necessary. The suppression capacitors and chokes available from auto-electrical suppliers for entertainment receivers will usually give the required results with CB equipment.

Other vehicle radio transmitters

Besides CB radio already mentioned, a considerable increase in the use of transceivers (ie combined transmitter and receiver units) has taken place in the last decade. Previously this type of equipment was fitted mainly to military, fire, ambulance and police vehicles, but a large business radio and radio telephone usage has developed.

Generally the suppression techniques described previously will suffice, with only a few difficult cases arising. Suppression is carried out to satisfy the 'receive mode', but care must be taken to use heavy duty chokes in the equipment supply cables since the loading on 'transmit' is relatively high.

12 Bodywork and fittings

General

1 The Estelle range has undergone several cosmetic changes whilst retaining its original body shape. Such items as bumpers and body moulding panels/strips, front grille etc have changed, being of different design or material.
2 The general procedures for servicing given in Chapter 11 are adequate to enable the owner to tackle most bodywork and related trim servicing operations. Where major differences occur, they will be dealt with here.

Spare wheel carrier

3 The spare wheel carrier is located under the front luggage compartment, welded to the chassis. The spare wheel sits in this carrier and is retained in place by a spring-loaded rod (photo).
4 The handle for this rod is in the luggage compartment, and turning it through 90° will allow the spare wheel to be removed.

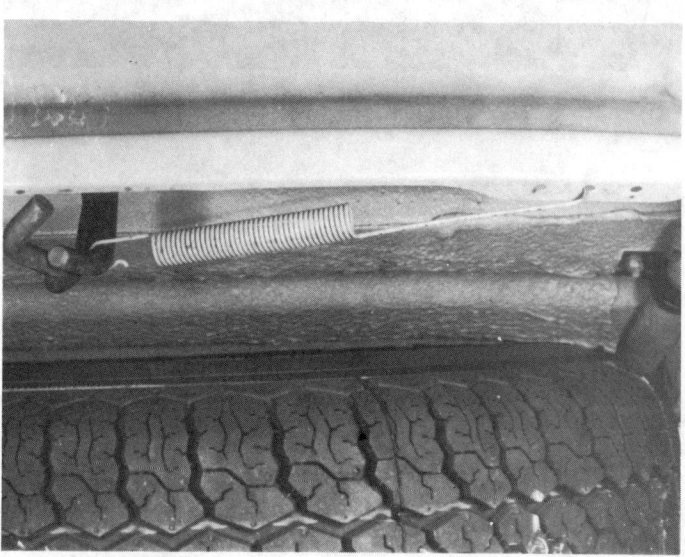

12.3 Spare wheel retaining rod spring

Front radiator grille

5 The front radiator grille is in left and right halves. The grille is removed by undoing two screws on the outboard edges and removing the centre screw and bracket (photo).
6 Refitting is a simple reversal of the removal procedure.

12.5A Radiator grille securing screws at the outboard edge ...

12.5B ... and centre

Sunroof frame – removal and refitting

16 It is recommended that this operation is entrusted to a specialist agent, but the procedure is given here for information.

17 Remove the glass sunroof. Unscrew and remove the latch and hinge blocks from the frame.

18 Unscrew and remove the black trim strips and peel back the head lining, exposing frame inner ring retaining screws.

19 Using clamps with large faces (approximately 2 to 3 in) and also using suitable protection to the frame and paintwork, clamp the frame on both corners to be released.

20 Unscrew the inner frame screws, starting at the corners.

21 When all four corners are unscrewed, remove the side screws, then the front and rear screws, and lastly the four central screws.

22 Carefully remove the frame, inspecting it as you do so for evidence of leaks.

23 Clean all traces of old sealant from the car roof and the frame.

24 Apply mastic sealant strip around the edge of the roof skin.

25 Carefully lower the outer frame into the aperture, being careful not to displace the mastic from the car roof.

26 Centralise the frame in the aperture.

27 Fit the lower frame, and carefully tighten the four central screws progressively, so as to keep the frame central.

28 Apply pressure to each corner to ensure a clean fit, and fit the remaining screws in the reverse order of removal, again tightening them progressively, and clamping each corner when fitting the corner screws.

29 Refit the trim strips and the latch and hinge blocks.

Sunroof
General

7 The sunroof is of the all glass type with tilt opening or it can be removed completely. A ceramic radio aerial is fixed inside the glass area.

8 To open the roof, slide the latch button forward and push the glass upward to one of two positions; half open or fully open.

Removal and refitting

9 To remove the glass completely, disconnect the aerial lead, open the roof and depress catch A, which will release the catch B – Fig. 12.38.

10 Push the glass upward at the rear until resistance is felt, then press both hinge locks upward. This will release the hinges and the glass may be lifted out.

11 Refit the glass by firstly resting its leading edge in place on the rubber seal.

12 Pull the glass downward, holding it at its rear edge, and applying inward pressure onto the leading edge.

13 This will engage the front hinges.

14 Reengage the latch, lower the glass fully and ensure the latch returns to its initial closed position.

15 Reconnect the aerial lead.

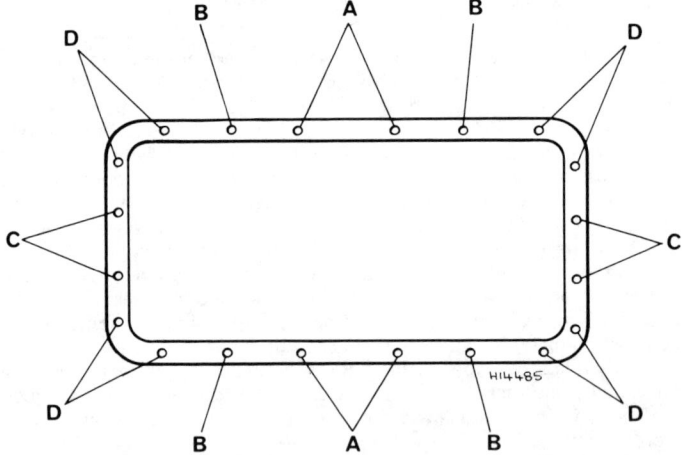

Fig. 12.39 Sunroof frame securing screws (Sec 12)

A Central screws   *C Side screws*
B Front and rear screws   *D Corner screws*

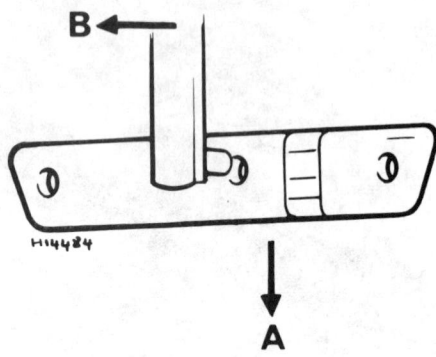

Fig. 12.38 Removal of the sunroof (Sec 12)

Depress catch A to release latch B

Sunroof – Rapid

30 Skoda have recently announced that it is now possible to fit a sunroof to the Rapid.

31 However, this must be of an approved type only, and must be fitted in accordance with Skoda's laid down procedures. These can be obtained from your local dealer.

Door mounted rear view mirrors – removal and refitting

32 To remove only the mirror for replacement undo the screw on the back of the arm (photo). When refitting make sure the seal is seated properly between the arm and mirror holder body.

33 To remove the complete assembly remove the two screws securing it to the door (photo).

34 When refitting make sure the seal on the base is seated properly before tightening the two screws.

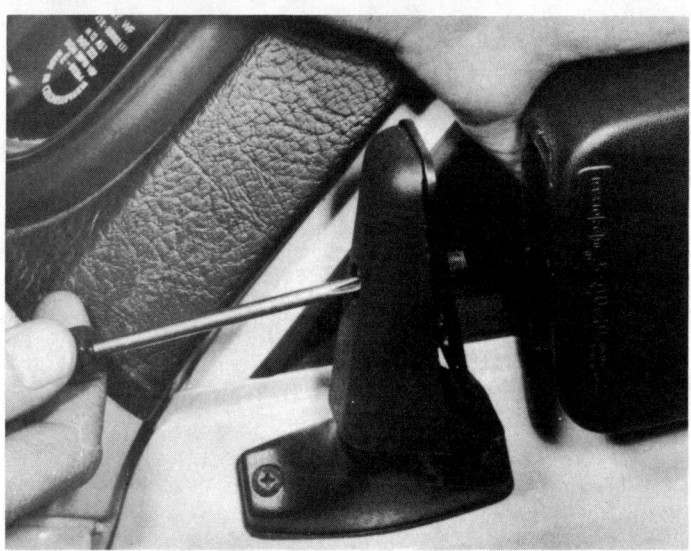 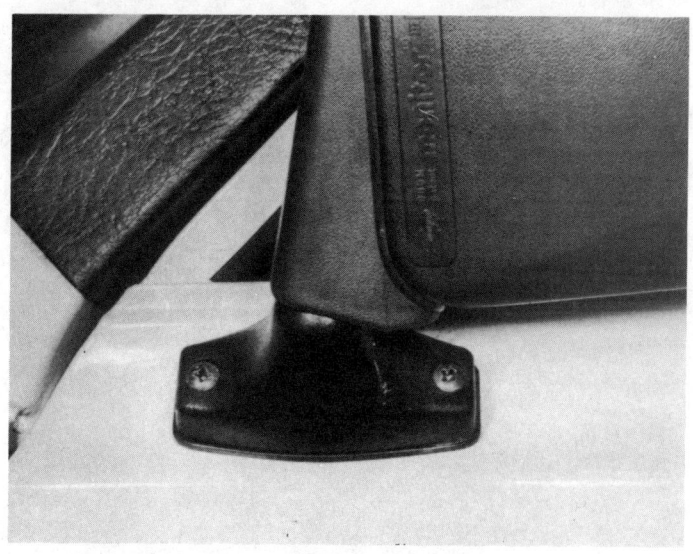

12.32 One screw holds the rear view mirror to the arm

12.33 Two screws secure the mirror arm to the door

General repair procedures

Whenever servicing, repair or overhaul work is carried out on the car or its components, it is necessary to observe the following procedures and instructions. This will assist in carrying out the operation efficiently and to a professional standard of workmanship.

Joint mating faces and gaskets

Where a gasket is used between the mating faces of two components, ensure that it is renewed on reassembly, and fit it dry unless otherwise stated in the repair procedure. Make sure that the mating faces are clean and dry with all traces of old gasket removed. When cleaning a joint face, use a tool which is not likely to score or damage the face, and remove any burrs or nicks with an oilstone or fine file.

Make sure that tapped holes are cleaned with a pipe cleaner, and keep them free of jointing compound if this is being used unless specifically instructed otherwise.

Ensure that all orifices, channels or pipes are clear and blow through them, preferably using compressed air.

Oil seals

Whenever an oil seal is removed from its working location, either individually or as part of an assembly, it should be renewed.

The very fine sealing lip of the seal is easily damaged and will not seal if the surface it contacts is not completely clean and free from scratches, nicks or grooves. If the original sealing surface of the component cannot be restored, the component should be renewed.

Protect the lips of the seal from any surface which may damage them in the course of fitting. Use tape or a conical sleeve where possible. Lubricate the seal lips with oil before fitting and, on dual lipped seals, fill the space between the lips with grease.

Unless otherwise stated, oil seals must be fitted with their sealing lips toward the lubricant to be sealed.

Use a tubular drift or block of wood of the appropriate size to install the seal and, if the seal housing is shouldered, drive the seal down to the shoulder. If the seal housing is unshouldered, the seal should be fitted with its face flush with the housing top face.

Screw threads and fastenings

Always ensure that a blind tapped hole is completely free from oil, grease, water or other fluid before installing the bolt or stud. Failure to do this could cause the housing to crack due to the hydraulic action of the bolt or stud as it is screwed in.

When tightening a castellated nut to accept a split pin, tighten the nut to the specified torque, where applicable, and then tighten further to the next split pin hole. Never slacken the nut to align a split pin hole unless stated in the repair procedure.

When checking or retightening a nut or bolt to a specified torque setting, slacken the nut or bolt by a quarter of a turn, and then retighten to the specified setting.

Locknuts, locktabs and washers

Any fastening which will rotate against a component or housing in the course of tightening should always have a washer between it and the relevant component or housing.

Spring or split washers should always be renewed when they are used to lock a critical component such as a big-end bearing retaining nut or bolt.

Locktabs which are folded over to retain a nut or bolt should always be renewed.

Self-locking nuts can be reused in non-critical areas, providing resistance can be felt when the locking portion passes over the bolt or stud thread.

Split pins must always be replaced with new ones of the correct size for the hole.

Special tools

Some repair procedures in this manual entail the use of special tools such as a press, two or three-legged pullers, spring compressors etc. Wherever possible, suitable readily available alternatives to the manufacturer's special tools are described, and are shown in use. In some instances, where no alternative is possible, it has been necessary to resort to the use of a manufacturer's tool and this has been done for reasons of safety as well as the efficient completion of the repair operation. Unless you are highly skilled and have a thorough understanding of the procedure described, never attempt to bypass the use of any special tool when the procedure described specifies its use. Not only is there a very great risk of personal injury, but expensive damage could be caused to the components involved.

Conversion factors

Length (distance)
Inches (in)	X	25.4	= Millimetres (mm)	X	0.0394 = Inches (in)
Feet (ft)	X	0.305	= Metres (m)	X	3.281 = Feet (ft)
Miles	X	1.609	= Kilometres (km)	X	0.621 = Miles

Volume (capacity)
Cubic inches (cu in; in^3)	X	16.387	= Cubic centimetres (cc; cm^3)	X	0.061 = Cubic inches (cu in; in^3)
Imperial pints (Imp pt)	X	0.568	= Litres (l)	X	1.76 = Imperial pints (Imp pt)
Imperial quarts (Imp qt)	X	1.137	= Litres (l)	X	0.88 = Imperial quarts (Imp qt)
Imperial quarts (Imp qt)	X	1.201	= US quarts (US qt)	X	0.833 = Imperial quarts (Imp qt)
US quarts (US qt)	X	0.946	= Litres (l)	X	1.057 = US quarts (US qt)
Imperial gallons (Imp gal)	X	4.546	= Litres (l)	X	0.22 = Imperial gallons (Imp gal)
Imperial gallons (Imp gal)	X	1.201	= US gallons (US gal)	X	0.833 = Imperial gallons (Imp gal)
US gallons (US gal)	X	3.785	= Litres (l)	X	0.264 = US gallons (US gal)

Mass (weight)
Ounces (oz)	X	28.35	= Grams (g)	X	0.035 = Ounces (oz)
Pounds (lb)	X	0.454	= Kilograms (kg)	X	2.205 = Pounds (lb)

Force
Ounces-force (ozf; oz)	X	0.278	= Newtons (N)	X	3.6 = Ounces-force (ozf; oz)
Pounds-force (lbf; lb)	X	4.448	= Newtons (N)	X	0.225 = Pounds-force (lbf; lb)
Newtons (N)	X	0.1	= Kilograms-force (kgf; kg)	X	9.81 = Newtons (N)

Pressure
Pounds-force per square inch (psi; lbf/in^2; lb/in^2)	X	0.070	= Kilograms-force per square centimetre (kgf/cm^2; kg/cm^2)	X	14.223 = Pounds-force per square inch (psi; lbf/in^2; lb/in^2)
Pounds-force per square inch (psi; lbf/in^2; lb/in^2)	X	0.068	= Atmospheres (atm)	X	14.696 = Pounds-force per square inch (psi; lbf/in^2; lb/in^2)
Pounds-force per square inch (psi; lbf/in^2; lb/in^2)	X	0.069	= Bars	X	14.5 = Pounds-force per square inch (psi; lbf/in^2; lb/in^2)
Pounds-force per square inch (psi; lbf/in^2; lb/in^2)	X	6.895	= Kilopascals (kPa)	X	0.145 = Pounds-force per square inch (psi; lbf/in^2; lb/in^2)
Kilopascals (kPa)	X	0.01	= Kilograms-force per square centimetre (kgf/cm^2; kg/cm^2)	X	98.1 = Kilopascals (kPa)

Torque (moment of force)
Pounds-force inches (lbf in; lb in)	X	1.152	= Kilograms-force centimetre (kgf cm; kg cm)	X	0.868 = Pounds-force inches (lbf in; lb in)
Pounds-force inches (lbf in; lb in)	X	0.113	= Newton metres (Nm)	X	8.85 = Pounds-force inches (lbf in; lb in)
Pounds-force inches (lbf in; lb in)	X	0.083	= Pounds-force feet (lbf ft; lb ft)	X	12 = Pounds-force inches (lbf in; lb in)
Pounds-force feet (lbf ft; lb ft)	X	0.138	= Kilograms-force metres (kgf m; kg m)	X	7.233 = Pounds-force feet (lbf ft; lb ft)
Pounds-force feet (lbf ft; lb ft)	X	1.356	= Newton metres (Nm)	X	0.738 = Pounds-force feet (lbf ft; lb ft)
Newton metres (Nm)	X	0.102	= Kilograms-force metres (kgf m; kg m)	X	9.804 = Newton metres (Nm)

Power
Horsepower (hp)	X	745.7	= Watts (W)	X	0.0013 = Horsepower (hp)

Velocity (speed)
Miles per hour (miles/hr; mph)	X	1.609	= Kilometres per hour (km/hr; kph)	X	0.621 = Miles per hour (miles/hr; mph)

Fuel consumption*
Miles per gallon, Imperial (mpg)	X	0.354	= Kilometres per litre (km/l)	X	2.825 = Miles per gallon, Imperial (mpg)
Miles per gallon, US (mpg)	X	0.425	= Kilometres per litre (km/l)	X	2.352 = Miles per gallon, US (mpg)

Temperature
Degrees Fahrenheit = (°C x 1.8) + 32   Degrees Celsius (Degrees Centigrade; °C) = (°F - 32) x 0.56

*It is common practice to convert from miles per gallon (mpg) to litres/100 kilometres (l/100km),
where mpg (Imperial) x l/100 km = 282 and mpg (US) x l/100 km = 235

Index

Printed by
J H Haynes & Co Ltd
Sparkford Nr Yeovil
Somerset BA22 7JJ England